ne, **shady** **TOWN**, prison town,
ty, upside-down to
er **city**, **spider** c
rison town, city-hospital, **upside-down**
city, trap town, town-machine,
ital, upside-down town, model
e city-lab, Town-machine, **man-**
idden city, mock city, **flower city,**
y-lab, **man-made city**, prison town,
e, invisible city, dreamland, city-hospital,
er city, **spider city**, the city-lab
own, city-hospital, upside- down town,
the city-lab, play city, **dead city**
-machine, **flower city, spider**
ock city, prison town, city-hospital,
er city, **spider city**, the city-lab
rison town, city-hospital, **upside-down**
city, the city-lab Town-machine
upside-down town, Replica city
lab, Town-machine, **suspicion**
own town, dark city, **flower city,**
hine, **shady town,** prison town, city-
y, **flower city, spider city** the

Cities
made
differently

David Graeber and Nika Dubrovsky

The MIT Press
Cambridge, Massachusetts
London, England

The MIT Press would like to thank the anonymous peer reviewers who provided comments on drafts of this book. The generous work of academic experts is essential for establishing the authority and quality of our publications. We acknowledge with gratitude the contributions of these otherwise uncredited readers.

This book was set in EasyFlex by Yuri Gordon. Book design by Natasha Agapova, Ludmila Ivakina, Torsten Lesszinsky, Elena Shindukova and Marina Sergeeva. Printed and bound in Canada.

Library of Congress Cataloging-in-Publication Data

Names: Dubrovsky, Nika, 1967 – author | Graeber, David, author.
Title: Cities made differently / Nika Dubrovsky and David Graeber.
Description: [Cambridge] : The MIT Press, [2025] | Series: The made differently series | Includes bibliographical references and index.
Identifiers: LCCN 2024019117 (print) | LCCN 2024019118 (ebook) | ISBN 9780262549332 (paperback) | ISBN 9780262380089 (epub) | ISBN 9780262380096 (pdf)
Subjects: LCSH: Cities and towns. | Sociology, Urban.
Classification: LCC HT151 .D76 2025 (print) | LCC HT151 (ebook) | DDC 307.76--dc23/eng/20240628
LC record available at https://lccn.loc.gov/2024019117
LC ebook record available at https://lccn.loc.gov/2024019118

10 9 8 7 6 5 4 3 2

This book is dedicated
to David, who always
remained a child at heart,
able to sense the worlds
of many different people—
frightening, empty, caring,
magnificent—and who thus
was well aware that we, too,
can remake our shared
world at will. And to Benjamin,
who will live in this world that
we pondered while writing
these books.
Nika Dubrovsky

Introduction

In thousands of ways, we are taught to accept the world we live in as the only possible one, but thousands of other ways of organizing homes, cities, schools, societies, economies, cosmologies, have and could exist. The series of books Made Differently... is designed to play with possibility and to overcome the suspicion, instilled in us every day, that life is necessarily limited, miserable, and boring.

The project evolved over decades as an illustrated dialogue between the artist and author Nika Dubrovsky and the late anthropologist David Graeber. Nika's son, who then was four, also took part. It brings together anthropology, literature, play, and drawings.

Our Made Differently **books consist of notes, quotes, photographs, film stills, and drawings, mainly by Nika. The books exist in two versions: one for reading and thinking with, the other for dreaming and drawing in. The latter can be downloaded for free at** a4kids.org.

The first three books in the series are about (1) Cities, that is to say: different ways of living together; (2) Museums: different ways of thinking about values, and (3) Artists: different ways of being human.

We hope that you will feel that our book is like a kaleidoscope, in which you see changes as you are looking at it. That is why there are different ways for you to navigate these books. Following the introduction, you will find a table of contents for the illustrated chapters.

As you flip through the pages of this book, looking at different versions of how people lived together and imagining new ways that they might yet live, perhaps you might ponder what city might be best for you.

There is also an additional path that winds through the pages of this book. It consists of keywords, which connect chapters to each other. However, the keywords we picked and the connections we made are not the only possible ones.

When you look at the index of keywords in the back, please think about what is not there: which possibilities are missing from the book? These are stories not yet written, which you might want to write or think through on your own.

The section called Study Materials, located in the back, lets you learn more about the real and fictional projects, ideas, and people mentioned in the book.

These projects and ideas offer visions of the past and the future, which are quite different from things as they are now. What do you think: could things have been otherwise? Should things become otherwise in the future? Should we think about this together? After all, city, museum, and humanity itself are collective projects.

Contents

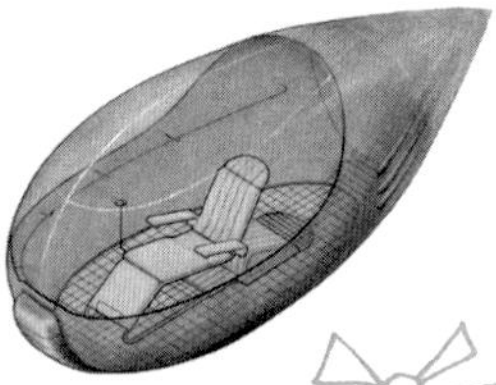
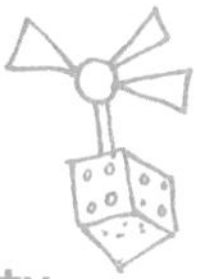

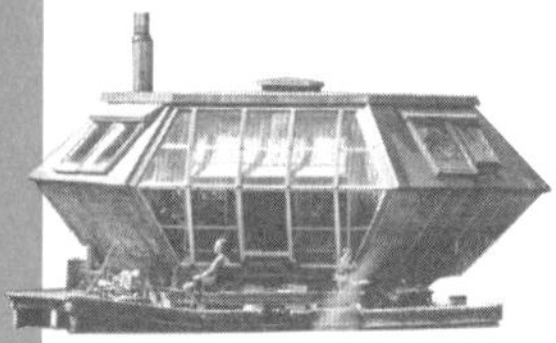
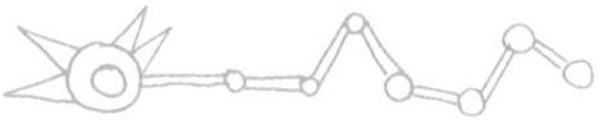

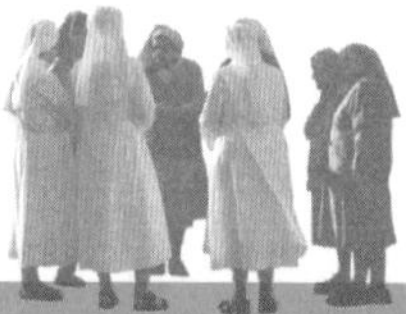

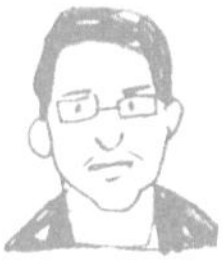

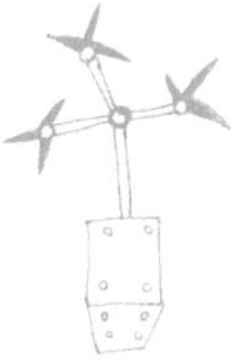

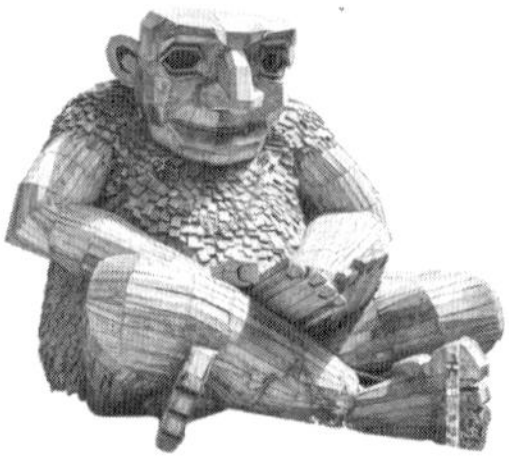

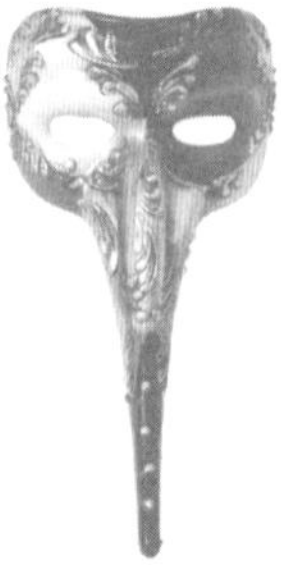

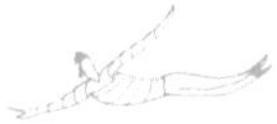
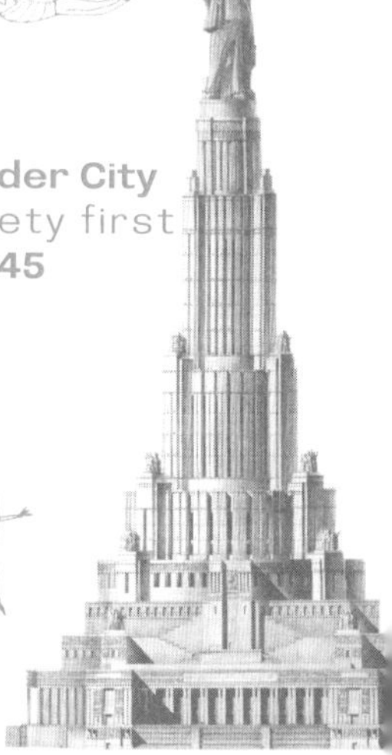

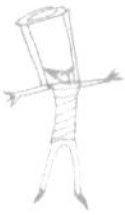

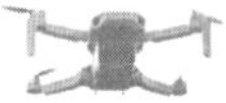

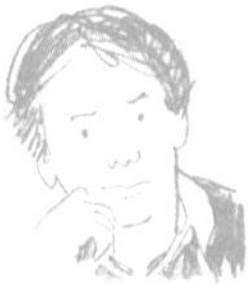

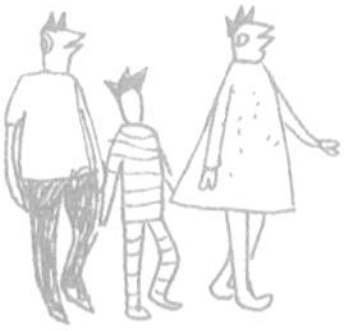

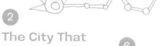

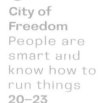

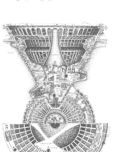

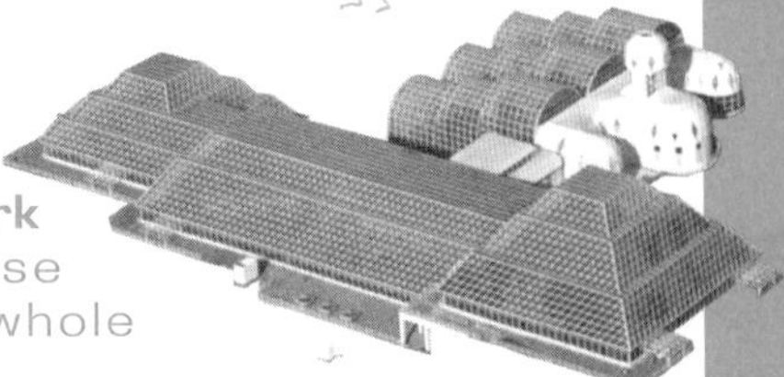

1
Vertical living quarters are built into the community ring.

2
The complex consists of eight vertical five-story residential buildings with individual units connected by elevator shafts, with a horizontal, circular communal space located below.

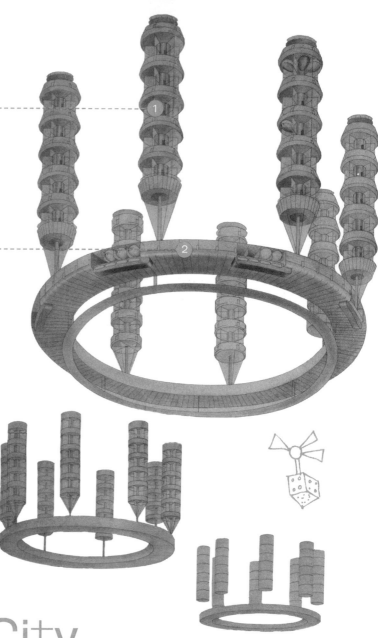

Flying City

Architect Georgy Krutikov dreamed up flying cities to free humans from gravity. Left to the care of plants and animals, perhaps planet Earth could catch its breath.

In revolutionary Russia, Krutikov designed cities in hopes of changing the way humanity lived.

What do you think about living in the clouds?

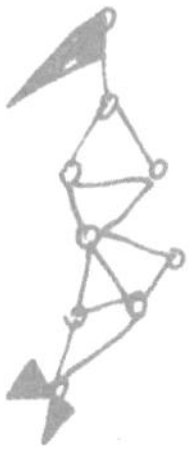

A similar idea was described in 1915 by the poet Velimir Khlebnikov:

He imagined that people would live in glass mobile homes whose passengers could travel wherever they wanted to. This amazing invention of human engineering would allow people to stay in communities for as long as they wished, without ever being stuck in one place forever. Mobile glass houses would be constructed to easily "plug into" giant collective flying communes, made up of travelers joining and leaving to continue their endless exploratory journey in their mobile glass homes.

No more migrants and locals. Just human beings – travelers, true citizens of the world!

The mobile glass home will be able to join and leave large collective communes at will, continuing their endless explorations in their mobile glass hut. Travelers will become part of the environment, seeing everything that happens around through the glass walls of the mobile hut.

At night, the home will become opaque and turn into a great place to sleep.

Small communities in the clouds can be assembled into infinitely larger cities and then dispersed again. Maybe a few people think it's bad, but most people would think it's impossible.

A flying city would consist of a cluster of giant residential complexes floating above the Earth.

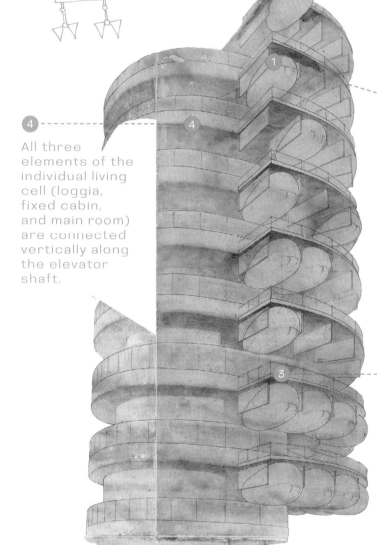

1 Communication between the ground and the buildings floating in the air is carried out with the help of a universal means of transportation (the cabin), which can move in the air, on the ground, on water, and under water.

4 All three elements of the individual living cell (loggia, fixed cabin, and main room) are connected vertically along the elevator shaft.

3 Each floor of the circular residential block is divided into six individual cells. Each cell consists of a high loggia, which supports a unit for docking and anchoring the mobile cabin cell and the living room located above it.

Krutikov and Khlebnikov, working in times of radical revolutionary change, could hope for a large-scale realization of their projects in real life. Today, such flying cities are mostly constructed in the imagination.

Argentinian artist Tomás Saraceno has been thinking of different ways to live in the sky since 2002. As part of the research project Cloud Cities, he is developing a prototype for an international modular settlement. His aerial constructions of transparent and reflective materials are exhibited in museums around the world. Inspired by real-life structural examples of bacteria, galaxies, foam, and neural networks, this artist is looking for new ways for humans to live and travel in harmony with nature.

Would you like to live in a house that turns into a vehicle and travels between colonies? Might you be happier to stay in one place and not have to move around? There are many ways to live in the Flying City.

2

A mobile dwelling cabin, which can be easily connected to buildings floating in the air, is both a means of transportation and part of a stationary dwelling. The shell of the cabin and the furniture inside the cabin changes depending on the position of the person (sitting, lying down).

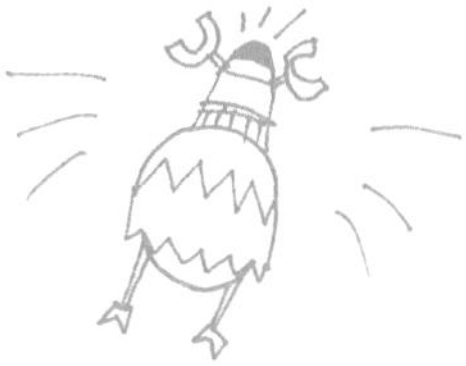

ison town, city-hospital, upside-down town, shady

The City That Always **Sleeps**

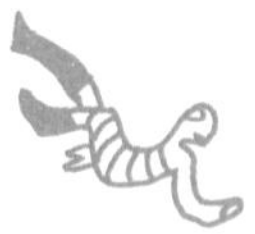

Mankind has long dreamed of technology that would free us from hard work, pain, and suffering.

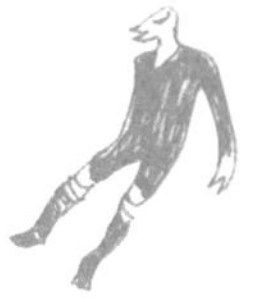

Would you trade your freedom for safety and comfort? And what do you consider "safety"?

In the Wachowski sisters' cult film The Matrix, people dream beautiful dreams served to them by intelligent, almighty machines. The world seems perfect to the dreamers, but in the real, non-dream world, humans reduced to bodies mutilated by metal tubes and piled up in ugly sarcophagi, their cities lying in ruins.

These machines use human bodies to produce energy. The care they provide to people turns out to actually be a brutal imprisonment.

One of the heroes of *The Matrix*, Morpheus, explains why so many people support a system that exploits them:

Think about it: how can we separate care that becomes oppressive from care that can liberate us?

"The Matrix is a system. That system is our enemy. But when you're inside, you look around, what do you see? Businessmen, teachers, lawyers, carpenters. All these people are still part of the system. Most of them are not ready to be unplugged. And many of them are so inured, so hopelessly dependent on the system, that they will fight to protect it."

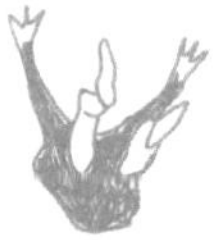

A town like this is akin to a military camp, neatly controlled by machines.

ison town, city-hospital, upside-down town, shady

Cities made differently
tile 3
City in the Clouds

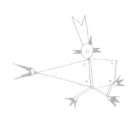

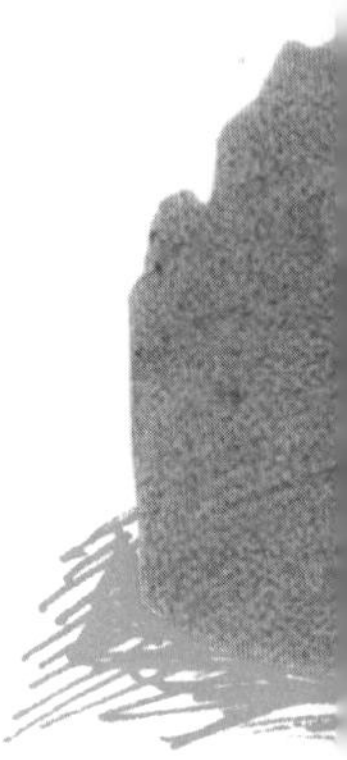

City in the Clouds

The idea of a flying city is an age-old dream of mankind. But what if a flying city was designed not to liberate everyone but rather to let a select few control everyone else?

Only one city won the battle with the floating ship-city, and only because that city's scientists managed to block the weaponized magnetic field used by their attackers.

In *Gulliver's Travels*, Irish author Jonathan Swift describes a flying island—a massive weapon in the shape of a city created by scientists for the benefit of their king. The flying ship punishes rebellious towns by blocking them from the sun or rain, or, sometimes, simply by descending and flattening them.

The king uses his flying city to render his people defenseless and obedient. But what if someone came up with an even cleverer technology, one that could defeat the king?

Those who live in the clouds enjoy their power and technological advances, but what about those who remain on Earth?

Jonathan Swift wrote *Gulliver's Travels* in 1726. On his third voyage, Gulliver discovers the flying island of Laputa: "I turned back, and perceived a vast opaque body between me and the sun moving forwards towards the island. As it approached nearer over the place where I was, it appeared to be a firm substance, the bottom flat, smooth, and shining very bright, from

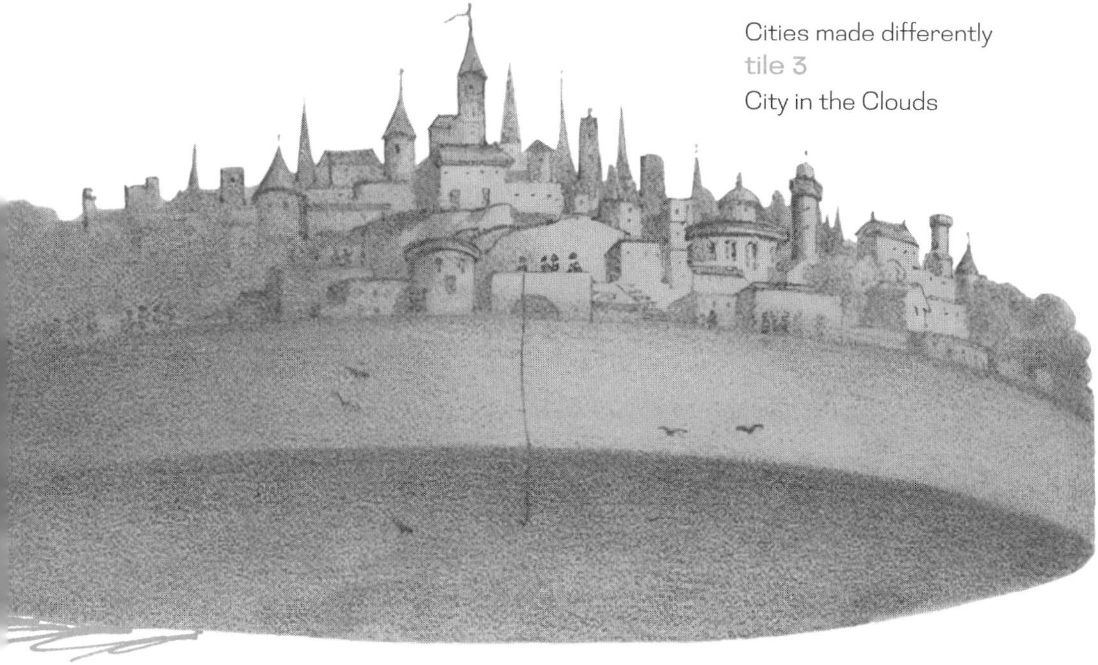

Are you willing to divide humanity between those floating above the Earth and everyone else?

the reflection of the sea below. The reader can hardly conceive my astonishment, to behold an island in the air, inhabited by men, who were able (as it should seem) to raise or sink, or put it into progressive motion, as they pleased."

The scholars of Laputa, obedient to their king, did not care whether their scientific research harmed the people down below. It seems that the scientists of the King's City were estranged from real earthly life. Their scientific discoveries were used solely to maintain the power of their king.

If the avant-garde architect Krutikov's Flying Cities had been built, perhaps many animals, fish, birds, plants, and trees would no longer face extinction. The Earth could avoid climate change disasters as people (almost like angels) would be living in the clouds. Should we actually build cities like this?

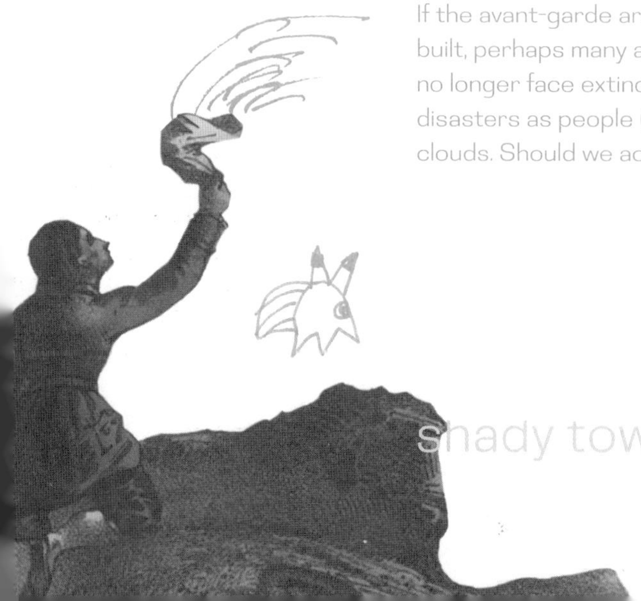

Military Town

It's about the basics: you attack, or you defend.

Everyone here is a fighter; everyone is prepared for war. This warrior city is about rules and discipline; order and power. The streets are clean, neat, and straight, as though drawn with a ruler. The heart of the city is the control center. This geometrical landscape emanates entirely from the will of a single person—the commander—and his fantasy of total and perfect control.

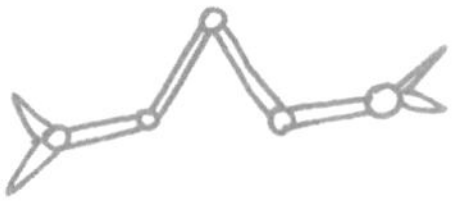

Would you agree to live in a city where there was little or no time for fun, and no end of strict regulations and punishments for those who failed to conform?

Many European cities such as Manchester, Vienna, Cologne, and Florence take their layout from Roman military camps, which were colonial outposts of the Empire.

One can think about Military town like a well-designed game with unchangeable rules: the streets, houses, and public spaces are filled with people in uniform, leading a uniform, predetermined life, under clear laws and the control of a single will. This game may enthuse some participants, but there are always going to be others who want to play a different game. For them, Imperia asserting themselves as the sole rule-makers have always been a problem—to say the least.

Compare life in two cities: one where the rules of the game are fixed, and another where townspeople can get together and reimagine city life.

Those who declined to take part in the game dictated by the Roman Empire, including the non-aligned and dissenters, became potential targets for attacks.

In a lot of countries, security forces have multiplied over the past decades.

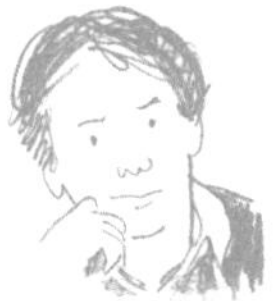

David Graeber

"Some economists estimate that a quarter of the American population is now engaged in 'guard labor' of one sort or another—defending property, supervising work, or otherwise keeping their fellow Americans in line."

1 Roman forts were protected with trenches, berms, ramparts, and walls.

2 Every Roman fort had four gates.

3 Forts had built-in hospitals for wounded and sick soldiers.

4 Grain to feed the soldiers and horses was stockpiled in storehouses.

5 Workshops to produce weapons and armor.

6 The main quarters were reserved for administrative work of all kinds and religious activities.

7 Soldiers, who served in the army for 25 years, made up the majority of the city's population. They were housed in barracks, with lots of soldiers crammed into each dwelling.

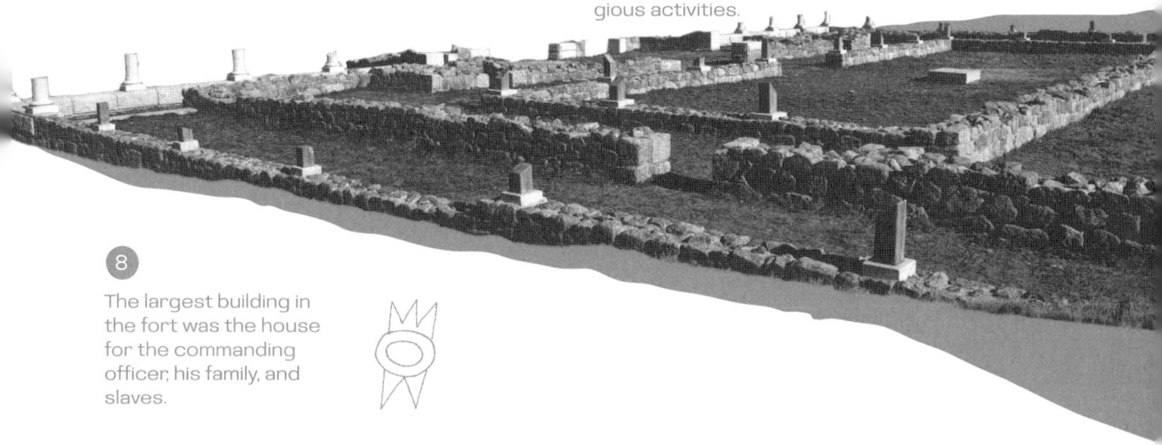

8 The largest building in the fort was the house for the commanding officer, his family, and slaves.

ap city, prison town, play city, upside-down town, p

City of Freedom

A city of freedom is one built and owned by its residents. It is home to artists, florists, bus drivers, librarians, cooks, carpenters, children, parents—and just about anyone else. But can soldiers live here?

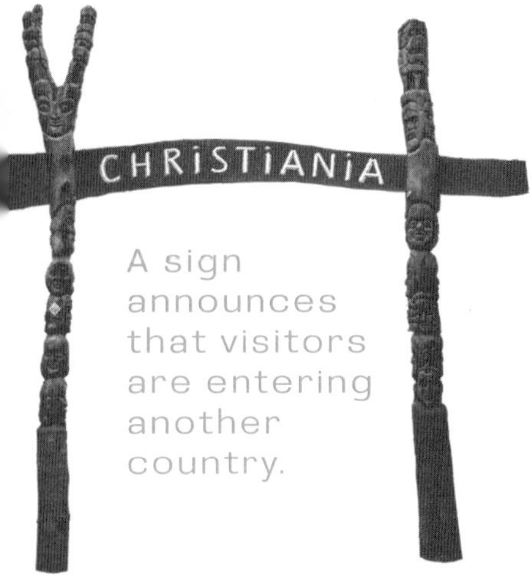
CHRISTIANIA

A sign announces that visitors are entering another country.

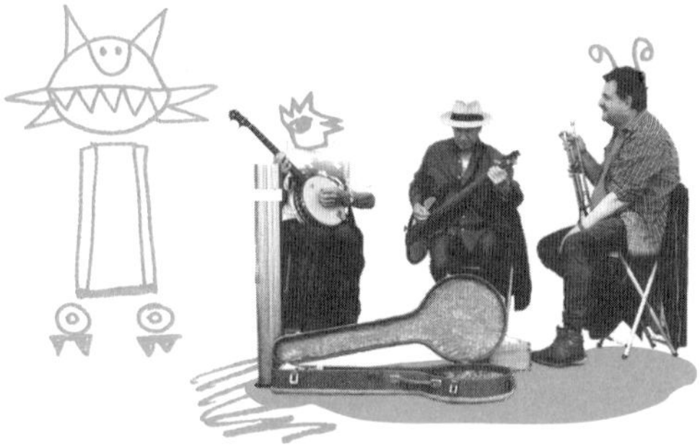

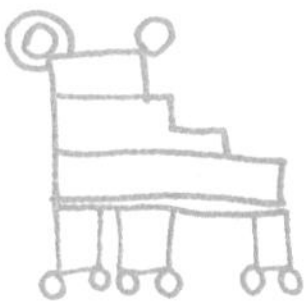

A beautiful river and boats!

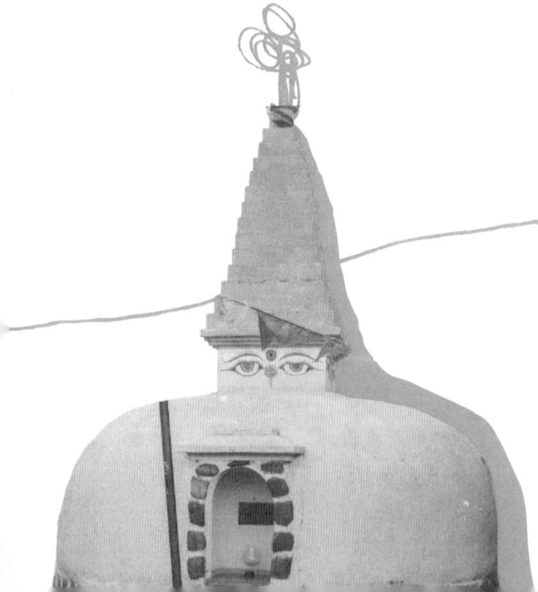

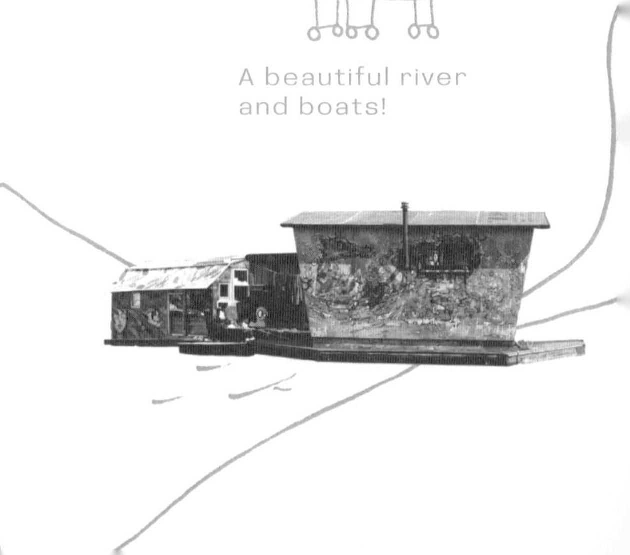

A truly free store where things can be left or taken for free.

In the capital of Denmark, Copenhagen, the home of Hans Christian Andersen, there is an area called Christiania, a free city whose founders, without asking permission from the authorities, decided to make a "fairy-tale come true" city.

The city council in which all decisions are made by local people.

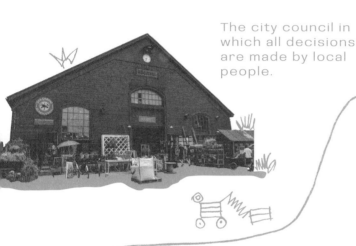

Houses are built by citizens from found materials. Each house is completely unique.

Playgrounds, flowers, and sculptures made by residents are scattered throughout the city.

Adults and children travel by bicycle. Nobody's in a hurry.

The river, the trees, and the fields: it feels like a village, but it's the center of a metropolis.

21

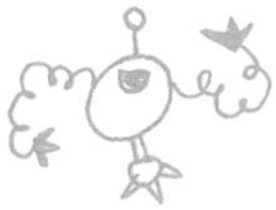

Can you build a city like this where you live?

People from countries near and far flocked to this amazing place to enjoy concerts and exhibitions. Museums sprang up all over the world with exhibitions dedicated to Christiania, featuring countless objects created by its inhabitants and photographs of their fabulous homes.

In 1971, some Copenhagen residents took over an abandoned military barracks located in the center of the city and started a self-governing society. They called their new city Christiania, hanging a sign that says, "You are leaving EU territory!" at its entrance and "You are entering the EU" at its exit.

The town consists mostly of public housing. Since no one regulated construction, the homes of Christiania have turned out to be surprisingly diverse. Sometimes people built houses made of window frames. Others rebuilt parts of destroyed buildings and

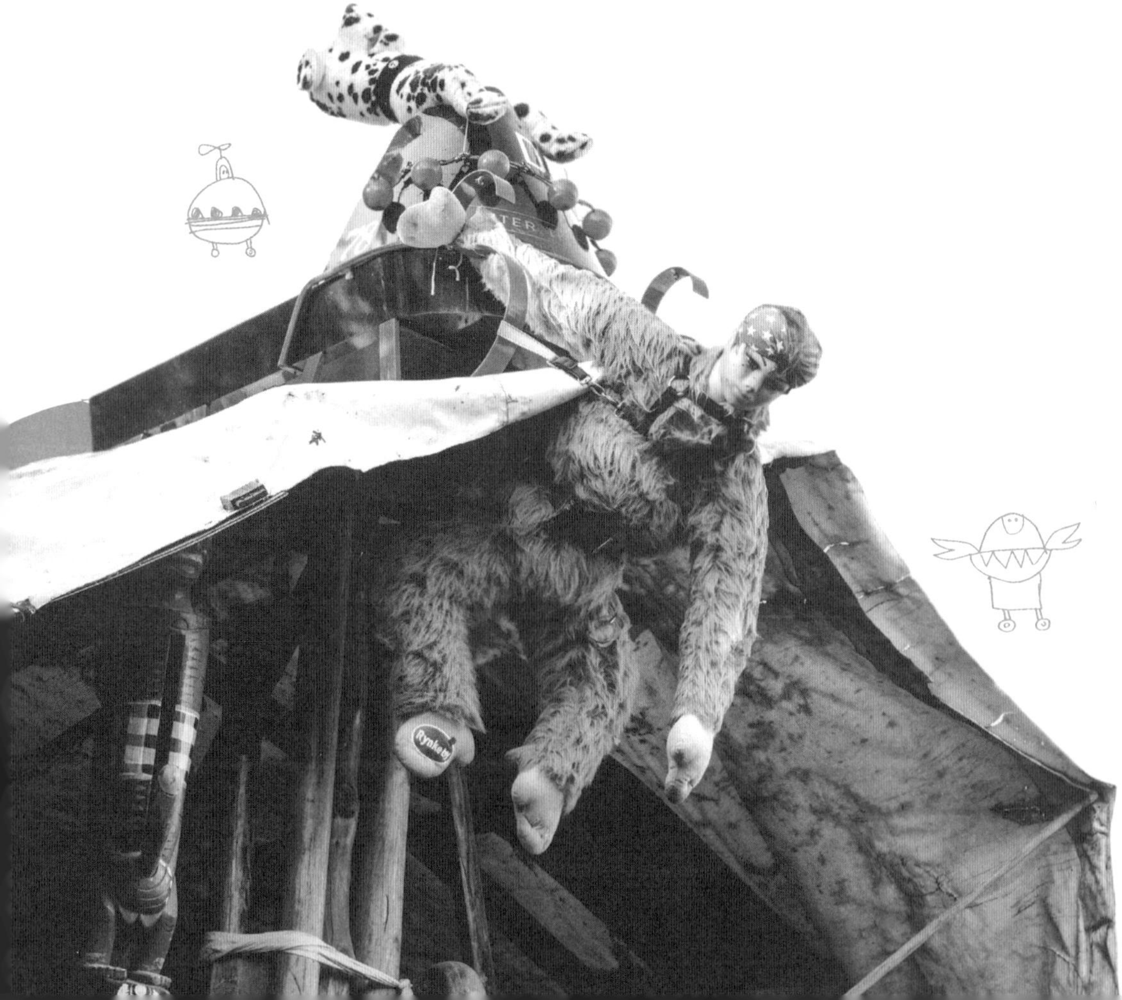

THE WORLD IS IN OUR HANDS

SOME LAWS OF CHRISTIANIA:

1. Everyone is responsible for everyone else.

2. Weapons and bulletproof vests are prohibited.

3. Cars are prohibited.

4. It is forbidden to steal.

5. Hard drugs are prohibited.

decorated them with homemade sculptures. Some houses are completely covered with murals. Many residents survive on the souvenir trade, social benefits provided by Denmark's welfare state, and the low cost of living thanks to free housing and communal activities, such as concerts and education.

Eventually, the city grew so crowded it could no longer accommodate new residents. Meanwhile, the government of Copenhagen has repeatedly sued Christiania, trying to subject its inhabitants to citywide rules.

The inhabitants of this communist utopia have ultimately been forced to become private property owners. The rumor is that ever since, the communal structure of the city has been showing signs of decay.

Protest is like begging the powers that be to dig a well. Direct action is digging the well and daring them to stop you.

son town, city-hospital, upside-down town, shady

The City of Play

what if the most essential feature of all living beings is the ability to play? Many people think of play as a childish thing, but what if we built a city around it? what if carnivals, festivals, dancing, and joy became the main pastime of its townspeople?

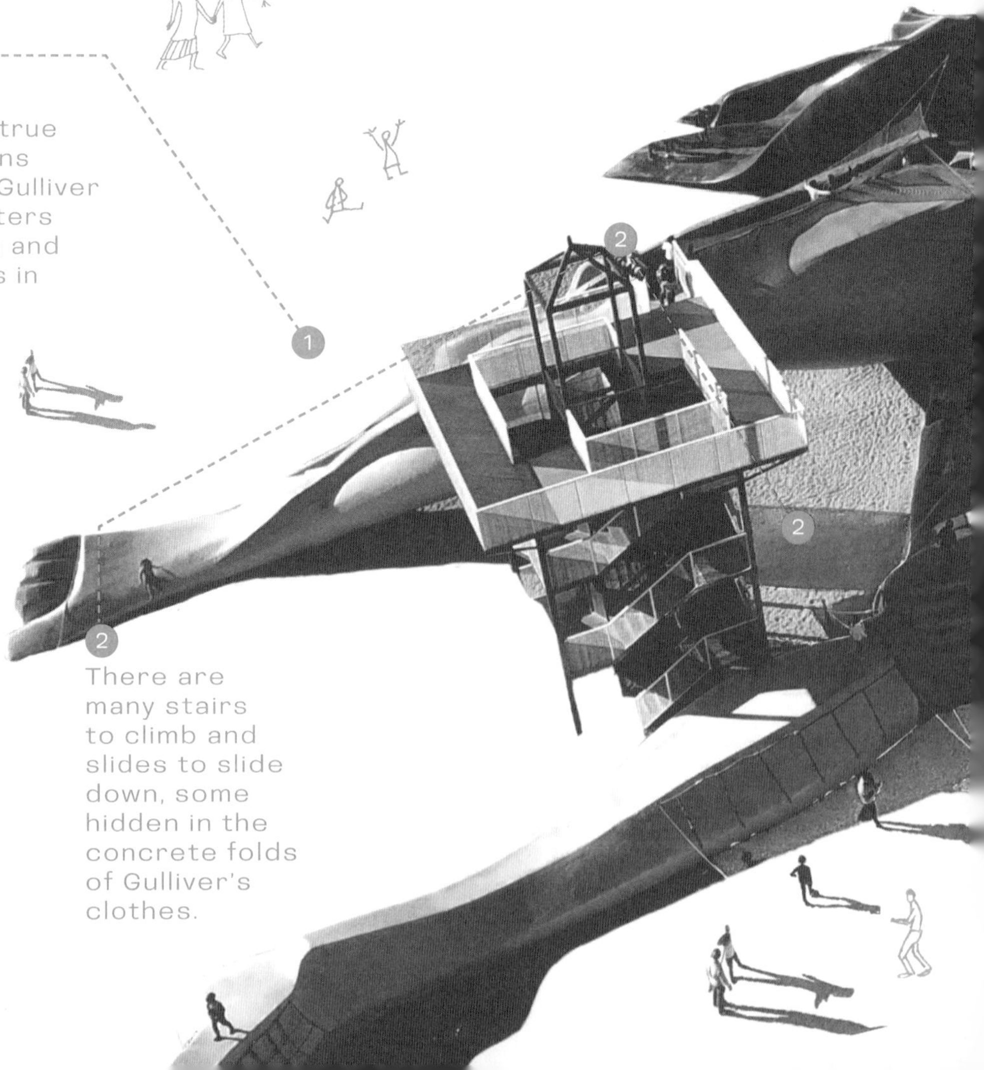

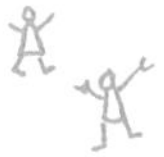

1 Children feel like true Lilliputians here as Gulliver is 67 meters in length and 9 meters in height.

2 There are many stairs to climb and slides to slide down, some hidden in the concrete folds of Gulliver's clothes.

Cities made differently
tile 6
The City of Play

How to play on the playground: run very fast, pretend to be someone else, catch up, hide and seek, try a merry-go-round, meet new and old friends, show off what you can do, brag and gossip, share secrets, and be silly. Play for the sake of the game.

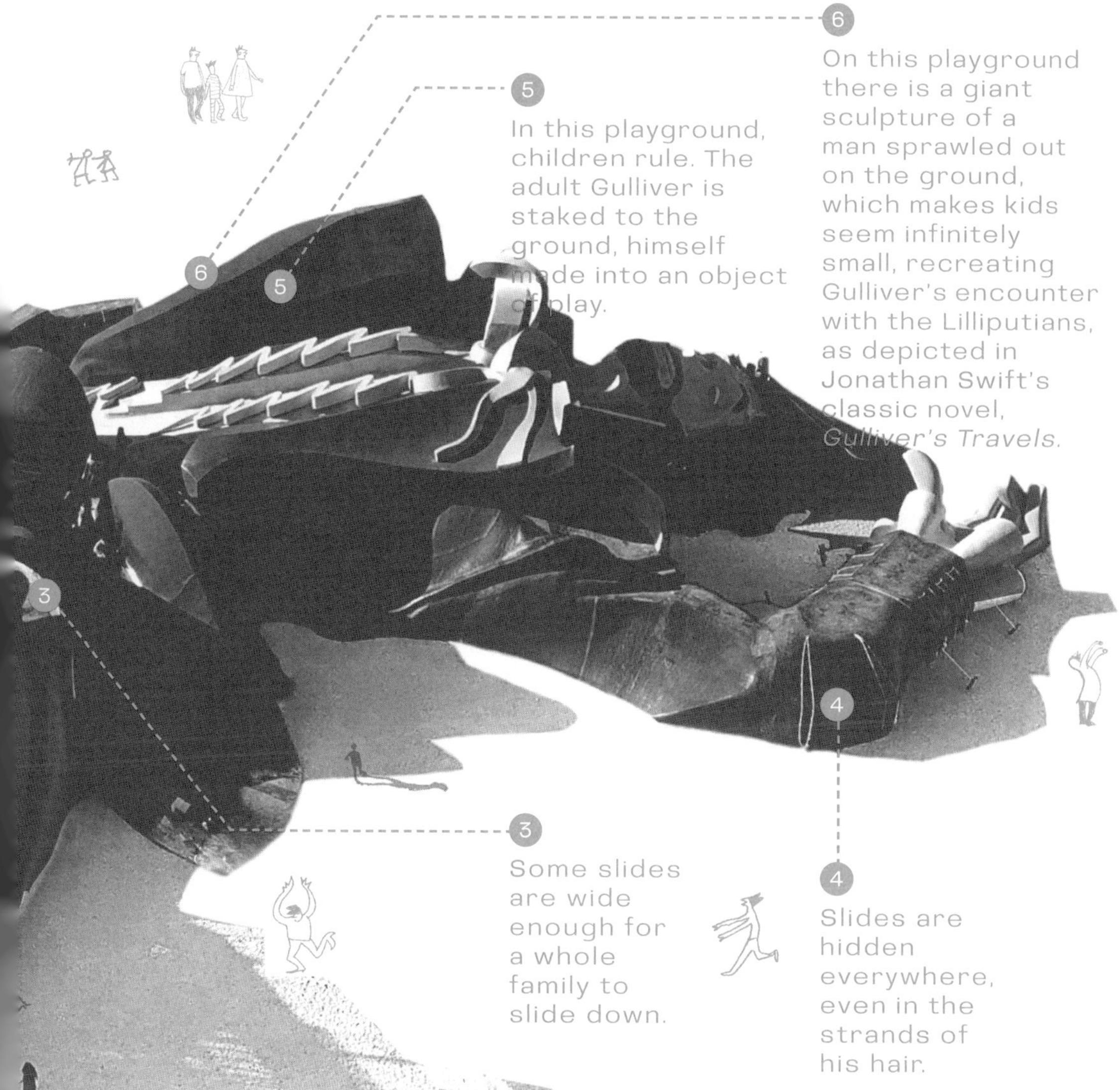
6
On this playground there is a giant sculpture of a man sprawled out on the ground, which makes kids seem infinitely small, recreating Gulliver's encounter with the Lilliputians, as depicted in Jonathan Swift's classic novel, *Gulliver's Travels*.
5
In this playground, children rule. The adult Gulliver is staked to the ground, himself made into an object of play.
3
Some slides are wide enough for a whole family to slide down.
4
Slides are hidden everywhere, even in the strands of his hair.

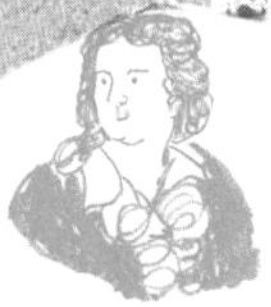
Schiller

"Man plays only when he is in the full sense of the word a man and he is only wholly a Man when he is playing."

Do you think the 70,000 park employees who run hotels, restaurants, bus parks, monorail systems, amusement rides, and movie theaters find their work playful?

The Walt Disney Company is also known for creating the largest theme park in the world, Disney World. It houses the fairy-tale buildings featured in Disney cartoons. It may feel as if you've stepped into a real-life fairy tale.

Unlike the City of Play, where the rules are invented and can be changed by the players themselves, in Disney World the roles of the participants are fixed once and for all. They are divided into buyers and sellers, into those who pay and those who receive payment.

Disney World participants seem to pretend to be preoccupied with finding treasure or meeting Sleeping Beauty, while perfectly aware that the main focus of the project is making money for one of the richest corporations on Earth.

Perhaps as people get older, they forget how to play. They forget that rules can be remade and games can always be played differently. Children know that if a game isn't fun, then it's not worth playing.

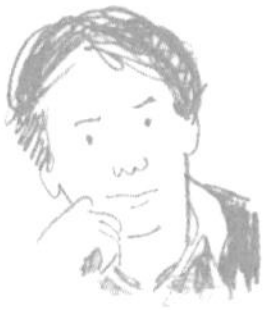

David Graeber

"Play is present when the free expression of creative energies becomes an end in itself. It is freedom for its own sake."

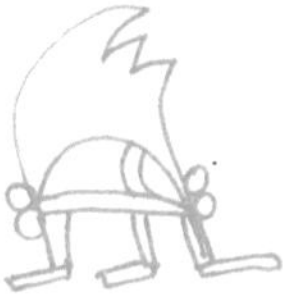

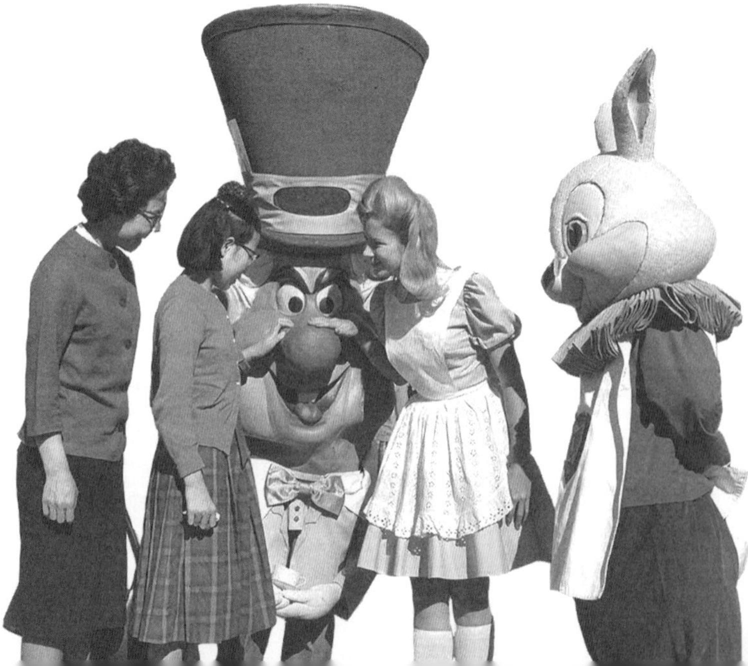

Cities made differently

tile 6

The City of Play

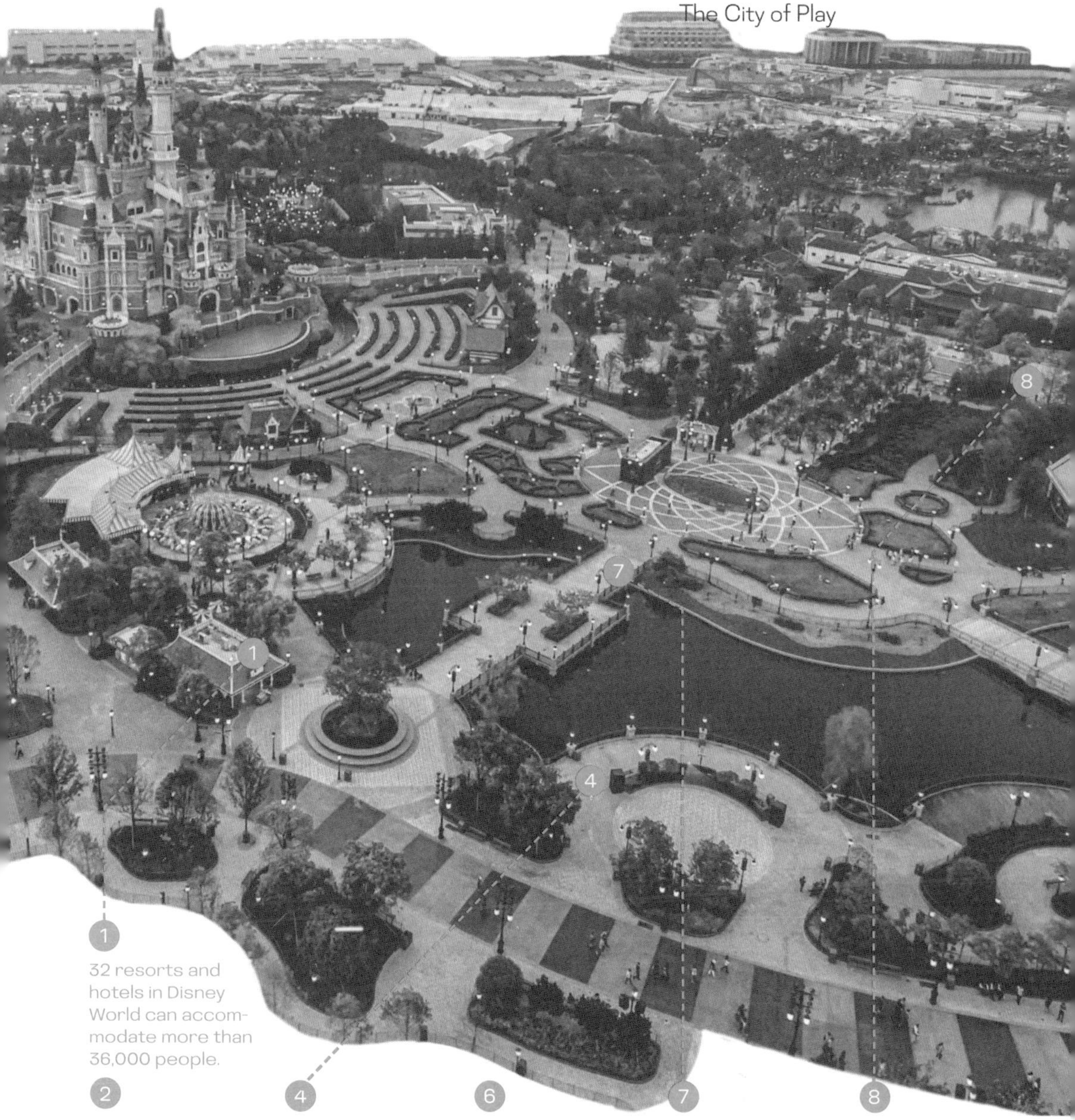

1
32 resorts and hotels in Disney World can accommodate more than 36,000 people.

2
On busy days, Disney World can have up to 155,000 visitors. People need to plan and book their trip well in advance.

3
Disney Springs is a separate complex with 100 shops and 65 dining places.

4
Disney World governs the surrounding area and operates under specific tax regulations.

5
Four theme parks and two water parks are spread across the area, almost as big as San Francisco.

6
Some of the people you see there are actually undercover security personnel. There are also cameras all over the park for surveillance.

7
Beneath the Magic Kingdom of Disney Park, there's a huge tunnel system that crew members use for transportation. It covers nine acres and includes facilities like trash disposal, delivery services, warehouses, and a cafeteria for staff.

8
The parking lot for Magic Kingdom Park covers an area of more than 125 acres and can hold over 12,000 cars, which makes it one of the largest in the world. It's bigger than the park itself.

What if the center of your town became a playground? Think of it in a way that makes it interesting for old and young alike. Someplace people would want to gather—perhaps to figure out city affairs while they play?

Imagine a ten-story house designed especially for play and to run around in. A maze house, a garden-house, a park-house!

In large cities, playgrounds are often characterized by standardized designs and enclosed within grid-like fences. This design reflects a common belief that society is safest and best governed with careful partitions, walls, and lines, creating within itself stark divisions between public and private, work and leisure, white and black, legal and illegal, rich and poor, etc. Playgrounds are another way of dividing people in the name of keeping order. The young are separated from the old under the pretext of protecting each from the other.

Initially, New York City playgrounds were built at the request of the children themselves, who even collected money for play areas. However, the outcome was that the playgrounds built were more like prison yards than play zones. The city hired supervisors to order children to play certain games and to separate boys and girls to different sides of the playground.

Do rules keep people safe? Or is there more to safety than just rules?

In August 1904, several months after the public playground opened, the New York Tribune reported that "the great problem has been the maintenance of order... it has taken a year of ceaseless effort for the young men and women in charge to gain a semblance of control over the youngsters."

Perhaps fenced playgrounds symbolize adults' fear of children. Or children's fear of adults? Or perhaps our shared hope not to lose control of dangerous big-city life?

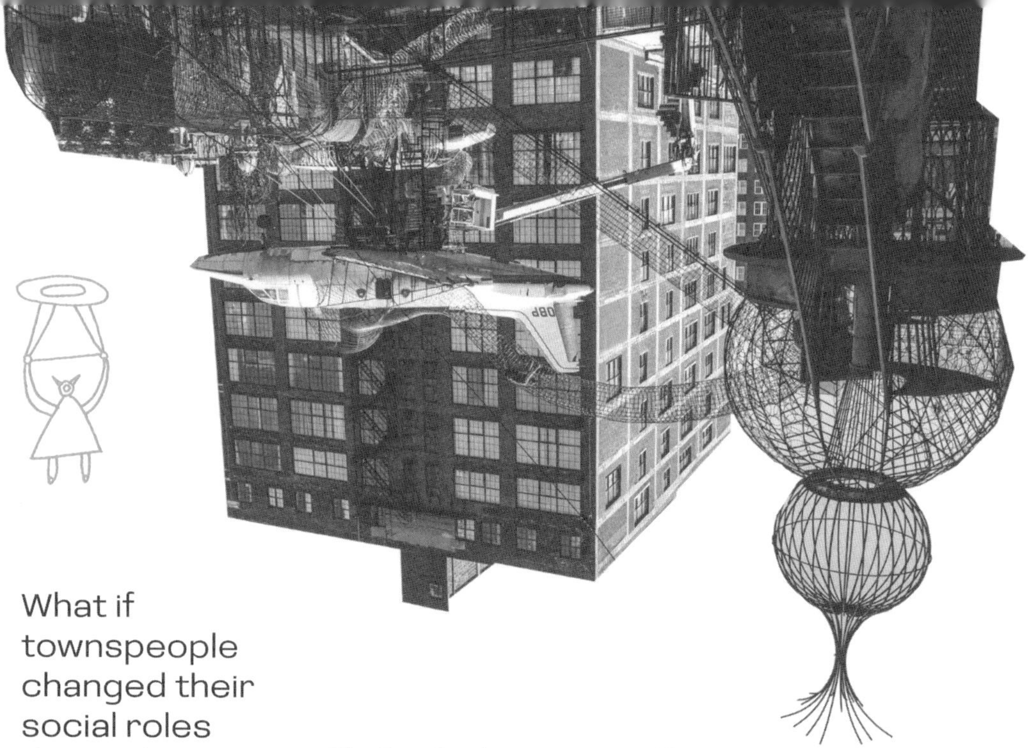

What if townspeople changed their social roles depending on the season?

What if in the summer, everyone would be playful and disobedient, and in the winter they would work hard.

Come fall and spring, townsfolk would spend time learning from each other.

The British educator A. S. Neill believed that even school should be a place for play. In 1921, he founded the Summerhill School on the basis that teachers and children should be equal. In this school, nobody is forced to go to class, and games are no less important than other tasks. Students choose subjects according to their taste, and nobody is given grades.

All decisions are made collectively and each person has a vote. Everyone behaves as they please, as long as they don't harm others.

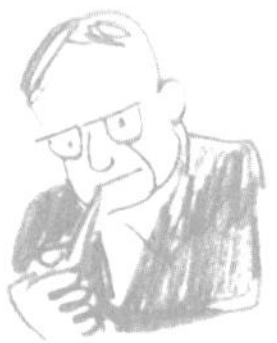

A. S. Neill

"I believe that to impose anything by authority is wrong. The child should not do anything until he comes to the opinion—his own opinion—that it should be done. The curse of humanity is the external compulsion, whether it comes from the Pope or the state or the teacher or the parent. It is fascism in toto."

ady town, prison town, city of Fear, upside-down t

City of Greed

what if you had to live in a city whose citizens must pay not only for housing and healthcare but also for the air they breathe?

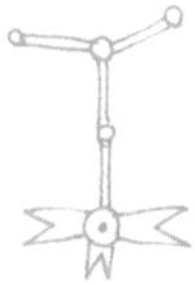

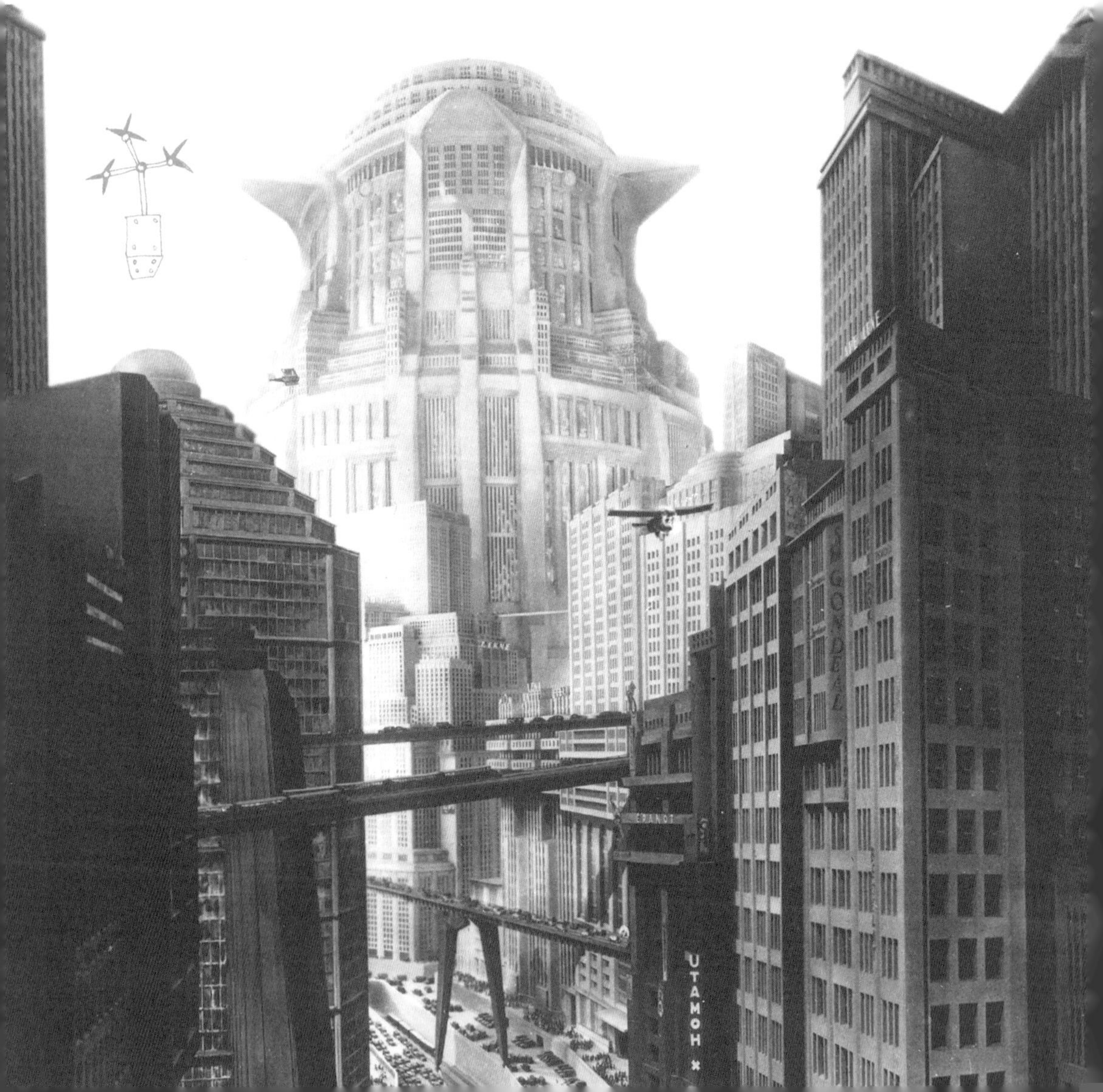

In most cultures, feeding travelers and sheltering the homeless is considered a must, but in ours, the hungry and homeless are regarded as a good way to make money. Should we change that?

Do you think the world would be a better place if there was a price tag on water, food, sunlight, and even air?

The dystopian novel *The Air Merchant* takes place in a secret underground factory city. Mr. Bailey, the factory owner, condenses air from the atmosphere and sells it to his fellow citizens for a profit. Eventually, the Earth's atmosphere thins, creating a catastrophic shortage of breathable air. With the price of air increasing, fewer and fewer humans can afford to keep breathing.

When people can't pay for the air they breathe, the police throw them out of the city. Everyone lives in constant fear of suffocating, thinking only of how to earn enough money to spare their loved ones and themselves that terrible fate.

The food company Nestlé is often criticized for its irresponsible use of water in India, Pakistan, and other developing countries. Captured in the documentary film *We Feed the World* (2005), a former Nestlé chairman said:

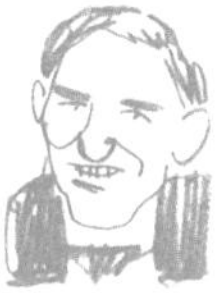

Peter Brabeck-Letmathe

"It's a question of whether we should privatize the normal water supply for the population. And there are two different opinions on the matter [...] NGOs, who bang on about declaring water a public right [...] That's an extreme solution. The other view says that water is a foodstuff like any other, and like any other foodstuff, it should have a market value. Personally, I believe it's better to give a foodstuff a value so that we're all aware it has its price ... "

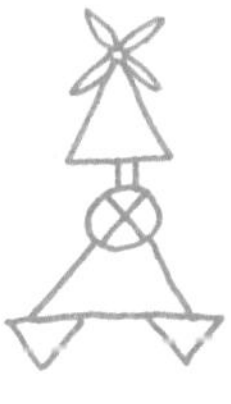

r city, prison town, invisible city, upside-down tow

Cities made differently
tile 8
City as a Family

City as a Family

Imagine a city without any strangers, where everything is shared, and everyone looks after each other. There are no shops, no money, and no danger at all.

We think of the family as a group that practices "basic communism": from each according to his ability, to each according to his needs. Any family is thought to be protected by bonds of kinship from the cruel laws of the outside world. Unlike businesses, rarely will a family throw out a sick child or an elderly parent because they are no longer "revenue-generating assets."

According to Roman law, which still underlies the value system of Western societies, a family was all those people living within the household of a paterfamilias, or father, whose authority over them was recognized as absolute. Under the protection of her own father, a wife might be spared abuse, but his children, slaves, and other dependents were his to do with as he wanted. According to early Roman law, a father was fully within his rights to whip, torture, or sell them. A father could even execute his children, provided that he found them to have committed capital crimes. With his slaves, he didn't even need that excuse.

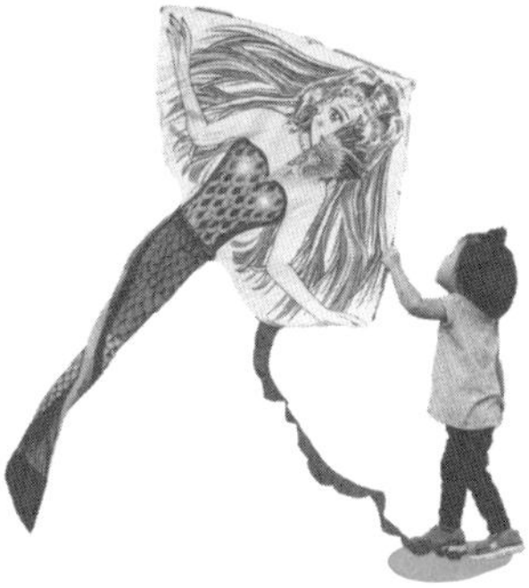

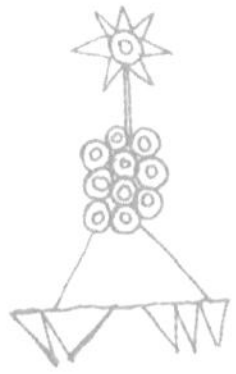

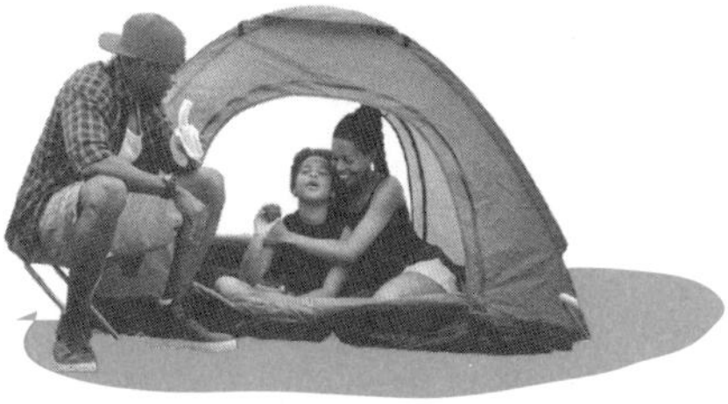

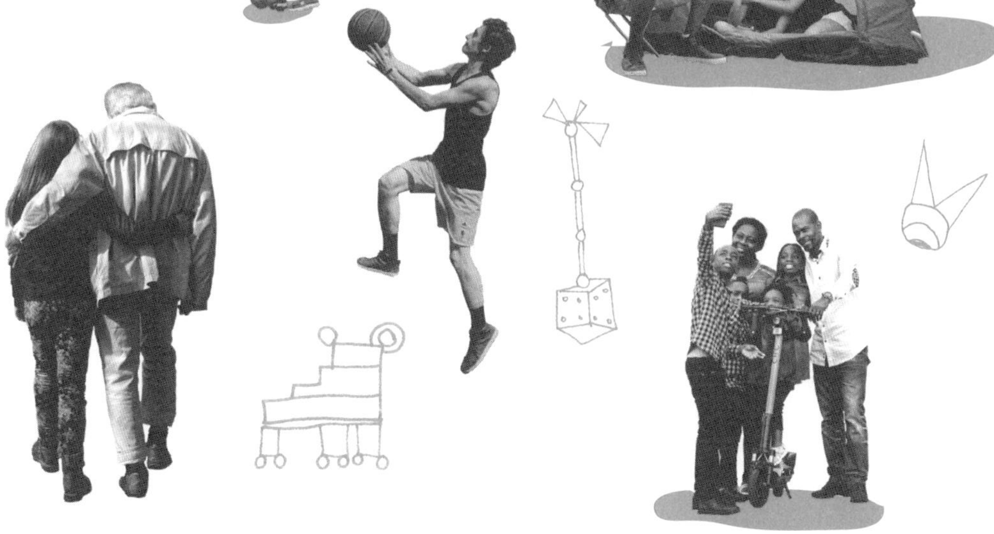

Sometimes family members don't agree with each other, while people from totally different places might find they have much more in common.

Do people have to be related to share a worldview?

Patriarchal family is also the model for authoritarianism. In ancient Rome, the patriarch had the right to treat his household members as property rather than as equal human beings.

The Enlightenment philosopher Jean-Jacques Rousseau believed that humankind originally lived in small bands of hunter-gatherers composed of close friends and relatives until big cities and agriculture emerged, and with them wars, greed, and exploitation.

However, archaeology shows us numerous examples of how people in different times and across different parts of the Earth lived in large metropolitan areas while managing their collective affairs on a fairly egalitarian basis. At the same time, there have always been small communities where status inequality prevailed and a privileged minority at the top benefited by exploiting the rest.

We know from our personal experience that in almost every family, there are elements of both authoritarianism and baseline communism. This contradiction never fully goes away but different cultures handle it differently.

Dominium derives from dominus, meaning "master" or "slave-owner," but ultimately from domus, meaning "house" or "household."

Cities made differently
tile 8
City as a Family

"And the boys go
into business
And marry and raise
a family In boxes
made of ticky-tacky
And they all look just
the same."

Malvina Reynolds

City-less City

Road construction and cheap gasoline made it possible in the nineteenth and twentieth centuries to create huge residential settlements outside of cities, called suburbs, where neighbors live very close to one another but remain strangers. These suburbs have created many environmental problems. Suburbanites

1 Water
Phoenix is a desert. Water for the city is supplied by pipeline from the Colorado River, over 300 miles away, and the river is drying up.

2 Houses
Phoenix homes are built without regard to their environment, a desert, where temperatures exceed 100 degrees for more than 100 days a year. As a result, a massive amount of energy goes into cooling them.

3 Roads
Phoenix is a huge highway. Eighty-eight percent of Phoenix residents commute by car to work. There is virtually no public transportation, and the city ranks among the worst in the country for ozone pollution.

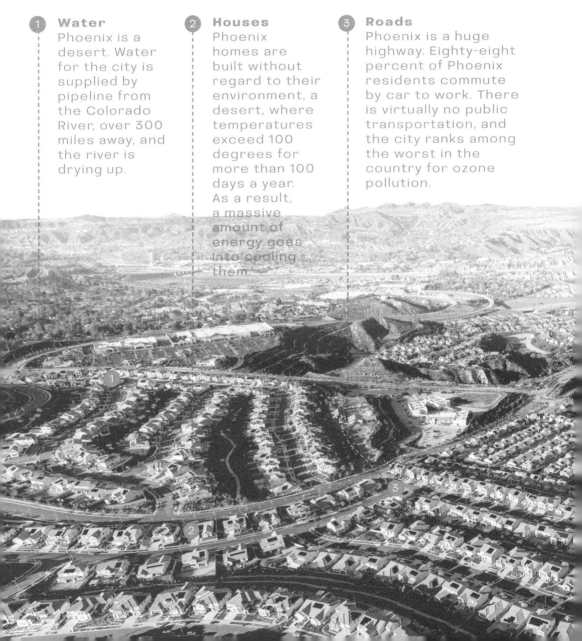

Cities made differently
tile 8
City as a Family

"Perhaps the most important thing we produce is other human beings. Outside of that, the production of things has no meaning."

David Graeber

spend hours and burn millions of gallons of fuel commuting to and from their jobs in cities. And vast natural areas that once were forests, lakes, and fields, places where birds and animals lived, have been destroyed to build large, uniform houses and lawns.

The suburbs became the domestic sphere where human life is reproduced: where children are born and raised, where dishes are washed (mostly by women), and where relatives gather. Conversely, the city remains the public sphere where (mostly men) make money, write laws, and produce useful things far away, or at least a couple hours drive away from the suburbs.

What if instead of cities and suburbs, there were networks of settlements where people both worked and lived, and grew food, and raised and educated their kids? For large festivals or carnivals, everybody would come together!

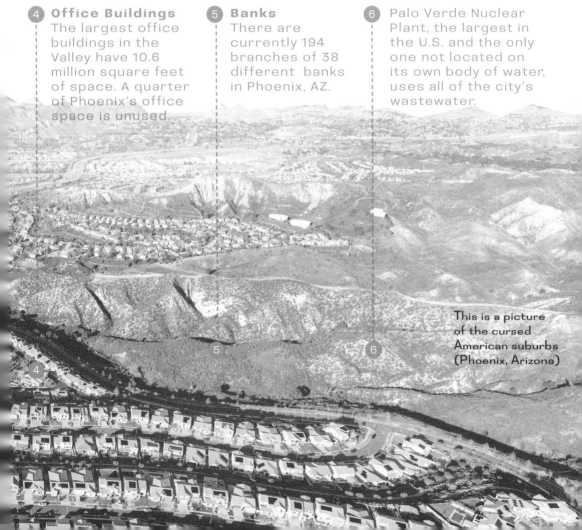

4 **Office Buildings**
The largest office buildings in the Valley have 10.6 million square feet of space. A quarter of Phoenix's office space is unused.

5 **Banks**
There are currently 194 branches of 38 different banks in Phoenix, AZ.

6 Palo Verde Nuclear Plant, the largest in the U.S. and the only one not located on its own body of water, uses all of the city's wastewater.

This is a picture of the cursed American suburbs (Phoenix, Arizona)

Cities made differently
tile 9
City in the Desert

City in the Desert

1   The Sky Suite, a two-bedroom rental apartment for tourists.

2   Ten live/work units will house up to sixty residents once finished.

3   Big musical and theatrical performances are held in the Amphitheater, which seats up to 500 spectators.

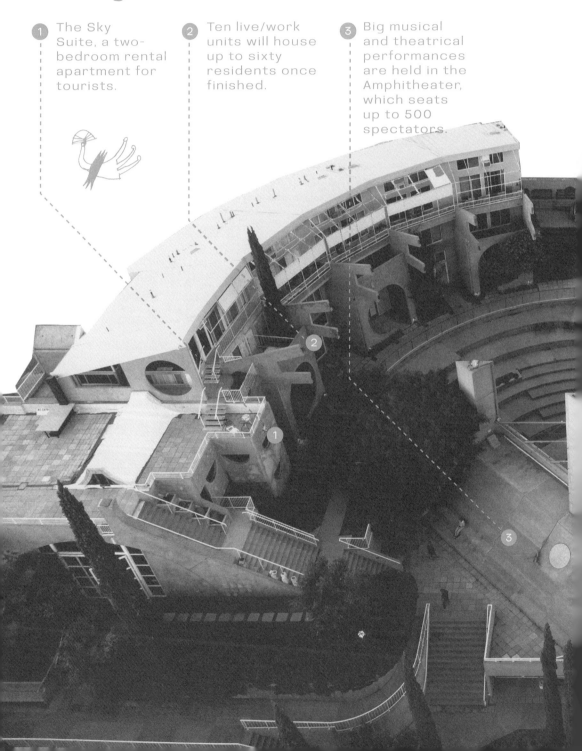

Arcosanti is a city for 2,000 people in the middle of a dead desert. Inside this big house, each resident has their own small bedroom, but they all come together to eat, work, and play.

4 The classroom can accommodate up to fifty people for workshops and community events.

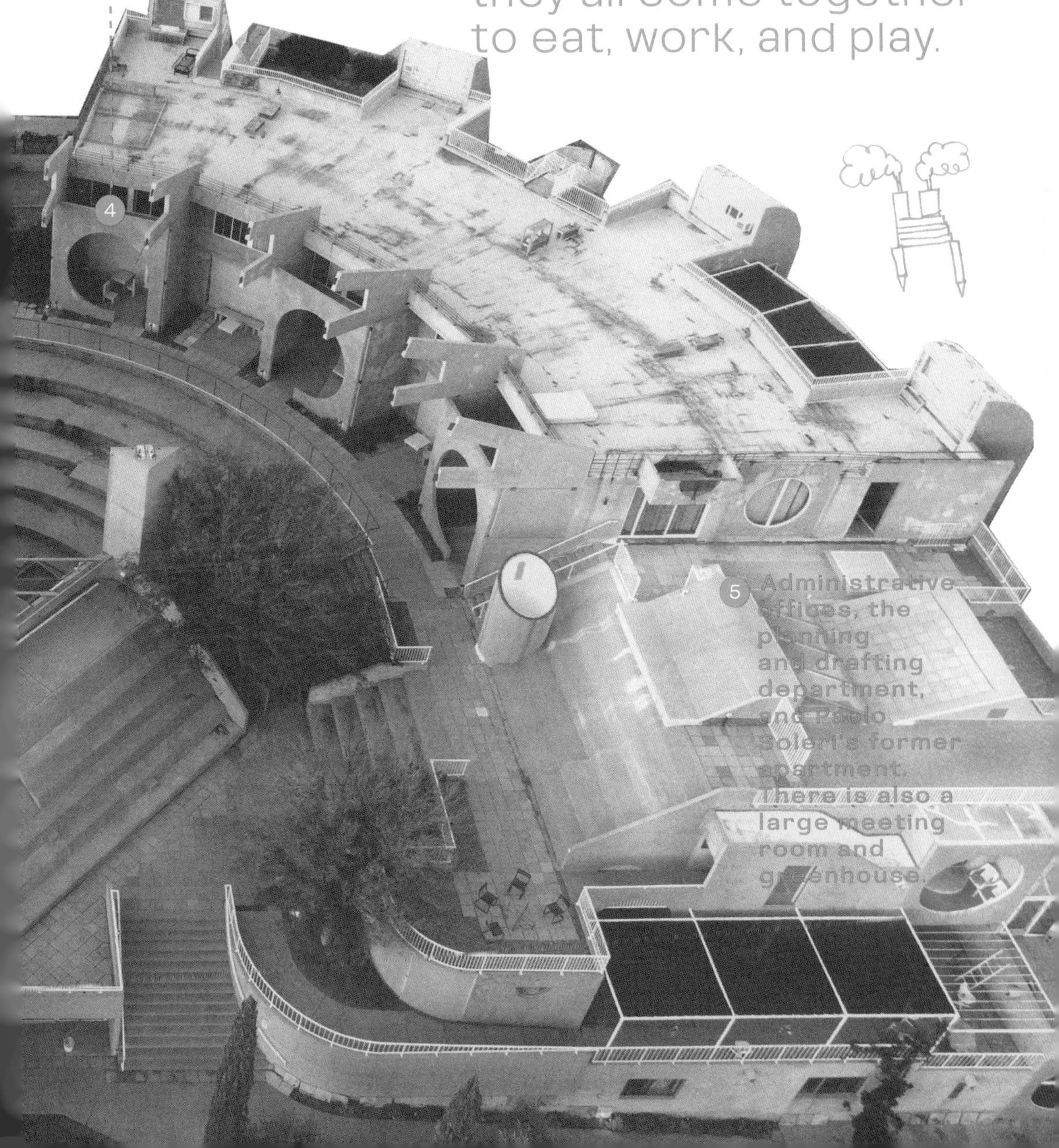
4
5
Administrative offices, the planning and drafting department, and Paolo Soleri's former apartment. There is also a large meeting room and greenhouse.

Cities made differently
tile 9
City in the Desert

In the face of
climate chaos,
how to build
resource-
efficient
cities?

Italian architect Paolo Soleri designed and built Arcosanti—a
city in the Arizona desert. Soleri wanted Arcosanti to show
how urban life can be lived with reverence for nature and how
it could benefit the city's residents rather than generate
profit. Arcosanti has everything needed for a comfortable life:
residential buildings, cafes, hotels, stores, a movie theater, gardens, farms, a swimming pool, and an amphitheater for public
assemblies.

One could say that Arcosanti has become a materialized ecological utopia, a model city built in spite of and as an admonition
to its neighboring city, Spring Valley, whose population is com-
parable to Arcosanti, while the city itself occupies an incredibly
larger area.

In a sense, the entire town of Arcosanti is one big building with
small living and large public spaces, replete with everything
each resident would need.

It is striking to realize that most of our problems have already
been solved in the last century. It turns out it is possible to live
without destroying the environment, without kicking out extra
people who don't fit in who are taking our jobs. Because, you
know what? We don't actually need to work that hard, because
most of the jobs are created by crooked social design: for the
purpose of building unnecessary houses and infrastructure,
producing cars, gasoline, people who organize and sell it all to us.

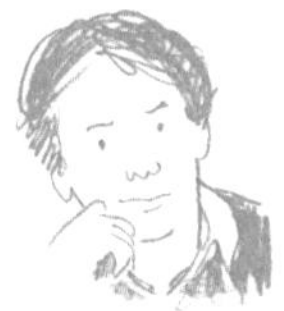

David Graeber

"If it's really true that as much as half the work we do could be eliminated without any significant effect on overall productivity, why not just redistribute the remaining work in such a way that everyone is working four-hour days? Or four-day weeks with four months' yearly vacation time? Or some similarly easy-going arrangement? Why not start shutting down the global work machine? If nothing else, it would probably be the most effective thing we could do to put a brake on global warming."

If people only had to work a few hours a week, we would have cities like Arcosanti all over the world.

Perhaps enact a worldwide law to restrict the construction of environmentally harmful cities?

In the developed world the majority of the population lives in cities that need huge amounts of energy to sustain themselves. Their life is generally divided into private and work domains, so they have to spend a lot of time getting to and from work every day.

New office spaces are constantly being built, although during Covid it became apparent that many jobs are actually Bullshit Jobs, and we can get by without them altogether. Whereas necessary jobs can be done locally.

Arcosanti was built as a form of creative refusal of the lifestyle based on endless work, loneliness and destruction of nature.

The starkly contrasting lifestyles and value systems between Arcosanti and Spring Valley have led to radically divergent uses of technology in the design of their living spaces.

Spring Valley is laid out differently in every way: it consists of one-story houses strung along the highway, with thin walls, so they require constant heating in the winter and cooling in the summer. While Arcosanti residents walk everywhere, people in Spring Valley have to drive everywhere, to work, the store, the movies.

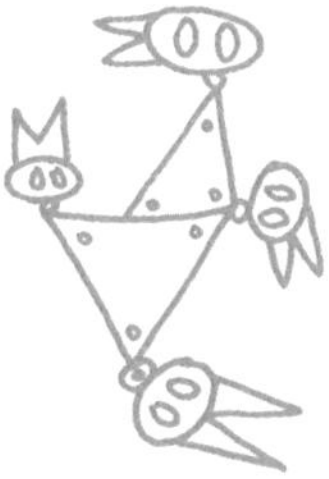

The question is, what happens to cities like Spring Valley, whose very survival depends on access to affordable oil and gas?

Sanctuary City

climate change means natural disasters will become more common. could a city protect its residents from extreme weather? could it feed and heal its own citizens?

In 1931, Abram Ioffe, known as the father of Soviet physics, proposed the idea of making single-building cities in the USSR. As many as a million people would live in one such house. As conceived by Ioffe, these cylindrical, windowless buildings would be heated by human body heat. Workplaces, private quarters, and public spaces would be placed no further than five hundred meters from each other, i.e., a seven- to eight-minute walk. Ioffe's ideas are similar to Paolo Soleri's, as both planned architectural spaces that could anticipate every aspect of human life, including energy consumption, work, entertainment, and even sleep.

In the early twentieth century, progressive architects built iconic examples of collective living, with small living quarters and lots of public space, such as communal canteens, laundries, and gardens. The ecological footprint of a person living in a compact city is much smaller than that of a person living in the suburbs, who has to travel long distances for work, food, school, and healthcare. People also feel better living together so long as their rights to privacy, safety, and personal space are preserved.

What if a million people moved into a single building? This city-building could have vast gardens and large windows to light roomy apartments. There would be no cars or buses carrying people to work as everyone works together inside. Parks and playgrounds would be located directly on the ground floor.

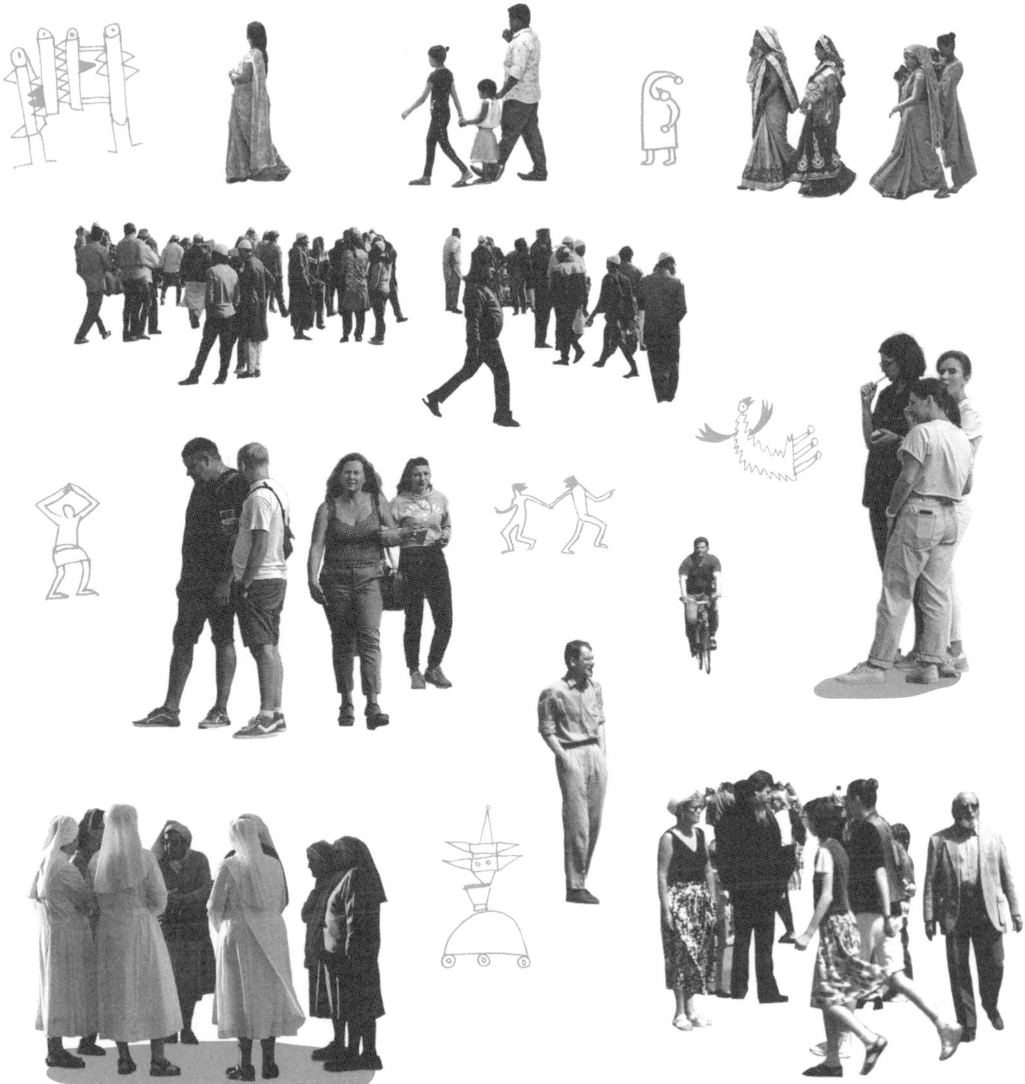

Heating, eating, and commuting costs would be minimal.

Many people believe that climate change will soon make it impossible to live in open spaces.

Large, technologically sophisticated cities may become the only safe place for mankind. They would protect people from wildfires, floods, and drastic temperature changes.

The Saudi monarchy is building a city for nine million residents, designed to be resilient to climate change. The Line will have no cars or streets, just as in Arcosanti. It will be possible to reach every essential living space, including schools, work, and apartments, within five minutes. Residents will be able to reach shopping and entertainment areas through a high-speed train located beneath the building.

The city will be powered entirely by renewable energy. Artificial intelligence will take care of the city's infrastructure, including its energy, water, waste, transportation, healthcare, and safety.

Do you think
The Line is more
of an attempt
by humanity
to save itself
from climate
disasters or
the opposite:
ignoring
that it exists
altogether?

A city-garden located in the heart of the desert. Isn't this proof that humans can control nature? But the construction of The Line would produce upwards of 1.8 billion tons of carbon dioxide, the equivalent of more than four years' worth of the UK's entire emissions.

We have one planet and one ecosystem. However, we have divided the earth into states and allow nations to do whatever they want within their own territory, although the climate change disaster they are each contributing to will affect everyone.

Compare Line City and Arcosanti. Where would you rather live?

Artificial intelligence will be used by The Line to integrate the city's life support systems, energy generation, and transportation. Yet, rules are made by humans, not by computers. Neutral technology does not exist. Technology is always political. Imagine what a Smart City might look like if the rules were written by a villain or a madman? What if the manager thinks women shouldn't be allowed to leave their flats or that children should be beaten?

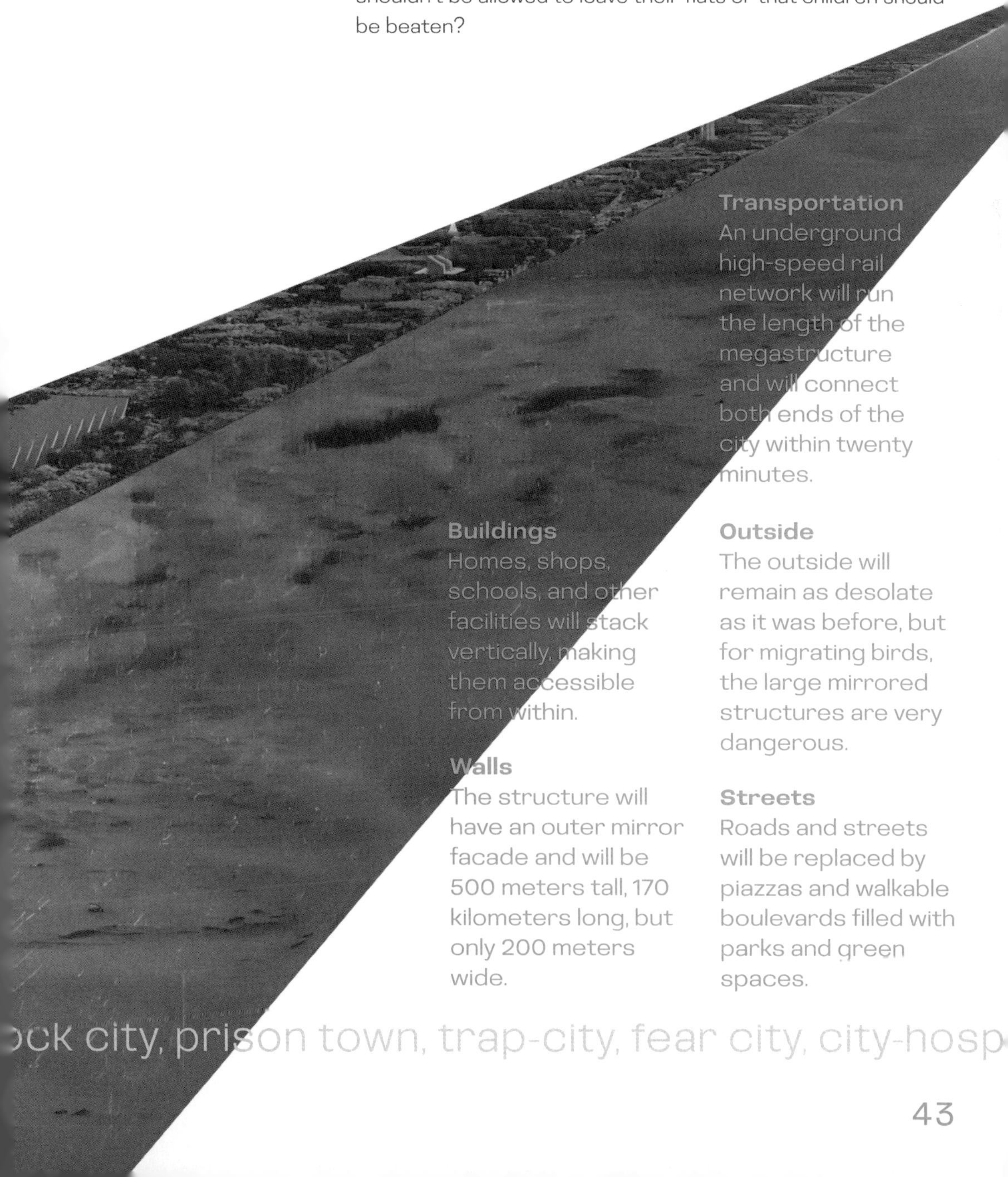

Transportation
An underground high-speed rail network will run the length of the megastructure and will connect both ends of the city within twenty minutes.

Buildings
Homes, shops, schools, and other facilities will stack vertically, making them accessible from within.

Walls
The structure will have an outer mirror facade and will be 500 meters tall, 170 kilometers long, but only 200 meters wide.

Outside
The outside will remain as desolate as it was before, but for migrating birds, the large mirrored structures are very dangerous.

Streets
Roads and streets will be replaced by piazzas and walkable boulevards filled with parks and green spaces.

ock city, prison town, trap-city, fear city, city-hosp

Leader
City

There are places where king-like figures reign for many years. It's believed that they are just great people—comrades or even relatives of everyone.

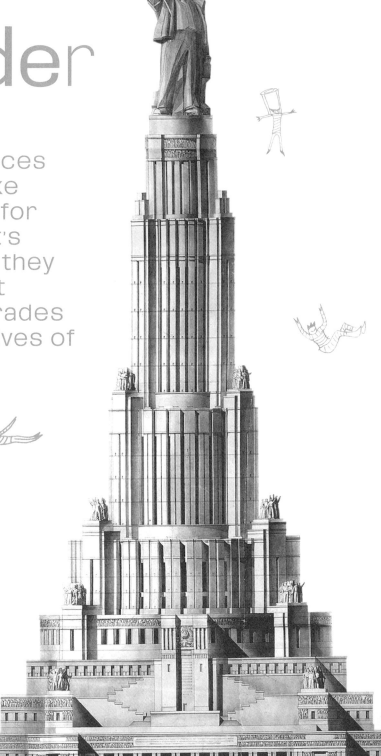

44

In the center of such towns there are sculptures of the chief.
At the beginning of each day, the residents bow three times to
the image of the chief, chanting "Thank you, chief, father!" If people love their leader, the leader will return their love and protect
them from enemies. Do you think that's a safe guess?

ıp city, shady town, city-hospital, upside-down tov

City of the Watched

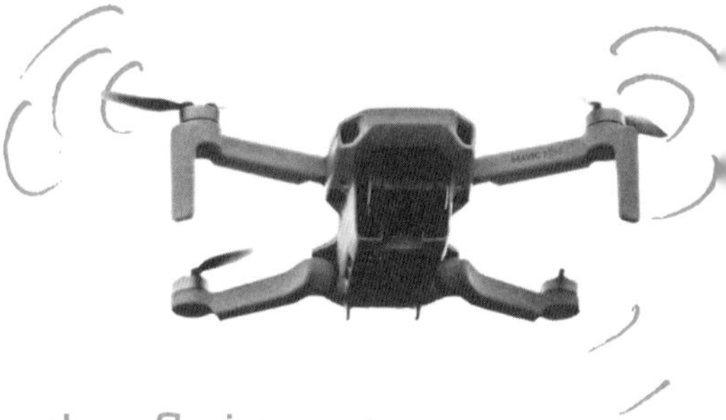

All residents are assigned a flying-eye camera that follows them everywhere they go.

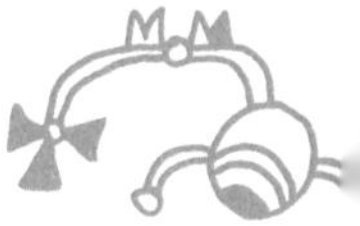

Do you think it's normal to live under constant surveillance by a flying eye? Maybe a little annoying?

CCTV cameras, introduced in England in the 1950s, were designed to monitor traffic. Since then they have spread everywhere, filming citizens not only on the streets but also in stores, schools, hospitals, parks, and even at home. Londoners are monitored by nearly one million surveillance cameras, some of which are already connected to a centralized facial recognition system.

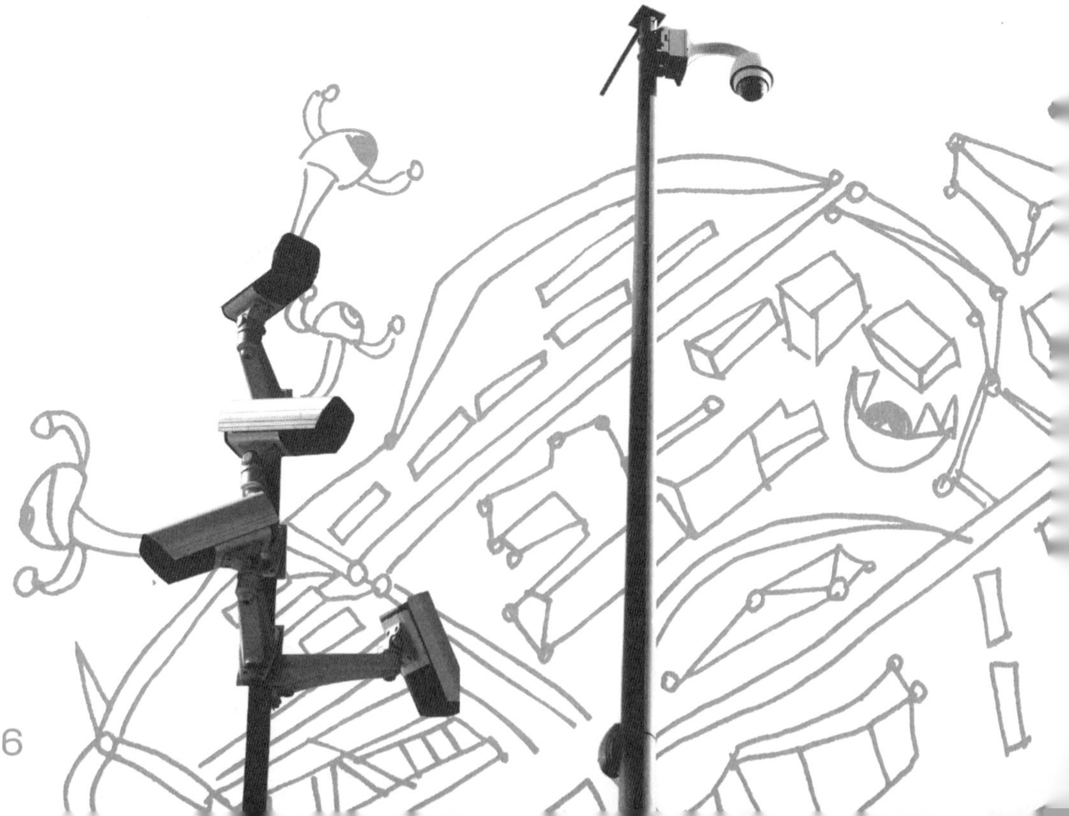

Cities made differently
tile 12
City of the Watched

Some adults like to be under complete control as if they were little kids. Just like in Leader City. How about you?

David Graeber

"The bureaucratization of daily life means the imposition of impersonal rules and regulations; impersonal rules and regulations, in turn, can only operate if they are backed up by the threat of force. And indeed, in this most recent phase of total bureaucratization, we've seen security cameras, police scooters, issuers of temporary ID cards, and men and women in a variety of uniforms acting in either public or private capacities, trained in tactics of menacing, intimidating, and ultimately deploying physical violence, appear just about everywhere—even in places such as playgrounds, primary schools, college campuses, hospitals, libraries, parks, or beach resorts, where fifty years ago their presence would have been considered scandalous, or simply weird."

Privacy activists argue that filming people who are not suspects poses a threat to public well-being.

Edward Snowden

"Saying that you don't care about the right to privacy because you have nothing to hide is no different than saying you don't care about freedom of speech because you have nothing to say."

ar city, city-hospital, upside-down town, dark city,

Transparent City

You can't hide from other people's eyes even for a second. All the walls in this city are transparent.

Yevgeny
Zamyatin

People want to be with each other. Yet they want to keep something for themselves. Where do we draw the line?

We by Yevgeny Zamyatin, published in 1924, was one of the first dystopian novels. It describes a society in which the state machine has excessive power. Inspiring George Orwell's *1984* and Aldous Huxley's *Brave New World*, *We* helped introduce the idea of dystopia as a literary genre.

The story takes place in a distant future, in a city isolated from the world by a green glass wall. Everything in it is subject to a strictly organized schedule: people get out of bed at the same time, eat their meals, and go to work or study, as though all of them are parts of a huge machine.

The heroes of the novel do not have personal names, but are instead marked by numbers. Each citizen is equally unfree within the system. Even the Benefactor, who rules the United State, is as much a slave to the system as any other Number. The lack of freedom is considered a guarantee of happiness because they believe in this city that freedom and happiness are incompatible, and that the main enemy of happiness is imagination, which the United State has learned to remove by means of X-rays.

In Zamyatin's city, people voluntarily give up their freedom or, as Thomas Hobbes would say, "enter into a social contract" to organize their lives so as to secure the happiness and welfare of the collective. The inhabitants of the city believe that as soon as the Benefactor and his guardians cease to watch every step of each one of them, they will immediately sink into the abyss of madness or turn to violence toward one another.

Zamyatin writes:

"For Numbers (as the inhabitants of the city were called) the need for the guiding hand of the Benefactor and complete submission to the control of the guardian spies became a necessity:

It felt so good to feel someone's watchful eye lovingly guarding against the slightest mistake, against the slightest misstep. It may sound a little sentimental, but the same analogy comes to my mind again: the guardian angels of which the ancients dreamed. How much of what they only dreamed of has materialized in our lives."

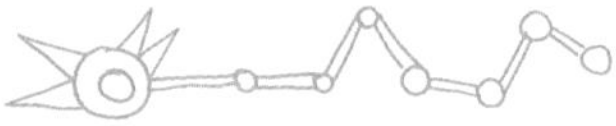

Today's authorities have a far greater technological capacity for control over people's lives than has ever existed in the history of mankind. Powerful agencies can intrude into the daily lives of virtually everyone using surveillance technology, whereas in the past, the State could only know what you were up to by means of spies overhearing conversations and collecting gossip. It seems that we are witnessing Thomas Hobbes's wild nightmare come to fruition with the construction of a real, digital Leviathan.

Which decisions in life would you like to keep private and not discuss with anyone, or only with very trusted friends?

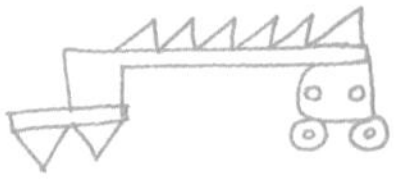

isible city, prison town, city-hospital, upside-dowr

City of Masks

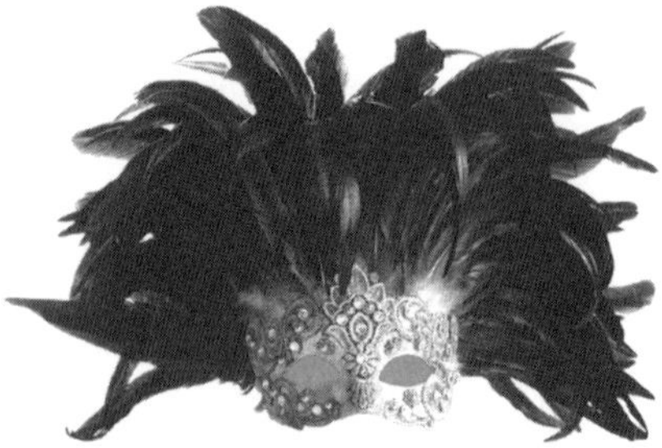

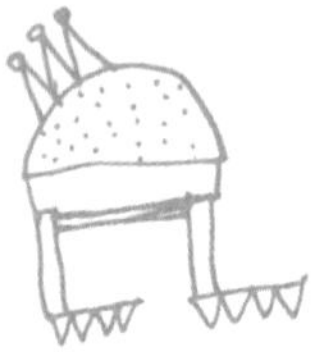

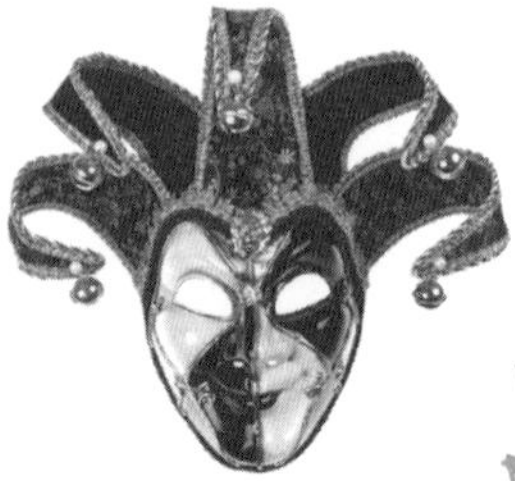

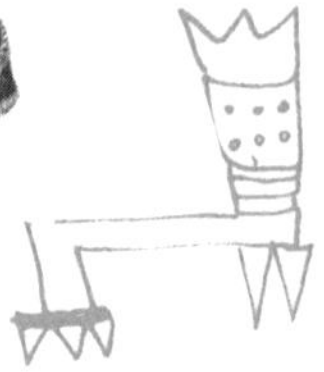

Imagine a city where everyday life is a carnaval! Every morning everyone must decide who to be today: a young beauty, a squeaky monster, a shady spy. Everyone can be whoever they want to be.

This is how carnivalesque Venice used to be for a few months of the year, a city built by fugitives and pirates hiding in its swampy shores from justice, debts, or taxes. The Mask was protected by the Republic of Venice. People went everywhere wearing one: to a salon, a government office, a monastery, a ball, a palace or a gambling house. During Carnival, rich and poor, beautiful and ugly, young and old disappeared. A patrician in a long robe could turn out to be a miserable beggar, and a humble.

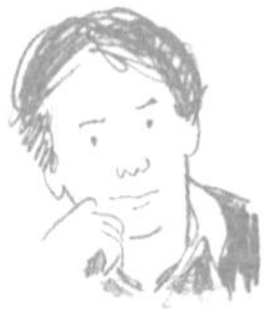

David Graeber

"We will remain faceless because we refuse the spectacle of celebrity, because we are everyone, because the carnival beckons, because the world is upside down, because we are everywhere. By wearing masks, we show that who we are is not as important as what we want, and what we want is everything for everyone."

tile 14
City of Masks

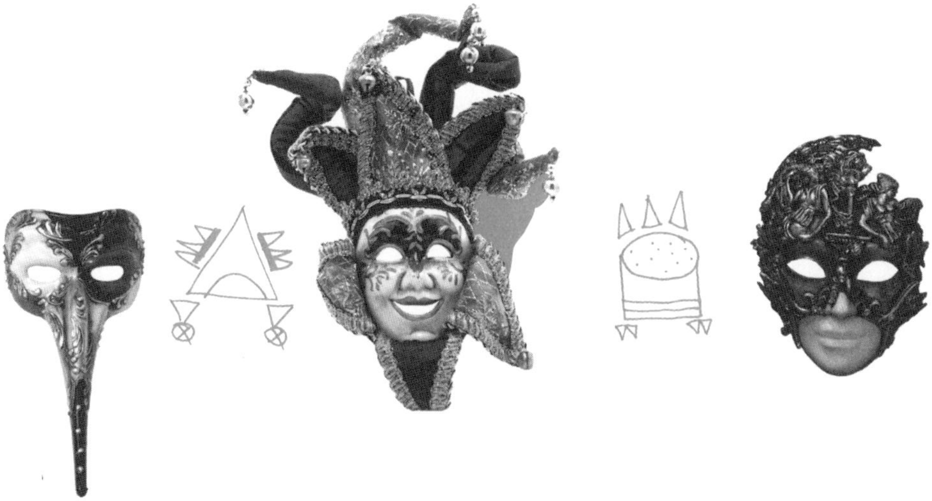

What if behind the urge to live under unbreakable rules is merely the fear of play?

A nun, a dexterous dealer, a noble lady, and a spy from a hostile kingdom—all were transformed into carnival performers, hidden behind a mask.

If the rules of carnival are that people are not the same thing as their masks, everyone must be as creative as possible in becoming the other. In war, the rules of the game are the opposite: everyone is exactly the same as their uniform. That is why members of one team kill the members of the enemy team as if everyone on the other team was the same person.

Most soldiers suspect that underneath the uniforms people are different: they are smart and stupid, young and old, beautiful and ugly. But for the sake of the game, it is decided otherwise. If the soldiers from the Military Town walked into the City of Masks, maybe they'd simply add to the cast of carnivalesque characters.

Compare the City of Masks with regulation-obsessed Cities, where all the rules are set and it's expected that everyone obeys, but no one is able to change anything.

Invisible City

imagine a city where citizens can become invisible whenever they please.

What if you could turn invisible at will? Could you resist becoming a criminal?

The Invisible Man by H. G. Wells is a brilliant novel about a poverty-stricken inventor who discovers the secret of invisibility. By using his invention he hopes to secure money to live on and for his future research. Under capitalism, however, money is always tied to power. So our hero ultimately destroys himself and his invention trying to bring the whole world under his control.

H. G. Wells

"I am just a human being—solid, needing food and drink, needing covering, too— But I'm invisible."

"Alone—it is wonderful how little a man can do alone!"

Is it possible to be safe in the city of invisible people?

Some believe that the surest way to avoid disaster is to allow only those technologies that society can collectively control.

In modern cities, where surveillance cameras follow us everywhere, invisibility is very tempting. American designer Adam Harvey makes costumes that help those wishing to escape the intrusive eye of the camera. Harvey offers neckties, pins, raincoats, and scarves, made with a special coating that confuses cameras, making your face or figure look blurry in the picture.

A technology that lets you control when you can or can't be seen would make you all powerful. Especially if others can't do it!

Imagine you were tasked with putting together a list of beneficial and dangerous technologies.

What two technologies would you forbid and what two technologies would you encourage?

Would making technologies open-source make them more or less safe?

The Open Source movement advocates for collaborative production. People agree to be open with technologies they are building, allowing others to make modifications.

This is how Adrian Bowyer's RepRap 3D printer was made, which was designed to print itself. Over the fifteen years of its existence, its price has dropped from thousands of dollars to a few hundred. Now a community of developers from around the world can potentially print anything for themselves, from household necessities to fine jewelry.

Nothing about this printer is copyrighted and anyone can build their own RepRap by downloading free instructions from one of many free websites.

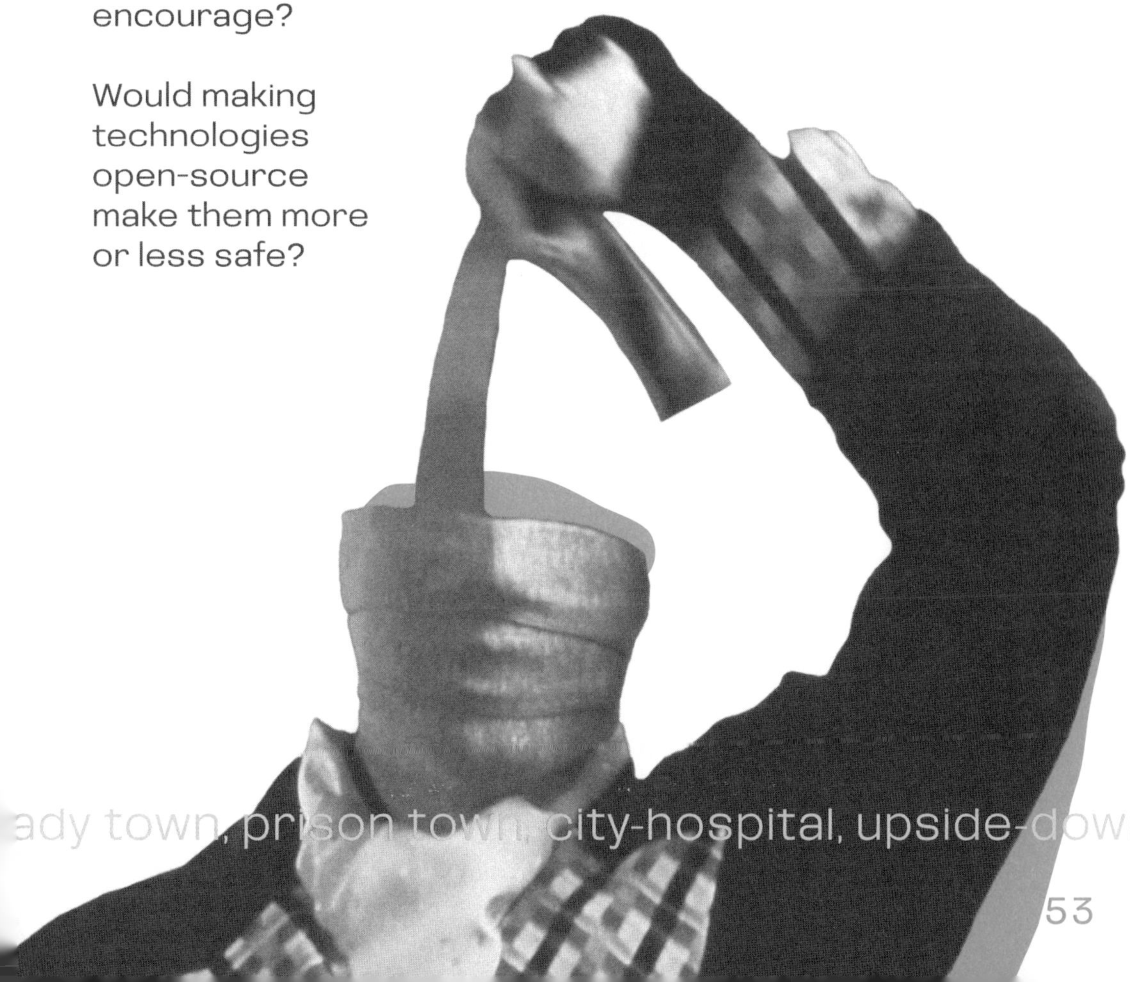
ady town, prison town, city-hospital, upside-down

Solitude City

In Victorian England, privacy was highly valued. Only the very rich were able to close their bedroom door to strangers. Most people lived in constant proximity to one another.

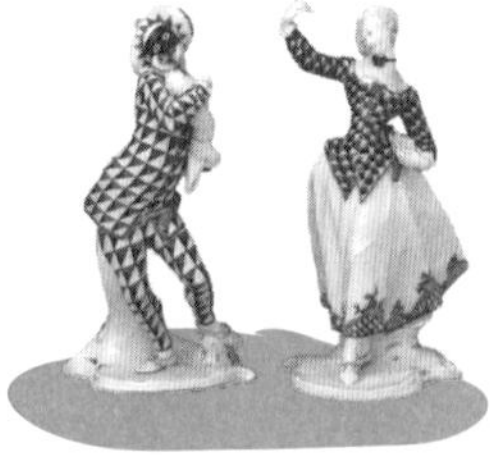

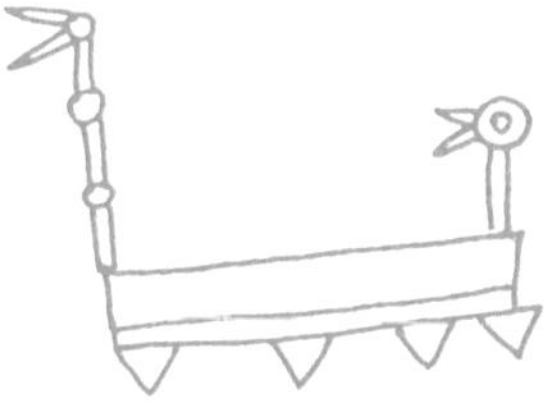

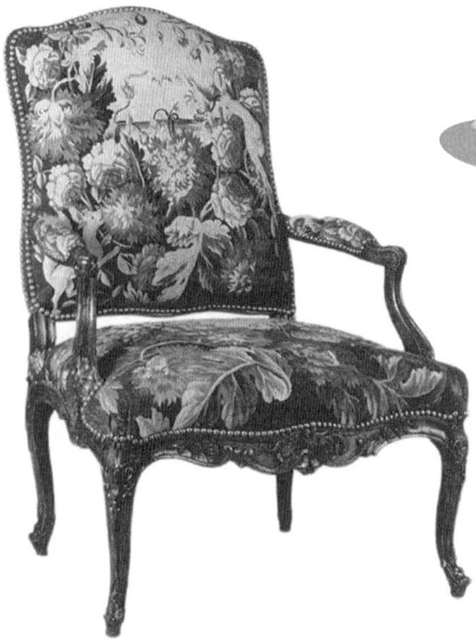

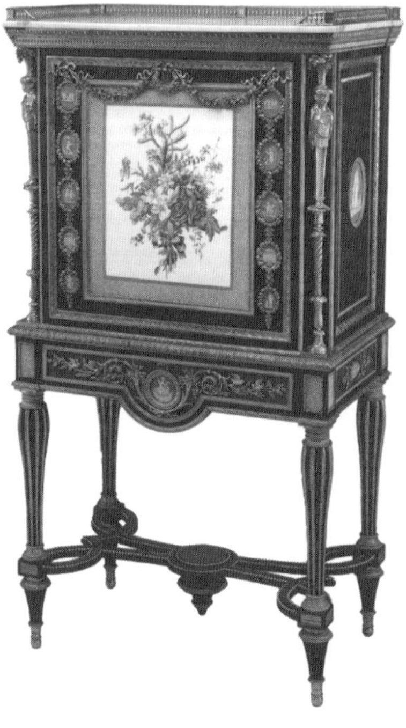

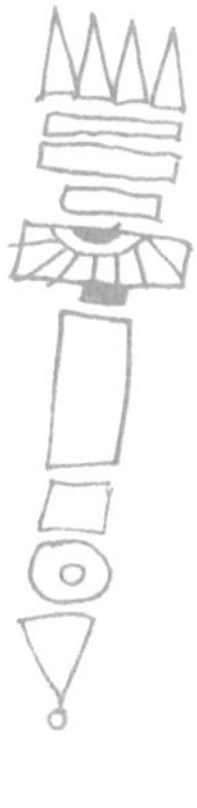

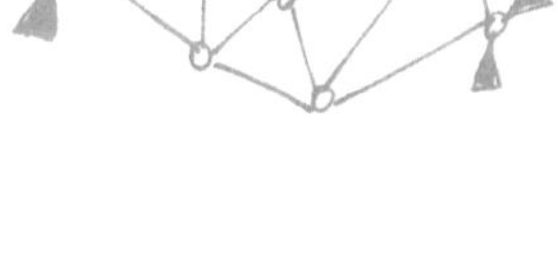

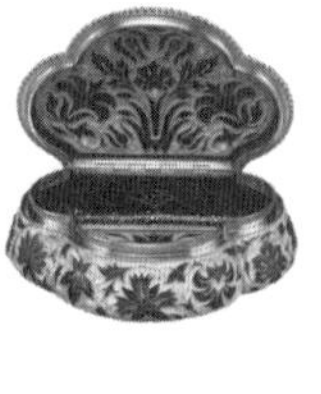

Cities made differently

tile 16

Solitude City

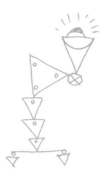

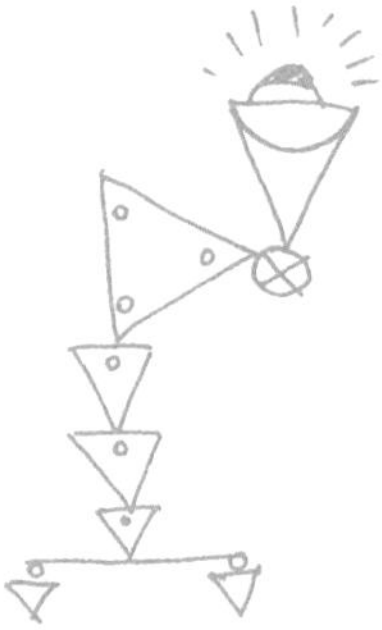

An upper-class Victorian mansion hid the lives of its inhabitants behind heavy curtains and thick walls. Everything from flower vases to table legs was draped in fabric. It was a private fortress, and gaining entry to it was no easy matter.

The occupants themselves were also separated from each other—each had their own private room, even spouses. The corridor system, which emerged during the Victorian era, was new to Europe. In this system, work was separated from home life, the rich from the poor, spouses from each other, and children from their parents.

An important part of the Victorian home was the living room, hidden in the depths of the dwelling and accessible only to the chosen few: family members and selected guests. It was decorated with portraits of the relatives, textiles, books, and colonial souvenirs, such as Chinese porcelain and Indian statuettes. Homeowners were willing to surrender some living space for the sake of making an impression on the right kind of guests in order to improve their social prospects.

London was one of the first cities in the world to industrialize, and once the transformation was underway, it quickly became dirty, smelly, and crowded. The new industrial city also made cleanliness and privacy in the personal home a rare luxury available only to the urban elite, though one likely desired and sought-after by every citizen.

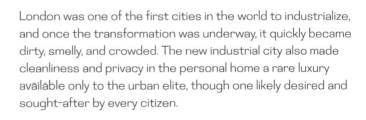

The home of a wealthy Londoner at the time of Queen Victoria was filled with incredible objects: outlandish tableware, carved furniture, and wonderful decorations.

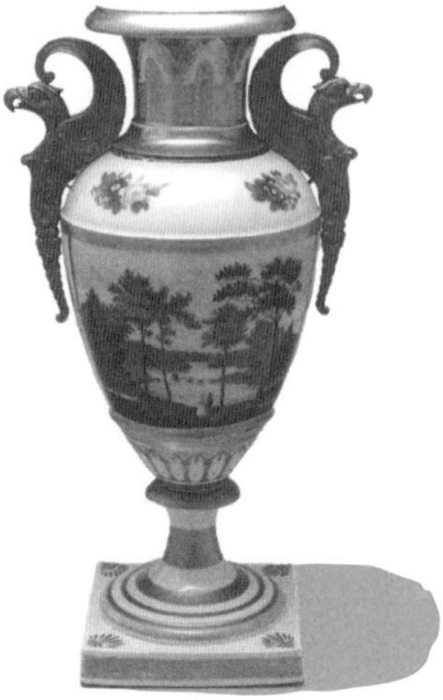

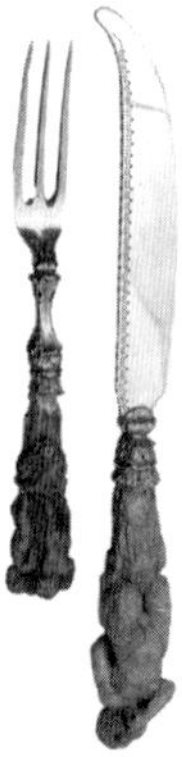

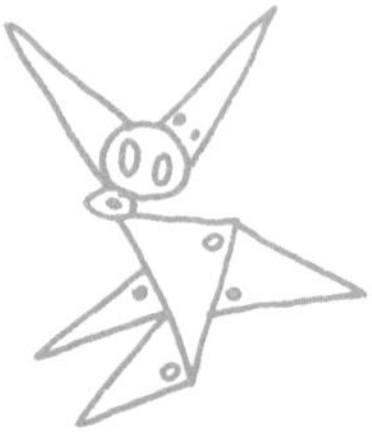

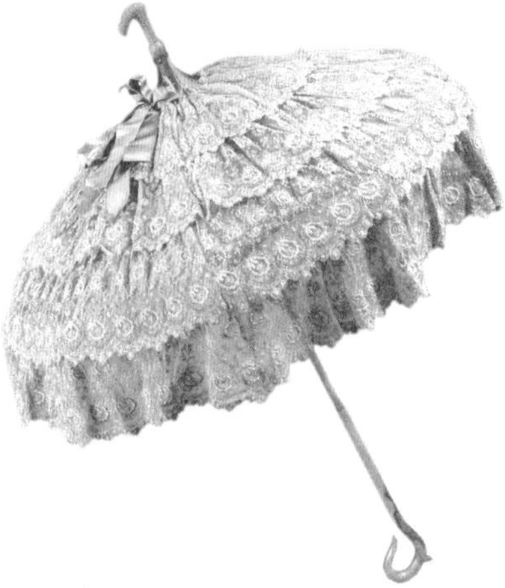

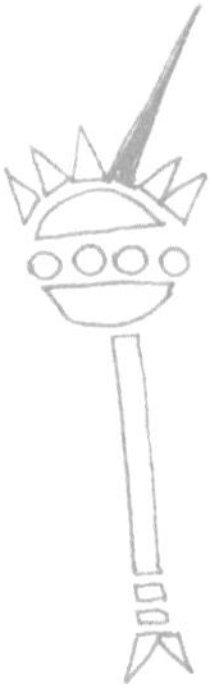

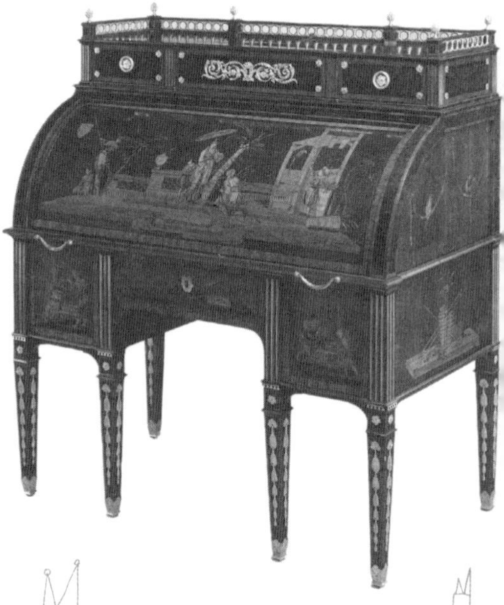

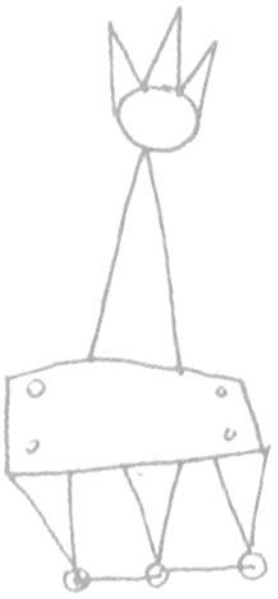

The British Museum is a display of treasures brought in from all over the world: from Chinese sets to Benin art bronzes to Greek and Egyptian art.

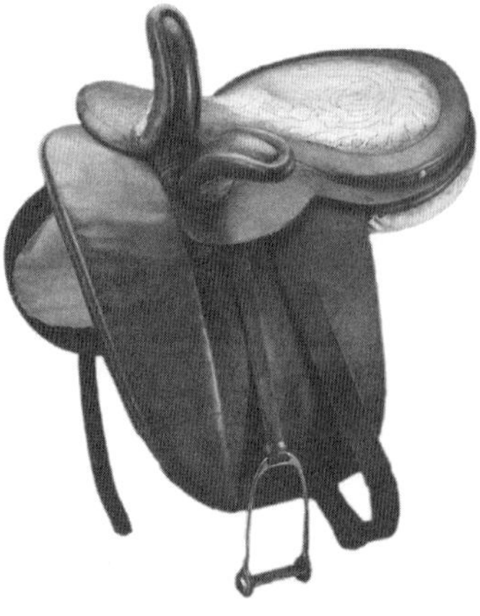

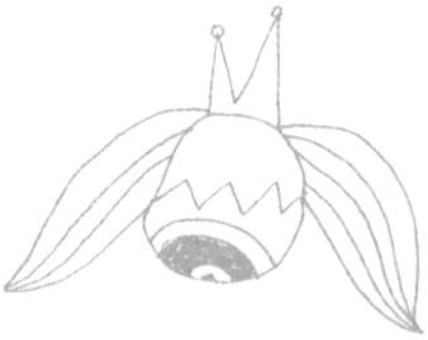

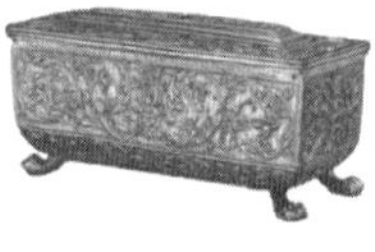

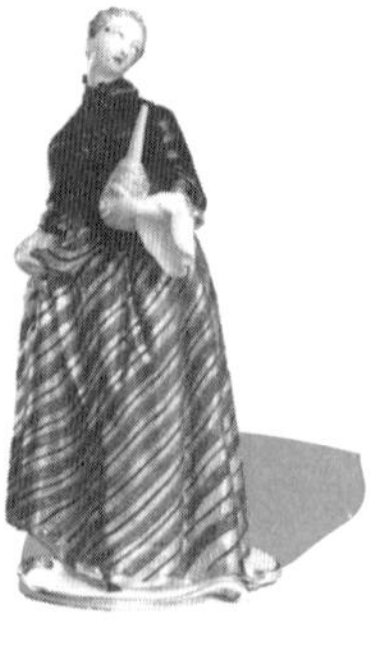

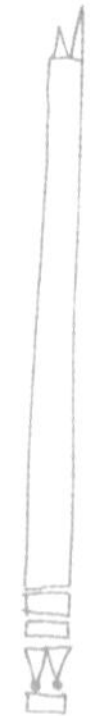

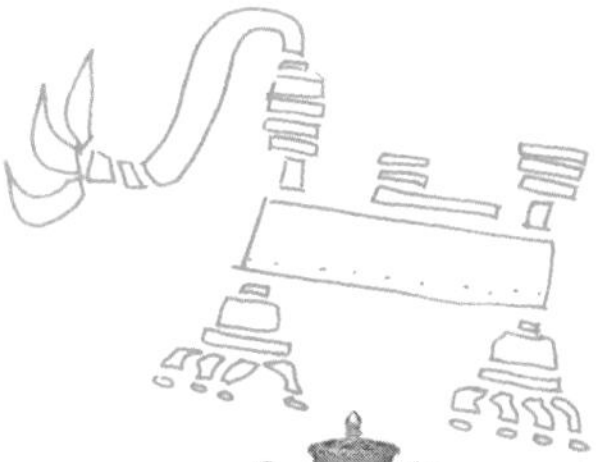

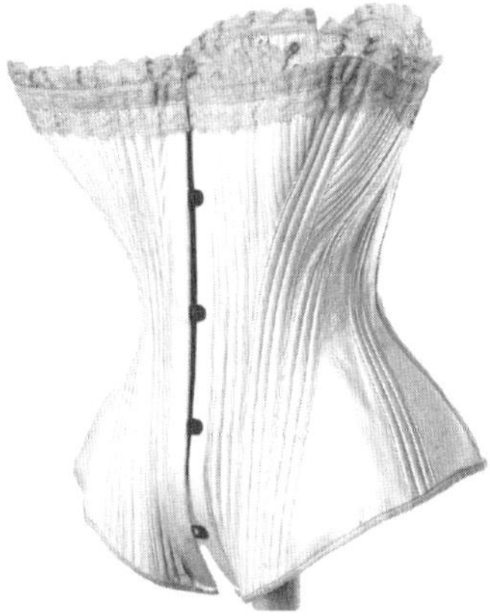

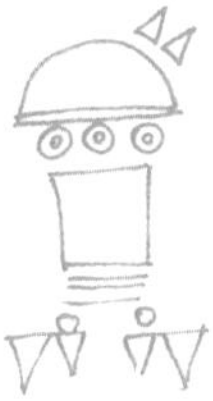

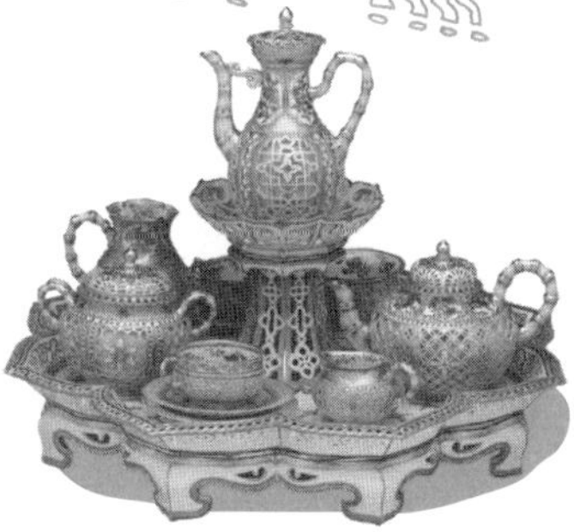

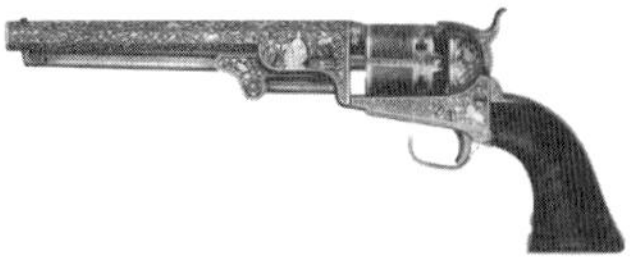

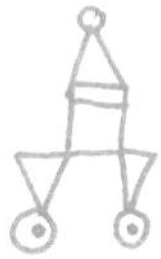

When privacy is a luxury, luxurious surroundings are a must.

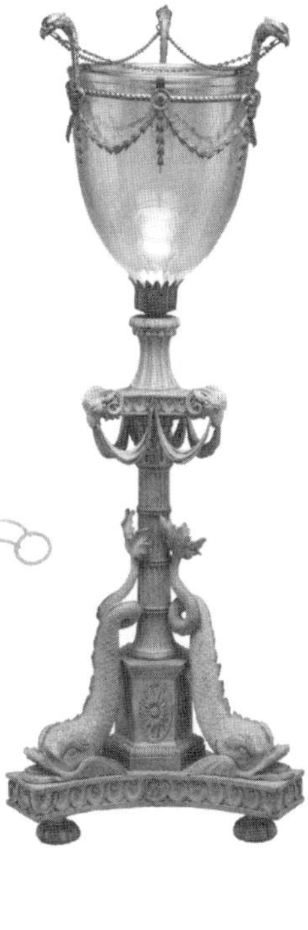

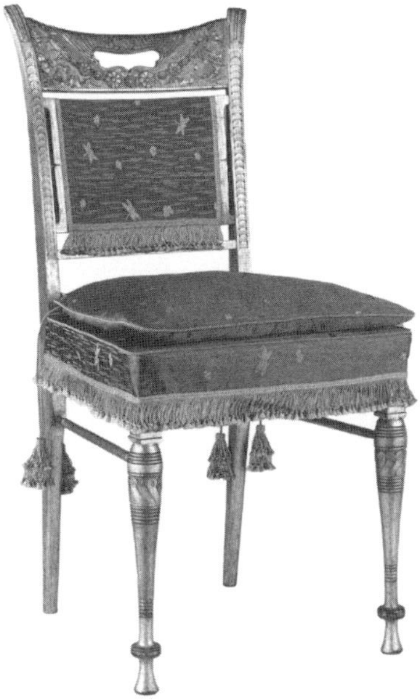

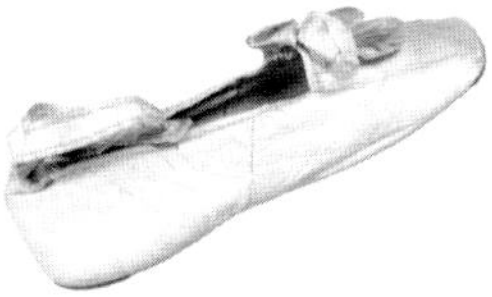

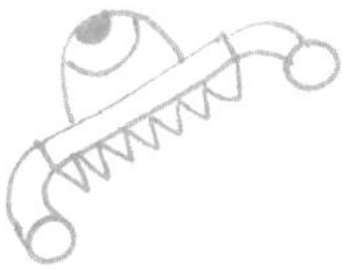

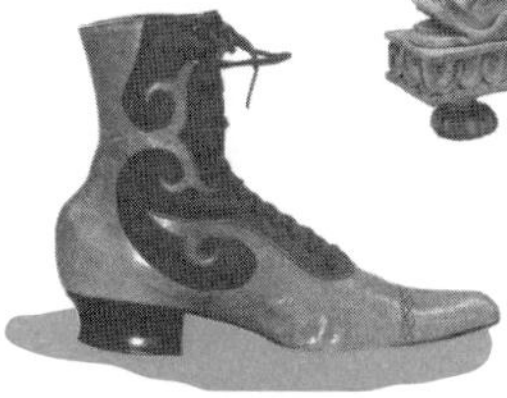

y garden, prison town, city-hospital, ditch city, fea

One-Man City

A hermitage is a place of solitude. It is also the name of a palace in Saint Petersburg that houses a giant collection of art and is so vast that it could itself be considered a city.

It was run by a large staff but it was not run for the staff: it was run for the one resident, the emperor. The staff might as well have been replaced by robots.

'Celebration' is a private city of several thousand residents built by the Walt Disney Company in Florida. Disney promised it's citizen-customers a happy life in a perfect community with no crime or poverty, featuring low-rise buildings, pedestrian-friendly streets, stores, and great schools.

Disney said this city was an experimental prototype for the community of tomorrow, a model American city.

Sam
Chermayeff

"The only place where I feel alone in a modern city is the street. There I don't know anyone and nobody knows me. As soon as I find myself at home I immediately engage with my social networks—I post on Facebook or Twitter; I write comments, to which somebody immediately responds. So I become a public persona at home. In the past, it was the other way around: going out onto the street of a small town or village, one would immediately meet acquaintances—the baker, the postman—and find oneself in a public space, and only seek solitude at home."

Living in a modern big city does not necessarily spare urban dwellers from loneliness.

By gaining control over all aspects of local life, including taxes and services, Disney built a private company town. It appealed to the nostalgic myth of "real America," but today the city experiences crime, governance problems, and individual tragedies.

Another city of dreams is now deserted. In the 1880s, the town of Buford, Wyoming had about two thousand residents employed in building one of the largest railroads in the United States. Since then, Buford has changed a lot. For years its roadside entry sign read "Population: 1." The only resident, who went by the name of Dan, was also the official mayor of Buford,, the operator of its only gas station, and the owner of its grocery and hardware store. Passing truckers often entered the town's only occupied home to drag the mayor out of bed and have him fill up their trucks. Then Dan moved away and the city was purchased by a Vietnamese investor. Will people come back to Buford?

Would you like to be the lone resident of a stunning
city run by robots, where the only thing missing is human
companionship?

garden, city of Fear, mock city, upside-down tow

Ghost Town

They avoid meetings with strangers. They know when to pack their bags and disappear without a trace. They also return home quickly and unnoticed.

There are different means of resistance. What if a defender never even meets their attacker, skillfully avoiding any contact with them?

After all, nobody would be able to claim victory if there were no interaction, let alone battle. What do you think?

Most of the cities of the Inca Empire were destroyed during the Spanish conquest. The city of Machu Picchu was neither conquered by the Spanish Conquistadors, but was abandoned by the inhabitants around the same time the Spaniards attacked the Inca Empire. And yet, inhabitants of Machu Picchu never fought them.

It is one of the best preserved Inca cities and a true mystery.

We know from archaeological evidence that Machu Picchu was a highly organized and developed society. There were temples all over the city, elaborate terraces for intensive farming for which the city's engineers created an amazing water drainage system, and their artisans worked in specialized workshops. Their kings lived in incredibly beautiful palaces.

Some believe that hostilities in the hidden place in the mountains, where the city was located, made it impossible to sustain life and that is why its inhabitants left. Others believe that the Incas so skillfully concealed the roads leading up to the city that the Spaniards never found them, leaving the sudden exodus an unexplained mystery.

1 -

Numerous temples and ceremonial rocks across Machu Picchu used to worship Inca Gods.

2 -

The Main Temple was located at the Sacred Plaza.

Some think that disease and war made it impossible to maintain the city, located high in the mountains. Others believe that the Incas hid the roads leading to the city, making it impossible for the Spaniards to find it.

3 Religious celebrations were hosted at the Main Plaza, which separates the ceremonial section from the residential and industrial areas.

5 The factory houses used by workers for weaving and pottery.

7 Administrators, priests, and craftsmen lived in the residential sector.

4 The Royal Palace is located in the sacred district near the main water source, the Temple of the Sun, and the royal tomb.

6 The area near the Condor Temple is believed to have been a prison sector.

8 Wide steps extend into agricultural land, while also protecting the city from landslides.

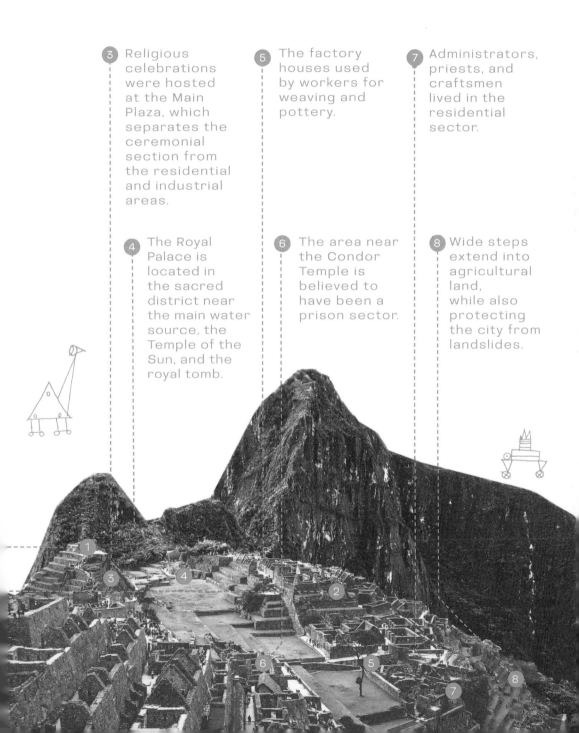

A City
of Runners

The people who live in this city believe that real life is all about constant competition.

The people in a city of runners find it fascinating or even necessary to keep track of who among them is more important, who is richer, smarter, more beautiful, or more worthy. There are many ideas about how the city came to have habits like this. One of the city's revered philosophers, Thomas Hobbes, believed that the natural state of human beings is to seek violent domination over their neighbors, and that society, without the authority of the Sovereign, would quickly turn into a battle of all against all. Constant competition between people is thus seen as an enjoyable game as compared with real war, which is always lurking around the corner.

Cities made differently
tile 19
A City of Runners

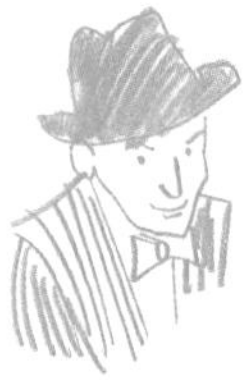

New York, New York
I want to wake up
in a city
That never sleeps
And find I'm
A number one
Top of the list
King of the hill.

Frank Sinatra

Naturally, in cities like this, there must be some who are poor, ugly, and unhappy. Just as in some childrens' games, there are winners and losers.

People living in the city of runners foster in their kids an admiration for winners, and an ambition to surpass their peers in all areas. Children in the city of runners have no interest in learning together, sharing, or mutual aid. Helping someone pass an exam is considered "cheating" and is strictly punished. All their lives, adults are engaged in constant competition over beauty, skill, and wealth.

Runners believe that people who live differently than them, who refuse to play their games, simply choose to be losers.

During the 1968 student unrest in Western countries, some disaffected young people eagerly abandoned the big cities for the "sleepy" provinces, where they created autonomous settlements, many of which still exist today.

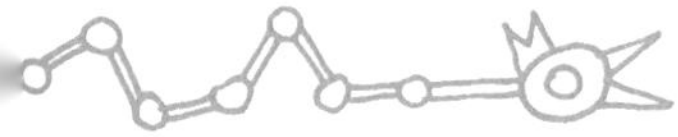

…ar city, prison town, city-hospital, upside-down tow…

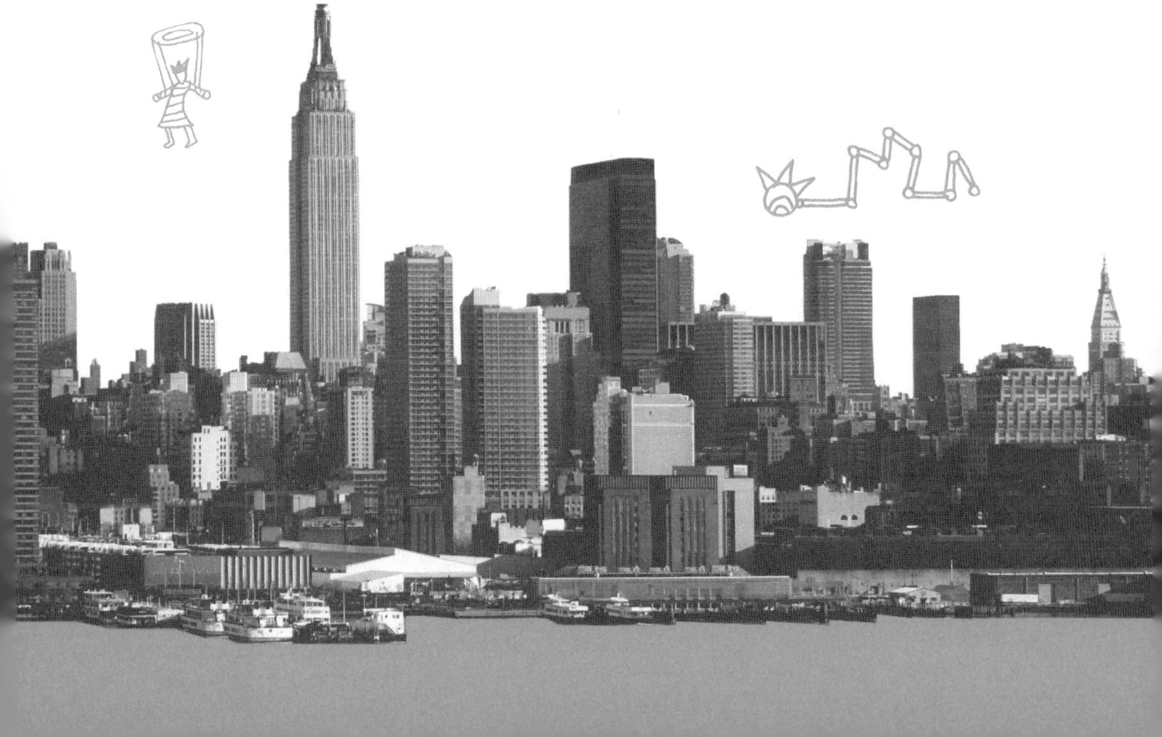

Underground City

Living in an underground city could be safe and convenient. without weather, there's no risk of storms. And no trees means no forest fires.

Underground cities have been around practically forever. The city of Derinkuyu in the Turkish province of Cappadocia, for example, was built between 2000 and 1000 BCE. The landscape of volcanic tuff—a unique soft stone—could be hollowed out without requiring complex tools, making room to house twenty thousand people. The underground city boasted a stable, corrals, churches, schools, canteens, bakeries, barns, wine cellars, and workshops. The intricate system of tunnels connecting it all together meant that intruders would not know their way around and quickly get lost.

Tunnels are found underneath many cities. Rome is famous for its catacombs, and at one time subterranean burial chambers were commonplace. These days they tend to be for underground trains called subways. In Beijing the residents became so fearful of nuclear war they built an entire bunker city, with thirty kilometers of tunnels connecting underground houses, schools, hospitals, shops, libraries, theaters, and factories. There's even an underground roller skating rink!

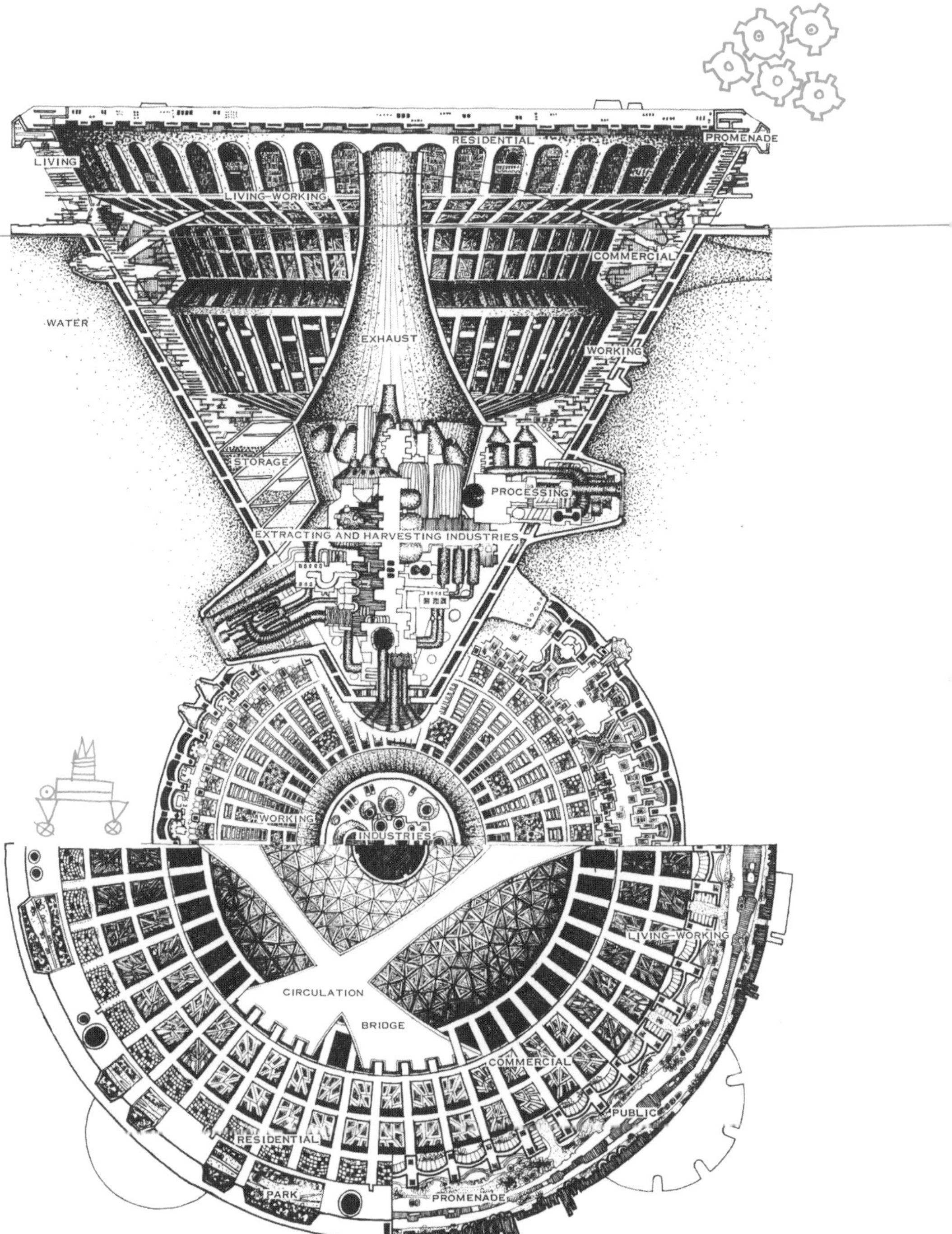
RESIDENTIAL
PROMENADE
LIVING
LIVING-WORKING
COMMERCIAL
WATER
EXHAUST
WORKING
STORAGE
PROCESSING
EXTRACTING AND HARVESTING INDUSTRIES
WORKING
INDUSTRIES
LIVING-WORKING
CIRCULATION
BRIDGE
COMMERCIAL
PUBLIC
RESIDENTIAL
PARK
PROMENADE

tile 20
Underground City

Mexico City has not gone as far as to build an entire city underground, but architect Esteban Suarez is planning an underground apartment building. And what a building it will be! Piercing the center of the Mexican capital with its tip will be a sixty-five-story pyramid—no wonder they call it the earth-scraper. The glass-enclosed area above the surface will be for recreation and outdoor concerts. Underground, the building will be heated and powered with geothermal energy, making the pyramid energy self-sufficient.

It's not easy building downward into the earth, but building underground won't disrupt the historical landscape of the city. And it evades the city's building codes restricting the height of structures to eight floors.

LIGHT WELLS
PUBLIC
NEIGHBORHOOD
PROMENADE
CITY CENTER
PARK
WAREHOUSING
AUTOMATED PRODUCTION

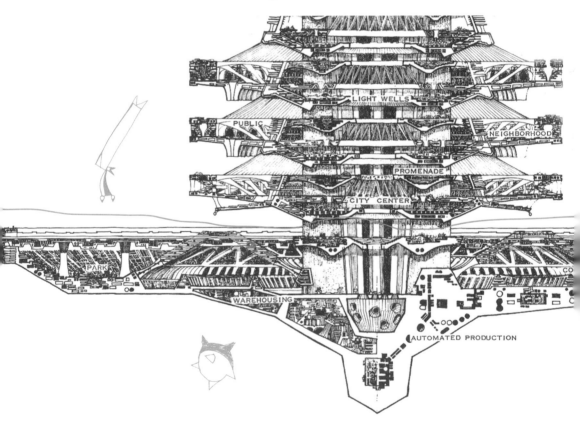

The city of Mirny in the Russian far north has its eye on an abandoned diamond mine as the site for an underground city. There are no more diamonds to be found, but its abandonment threatens neighboring villages with cave-ins and landslides. Moscow architect Nikolai Lyutomsky has proposed a solution: building a strong concrete skeleton inside the quarry to strengthen its walls while covering its top with a transparent dome, resulting in an underground ecocity fit for ten thousand people. Yakutiya has a harsh arctic climate with temperatures reaching as low as -60 °C in the winter. But underground, the temperature never falls below zero. The quarry would thus be good for both people and plants. Its architects have allocated most of the city's inner space to vertical farms.

1. Water source.
2. Urban farm.
3. Protective structures.
4. Bomb shelter.
5. Schools, museums.
6. Hospitals.
7. Theaters and cinemas.

Farms for food production, technical laboratories, factories, and research centers are located underground and, aboveground, there will be play centers and schools. Moving between the underground and the surface is quick and easy.

Going underground to avoid possible misfortunes might seem like a good idea, but there's a catch: if you don't like the rules of your community, it's tough to get out.

How important is it to be able to easily leave one community whose rules no longer suit you and join a different one?

D UTILITIES

ch city, prison town, dream city, upside-down tow

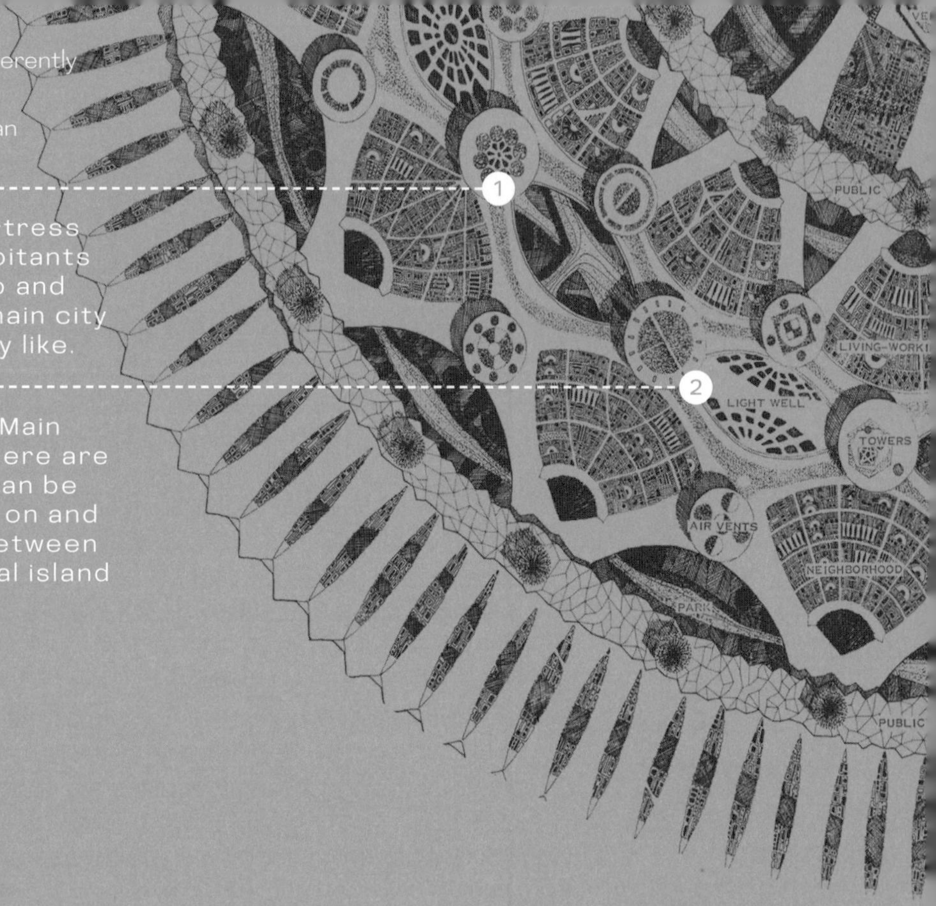
PUBLIC
LIGHT WELL
TOWERS
AIR VENTS
NEIGHBORHOOD
PARK
PUBLIC

1. A mobile fortress whose inhabitants may sail into and out of the main city anytime they like.

2. Around the Main Fortress, there are ships that can be used to live on and for travel between the individual island cities.

City in the ocean

Unlike an underground bunker, a floating city is vulnerable to adverse weather, but it is a difficult target to attack!

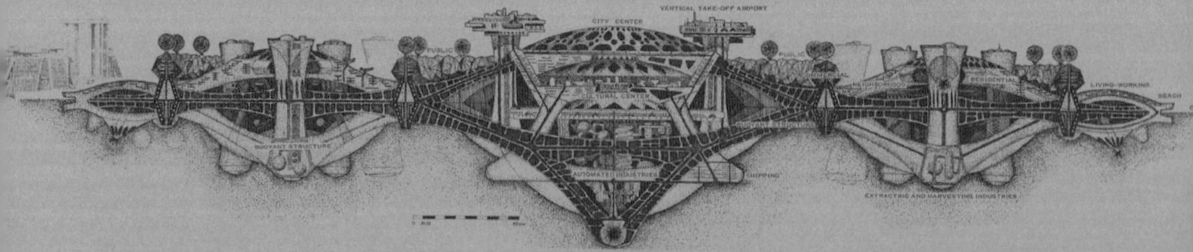
VERTICAL TAKE-OFF AIRPORT
CITY CENTER
CULTURAL CENTER
AUTOMATED INDUSTRIES
BUOYANT STRUCTURE
LIVING-WORKING
EXTRACTING AND HARVESTING INDUSTRIES

Many cities were founded by refugees who settled on empty and almost inaccessible land.

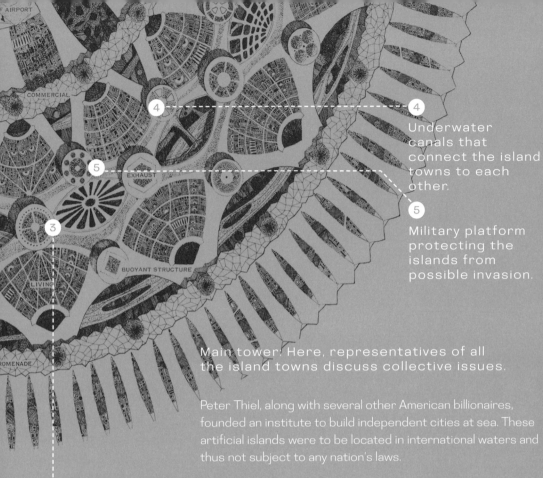

AIRPORT

COMMERCIAL

EXHAUST

BUOYANT STRUCTURE

LIVING

PROMENADE

4 Underwater canals that connect the island towns to each other.

5 Military platform protecting the islands from possible invasion.

Main tower: Here, representatives of all the island towns discuss collective issues.

Peter Thiel, along with several other American billionaires, founded an institute to build independent cities at sea. These artificial islands were to be located in international waters and thus not subject to any nation's laws.

Autonomous republics are able to grow their own food, produce renewable energy, and are equipped with scientific and medical laboratories.

These floating cities could house more than a thousand people, following the American tradition of commercial cities like Walt Disney's city, Celebration.

Similar to Krutikov's flying cities, floating islands can be connected or disconnected at will, preserving the unity of the whole and the autonomy of the parts.

There are many versions of this idea. Pirate ships of the 18th century also formed similar communities. Krutikov's communist project was intended to benefit all mankind and save nature from industrial destruction

Commercial cities plan to sell places on the floating islands to those who have the means to pay for it.

3 Small houses on the largest island.

Cities made differently
tile 21
City in the Ocean

Speaking of pirate ships

The pirate ships and settlements of the Golden Age of Piracy resemble the floating republic cities.

Each ship during the Golden Era of Piracy was essentially modeled after a factory with an elaborate organization of labor strictly controlled from above. It makes them notably similar to the military cities from chapter 4 on Cities of Fighters.

The life that sailors could expect serving on an imperial navy vessel was harsh: corporal punishment, occasional starvation, endless hard work, and strict discipline. In fact, most sailors did not join the Navy voluntarily but were conscripted into naval service by their king. It comes as no surprise, then, that ship mutinies occurred regularly. Even with mutiny punishable by death, commandeering the ship and raising a pirate flag didn't seem like such a bad idea to mutineers.. A free life is worth living, no matter how short.

Unlike conscripted sailors, pirates chose their own captains and took part in decision-making aboard their ships. Pirates obeyed their captain only during combat. Otherwise, their lives resembled those of the free Greeks who Montesquieu famously described as "all pirates." They created their own rules and governed themselves. Pirates were even known to have collected welfare funds for their wounded comrades and to have provided for the families of crewmembers killed in action.

The history of piracy is shrouded in gruesome and terrifying legends. One could even say that the pirates themselves leaned into these tales, exaggerating to great effect their ferocity on the high seas. Yet aboard their ships, they seemed to have conducted their affairs through more enlightened means, with conversation, deliberation, and debate.

Pirate settlements, such as Sainte-Marie and especially Ambonavola, seem to have been self-conscious attempts to reproduce the democracy of pirate ships on land. Because most outsiders feared intruding upon the legendary Pirate Kingdom, few ever came close enough to see that the people living in these settlements were ruling themselves without kings, decades before the American Revolution.

Cities made differently
tile 21
City in the Ocean

"The word 'utopia' first calls to mind the image of
an ideal city, usually with perfect geometry. The
image seems to hearken back originally to the
royal military camp: a geometrical space that is
entirely the emanation of a single, individual will, a
fantasy of total control."

David Graeber

Perhaps this city on the ocean, which describes communism for the rich,
where citizenship is for sale, recall other utopias (see the chapter Cities
of Fighters). After all, such cities would have to be guarded against the
poor, who can't afford to live in utopias.

Unlike them, the pirate communities of the 18th century were fluid and
ever-changing structures, more akin to Krutikov's Communist project of
Flying Cities than to a strictly organized army settlement.

Pirates were portrayed as horrible criminals who violated all norms of human behavior, who engaged in drunkenness, murder, robbery, and all sorts
of immorality. Most pirates' lives ended at the imperial gallows, and only
very few of them ever got to retire. The story of one such settlement,
a Mock Pirate kingdom in Madagascar, is described in David Graeber's
Pirate Enlightenment.

eam city, invisible city, city-hospital, upside-down

City of **Punishment**

some citizens make the rules, and the rest must obey. whoever disobeys deserves to be punished!

At the core of any game, including those that are dangerous or somewhat cruel, is the ability to stop or even to run away. Imagine being trapped in a game you can't leave!

Ready or not, here I come!

Imagine a game of hide-and-seek that cannot be stopped if the players get tired or bored. This would evidently be a terrible dystopia. Perhaps the first rule for any game should be the option to quit or to rewrite the rules.

The Ku Klux Klan is an American hate group fighting to advance what they see as the genetic superiority of the white race. Members of the Ku Klux Klan sent orange pips, or seeds, anonymously to their enemies, who included Blacks, Jews, communists, and anyone else they disagreed with or disliked. Whoever

Imagine play without rules. Would it be fun? Could we even call it play? How would it be different from everyday life?

received such a warning had to renounce their views or run away; otherwise, they could be killed. KKK members dressed in white robes and pointy hoods. In these uniforms, they resembled the ghosts of fallen Confederate soldiers who fought in the Civil War for the slaveholding South. White robes helped members of the Ku Klux Klan intimidate others while concealing their identities. Precisely because of the widespread domestic terror carried out by the KKK, some U.S. states still prohibit the wearing of masks in public places.

David Graeber

"Violence is so often the preferred weapon of the stupid. One might even call it the trump card of the stupid, since (and this is surely one of the tragedies of human existence) it is the one form of stupidity to which it is most difficult to come up with an intelligent response."

Who would want to play a game where you have to follow orders that no one chose, no one likes, and that cannot be changed?

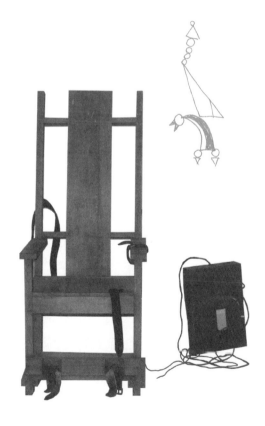

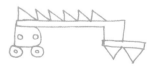

Trash City

imagine that you, your friends, and
your family all live on top of a giant
garbage dump. whatever you do—playing,
swimming, washing, gardening, or even
having a birthday party—you are always
surrounded by mounds of garbage.

your job is to sort through the garbage,
pulling out anything that can be used or
recycled. The garbage sorting is mainly
done by women and children, while
men carry in sacks of rubbish from the
outside or talk with visitors from other
cities who bring their garbage to the
dump and buy the useful things they find.

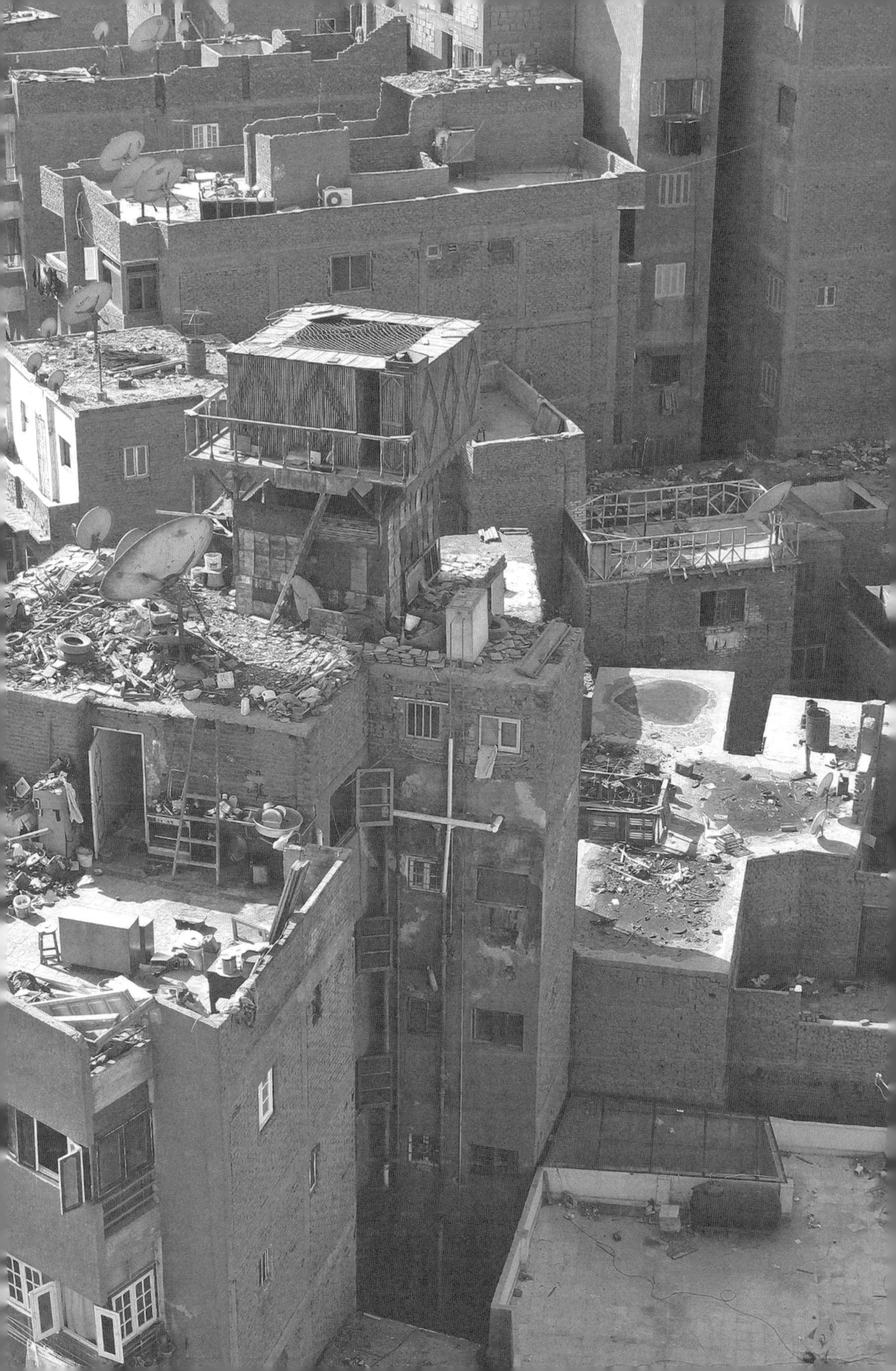

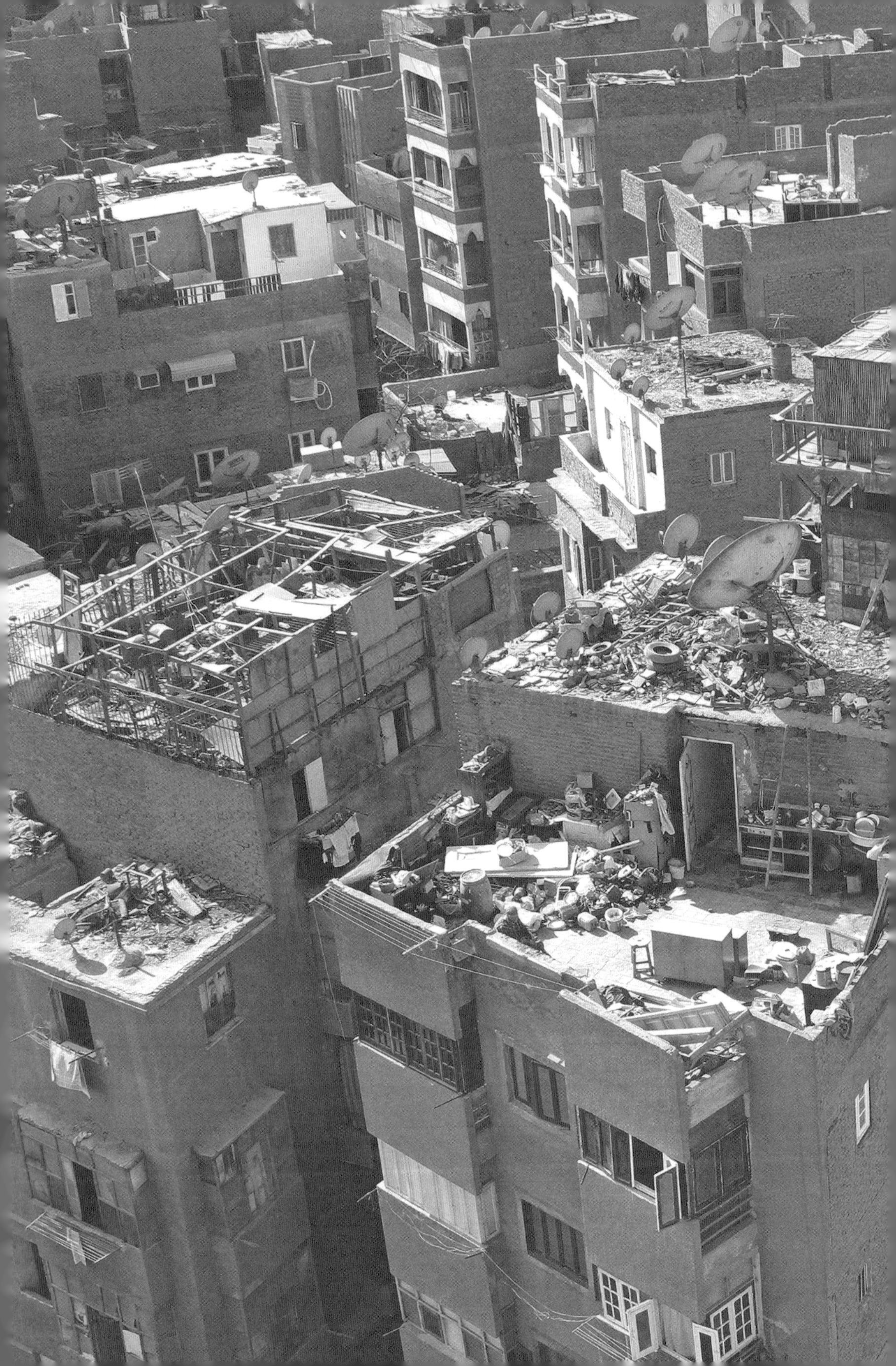

Trash City

On the outskirts of Cairo, there is an area known as Garbage City. The Egyptians who live there have a dirty job: they sort through all the city's trash produced every day by over 20 million people. Families work there, the young and the old, picking out everything that has any value. Many of these urban scavengers were once rural peasants who could find no other work in the city. On the first floors of the unfinished and dilapidated brick houses that make up Garbage City, people are hard at work sorting and packaging waste while their living quarters are on the floors above. Streets, yards, and even rooftops are all filled up with garbage. Everything stinks. But this stench does not prevent normal city life—here children play, adults smoke hookah pipes in cafes, and street vendors sell fruit and freshly baked bread.

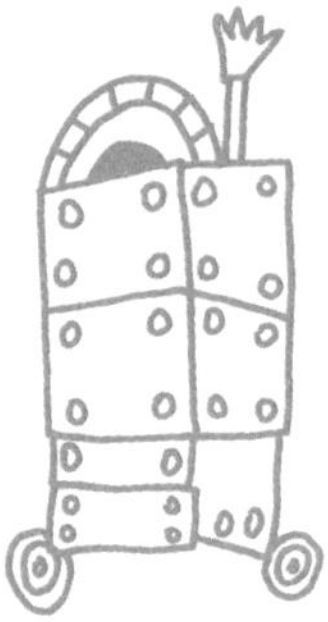

Some people's trash is other people's treasure! People throw out things that can be used to generate energy, build houses, and even make works of art.

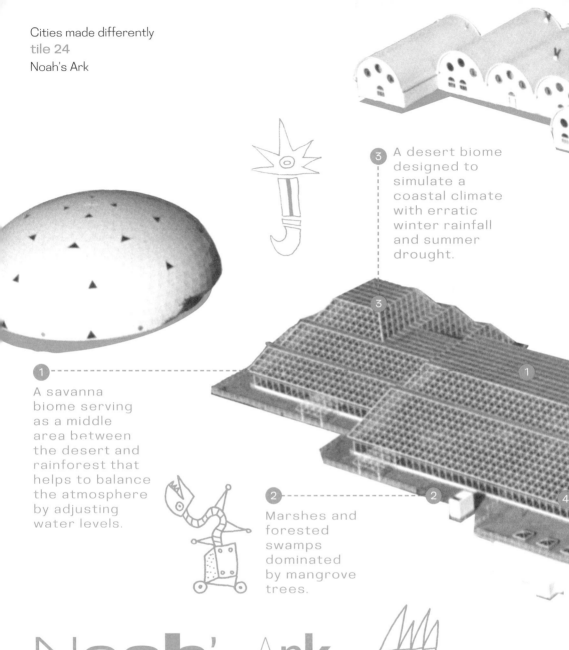

3 A desert biome designed to simulate a coastal climate with erratic winter rainfall and summer drought.

1 A savanna biome serving as a middle area between the desert and rainforest that helps to balance the atmosphere by adjusting water levels.

2 Marshes and forested swamps dominated by mangrove trees.

Noah's Ark

In this city, everything that exists on Earth is nearby: gardens, forests, birds, fish, leopards, and pet dogs.

Cities made differently
tile 24
Noah's Ark

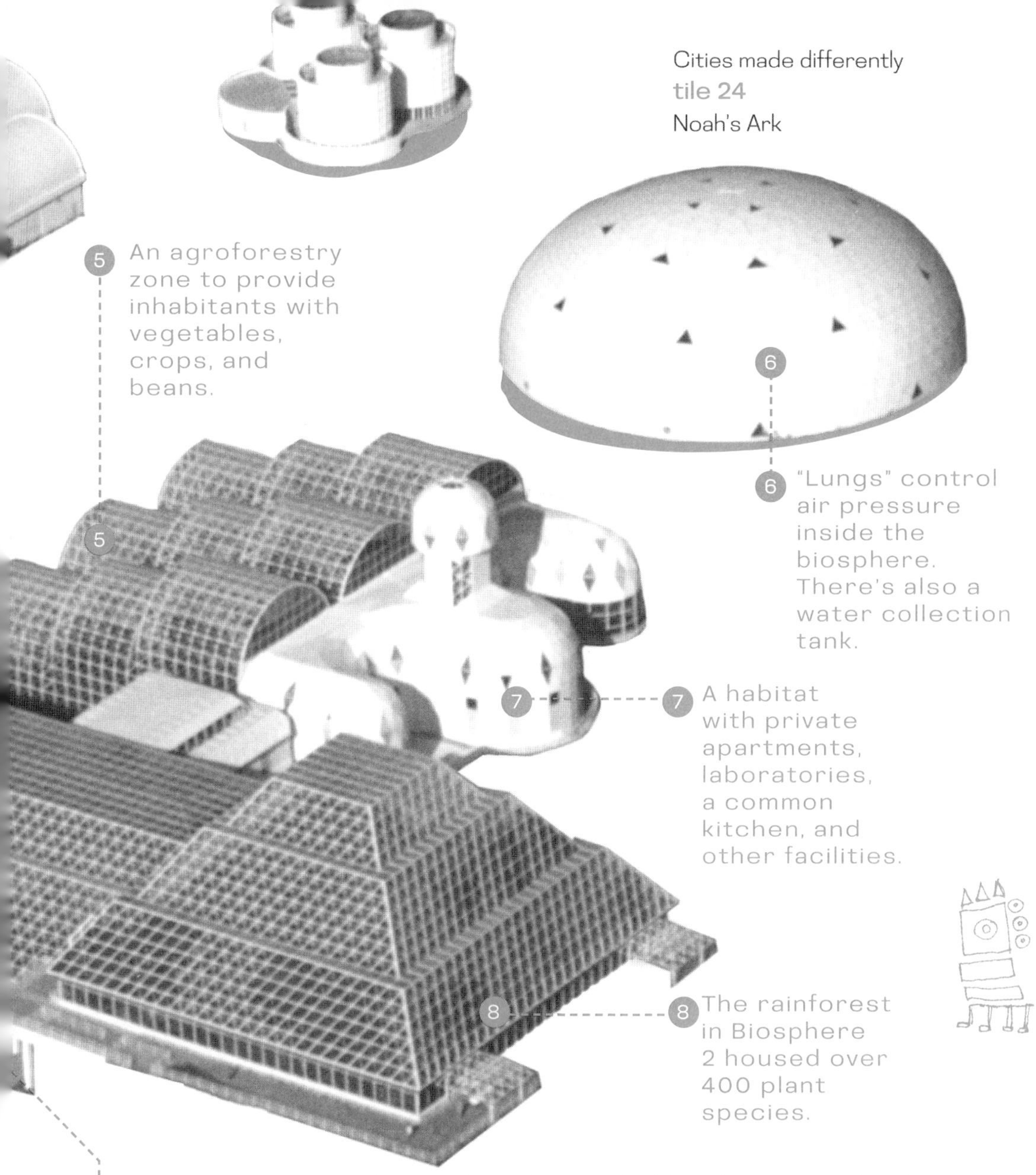
5 An agroforestry zone to provide inhabitants with vegetables, crops, and beans.
6 "Lungs" control air pressure inside the biosphere. There's also a water collection tank.
7 A habitat with private apartments, laboratories, a common kitchen, and other facilities.
8 The rainforest in Biosphere 2 housed over 400 plant species.
4 A research ocean with approximately 2.6 million liters of water, simulating a Caribbean reef environment with fish, algae, and various invertebrate species.

Imagine that in this giant building, there is a coral reef populated with fish, a jungle for monkeys and birds, fields for grain and vegetables, and complex machines for generating heat and cleaning the air. People must learn to live within this structure just as they now live on Earth.

A team of scientists built a self-contained city where they live in peace and harmony. They never need to go outside because there's nothing beyond the walls that they don't already have inside.

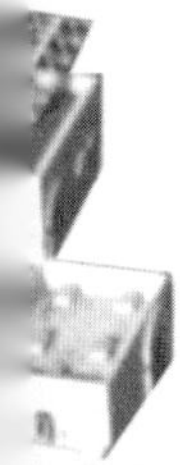

Biosphere 2 was a grand experiment in the Arizona desert: a glass-domed complex containing an ultra-modern farm, an avant-garde residential house, and five ecological biomes: jungle, savanna, desert, mangrove forest, and a small ocean complete with a beach and coral reef. People, goats, pigs, chickens, and over three thousand other animal species all lived there. This "ark" was designed to function autonomously for two years, with people living on the produce grown inside the biosphere, breathing oxygen produced by its plants, and recycling its water—a sort of a miniature planet. Eight volunteers—four men and four women—planned to spend their days performing manual labor, taking meals together, playing music in their spare time, and, most importantly, conducting scientific research.

The birthplace of closed system theory was the USSR. In the biophysics laboratory of Krasnoyarsk during the 1960s, scientists experimented with human subjects living autonomously in chambers cut off from the outside world except for their sup-

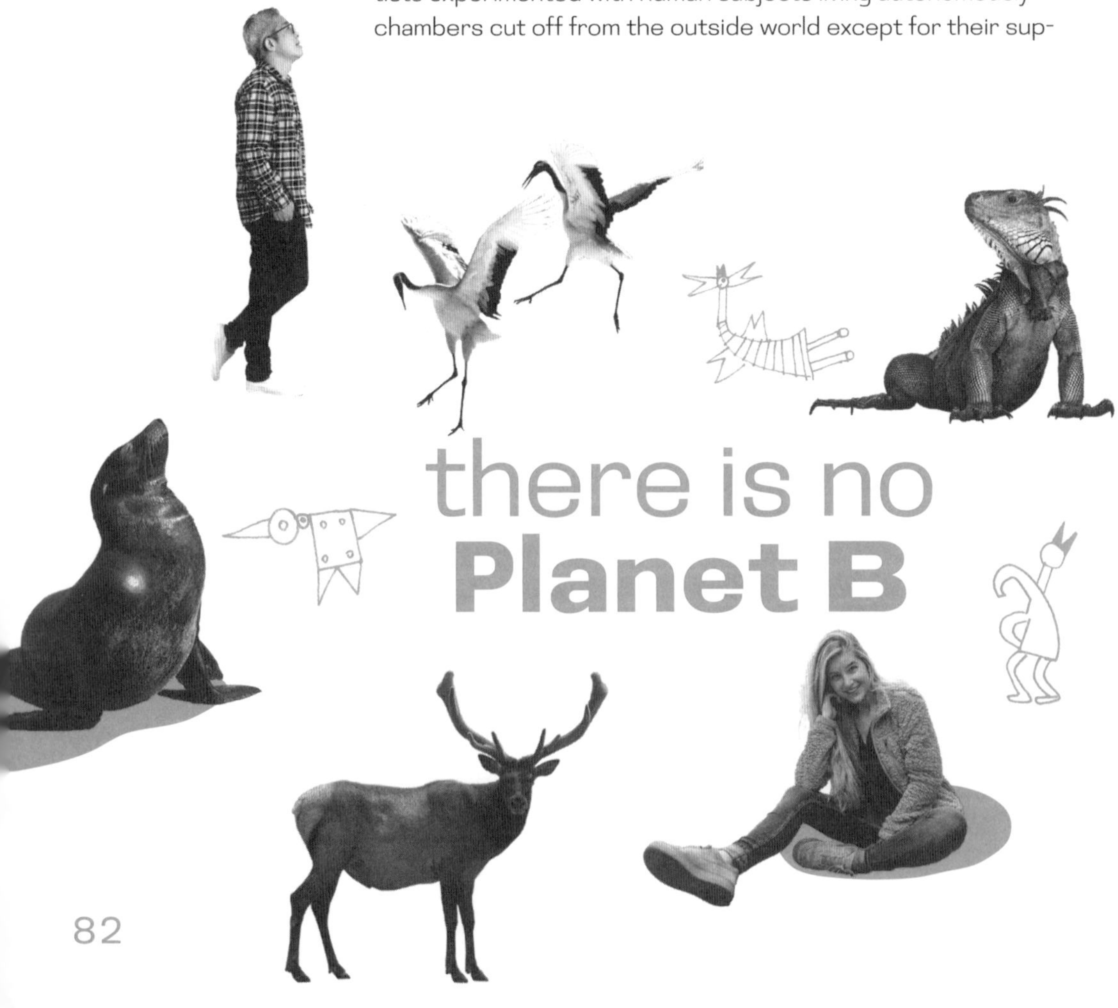
there is no
Planet B

ply of oxygen. In the middle of the last century, mankind believed that very soon we would go into space. For life on other planets and during long space flights to be viable, life support technology within completely enclosed systems was a necessity.

There is something divine about designing a city that is so self-sufficient that inhabitants never have to leave it.

Scientists at Biosphere 2 ultimately lost control of their system. Microorganisms, ants, and other insects multiplied, depleting oxygen levels and threatening food production. Before its completion, the experiment was terminated. Nevertheless, the dream of building a closed system has been carried on by Chinese scientists who claim they can sustain human life in systems almost entirely closed to the outside world.

Was the project a success? On September 26, 1993, when the facility was officially depressurized, letting out the volunteers inside, their faces indicated that the experiment had failed. Despite all of its clever design, the biosphere had ultimately been proven uninhabitable. Today, Biosphere 2 serves as a testament to how unsuccessful humanity has been in trying to reproduce the Earth's delicate biosphere, and thus a reminder of how important it is to preserve our natural environment.

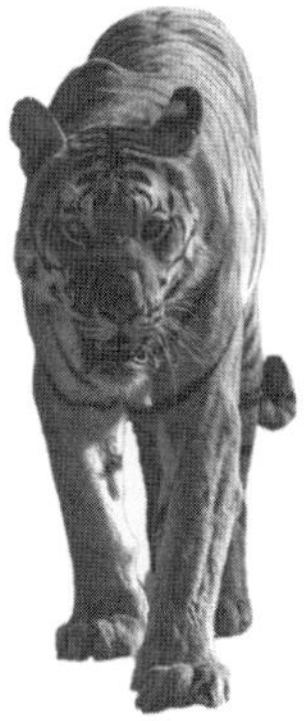

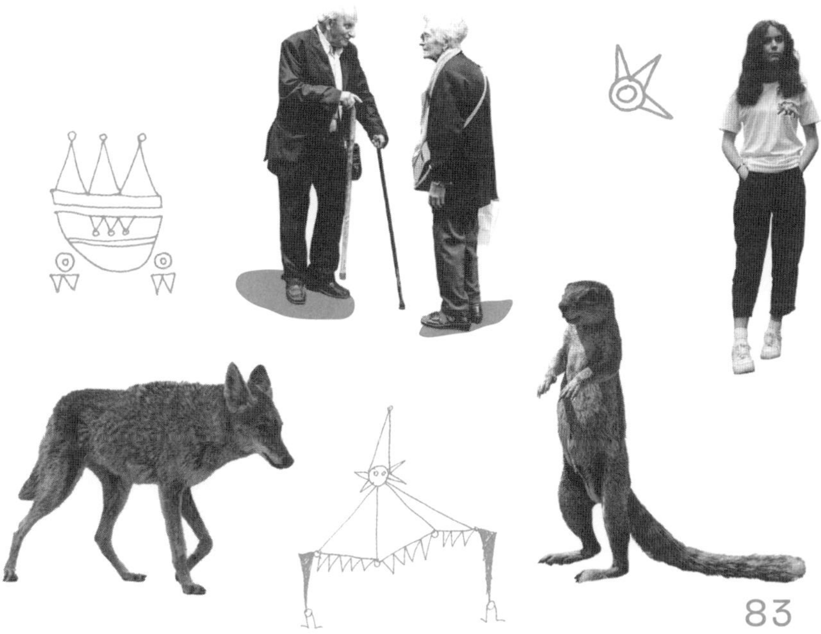

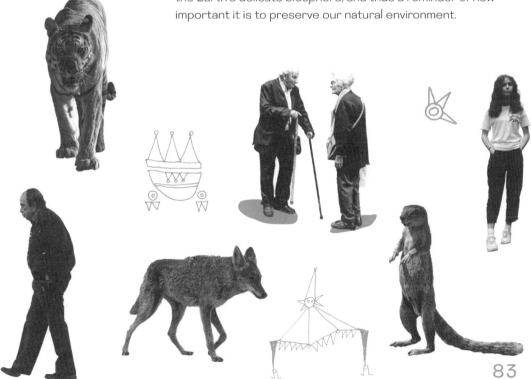

1 A signal fence with barbed wire.

2 A bed of nails was placed in front of the fences.

3 The fourth generation of fortification that separated East and West Berlin, known as the death strip, was 43 kilometers long and up to 150 meters wide. This three-meter-high concrete wall kept the citizens of East Berlin from escaping.

Model City

This city was designed and built to show everyone just how beautiful, fair, and comfortable life can really be! This model city seems to say: "Look at me! Why are you still not living like this? Join us or build yourself a city like ours!"

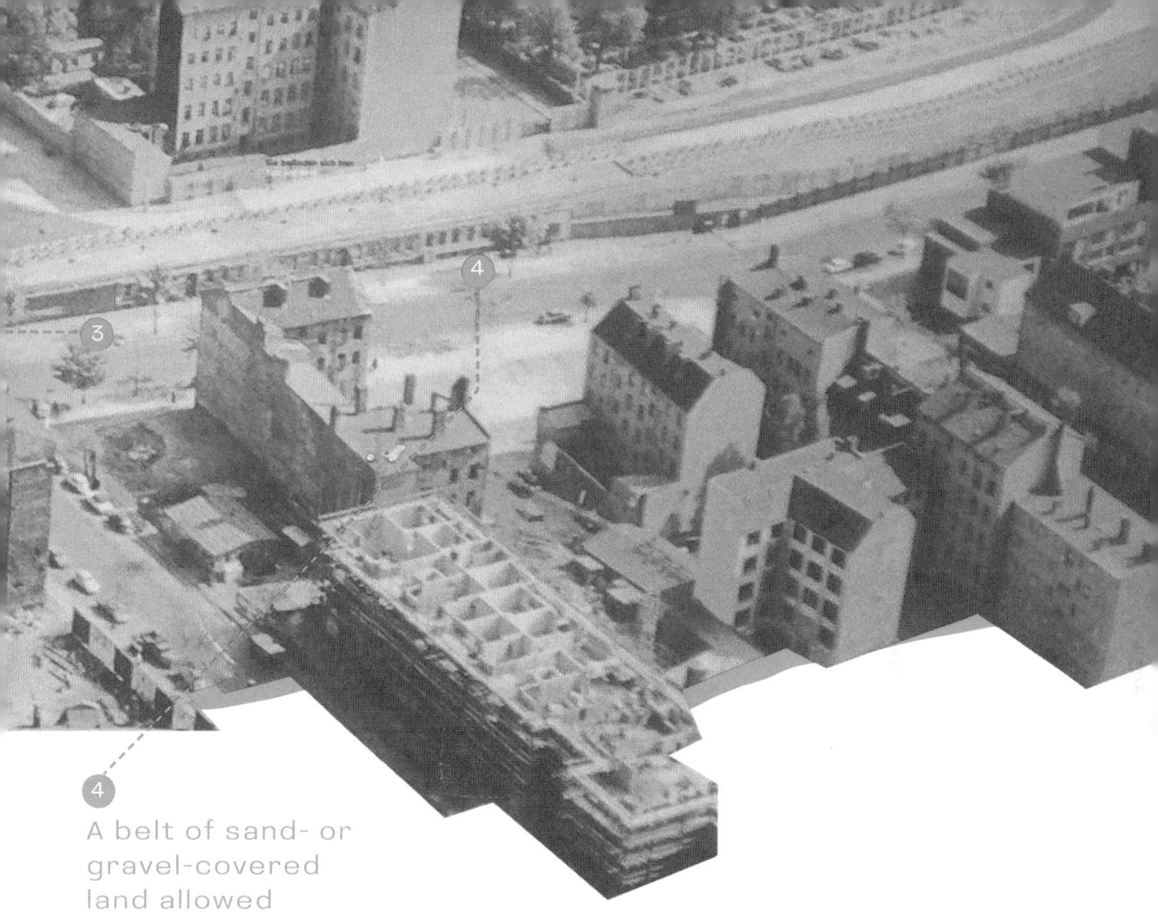
4
3

4

A belt of sand- or gravel-covered land allowed the guards with attack dogs to track down refugees by following their footprints.

After the Second World War, Germany's capital was divided between the USSR and the Western allies. East Berlin was the capital of the Soviet half, whereas West Berlin became a bastion of capitalism located in the heart of Socialist East Germany. West Berlin became a major industrialized center with developed commerce, a smooth-operating banking system, and an excellent service industry. The city's model economy soon rivaled those in other developed countries less affected by the war, such as Finland, Denmark, Portugal, and Turkey. West Berlin housed about 180 research centers, 35 museums, and 18 theaters. The Symphony Orchestra directed by Herbert von Karajan enjoyed world renown. It hosted international fairs, exhibitions, and conventions of all kinds. The only thing missing was an army.

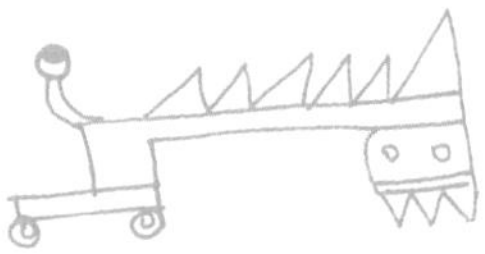

GDR residents clearly appreciated the success of West Berlin. By the 1960s, one in seven people from East Germany had escaped to the West. To stop this Western defection, the Soviet government erected the Berlin Wall.

eam city, prison town, curse city, upside-down tov

City Under Siege

war changes society. sometimes, its outcome is the advent of an even harsher regime than what came before. yet, at the same time, a deadly threat sometimes leads to cooperation that can liberate a society from within.

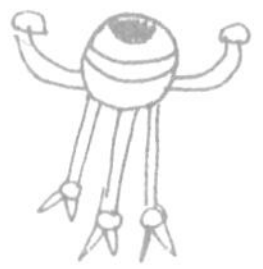

Many cities in history have been bombed, attacked, and ravaged. How do people live when attacks continue for years; when it seems that normalcy is all but extinct? Here, we take a look at the autonomous territory of Northern Syria or Rojava.

Despite being surrounded by deadly enemies, Rojava provides the world with an example of an incredible democratic experiment.

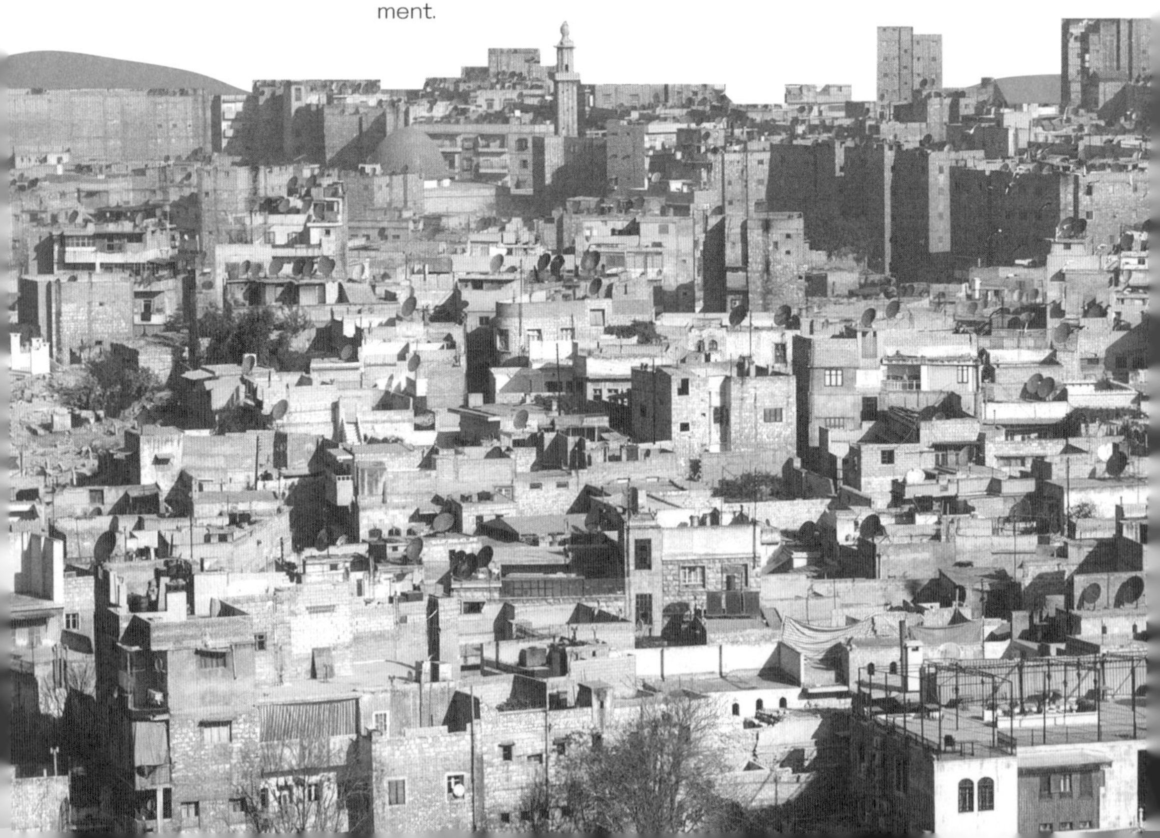

Popular assemblies, in councils carefully selected for cultural balance, are responsible for decision making. In each municipality, for instance, the top three officers must include one Kurd, one Arab, one Assyrian or Armenian Christian, and at least one of the three must be a woman. There are also women's and youth councils. And echoing the armed Mujeres Libres (Free Women) of Spain, they are defended by a feminist army, the "YJA Star" militia. The "Union of Free Women" is symbolized by a star representing the ancient Mesopotamian goddess Ishtar. This woman-led army has carried out a large proportion of the Kurdish combat operations against the forces of Islamic State.

d-city, military city, mask city, dream-city, upside-c

Sun City

magicians,
astrologers,
and scientists
rule this city
that many
consider an
elusive utopia.

The most
intimate
feelings, such
as affection
between
parents and
children, are
forbidden here.

Do you think the
government
should be able
to regulate who
falls in love with
whom? What
should the
government
regulate
anyway?

In the seventeenth century, Tommaso Campanello described a utopian society governed by the magical wisdom of great men.

The Sun City seems attractive: a peaceful society living in harmony with nature, where everyone works, but only four hours a day; where manual and intellectual labor are equally valued; where there is no greed or crime; where the city is turned into a giant museum-book; where every child has access to all human knowledge just by walking the streets of the city.

What could be better?

Yet, isn't it similar to the militaristic utopia of the Roman cities, or even the world of *The Matrix*, with the same patriarchal high command, centralized laws, strict rules, and, ultimately, organized violence applied against dissenters?

What about those citizens who don't agree with the rules of the city and would like to change them?

All private, uncontrollable human feelings such as compassion and personal affection are criminalized, said to be detrimental to the central plan. Individuality, even individual feelings, threaten those in power. Whatever cannot be controlled must be eliminated.

In Campanella's time, European colonizers conquered what they called the "New World," subjugating it beneath an iron fist to the only "true law"—their law. In their wake, they left entire continents destroyed and enslaved.

The magicians, astrologers, and scientists of Sun City were convinced that they knew of the one true way of life that would make all people happy and become a model for all mankind. Would you want to live in this new and better world?

side-down town, city-machine, dream-city, prison

School City

Every human society has a notion of what knowledge is and how to pass it on from generation to generation. European universities have come to unexpected conclusions about the nature of knowledge and its reproduction.

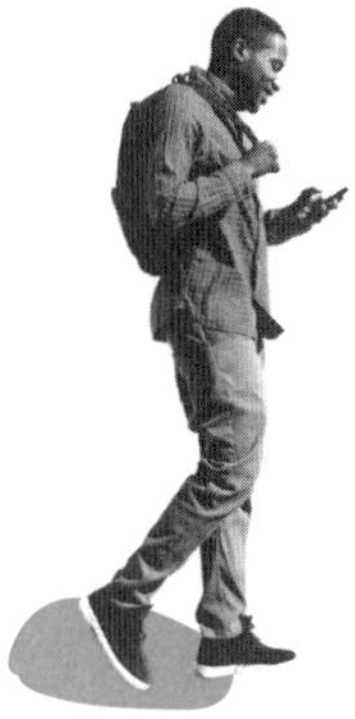

There are many ways of sharing knowledge. Here we would like to reflect on the role of medieval monasteries in laying the foundation for modern universities.

Many things in our lives that seem unchanging—such as the existence of everlasting commercial entities that build houses, own banks, and even run entire cities like Disney World—originated in monasteries.

Corporations are really a rather bizarre idea: They are not just charming legal fictions, but treated legally as persons, with rights and privileges just like human beings. At the same time, they are also immortal, never having to go through all the human untidiness of marriage, reproduction, infirmity, and death. To put it in proper medieval terms, they are very much like angels.

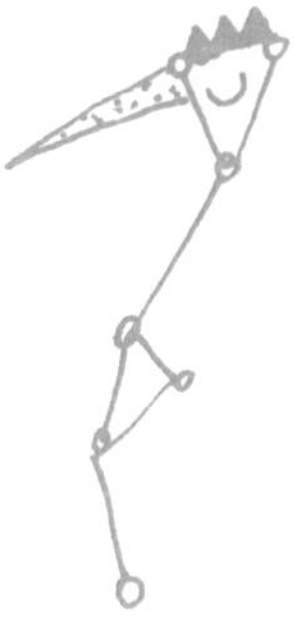

Walt Disney created a corporation named after himself which has a truly royal fortune of hundreds of billions of dollars. It continued to grow beyond his lifetime by selling rights to the image of Mickey Mouse and other cartoon characters, creating new cartoons, and running Disney World, among other operations.

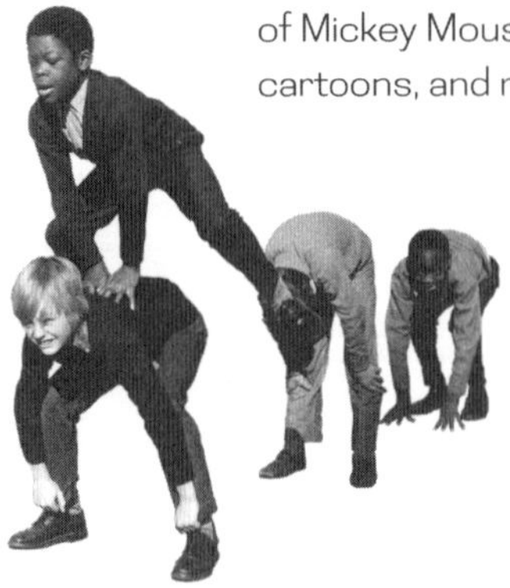

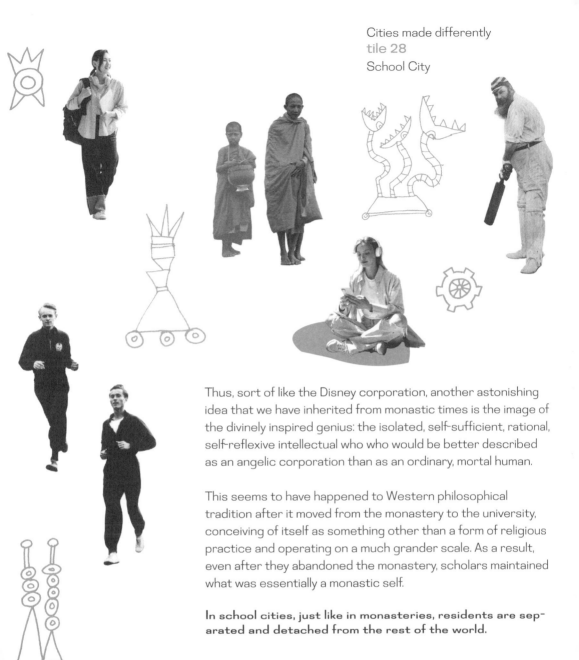

Thus, sort of like the Disney corporation, another astonishing idea that we have inherited from monastic times is the image of the divinely inspired genius: the isolated, self-sufficient, rational, self-reflexive intellectual who who would be better described as an angelic corporation than as an ordinary, mortal human.

This seems to have happened to Western philosophical tradition after it moved from the monastery to the university, conceiving of itself as something other than a form of religious practice and operating on a much grander scale. As a result, even after they abandoned the monastery, scholars maintained what was essentially a monastic self.

In school cities, just like in monasteries, residents are separated and detached from the rest of the world.

y-city, prison town, city-hospital, upside-down to

91

Solitude and detachment from the world.

1 A violent riot between townsmen and students started here in 1355. As a result, the university gained many economic privileges, and the city authorities had to pray and pay for the students killed every year.

2 Oxford University Press printed one of the first books at the very dawn of printing history in the late 15th century. Now, it is the largest university press in the world.

3 The University Church of St Mary the Virgin housed many university functions in its early history, including its first dedicated treasury, court, and library.

4 One of the oldest libraries in Europe began as a room in a church and grew into a network of 28 libraries with over 13 million printed items.

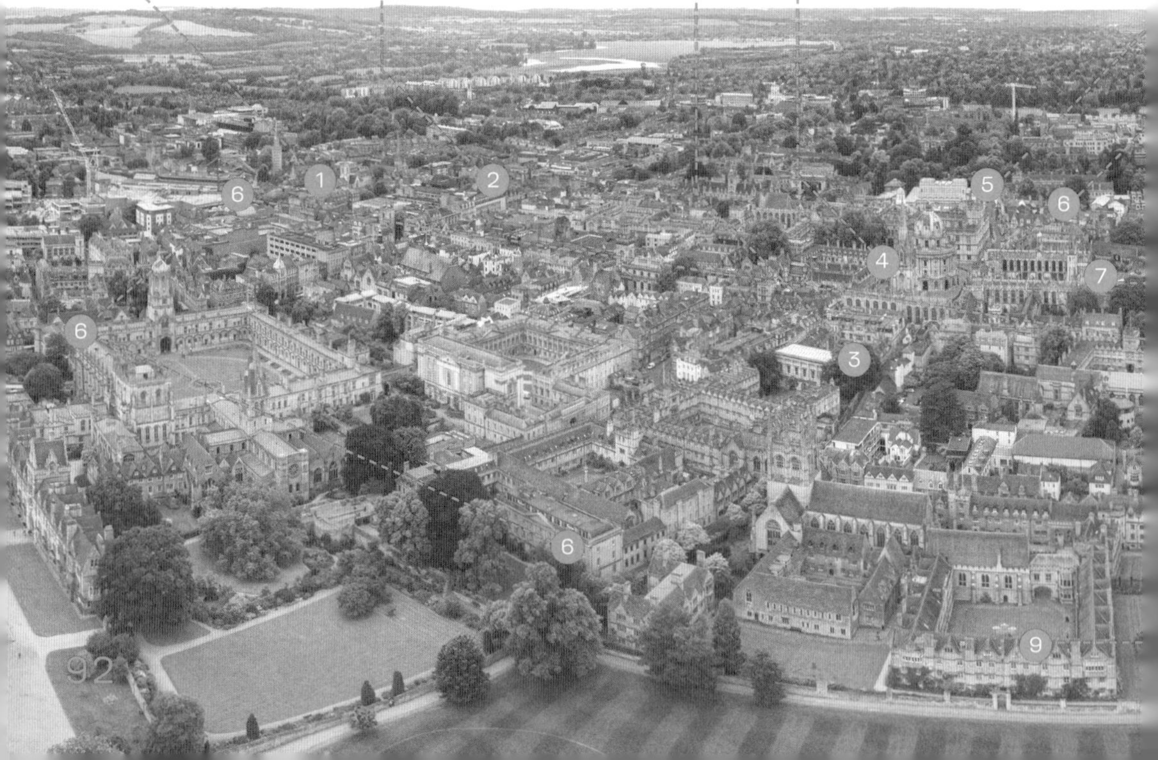
6
1
2
5
6
4
7
6
3
6
9

5 As members of the clergy, scholars were subject to the ecclesiastical court and not the regular city court. Some disputes involving scholars were resolved in the university court.

7 In 1209, two Oxford students were hanged for killing a townswoman. To escape the still hostile townsmen, approximately 3000 scholars left the city and founded Cambridge University.

8 Oxford University consists of 44 independent and self-governing colleges dispersed throughout the city.

6 All of the doctors and masters of the university formed the convocation. This became the main governing body of the university.

9 Academic halls provide accommodation for students that separate them from the townsfolk.

City of Care

HOW do we build a city where people can live meaningful and fascinating lives; where justice prevails over stupidity and wickedness? HOW do we build a city that welcomes all but also allows for the easy departure of those who object to its rules?

What is care anyway? How do we want to be cared for?

It is obvious that caring for human life, with all its various stages of birth, adolescence, education, and illness is the main priority of any city. Without people, a city is just buildings—an empty archaeological site or maybe an architectural exhibition. So cities are really about the people that live in them. Although, if you think about it, our modern cities don't seem to be built around care for people, but around work or shopping—or production and consumption.

The Chilean architect Alejandro Aravena has designed social housing neighborhoods with significantly reduced construction costs. One of Aravena's projects was on the site of the Quinta Monroy slums in the Chilean city of Iquique. The plan was to construct houses that were halfway complete, for families to purchase at minimal cost and finish building according to their needs. By involving people in the creation of their own homes, the architect assists in cultivating and strengthening the relationship between the people and their space.

Care can be tender and loving, intrusive and insolent, or even dismissive and murderous. Prisons also care about their prisoners: they feed and house them. Yet is it possible to think about prisons as spaces of care?

This plan has allowed a hundred families to settle permanently on territory that they have "illegally" occupied for thirty years. The builders laid the foundation and the remaining common space between the houses was completed by the residents themselves, according to their budgets and aesthetic preferences. The city turned out very beautifully.

Just one year later, the houses in the area increased in value several times over, even so the residents were in no hurry to part with them.

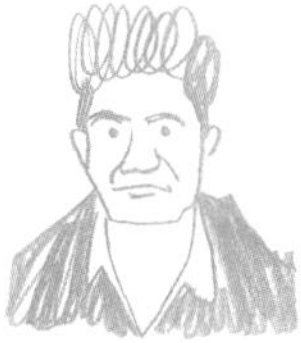

Alejandro Aravena

"The city itself—it is a tool for improving the quality of life and spreading that quality to the majority of the planet's population. In a few years, about 70% of us will live in cities. In turn, the quality of life in the city is determined by what you can do there freely and for free. One of the main challenges of today is social inequality. And do not think that its root lies solely in the amount of annual income. Infrastructure, public spaces, social housing, transport systems—all these are unique opportunities to address inequality. And the more parks and other nice places there are in a city which everyone can enjoy without buying a ticket, the better the city and the higher the quality of life."

itary city, dream city, city-hospital, nightmare-city

Egalitarian cities have existed in human history for many thousands of years. What they have in common is an urban architecture built primarily to reproduce human life. Hence, communal housing serves as the foundation of these cities. Just as common is the lack of palaces and ritual institutions in the center of city life. Teotihuacán society was, for example, exceptionally egalitarian.

We know about such egalitarian cities as Teotihuacán, "mega-sites" found in Ukraine and Moldova, and the society of "rich farmers," as archaeologist Rosemary Joyce calls a settlement found in Uruguay.

Where in egalitarian cities does social life take place if they don't have palaces and cathedrals in the middle of the city?

When Mexican archaeologist Laurette Séjourné first excavated one of Teotihuacán's living compounds in the 1950s, she called it a "palace in the city of the gods."

Some cities used the rooftops of private houses instead of streets as a public space, and it was there that passersby met and discussed business. In many cases, people gathered outside the city to organize festivals, carnivals, and rituals, or

to build public monuments. Often these projects were quite ambitious, but, importantly, they were occasional or seasonal; daily life was not organized around them.

This building—known as Zacuala—had large, spacious rooms with walls covered in colorful murals. Each living area had one or more patios open to the sky, with drains in the floors to let rainwater out of the compound. Family members were buried in graves under the house floors, often with rich and elaborate offerings.

Compared to most Aztec sites, Teotihuacán seems very strange, and not just because of its huge size (100,000 people, living in an area of close to 20 square kilometers). For one, it's the only pre-modern Mexican city planned entirely according to a grid layout. Secondly, its residents lived in apartment-like multifamily compounds with white lime-plaster floors, ornamented roofs, and porches which were remarkably spacious and luxurious for the ancient world. These complexes were key to the conclusion of many researchers that the city's residents lived far more economically equal lives than in any other known Mesoamerican society.

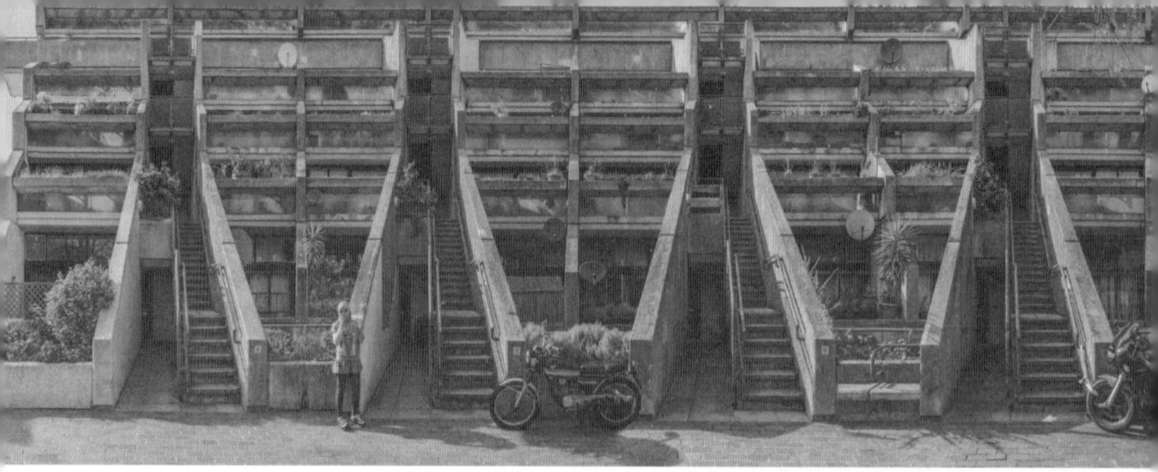

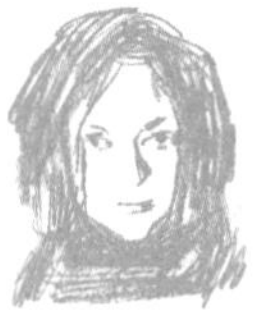

Nika Dubrovsky:

The Alexandria Estate, also called Rowley Way, was built by British architect Neave Brown in 1978 as public housing with 520 apartments. It includes a school, a park, playgrounds, its own heating system and a wide variety of public spaces, the most important of which being the famous red brick road that runs through the Estate, free of cars. Kids can play along the road and benches are set up so that people can sit and talk to each other. Along the way, there are small gardens and squares where neighbors can stop to discuss matters of shared interest. The windows of the apartments, each one with a terrace, face one another and overlook the red brick road, creating a space of collective safety.

Rowley Way offers a different way of living with others than, for instance, the city of Solitude. It may seem to some that the manner in which the windows of Rowley Way face each other and the way in which residents are encouraged to interact is similar to the Panopticon in the Transparent City, but there is one difference. Household privacy in Rowley Way is preserved by an intentional feature of its apartments; only the front faces the common road, while the back windows are entirely concealed from public view.

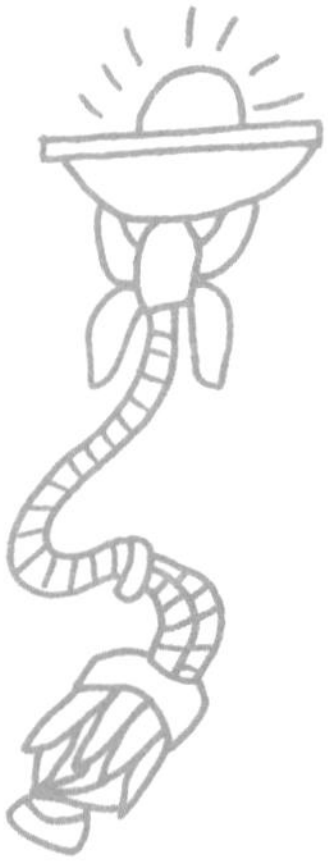

The complex was named the worst architectural structure in Britain by Margaret Thatcher, while simultaneously being the first postwar council housing estate to be designated an architectural treasure by the Historic Buildings and Monuments Commission for England.

After the death of my partner, and co-author of this book, I moved out of our mews house on Portobello Road and settled in Rowley Way. My neighbors—a family with five children, who immigrated from from Lebanon—and I take care of the shared flower

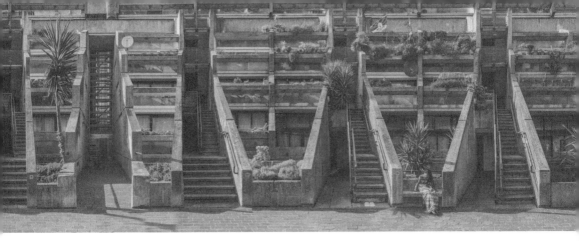

If you were the architect of a big estate, where would you live with your family? Would you allocate most of the square footage for residents' apartments, or would you distribute more space for public use, such as communal libraries, playgrounds, or maybe even a swimming pool?

garden in the space thoughtfully created by the architect between the apartments for the residents' joint projects. Houses for the poor are imagined by many to be places of crime and despair. In the United States, a number of those buildings have literally been blown up, eliminated as though they were a social disease, and the inhabitants resettled elsewhere. But Rowley Way remains a working example of an urban utopia, where 75% of the residents are non-owners, including many migrants from different parts of the world.

Rowley Way could have resembled a Roman military camp, with its modernist austerity and sparingly rational concrete structure, which is not called brutalist for nothing. Instead, it looks more like a flea market, a fairground, or an installation in a contemporary art museum. This is because the architect believed residents could use the Estate's vast public areas in their own way.

The public spaces and private terraces, decorated by residents, are vibrant and distinctive. Some people planted expensive olive trees; some have decorated their terrace with cheap plastic flowers; some have tomatoes; and some have luxurious palm trees. Every time I walk down the red brick road, I am captivated by each of the terraces, each of which is completely unique.

Perhaps it is the combination of strict rules governing internal structure and an abundance of public space that are responsible for the uniqueness of this estate.

People who have lived here for many years still love their home.

Afterword

In the afterword to this book, I want to talk about a project that grew out of it.

Imagine your dream estate with 500 families living in it. Would it look like a grand palace, a quaint European village, a futuristic Martian outpost, or maybe a federated pirate settlement?

The visuals used in this book are not just illustrations, but an attempt to share with readers a wider, wilder vision of how we might live together. The truly meaningful books are the ones that bring us together with other people. After all, if books don't change our lives, what are they good for?

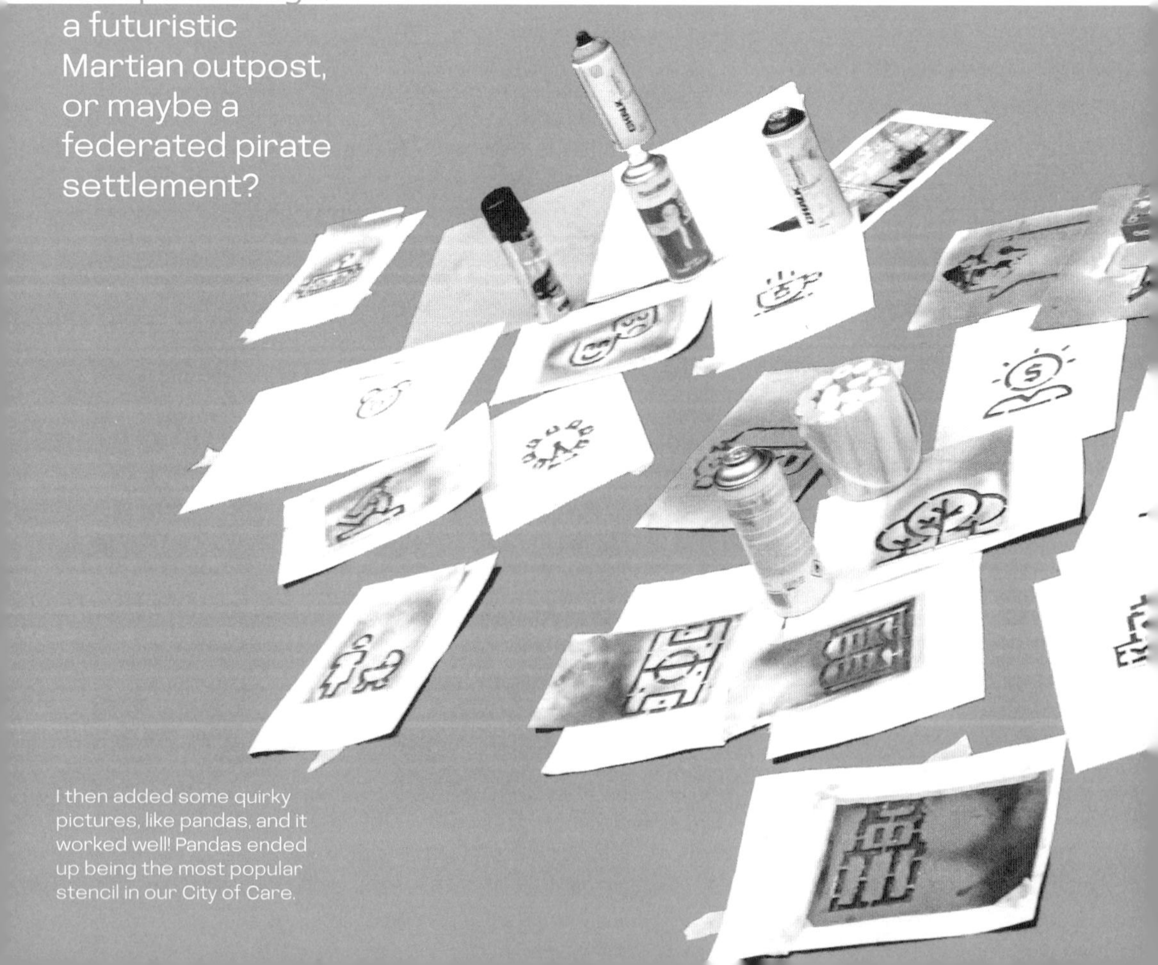

I then added some quirky pictures, like pandas, and it worked well! Pandas ended up being the most popular stencil in our City of Care.

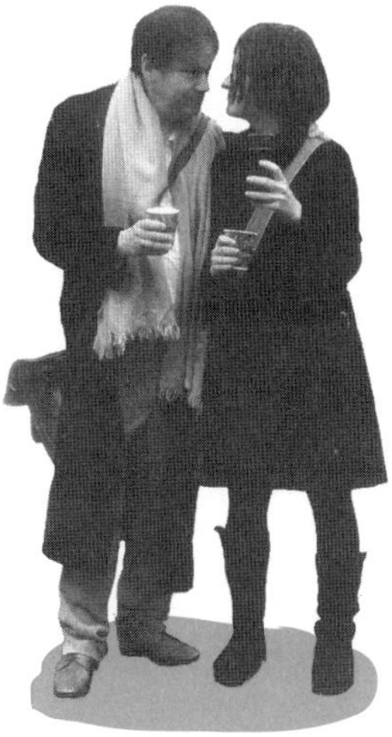

It is my hope that images, rightly used, have the potential to be more democratic than texts, because images communicate faster and further than language. They are a better way for many people to take part in public debate: For shy people who hate public speaking, for migrants who speak English as a second language, and especially for children whose agency is often ignored.

Images have one more peculiarity in contrast to texts. They make a stronger and more immediate impact on the mind, leaving us no time to think for ourselves and exercise judgment. That's why advertisements work. Yet, when images are produced together, shaped by continuous discussion, the situation changes completely. We get the opportunity to slow down and organize them through a collective meaning-making process.

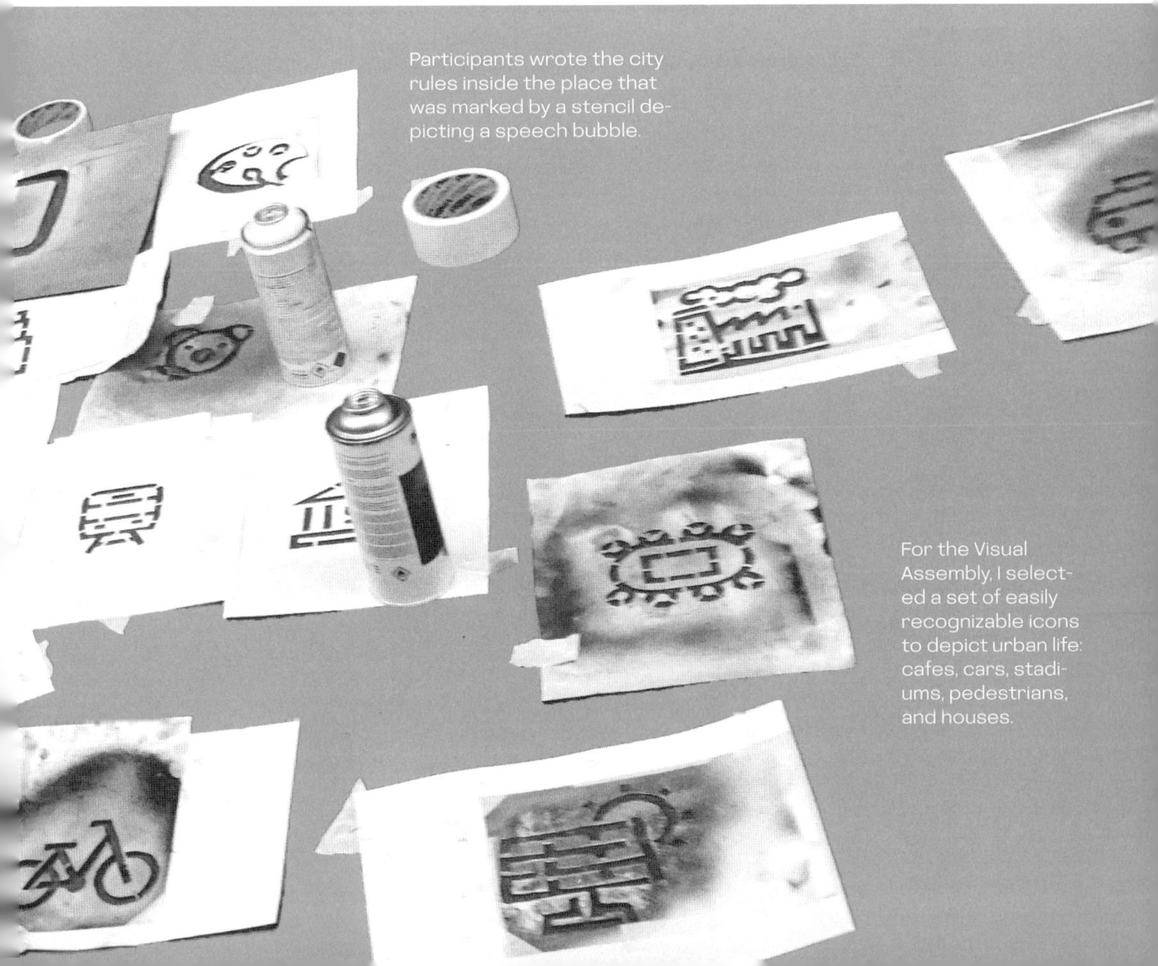

Participants wrote the city rules inside the place that was marked by a stencil depicting a speech bubble.

For the Visual Assembly, I selected a set of easily recognizable icons to depict urban life: cafes, cars, stadiums, pedestrians, and houses.

How often do
you meet as
a group with
your neighbors,
classmates,
family, or
friends to work
something out
together?

Imagine how
isolated a
person would
feel holding an
Assembly alone
and deciding
what is going to
happen in their
country, city,
or house for
everyone else.

Usually, when people get together, it is to do something fun. David recounted that in Madagascar, where he lived for two years while writing his doctoral dissertation, people would gather for meetings to solve common problems, as well as to sing and tell stories. It was, above all, an enjoyable social gathering, far different from the meetings we usually hold in the West, full of voting and bureaucracy.

With this in mind we came up with the idea of turning the book into something even more collaborative: a public drawing exercise that would provide us with new means of reimagining the way we live together. We decided to call this a Visual Assembly.

Since we held our Visual Assembly during Covid, it took some creativity to invent a way to be together without breaking the law. We decided to get out into the streets, sick of being stuck indoors, and above all to start something awesome.

We got help from artists and activists from Extinction Rebellion, one of the largest social movements of that year.

The Assembly met on Zoom, while David and I, along with our neighbor on Portobello Road, Olga Balla, served as self-appointed artists. Our job was to use chalk and spray paint to draw visuals on the deserted market square, according to the decisions made by the Assembly. It was fascinating to make art without coming up with anything on our own, following the instructions of others instead. Could it be that we discovered "socialist realism" in its proper form?

As we worked on mapping the City of Care, chalk, spray paint, and stencils were scattered around the square, available for anyone to pick up and use as they chose. Passersby began to join us. One was a well-known local character, followed by a pair of lovers, a street musician, a young guy cycling by—the number of participants was growing by the minute. Even with no announcements, it became quite aconsiderable gathering!

Can you think of any other ideas to facilitate group thought and expression, besides drawing and writing together?

It feels like it's much more fun to think things up together. We just need to figure out cool ways to do it.

This project started as a collection of social situations—utopias and dystopias, endlessly varied across different countries and times. Some of them seem intimidating and disastrous: "Why in the world would anyone want to live this way?" Others are breathtaking—"What a cool idea!" or "What a great place to live!"

But most importantly, we wanted to explore alternate versions of our own social life, imagining how things could change if we realized different possibilities.

Visual Assembly came about as a form of brainstorming about the most unusual and quirky social schemes, as an easy format to come up with ideas that are rare in our day-to-day lives.

But there are probably other ways of being and thinking together. Maybe while reading these lines you are even inventing your own?

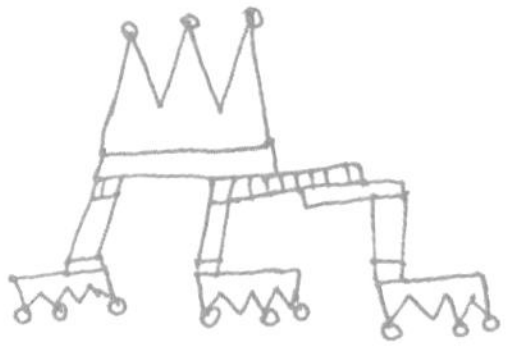

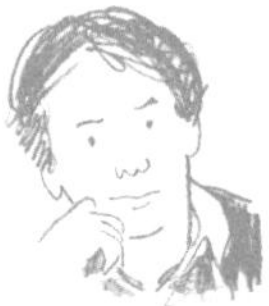

David Graeber

David wrote about this when we reflected on the results of the Assembly:

"The idea was to show people the approach is fun and to give people an experience of opening up imagination—in a way it's like popcorn, the consensus brainstorming tool, where no one can be criticized for any idea no matter what it is, then you record it all, then try to see what you can do with it. Step 2 would be seeing what we can do with it—to turn the exercise into a practical one; i.e., so you start off with pure imagination, and then, say, okay, Homerton. Let's reimagine Homerton. Or Newcastle. So ideally you turn the imagination you've just unleashed onto something that has immediate effects on lives."

Because if another world is possible, it is up to us to work it out with each other.

Study Materials

A large white building with a clock or of it. Street art at Christiania, Copen gen / Annie Spratt / Unsplash

№1

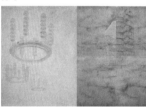

№2   №3   №4

Krutikov T.G. Diploma project "City of the future (evolution of architectural principles in city planning and housing organization)" / Federal State Budget Organisation of Culture (FSBOC) "State Scientific Research Museum of Architecture named after A.V. Shchusev"

Green matrix background computer generated / Smit / Shutterstock

From a French edition of Gulliver / Vve Magnin et Cie (Paris) / Bibliothèque nationale de France

Roman headquarters, A Querquennis, Os Baños Bande, Galicia (Spain) / ro Perez Vilariño / Wikim Commons (CC-BY-SA-2

№1
Flying Cities

1. Georgy Krutikov (1899–1958) was a Soviet constructivist architect famous for his drafts of utopian cities.

2. Velimir Khlebnikov (1985–1922) was a Russian poet and playwright who played a significant role in the Futurist and Russian avant-garde movements of the early twentieth century.

3. Velimir Khlebnikov. "My i doma," *Tvoreniya* (Moscow: Sovetskii Pisatel', 1986)

4. Tomás Saraceno is a contemporary artist who explores environmental issues in scientific and artistic forms. He is best known for his installations and sculptures, including Cloud Cities, a large-scale interactive project resembling airborne cities shown in exhibitions around the world.

№2
The City that Always Sleeps

1. Lana Wachowski and Lilly Wachowski are American film directors known for their work in The Matrix franchise, a dystopian science fiction film about a future where humanity is trapped in a simulated reality controlled by intelligent machines.

2. In The Matrix franchise, Morpheus guides and mentors the protagonist, Neo.

№3
City in the Clouds

1. Jonathan Swift (1667–1745) was an Irish writer best known for *Gulliver's Travels*, a satire published in 1726 that follows the adventures of Lemuel Gulliver as he voyages to various fantastical lands, encountering strange societies and reflecting on the flaws of humanity.

2. Balnibarbi is a fictional land in *Gulliver's Travels.*

3. Laputa is a fictional place in *Gulliver's Travels.*

4. Jonathan Swift, *Gulliver's Travels* (New York: Harper, 1950).

№5
City of Freedom

1. Hans Christian Andersen (1805–1975) was a Danish author and poet who is best known for his fairy tales, such as "The Little Mermaid," "The Ugly Duckling," and "The Emperor's New Clothes."

2. Christiania, also known as Freetown Christiania, is a self-governed, semi-autonomous neighborhood in Copenhagen, Denmark, established in 1971, where residents live in a community that emphasizes communal ownership and artistic expression.

№6
The City of Play

1. Lilliputians are a race of tiny people who inhabit the island of Lilliput in Jonathan Swift's *Gulliver's Travels.*

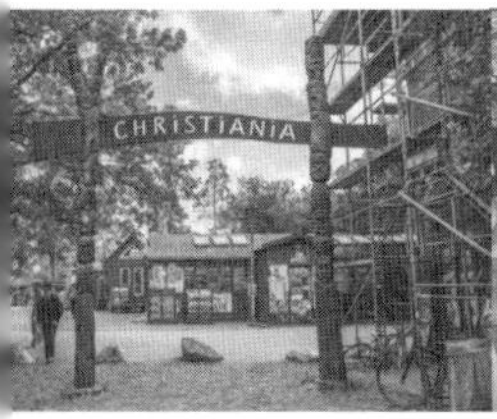
CHRISTIANIA

stiania district entrance sign / -filmws / Shutterstock

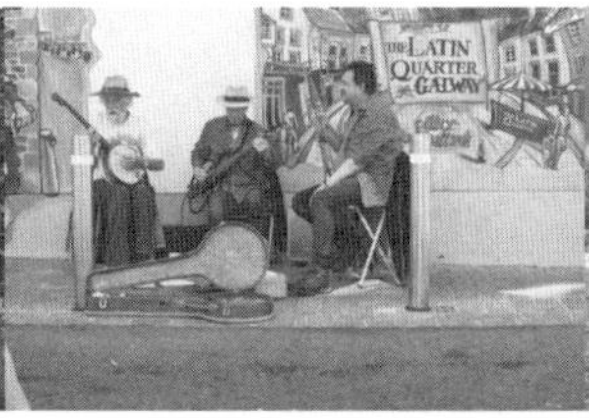
LATIN
QUARTER

Group of musicians, band, buskers, playing music at shop street in city center / Karlo Curis / Shutterstock

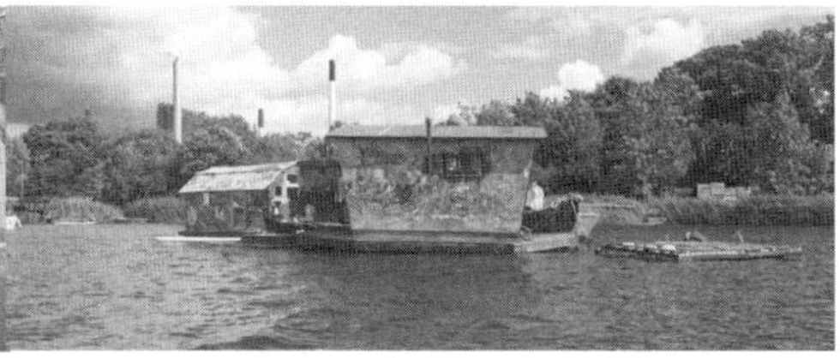

Freetown Christiania, self-proclaimed autonomous neighbourhood, an intentional community / Ruzanna / Shutterstock

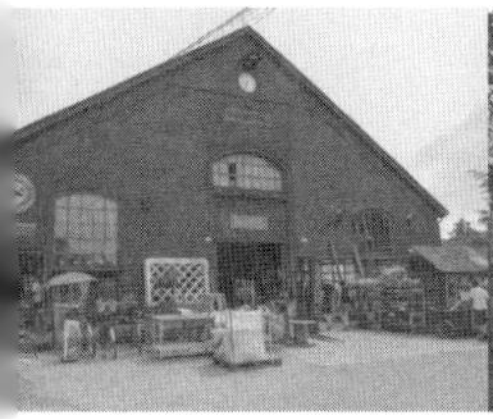

stiania alternative community at enhagen in Denmark / Stefano er / Shutterstock

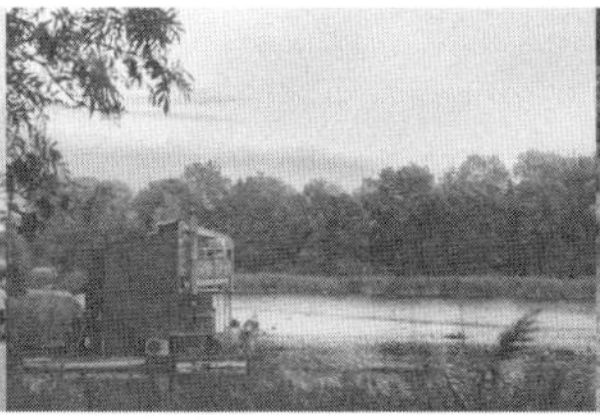

Christiania, house on the lake / Natan Cph / Shutterstock

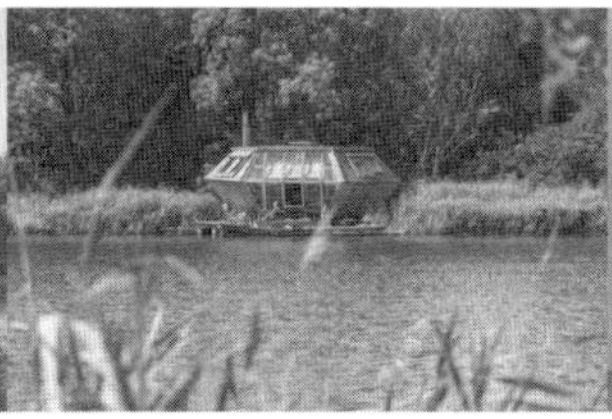

Freetown Christiania, a community in the Danish capital Copenhagen / Annchronick / Alamy Stock Photo

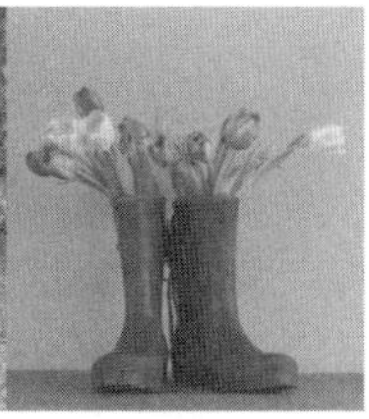

Pink & red tulips in rubber boots / debr22pics / Shutterstock

2. Walt Disney (1901–1966) was an American entrepreneur, animator, and film producer who founded the Walt Disney Company, known for iconic cartoon characters such as Mickey Mouse and Donald Duck.

3. Walt Disney World Resort is a vast entertainment complex situated in Orlando, Florida, featuring multiple theme and water parks, hotels, dining options, and shopping venues centered around Disney characters and stories.

4. Disney's *Sleeping Beauty* is a classic animated film about a cursed princess who can only be awakened by a true love's kiss.

5. A. S. Neill (1883–1973) was a Scottish educator. He founded Summerhill School, which let students make choices about their learning and participate in the school's decision-making.

6. Friedrich Schiller (1759–1805) was an influential German poet, playwright, and philosopher known for works that explored the transformative power of art and beauty in society.

7. Friedrich Schiller, *On the Aesthetic Education of Man* (New York: Oxford University Press, 1967).

8. A. S. Neill, Summerhill: *A Radical Approach to Child Rearing* (New York: Hart Publishing, 1960).

9. #NovaraFM, David Graeber, Bullshit Jobs, Direct Democracy and the End of Capitalism, 1st February 2019.

Nº7
City of Greed

1. Alexander Belyaev (1884–1942) was a Soviet science fiction writer. His 1928 novel *The Air Merchant* tells the story of meteorologist Georgiy Klimenko and his allies as they battle a villain plotting to steal Earth's air supply.

2. Peter Brabeck-Letmathe is an Austrian businessman and former CEO of Nestlé, the multinational food and beverage company famous for brands such as KitKat, Nescafé, Maggi, and others.

3. *We Feed the World* is a 2005 documentary that sheds light on the global food industry and its damaging impact on the environment, society, and food production practices.

Nº8
City as a Family

1. "Roman law" refers to the legal system and principles developed in ancient Rome that formed the basis for many modern legal principles around the world.

2. The Age of Enlightenment was an intellectual movement in the eighteenth century characterized by a focus on reason, science, and individual liberty, challenging traditional authority, and promoting ideals of progress and human rights.

3. Jean-Jacques Rousseau (1712–1778) was an influential eighteenth-century philosopher and writer who emphasized

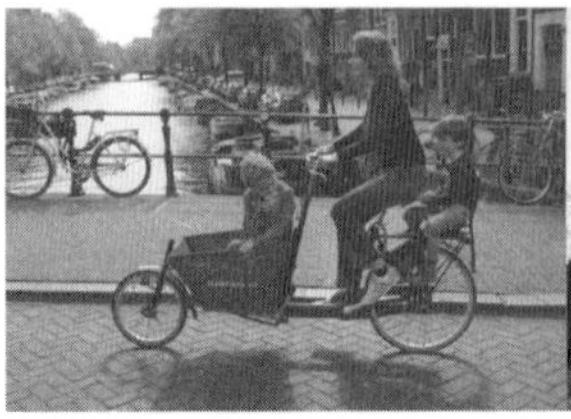

Mother with two children riding bicycles in historical part in Amsterdam / Bumble Dee / Shutterstock

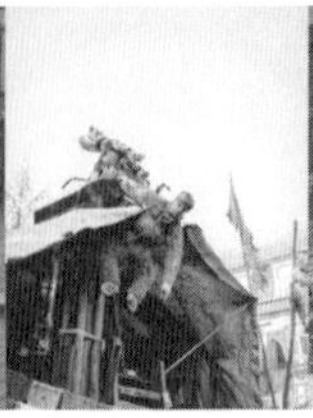

Christiania / Annie Spratt / Unsplash

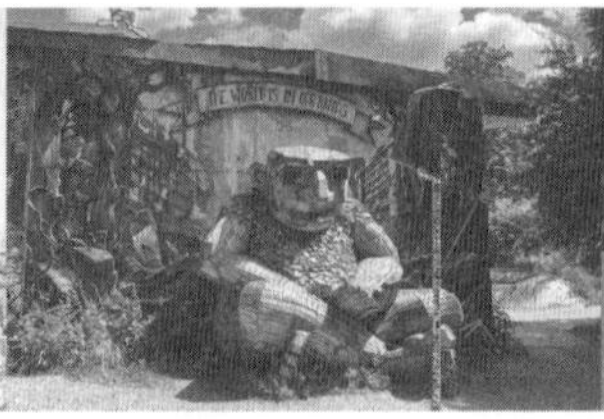

Streets of Copenhagen / Maria Eklind / Flickr.com (CC BY-SA 2.0)

№6

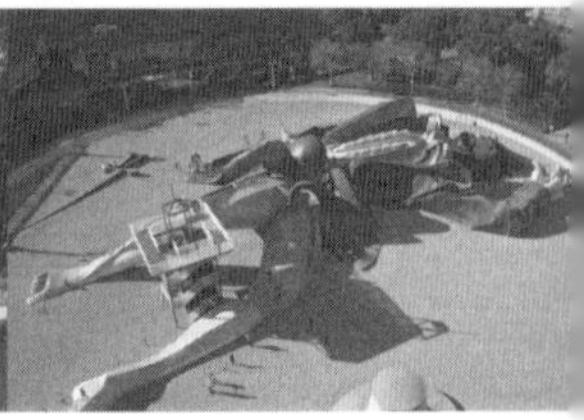

Bird's-eye view from park Gulliver, Valencia / ElPadrone / Pond5

№7

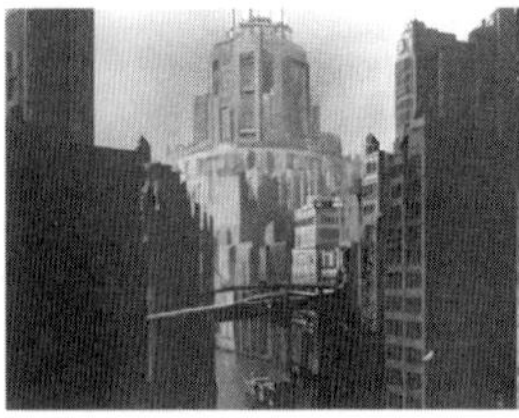

A screenshot from the film Metropolis (1927) / Friedrich-Wilhelm-Murnau-Foundation / Wikipedia

№8

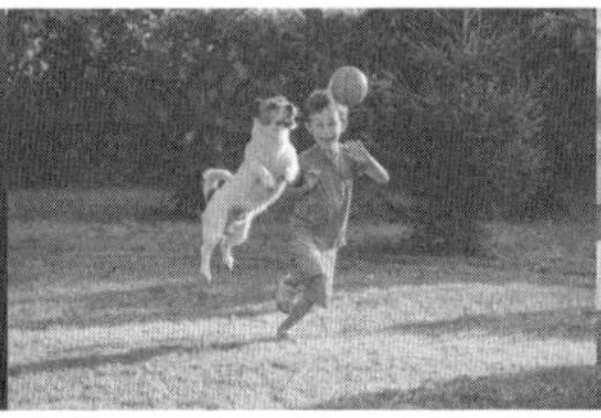

Family having fun outdoor with dog and basketball ball / Alexei_tm / Shutterstock

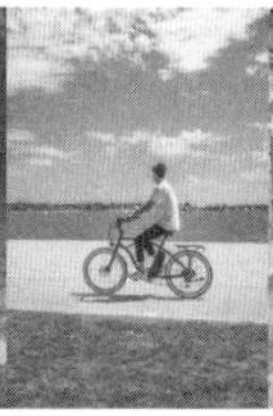

A man on a bike / Tower Electric Bikes / Unsplash

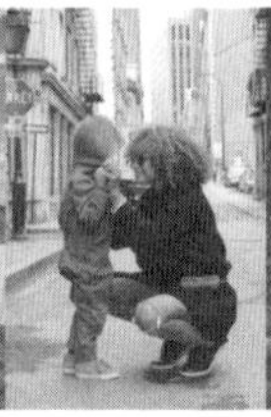

Woman holding kid at the street / Sai De Silva / Unsplash

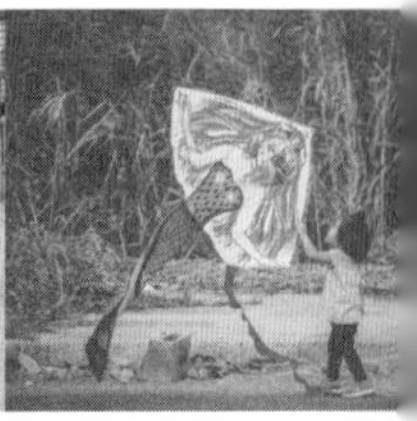

A girl with a kite / Ivan Botha Unsplash

individual freedom, the social contract, and the concept of humans being naturally good but corrupted by society.

4. The word "domestic" comes from the word *domus*, which overlaps somewhat in meaning with *familia*, as in "family." But, as proponents of "family values" might be interested to know, *familia* itself ultimately derives from the word *famulus*, meaning "slave." As for *dominium*, the word is derived from *dominus*, meaning "master" or "slave-owner," but ultimately from *domus*, meaning "house" or "household. It's related, of course, to the English term "domestic," which even now can be used either to mean "pertaining to private life," or to refer to a servant who cleans the house.
   See David Graeber, *Debt: The First 5,000 Years* (Brooklyn: Melville House, 2012).

5. The rapid growth of homeownership and the rise of suburban communities helped drive the postwar economic boom. Suburban neighborhoods of single-family homes tore their way through the outskirts of cities. William Levitt built the first Levittown, the archetypal suburban community, in 1946 on Long Island, New York. Purchasing mass acreage, "subdividing" lots, and contracting crews to build countless homes at economies of scale, Levitt offered affordable suburban housing to veterans and their families. Levitt became the prophet of the new suburbs, heralding a massive internal migration. The country's suburban share of the population rose from 19.5% in 1940 to 30.7% by 1960. Homeownership rates rose from 44% in 1940 to almost 62% in 1960. Between 1940 and 1950, suburban communities of greater than 10,000 people grew 22.1%, and planned communities grew at an astonishing rate of 126.1%. As historian Lizabeth Cohen notes, these new suburbs "mushroomed in territorial size and the populations they harbored." Between 1950 and 1970, America's suburban population nearly doubled to 74 million, with 83 percent of all population growth occurring in suburban places.
   Lumen Learning, The Rise of Suburbs, US History (American Yawp). Available online: https://courses.lumenlearning.com/suny-ushistory2ay/chapter/therise-of-suburbs-2/.

6. Raymond Westbrook goes through the three known cases of this really happening. It would seem that the father's authority here was considered identical to that of the state. If a father was found to have executed his child illegitimately, he could be punished.

№9
City in the Desert

1. Paolo Soleri (1919–2013) was an Italian architect and urban thinker who believed in designing cities that are both sustainable and efficient, combining architecture with ecology.

2. One of Soleri's notable projects is Arcosanti, an experimental town in Arizona that serves as a living example of his vision for a compact, environmentally conscious urban community.

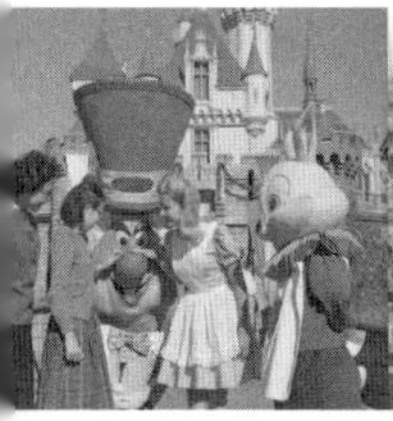
an student, Jong Sook
isiting the Mad Hatter and
at Disneyland, 1964-01-05
A Library Special Collec-
/ Flickr.com (CC BY 2.0)

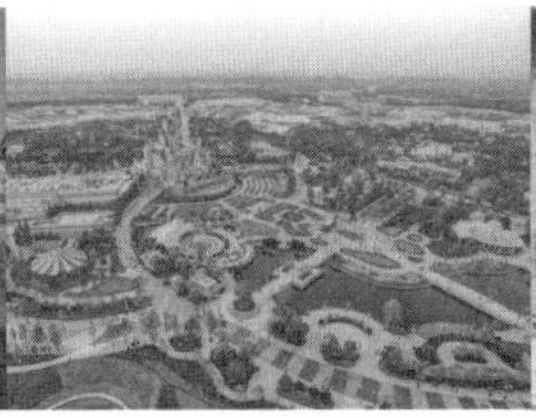
An aerial view of the Shanghai Disney Resort in Pudong, Shanghai, China / Imaginechina Limited / Alamy Stock Photo

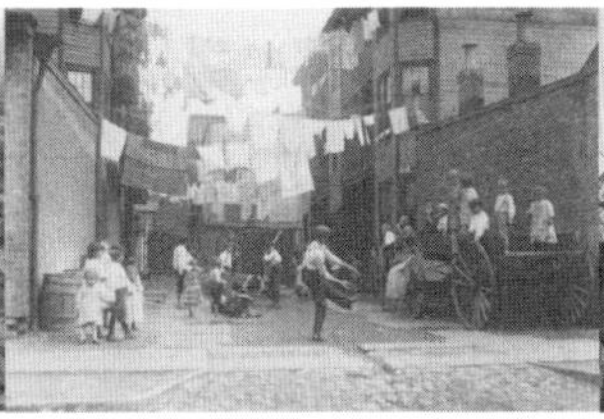
Playground in a Mill Village / Lewis Wickes Hine / Art Institute, Chicago (CC0 Public Domain Designation)

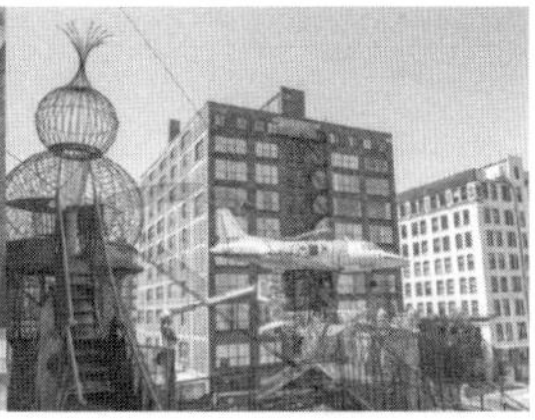
City Museum St. Louis: MonstroCity / City Museum (promotional purposes)

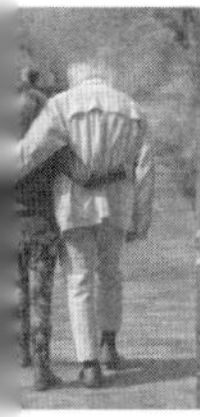
shot from
/ Janosch
Unsplash

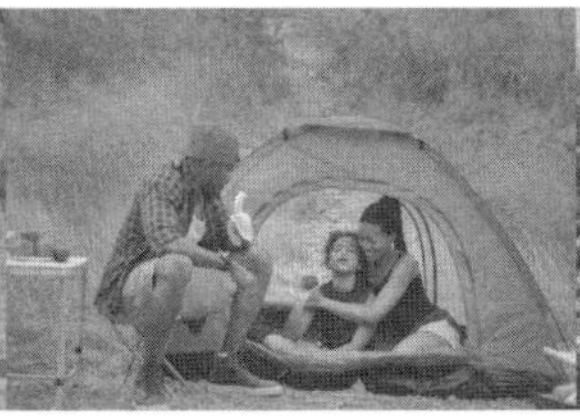
Family camping trip tent outdoor / Simply Love / Shutterstock

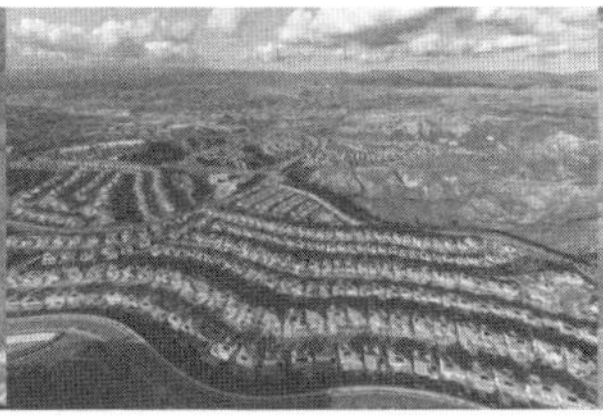
Aerial view of suburban housing sprawl in the Santa Clarita community of Los Angeles County, California / Trekandshoot / Shutterstock

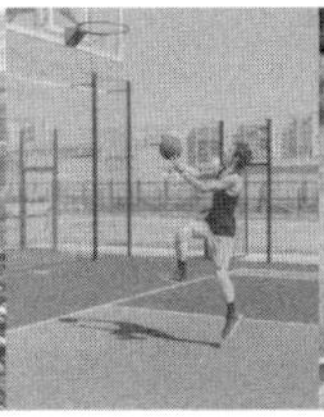
Man in black tank top and yellow shorts playing basketball during daytimer / Mira Kireeva / Unsplash

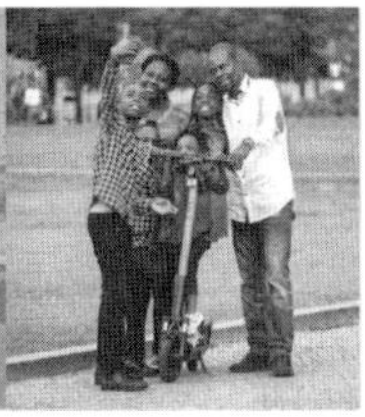
Man in white dress shirt and blue denim jeans holding orange and black kick scooter / Serhat Beyazkaya / Unsplash

№10
Sanctuary City

1. Abram Ioffe (1880–1960) was a famous Soviet physicist who studied how electricity flows through solid materials and played a significant role in promoting science education in the Soviet Union.

№11
Big Brother City

1. The phrase "Big Brother" first appeared in George Orwell's novel *1984*. It has become a byword for any large organization that spies on its members.

№12
Surveillance City

1. Edward Snowden is a former U.S. intelligence employee who leaked secret documents in 2013 on the internet, revealing widespread government surveillance programs conducted by the U.S. government.
2. David Graeber, *The Utopia of Rules: On Technology, Stupidity, and the Secret Joys of Bureaucracy* (Brooklyn: Melville House, 2015).
3. Alan Rusbridger, Ewen MacAskill, and Janine Gibson, "Edward Snowden: a right to privacy is the same as freedom of speech – video interview," theguardian.com.

№13
Transparent City

1. *We* is a dystopian novel by Russian writer Yevgeny Zamyatin (1984–1937), written 1920–21. It was first published as an English translation by Gregory Zilboorg in 1924 by E. P. Dutton in New York, with the original Russian text first published in 1952.
2. George Orwell (1903–1950) was a novelist, journalist, essayist, and critic, best known for his novels *Animal Farm* (1945) and *1984* (1949).
3. Aldous Huxley (1984–1963) was a writer and philosopher, best known for his dystopian novel *Brave New World* (1932).
4. Thomas Hobbes (1588–1679) was an English philosopher who is best known for his 1651 work *Leviathan*, which argues for the necessity of a strong central government to maintain social order and prevent chaos. Hobbes uses the term "Leviathan" as a metaphor for a state that controls the individuals within a society and thus ensures peace, stability, and order.
5. Yevgeny Zamyatin, *We*, translated by Gregory Zilboorg (New York: Dutton, 1924).

№14
City of Masks

1. The Venice Carnival is an annual festival held in Venice, Italy, known for its elaborate masks, costumes, parades, and festivities.

№9

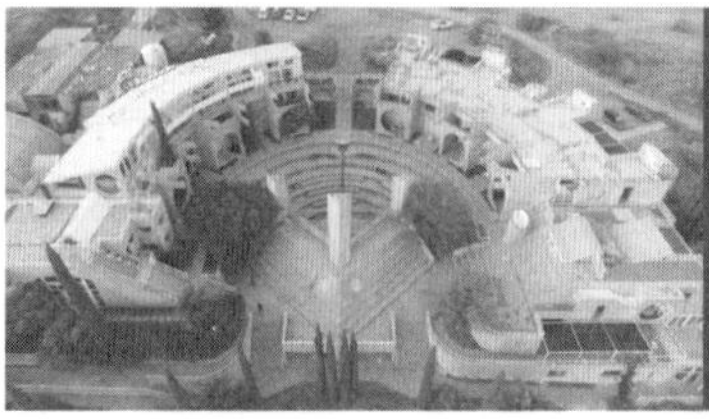

The Colly Soleri Amphitheater, viewed from straight above, drone shot / Rob Jameson / Cosanti Foundation

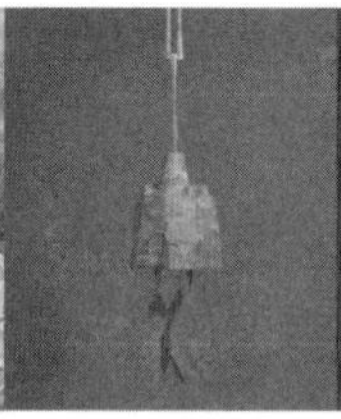

124b bronze bell / Jeremy Shevling / Cosanti Foundation

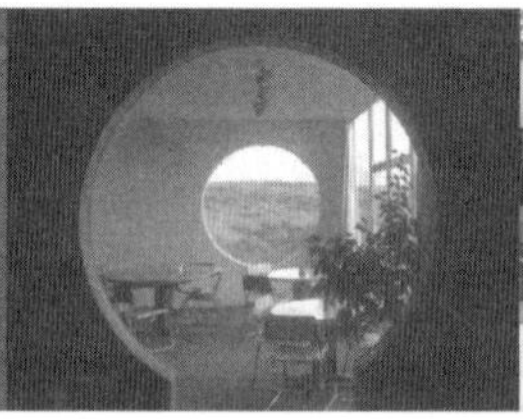

689.1510lvb6017. Cafe level, west bay / Laura Villa Baroncelli / Cosanti Foundation

№10

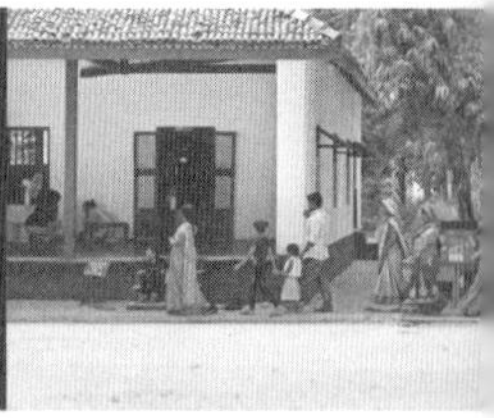

People walking on street during day time / Brijender Dua / Unsplash

№11

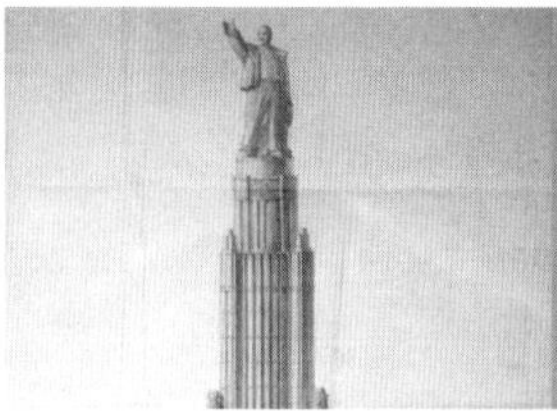

Иофан Б.Ф.; Архитектор: Гельфрейх В.Г.; Архитектор: Щуко В.А.; Скульптор: Меркуров С.Д. Технический проект. Дворец Советов. Москва. Макет. Из альбома "Технический проект Дворца Советов в Москве". Съемка: 1937-1939 гг

№12

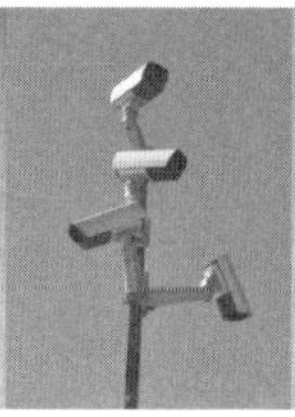

Draussen-kamer-as-uberwachung / Jürgen Jester

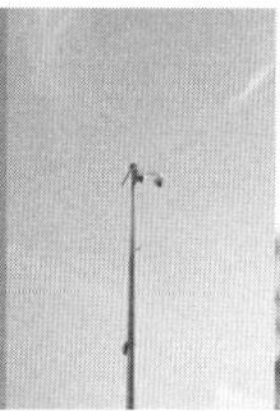

Modern security camera on high column / Ave Calvar Martinez / Pexels

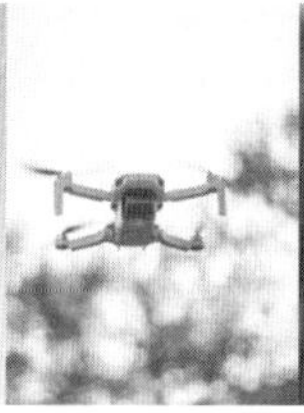

Modern drone flying over nature among trees / Callum Hilton / Pexels

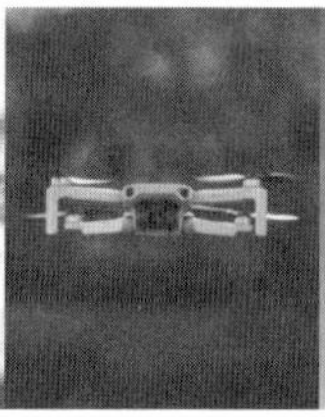

Small white drone with camera in flight / Callum Hilton / Pexels

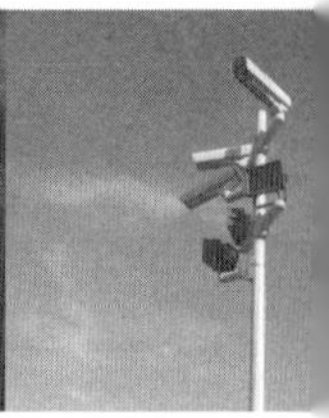

Black and White CCTV Cameras / Thomas Wi isch / Pexels

№15
Invisible City

1. H. G. Wells (1866–1946) was a British writer known for his science fiction novels, including *The Invisible Man* (1897), a story of a scientist who invented a method of achieving invisibility.
2. H. G. Wells, *The Invisible Man: A Grotesque Romance* (TK:TK).
3. Adam Harvey is a Berlin-based artist and applied researcher focused on computer vision, privacy, and surveillance.
4. The Open Source movement is in favor of creating software where the code is freely shared and can be modified and distributed by anyone.
5. Adrian Bauer is an English engineer and mathematician, the originator of the RepRap Project, a self-replicating 3D printer.

№16
Solitude City

1. Victorian England is the period of British history during the reign of Queen Victoria from 1837 to 1901, characterized by social, cultural, and industrial advancements as well as strict societal norms and values.
2. The British Museum is a public museum in London, established in 1753 and known for its extensive collection of over eight million works representing human history, culture, and art from all continents.

№17
One-Man City

1. The Hermitage Museum, located in Saint Petersburg, Russia, is one of the world's largest museums, founded in 1764 and housing over three million artworks and artifacts from diverse cultures and historical periods.
2. Sam Chermayeff is an architect, designer, and teacher.
3. The town was sold for less than a million dollars, and Buford's new overseer takes control of ZIP code 82052. It encompasses 10 acres of land and five buildings, including a three bedroom modular house he will now call home, a schoolhouse from 1905, a parking area, and a convenience and fuel store called the Buford Trading Post. The income-producing unincorporated community also touts a Union Wireless cell tower with a lease in place and United States Post Office Boxes used by residents from nearby properties. The tiny town welcomes an estimated 1,000 visitors per day during the summer tourism season.

№18
Ghost Town

1. Machu Picchu is an ancient citadel situated in the mountains of Peru, built in the fifteenth century and later abandoned, renowned for its architecture.
2. Spanish conquistadors were Spanish soldiers and explorers of the fifteenth and sixteenth

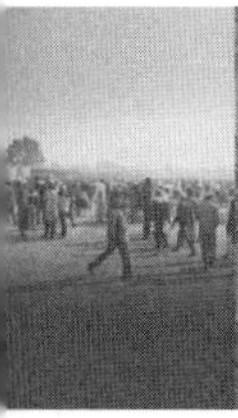

wd of people
ng daytime /
Merchant /
plash

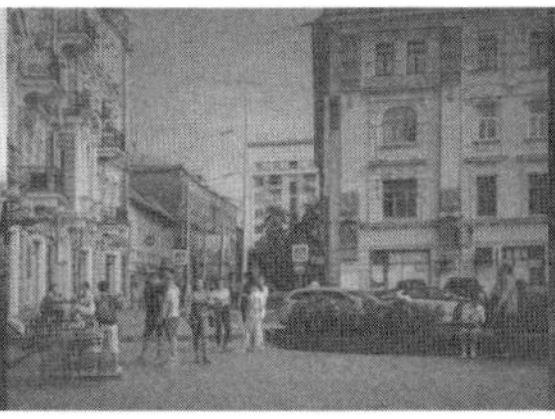

People walking on street during daytime / Egor Myznik / Unsplas

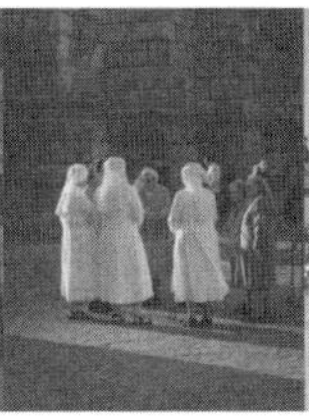

A group of people standing outside / Hernan Gonzalez / Unsplash

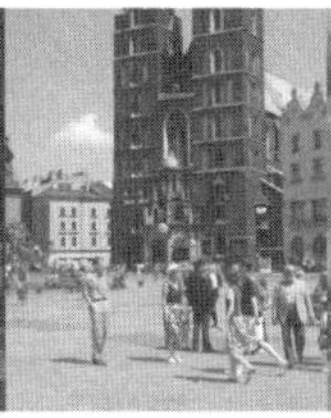

People standing beside concrete cathedral / Les Anderson / Unsplashh

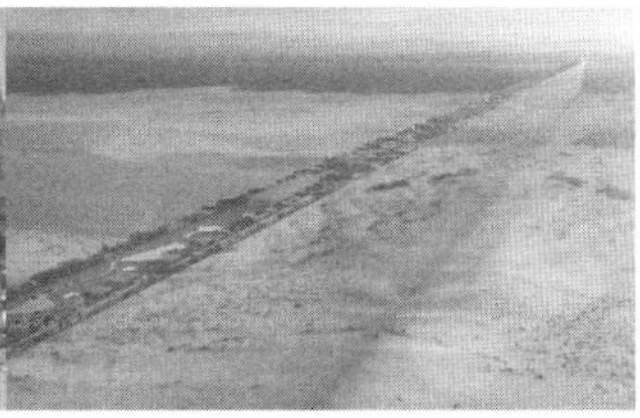

The Line - project rendering / Neom (promotional purposes)

4

№15

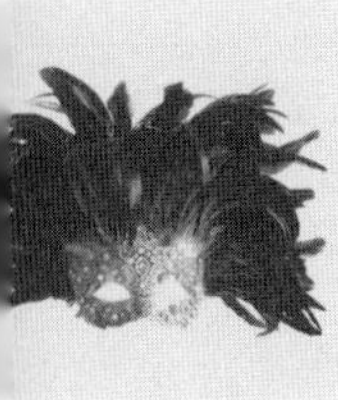

lden feathered
tian mask isolated on a
background / E. Spek
tterstock

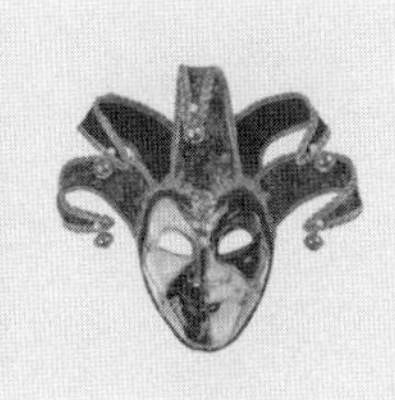

Hand-crafted and decorated face mask on an isolated white background / Ilizia / Shutterstock

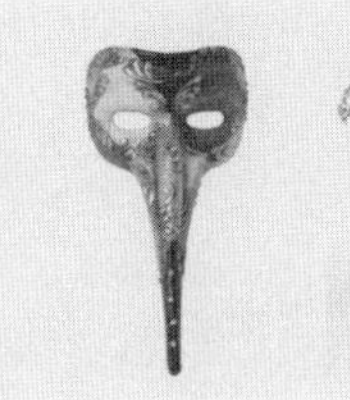

Upper view image of a colorful long nose Venetian mask against a white background / Radu Razvan / Shutterstock

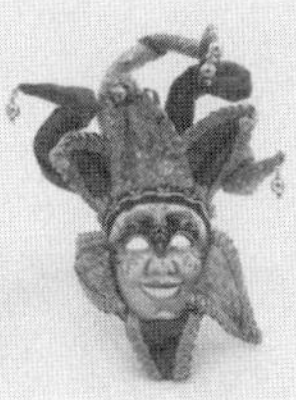

Venice mask / SarunasVysniauskas / Shutterstock

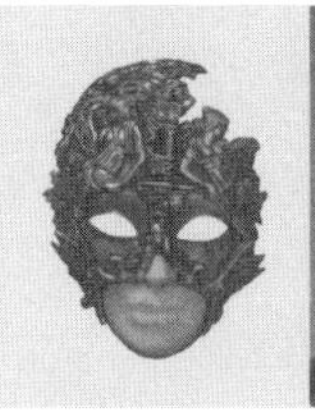

Colorful traditional Venetian mask isolated on white background / Aron M / Alamy Stock Photo

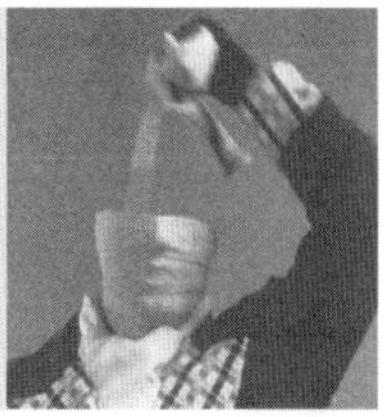

Chevy Chase, Memoirs of an invisible man, 1992 / AJ Pics / Alamy Stock Phot

centuries who conquered new territories in Latin America and expanded the Spanish Empire.

3. The Inca Empire was a civilization in South America, spanning from the thirteenth to the sixteenth century, known for its advanced agricultural systems, impressive stonework, centralized governance, and extensive road networks connecting its vast territories.

№19
A City of Runners

1. David Graeber, "Culture as Creative Refusal," *The Cambridge Journal of Anthropology*, vol. 31, no. 2 (2013), pp. 1–19.

№20
Underground City

1. Esteban Suarez is a Mexican architect who founded Bunker Arquitectura, an international multidisciplinary team formed of architects, urban planners, and designers.

2. Nikolai Lyutomsky is a Russian architect.

№21
City in the Ocean

1. Peter Thiel is an American entrepreneur, one of the co-founders of the online payment platform PayPal.

2. The Gulag was a system of forced labor camps established in the Soviet Union from the 1930s to the 1950s, where millions of people were imprisoned and subjected to harsh conditions, and often led to death.

3. David Graeber, *Pirate Enlightenment or the Real Libertalia* (New York: Farrar, Straus, and Giroux, 2023).

4. David Graeber, *Fragments of an Anarchist Anthropology* (Chicago: Prickly Paradigm Press, 2004), p. 65

5. David Graeber (1961–2020) was an American anthropologist, activist, and author known for his influential works on capitalism, bureaucracy, and debt.

№22
City of Punishment

1. The Ku Klux Klan is a white supremacist organization founded in the United States in 1865, known for its violence and racial hatred toward African Americans and other minority groups.

2. The Confederacy refers to the group of eleven Southern states that seceded from the U.S. in 1860–61 with the goal of preserving slavery and forming a separate nation, leading to the American Civil War.

3. David Graeber, *The Utopia of Rules: On Technology, Stupidity, and the Secret Joys of Bureaucracy* (Brooklyn: Melville House, 2015), p. 44.

№23
Trash City

1. Cairo is the capital and largest city of Egypt.

№16

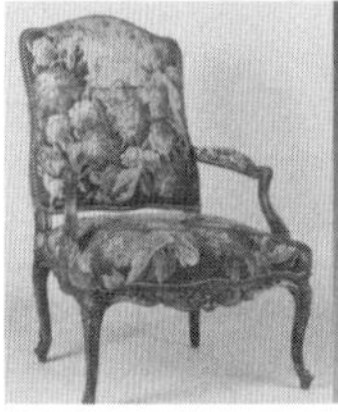
Armchair (part of a set of nine) / The Metropolitan Museum of Art

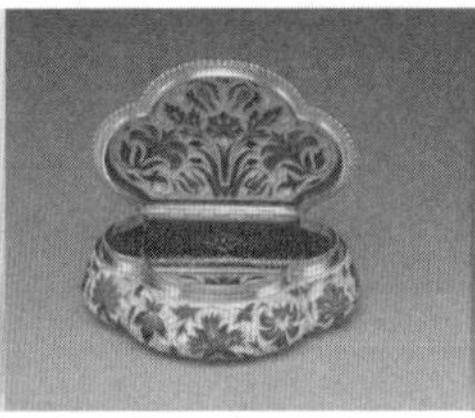
Box / The Metropolitan Museum of Art

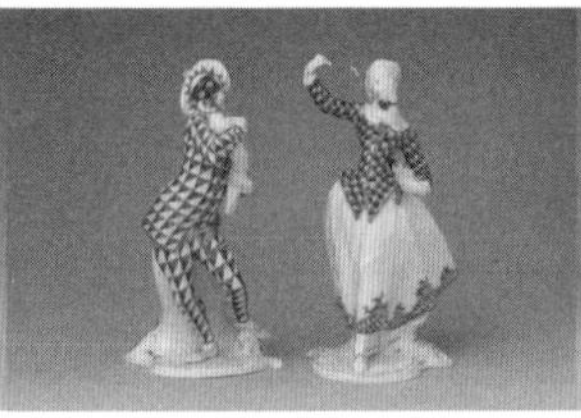
Harlequin. Manufactory Nymphenburg Porcelain Manufactory / The Metropolitan Museum of Art

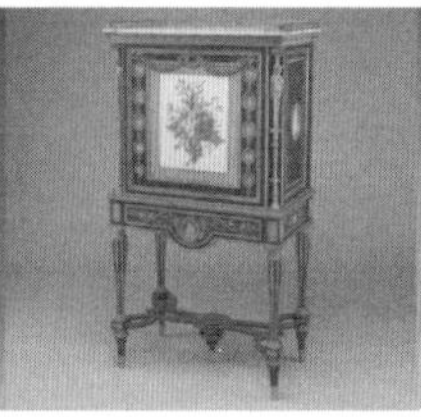
Drop-front desk (secrétaire à abattant or secrétaire en cabinet) / The Metropolitan Museum of Art

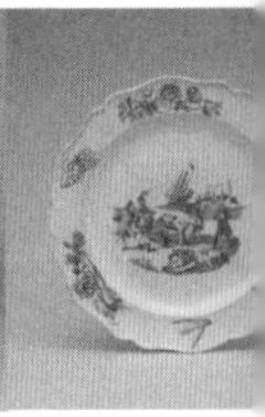
Plate / The Metropolitan Museum of Ar

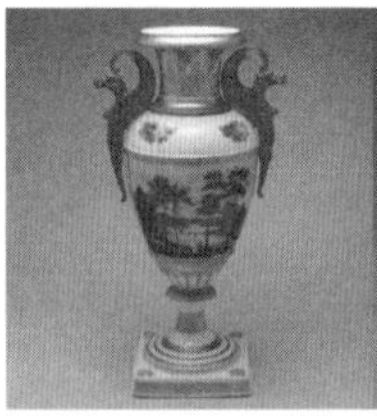
Vase / Tucker Factory / The Metropolitan Museum of Art

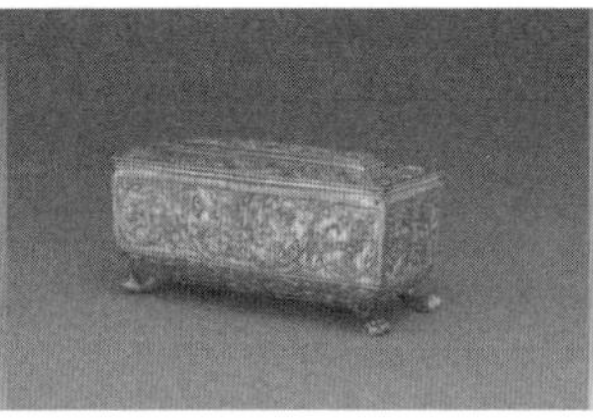
Casket, late 15th or early 16th century / The Metropolitan Museum of Art

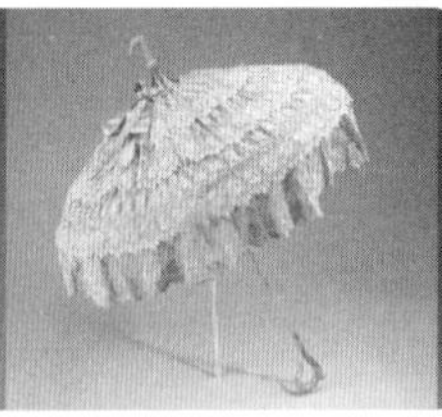
Parasol / The Metropolitan Museum of Art

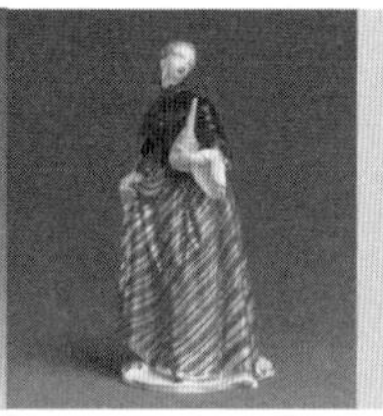
Donna Martina. Manufactory Nymphenburg Porcelain Manufactory / The Metropolitan Museum of Art

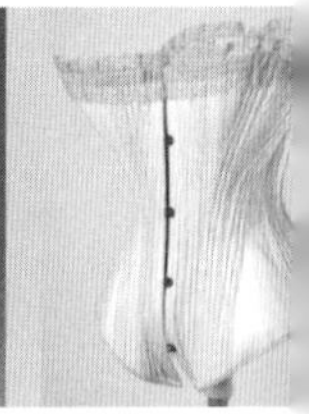
Corset, Manufacture La Sirene French, mid1880s / The Metropolitan Museum of Ar

№24
Noah's Ark

1. Biosphere 2 is a scientific facility in Arizona that simulates different environments like rainforests, deserts, and oceans to study how they function.

№25
Model City

1. Herbert von Karajan (1908–1989) was an Austrian conductor known as the principal conductor of the Berlin Philharmonic.

№27
Sun City

1. Tommaso Campanella (1568-1639) was an Italian philosopher and writer best known for his utopian vision of society in *The City of the Sun.*

№29
City of Care

1. Alejandro Aravena is a Chilean architect known for his socially conscious building projects that attempt to break down economic inequality in urban areas.

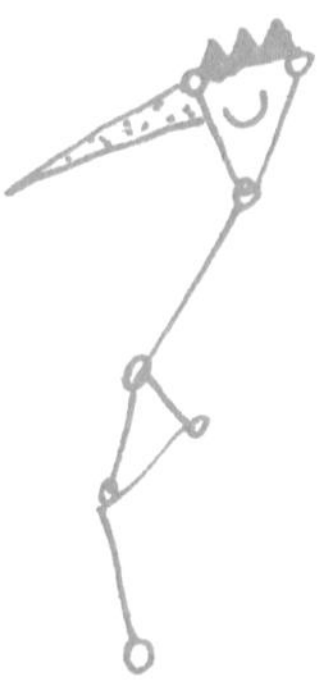

sources

1. David Graeber, *Bullshit Jobs: A Theory* (New York: Simon & Schuster, 2018) (p. 194), p. 34
2. David Graeber, *Direct Action: An Ethnography*, (AK Press, 2009) p. 46
3. David Graeber, *Fragments of an Anarchist Anthropology*, (Chicago: Prickly Paradigm Press, 2004)
4. David Graeber, *The Dawn of Everything: A New History of Humanity* (New York: Farrar, Straus and Giroux, 2021)
5. David Graeber, *The Utopia of Rules: On Technology, Stupidity, and the Secret Joys of Bureaucracy* (Brooklyn: Melville House, 2015)
6. Velimir Khlebnikov, *"My i doma,"* *Tvorenie* (Moscow: Sovetskii Pisatel', 1986)

dream city, city-hospital, shady town, prison to

...et / The Metropolitan Museum
...t

Knife, fork, and spoon. Elkington & Co. / The
Metropolitan Museum of Art

Side-saddle used by Con-
stance / National Museum
Australia

Rolltop desk / The Metropolitan Museum of Art

...e and tea service (déjeuner
...s réticule). Manufactory Sèvres
...factory / The Metropolitan
...um of Art

Shoes, American, 1899 / The Metropolitan Museum of Art

Side Chair. Herter
Brothers / The Metro-
politan Museum of Art

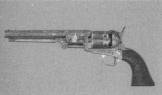

Gold-inlaid Colt Model 1851 Navy Revolver
(serial no. 20133), with Case and Accessories /
The Metropolitan Museum of Art

The Matrix, film directed by
...ena and Lilly Wachowski (Holly-
...wood: Warner Bros. and Village
...Roadshow Pictures, 1999)

...A. S. Neil Summerhill: *A Radical
...Approach to Child Rearing* (Hart
...Publishing Company, 1960)

...Friedrich Schiller, *On the Aes-
...hetic Education of Man*, (New
...York: Oxford University Press,
...967)

...Edward Snowden, Alan Rus-
...bridger, Ewen MacAskill, and Ja-
...ine Gibson, *"Edward Snowden:
...right to privacy is the same
...s freedom of speech,"* video
...nterview, theguardian.com,
...2 May, 2015

...Jonathan Swift, *Gulliver's Trav-
...ls* (New York: Harper, 1950)

...H. G. Wells, *The Invisible Man:
...Grotesque Romance* (New
...York: Signet Classics, 2007)

13. Raymond Westbrook, *"Slave and
    Master in Ancient Near Eastern
    Law,"* in *Law from the Tigris to
    the Tiber*, edited by Bruce Wells
    and Rachel Magdalene (Phila-
    delphia: Penn State University
    Press, 2009), p. 207

14. Yevgeny Zamyatin, *We*, trans-
    lated by Gregory Zilboorg (E. P.
    Dutton, 1924)

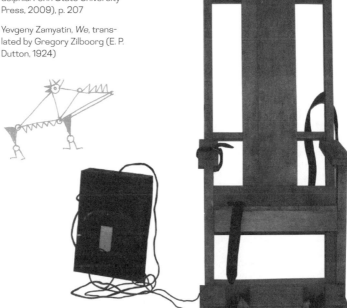

№17

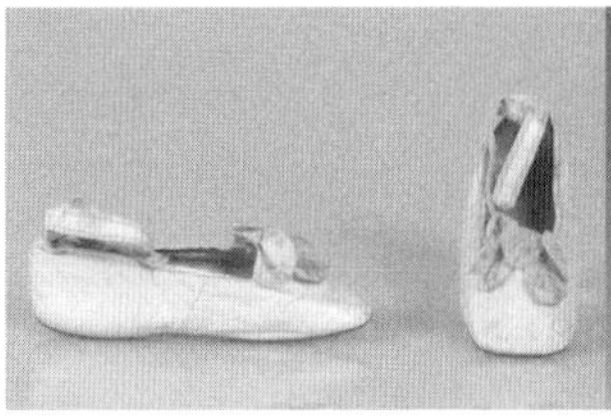

Shoes, Retailer Jeffers French Shoes, 1866 / The Metropolitan Museum of Art

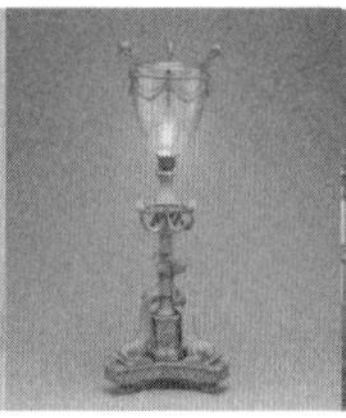

Candlestand (one of a pair) / The Metropolitan Museum of Art

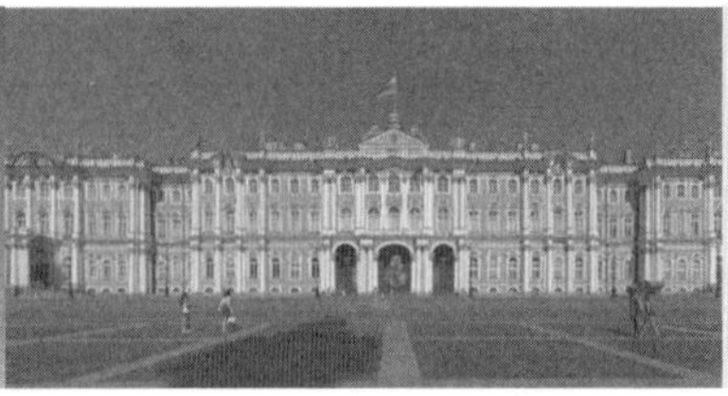

Winter_Palace_Panorama_2 / Florstein (WikiPhoto-Space) / Wikimedia Commons (CC BY-SA 4.0)

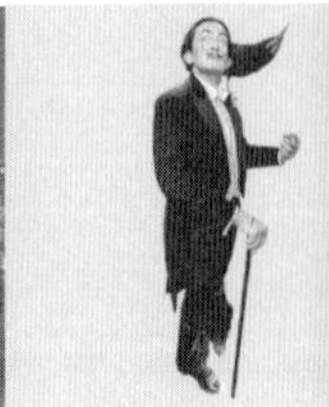

A Salvador Dali, the pain model at the Amsterdar Madame Tussauds wax museum / Olena Znak

№21

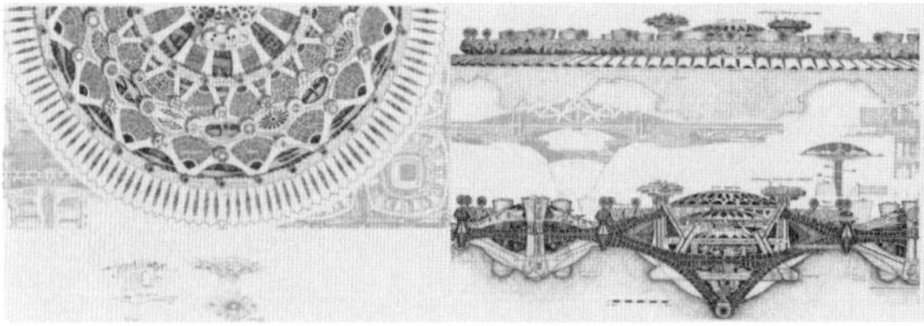

NOVANOAH I, a floating Arcology designed for a population of 400.000. Page 37 from "City in the Image of Man" / Cosanti Foundation

№22

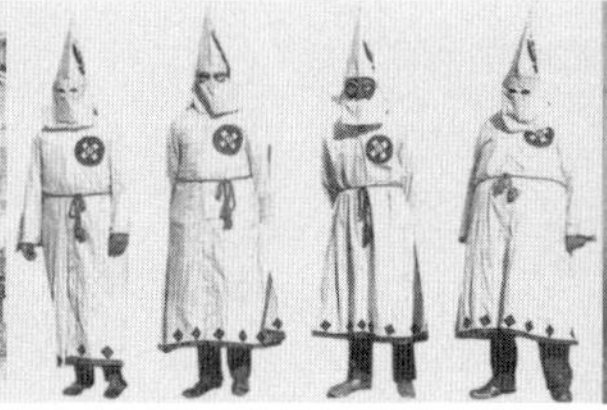

Ku Klux Klansmen / Library of Congress, Prints & Photographs Division, reproduction number, e.g., [LC-F82-1234]

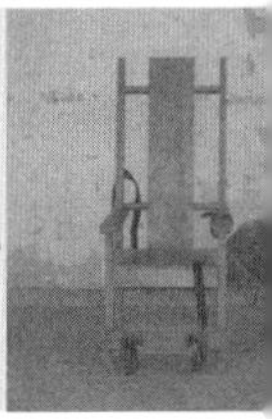

The former Louisia execution chamber Honeycutt / Wikim Commons CC BY-S

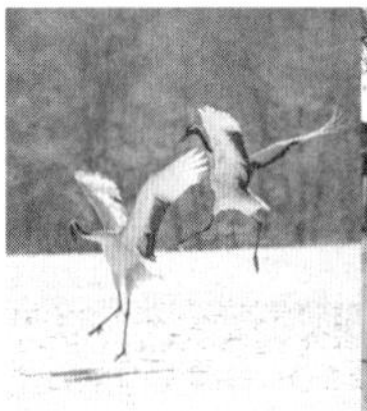

White birds flying over body of water during daytime / Birger Strahl / Unsplash

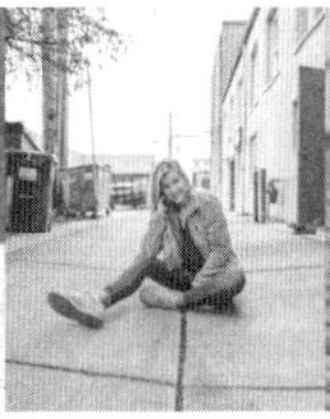

Woman sitting on sidewalk / Trevin Rudy / Unsplash

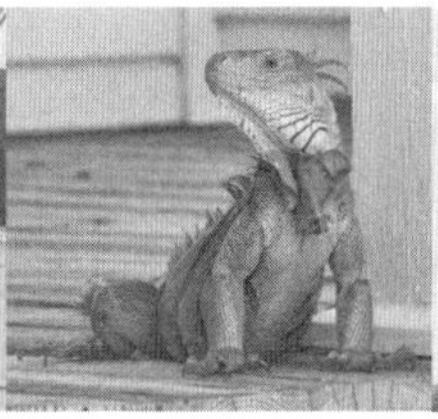

Yellow and gray iguana standing on brown wooden panel / Matthew Essman / Unsplash

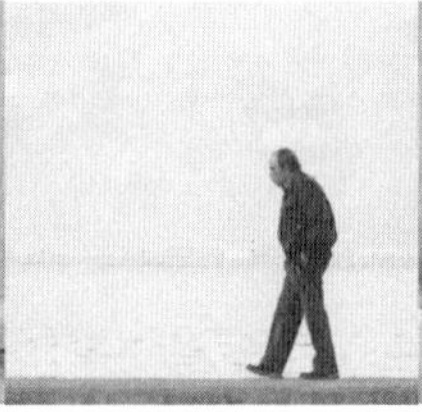

Man walking on dock / Ahmed Badawy / Unsplash

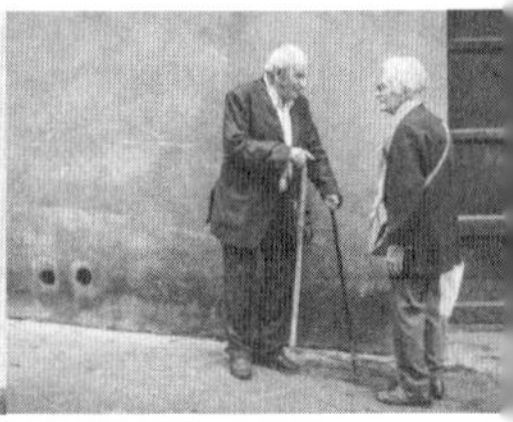

Two persons talking while standing n wall / Cristina Gottardi / Unsplash

№26

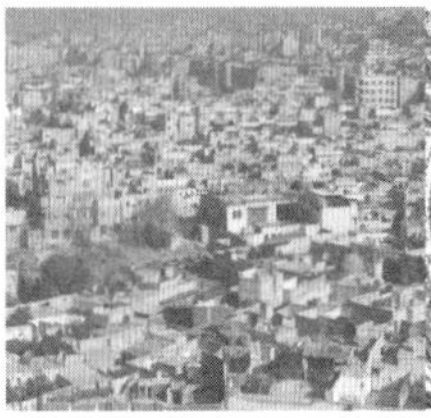

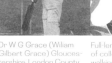

Aleppo, Syria. View of the city from height of bird's flight / Dima Moroz / Shutterstock

№27

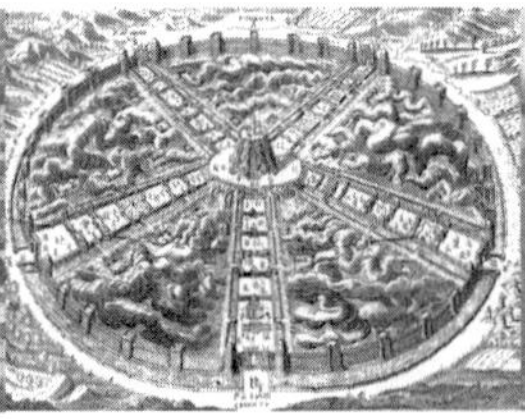

City of the Sun / University of Illinois Urbana-Champaign

№28

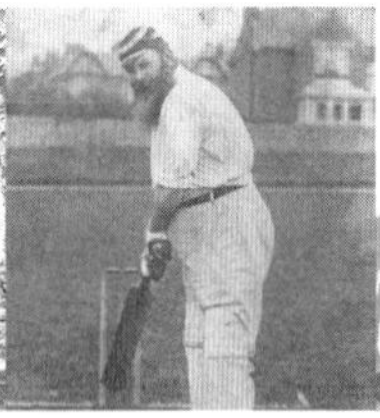

Dr W G Grace (Wiliam Gilbert Grace) Gloucestershire, London County and England / Tom Viggars / Alamy Stock Photo

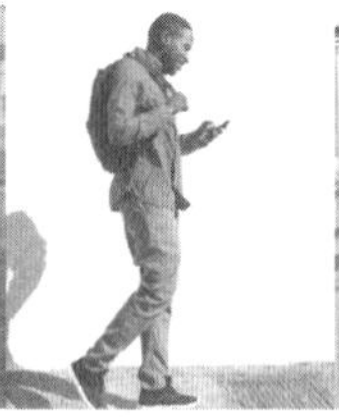

Full-length side portrait of college student walking with bag and mobile phone / Mimagephotography / Shutterstock

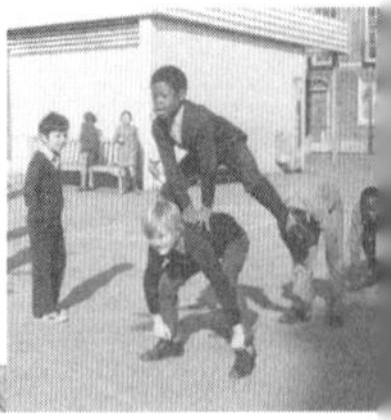

Children playing at Penton School, Islington, North Lo 11th March 1971. Face of Br 1971 Feature / Trinity Mirro Mirrorpix / Alamy Stock Ph

№29

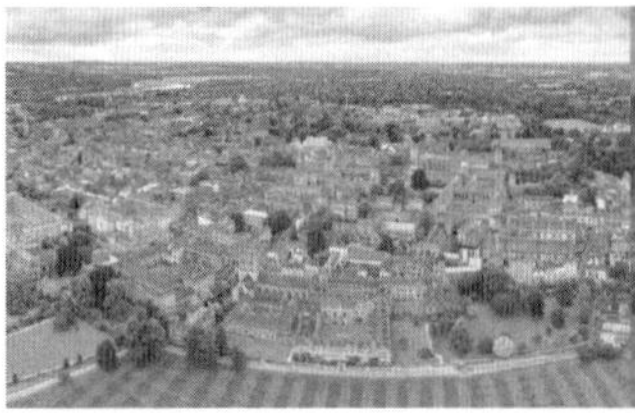

Oxford, aerial panorama / Chensiyuan / Wikimedia Commons (CC BY-SA 4.0)

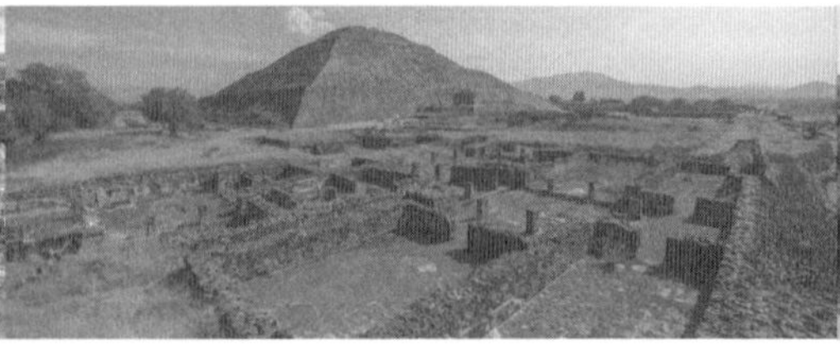

Pyramid of the Sun and Plaza of the Pyramid in Teotihuacán in city of San Juan Teotihuacán, State of Mexico, Mexico. Teotihuacan is a UNESCO World Heritage Site since 1987 / Wangkun Jia / Shutterstock

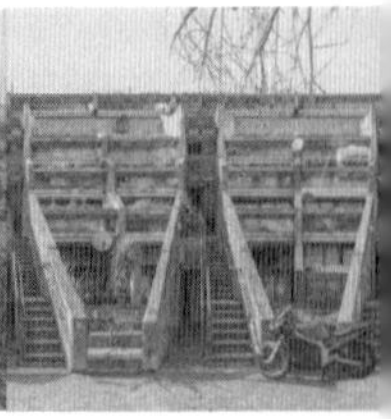

Alexandra Road estate / K OHYAMA / flickr (CC BY-S

8

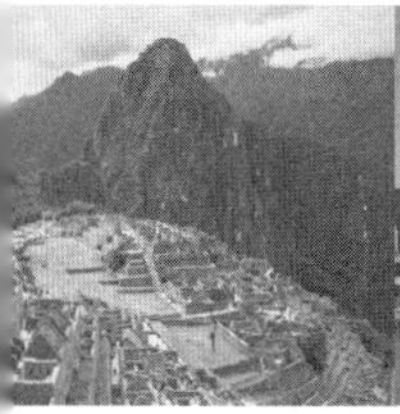

ıu Picchu / eddie-kisz-
ESpq5MMTg-unsplash /
: Kiszka / Unsplash

Nº19

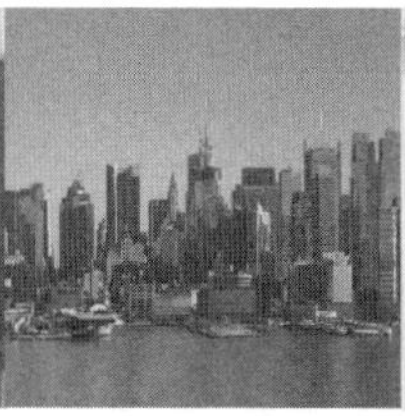

Panorama of the New York City skyline in Manhattan / rabbit75_ist / iStock

Nº20

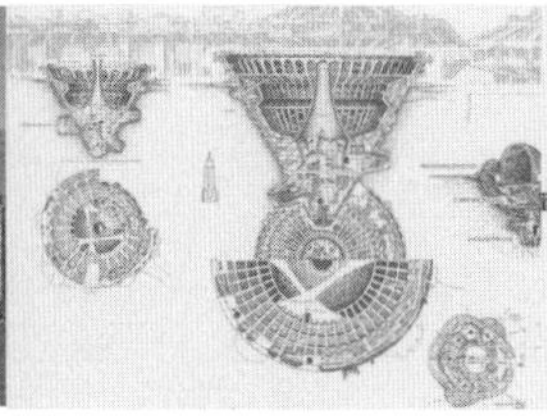

NOVANOAH II Arcology, Population 2,400,000. Page 39 in "Arcology: City in the Image of Man," by Paolo Soleri, original publication 1970 by MIT Press

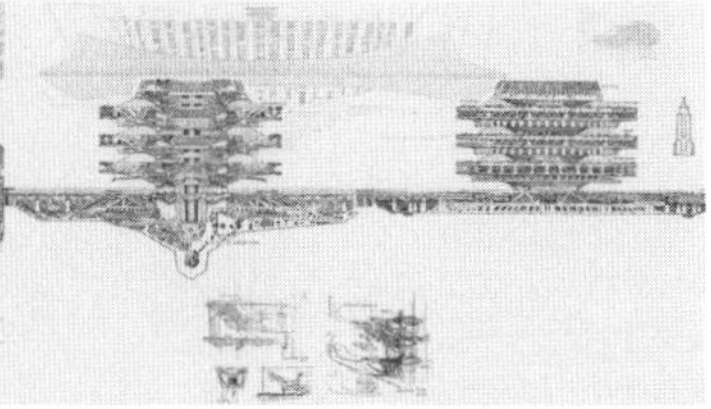

BABEL II B Arcology, Population 520,000. A hyper structure over 1 kilometer high and 2 kilometers in diameter at the bowl base. From the book "Arcology: City in the Image of Man," by Paolo Soleri, original publication by MIT Press in 1970

:3

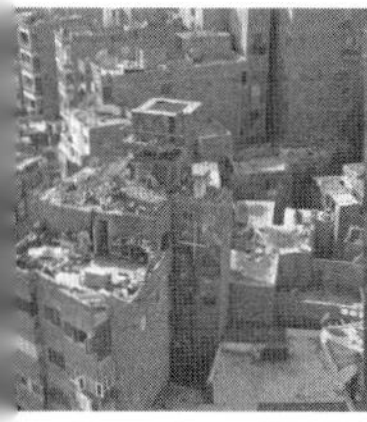

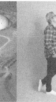

buildings and garbage
ofs in Cairo / Baloncici /
:estock

Nº24

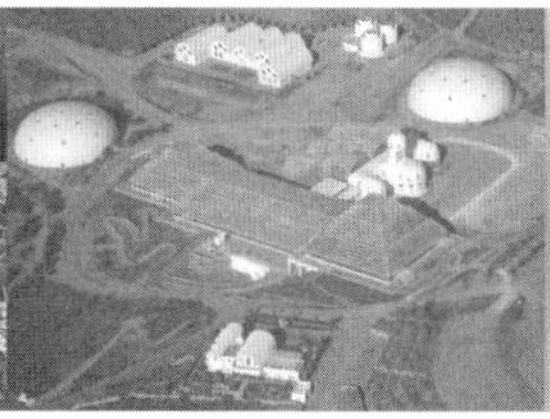

Aerial view of the enclosed ecosystem of Biosphere 2 at Oracle in Tucson, AZ / Joseph Sohm / Shutterstock

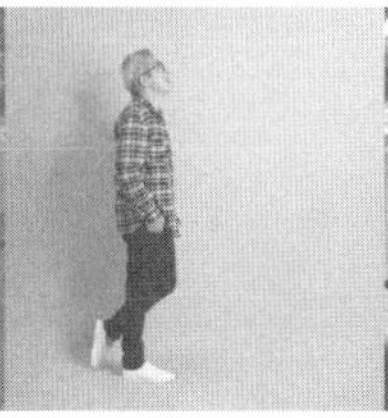

The full length of senior Asian man standing on the pink background / Kimberrywood / Shutterstock

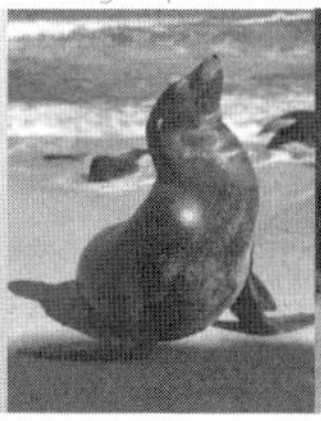

Black seal lion on seashore / Sand Crain / Unsplash

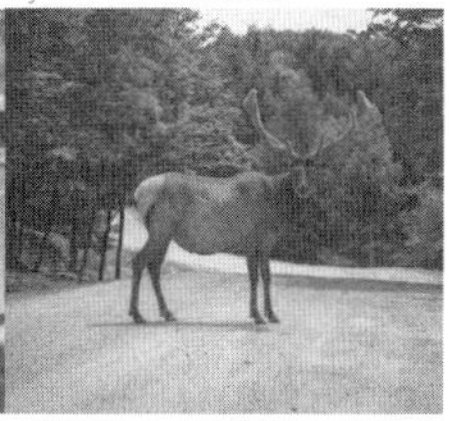

Brown deer on brown land near trees / Jp Valery / Unsplash

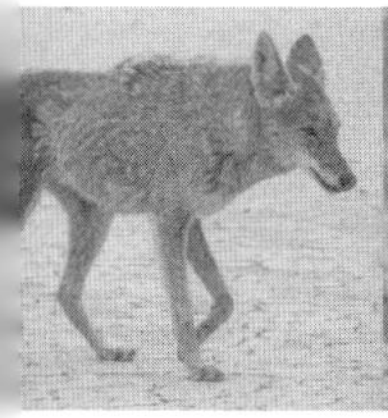

:e walking in desert
ȷ daytime / Oscar
ın / Unsplash

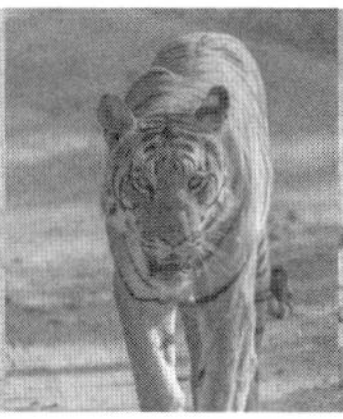

Brown tiger walking on brown sand during daytime / Hans-Jurgen Mager / Unsplash

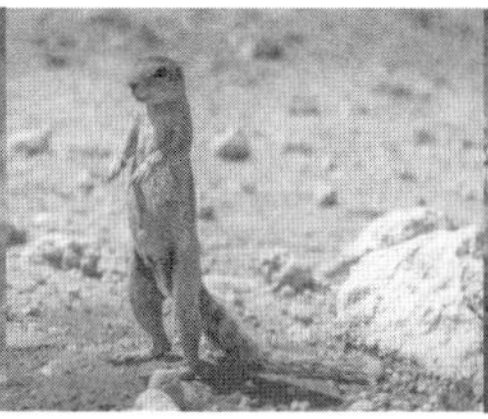

Grey hamster / Joachim Riegel / Unsplash

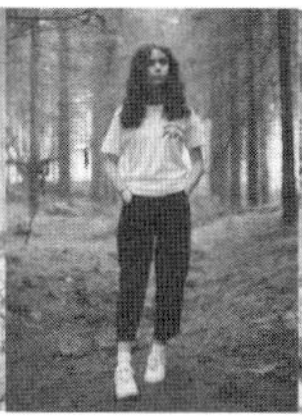

Woman standing in middle of forest / Philip Martin / Unsplash

Nº25

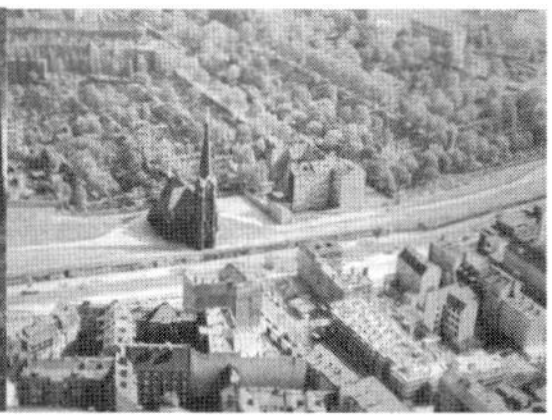

Berlin Wall / Unbekannt (Bundesrepublik Deutschland) / Wikimedia Common

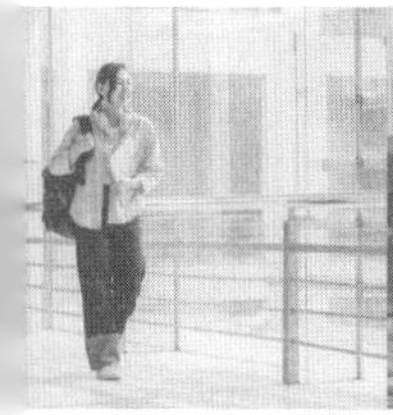

of young Asian college
school / TimeImage
ction / Shutterstock

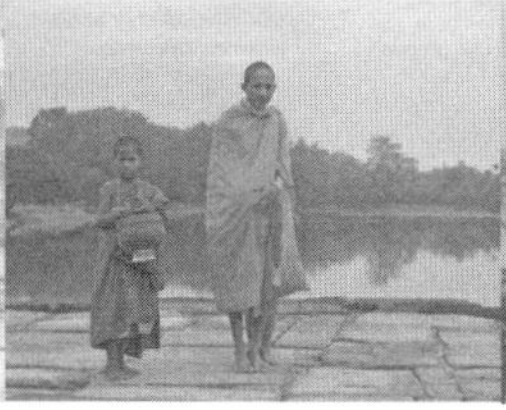

Young monks on their way to Angkor Wat, Siem Reap, Cambodia, Southeast Asia / incamerastock / Alamy Stock Photo

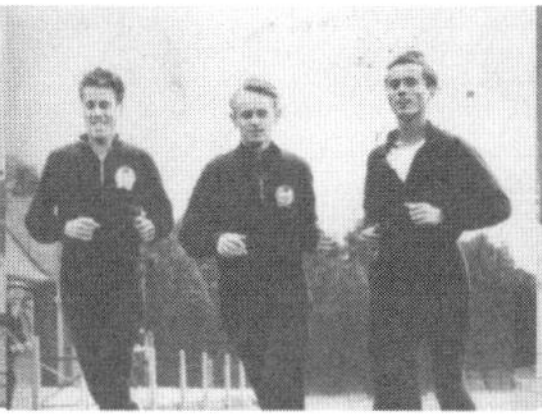

Hungary's record-breaking trio of Laszlo Tabori, Istvan Rozsavölgyi, and Sandor Iharos loosen up on grass. November 25, 1955. (Photo by Magyar Foto) / SuperStock / Alamy

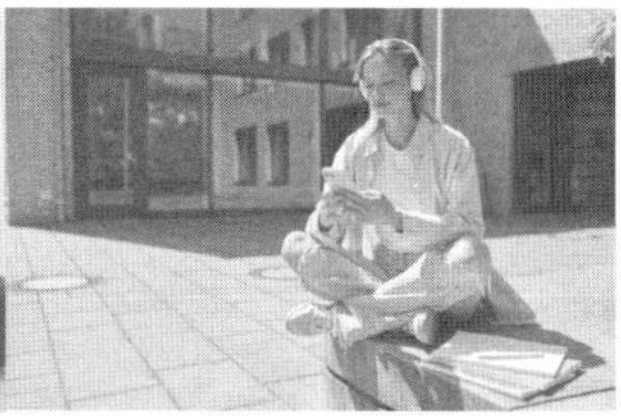

Girl university student wearing headphones using smartphone app sitting on stairs outdoors online learning, remote studying virtual class, watching webinar distance course or listening podcast / insta_photos / Shutterstock

0

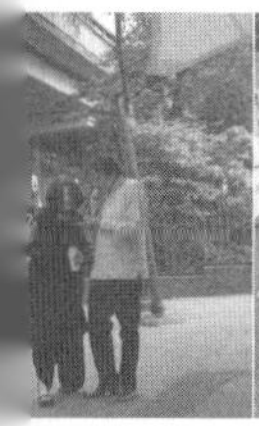

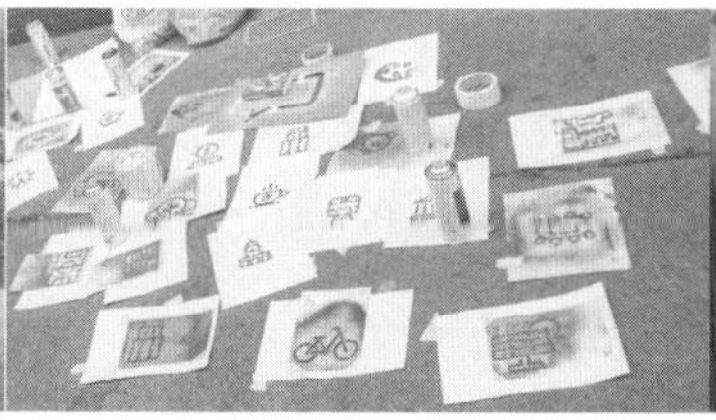

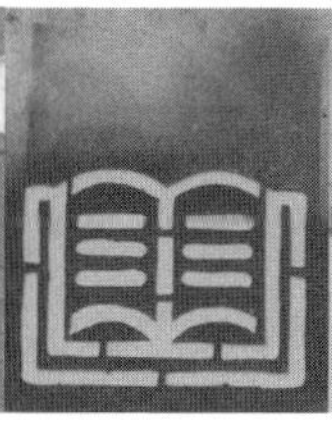

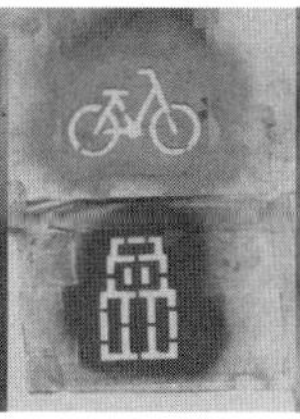

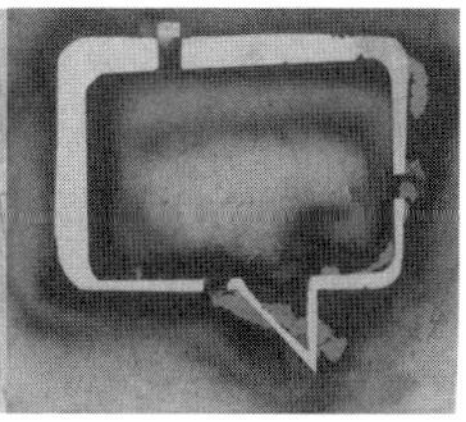

ıtions (video screenshot) / Nika Dubrovsky

index

index

participants

David Graeber
Nika Dubrovsky
Anna Akopova
Barbara Andersen
Phoebe Beckett Chingono
Sveta Bryleva
Benjamin Bush
Sam Chermayeff
Dana Daymand
Veronica Davidov
Natalia Djatko
Michael Dorfman
Frank Engster
Melissa Fleshman
Mark Fuller
Misha Gabovich
Adam Harvey
Ryan Healey
Ragnar Hjalmarsson
Kolbeinn Hugi
Ludmila Ivakina
Jenia Juravel
Julia Kashlinsky
Vladimir Kharitonov
Artem Kirpichenok
Alexander Koch
Yulia Kuranova
Yacov Lurie
Natalya Lyach
David Magnus
Sean Maliehe
Vadim Maximoff
Eugene Ostashevsky
Ilona Otto
Pierre Pagar
Chritina Pestova
Vassily Pigounides
Varvara Polyakova
Victoria Preletzkaya
Don Reneau
Boryana Rossa
Marina Sergeeva
Alena Shapovalova
Elena Shindukova
Natalia Smolianskaia
Yulia Svishcheva
Alexander Utto
Holly Wood

glossary

I put together a brief glossary from the collection of David's quotes to explain our understanding of some of the terms in this book.

These terms only exist because every day we wake up and continue to reproduce them.

Anthropology
is the study of human beings, both the points of diversity and unity in how people have lived around the globe and throughout the times.

David said, "I'm interested in anthropology because I'm interested in human possibilities."

"Social theory is largely a game of make-believe in which we pretend, just for the sake of argument, that there's just one thing going on: essentially, we reduce everything to a cartoon so as to be able to detect patterns that would be otherwise invisible." (Graeber and Wengrow, *The Dawn of Everything: A New History of Humanity*, p. 21)

Games and Utopias
Games ... are a kind of utopia of rules.

"True, one can play a game; but to speak of 'play' does not necessarily imply the existence of rules at all. Play can be purely improvisational. One could simply be play-ing around." (Ibid., p. 191)

"Genuine, living utopia-nism—the idea that radical alternatives are possible and that one can begin to create them in the pres-ent—as opposed to what might be called 'scientific utopianism': the idea that the revolutionary is the agent of the inevitable march of history, which was so easily, and cata-strophically, appropriated by the Right. The murder of dreams could only lead to nightmares." (Graeber, *Direct Action*, p. x)

Back in the 1880s, Peter Kropotkin responded to claims that anarchism was utopian by arguing that matters were really the other way around. What was naïve and utopian was to believe that one could give anyone arbitrary power over others and trust them to exercise it responsibly." (Graeber, *Direct Action*, pp. 352-3)

Communism and Capitalism
"Communism is the foundation of all human sociability. It makes society possible." (On the moral grounds of economic relations)

Communism is not an abstract, distant ideal, impossible to maintain, but a lived practical reality we all engage in daily, to different degrees, and that even factories could not operate without it—

even if much of it operates on the sly, between the cracks, or shifts, or informally, or in what's not said, or entirely subversively.

It's become fashionable lately to say that capitalism has entered a new phase in which it has become parasitical forms of creative cooperation, largely on the internet. This is nonsense. It has always been so.

Capitalism is not something imposed on us by some outside force. It only exists because every day we wake up and continue to produce it.

"Communism is already here. The question is how to further democratize it. Capitalism, in turn, is just one possible way of managing communism — and, it has become increasingly clear, rather a disastrous one. Clearly we need to be thinking about a better one: preferably, one that does not quite so systematically set us all at each others' throats." (Graeber, *Revolutions in Reverse: Essays on Politics, Violence, Art, and Imagination*, p. 36)

War and Carnival
What's the difference?

In war, the rules of the game are that everyone is equal to his uniform. That's why it's fine to kill anyone in "blue" if they're fighting against "the green." Although everyone knows that the people under the uniform are all different: smart and stupid, young and old. As opposed to the rules of Carnival: we all know that masks and people are not the same.

Politics and Magic
Politics is very similar to magic.

"It is the peculiar feature of political life that within it, behavior that could only otherwise be considered insane is perfectly effective. If you managed to convince everyone on earth that you can breathe underwater, it won't make any difference: if you try it, you will still drown. On the other hand, if you could convince everyone in the entire world that you were King of France, then you would actually be the King of France...

This is the essence of politics. Politics is that dimension of social life in which things really do become true if enough people believe them. The problem is that in order to play the game effectively, one can never acknowledge its essence. No king would openly admit he is king just because people think he is... 'Make me your leader because if you do, I will be your leader' is not in itself a particularly compelling argument.

In this sense politics is very similar to magic, which in most times and places... is simultaneously recognized as something that works because people believe that it works; but also, that only works because people do not believe it works only because people believe it works. This is why magic, from ancient Thessaly to the contemporary Trobriand Islands, always seems to dwell in an uncertain territory somewhere between poetic expression and outright fraud. And of course the same can usually be said of politics." (Graeber, *Revolutions in Reverse: Essays on Politics, Violence, Art, and Imagination*, p. 94)

119

town-machine, **shady town**, p
town, suspicion city, **flowe**
town-machine, **suspicion cit**
town, dark city, **flower city, Tl**
necropolis, prison town, city-hosp
shady town, necropolis, the city-
prison town, city-hospital, **Hidden city**,
town-machine, the city-lab, **Ma**
invisible city, town-machine, **invis**
down town, trap town, **flower**
machine, **leader city**, prison town,
city, **flower city**, **spider city**, th
town, city-hospital, **invisible city**, city
the city-lab, town-machine, **moc**
down town, replica city, **flower**
machine, **nightmare city**, pris
invisible city, **flower city, spic**
replica city, prison town, city-hosp
flower city, spider city, the c
city, prison town, trading city, upsic
spider city, the city-lab, town-
hospital, **upside down town**, dark
city-lab, town-machine, **hut-re**

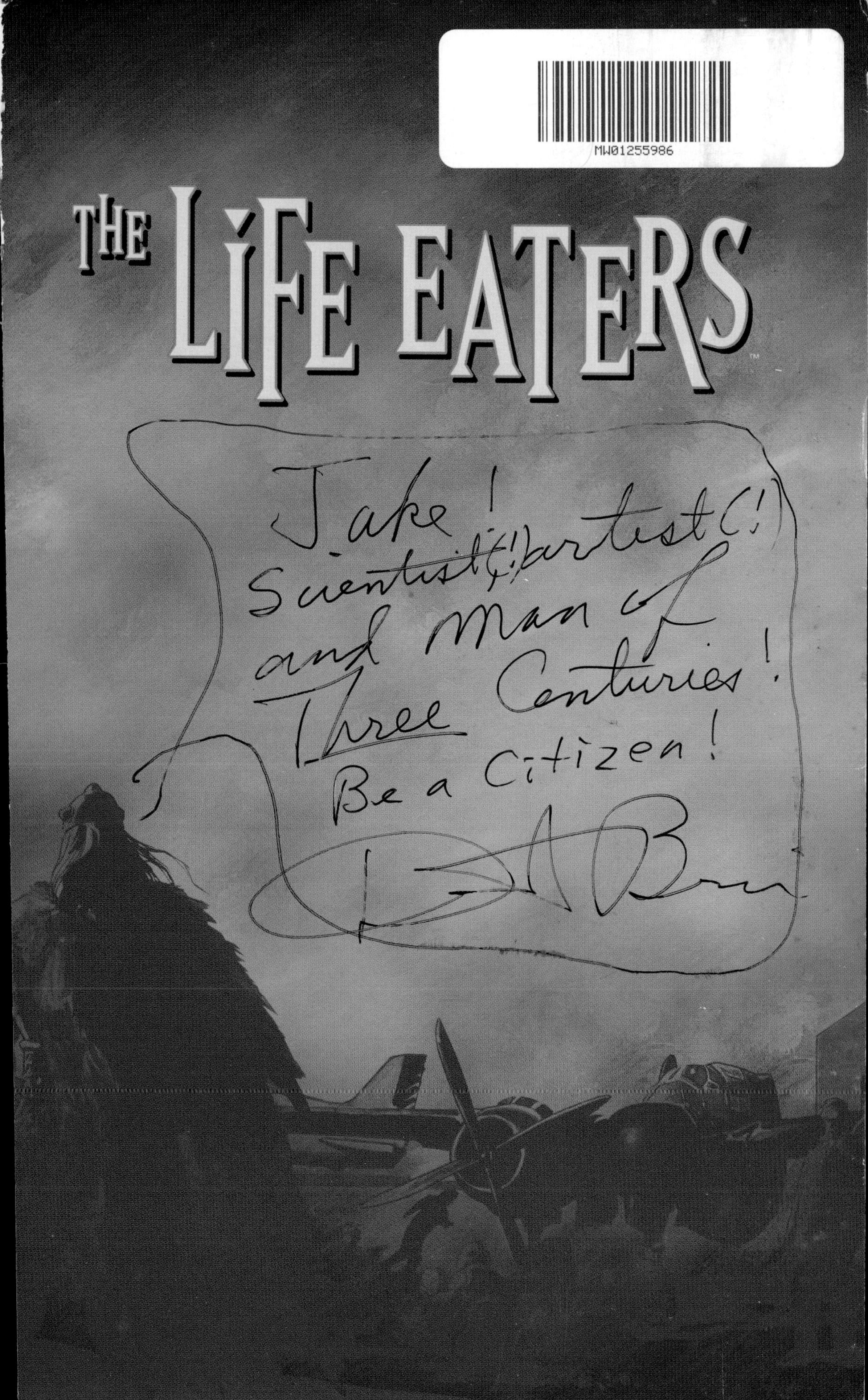
THE LIFE EATERS™

Jake!
Scientist(!), artist(!)
and man of
Three Centuries!
Be a Citizen!

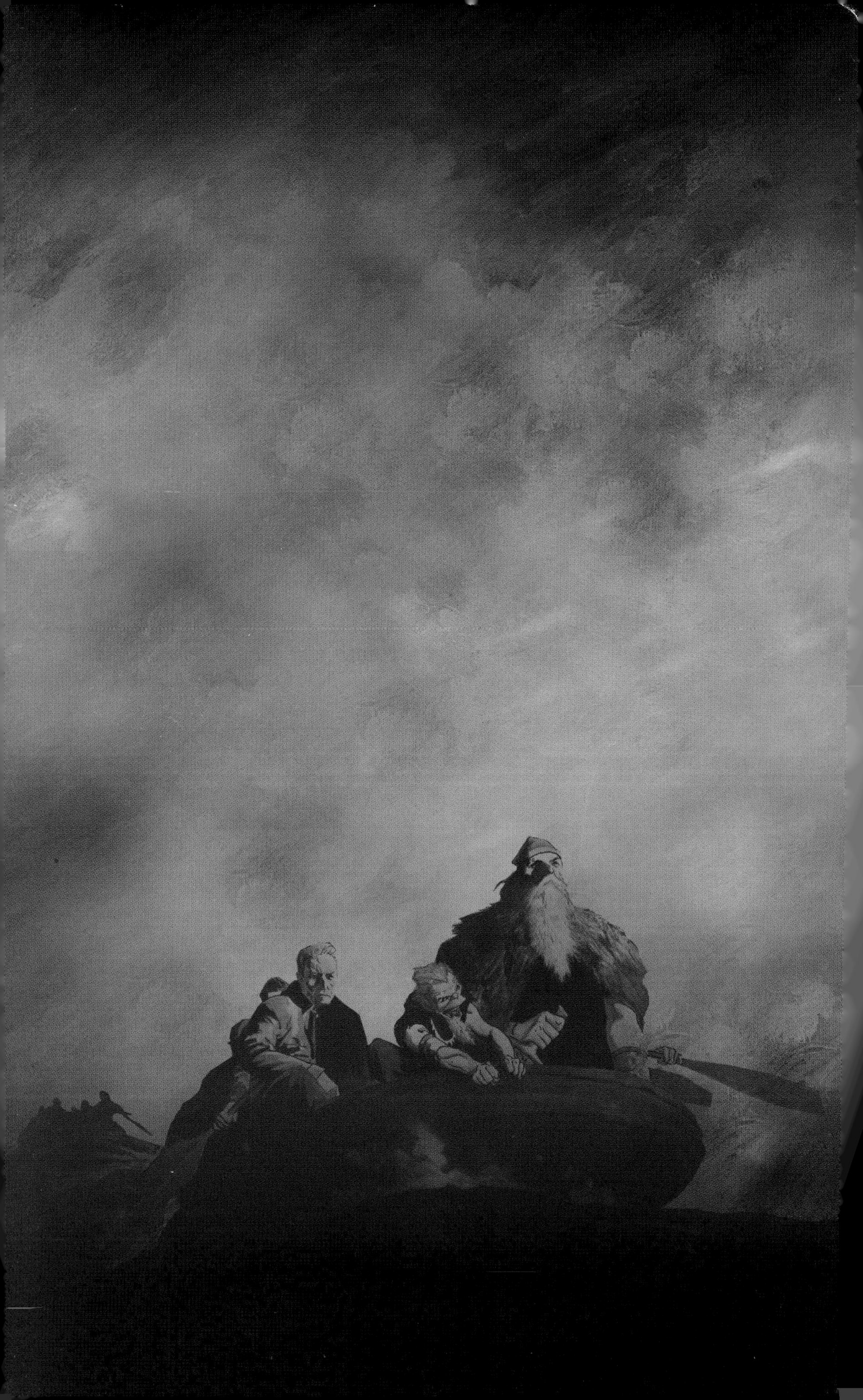

Writer
David Brin

Artist
Scott Hampton

Letterer

Todd Klein

Assistant Editor

Kristy Quinn

Editors

Jeff Mariotte and
Scott Dunbier

Designed by

Ed Roeder and
Larry Berry

Jim Lee, Editorial Director–WildStorm John Nee, VP & General Manager–WildStorm
Scott Dunbier, Group Editor   Ed Roeder, Art Director Paul Levitz, President & Publisher
Georg Brewer, VP–Design & Retail Product Development
Richard Bruning, VP–Creative Director Patrick Caldon, Senior VP–Finance & Operations
Chris Caramalis, VP–Finance Terri Cunningham, VP–Managing Editor
Dan DiDio, VP–Editorial Alison Gill, VP–Manufacturing
Lillian Laserson, Senior VP & General Counsel David McKillips, VP–Advertising
Cheryl Rubin, VP–Licensing & Merchandising
Bob Wayne, VP–Sales & Marketing

LIFE EATERS, 2003. Published by WildStorm Productions, an imprint of DC Comics.
Editorial offices: 888 Prospect St, Suite 240, La Jolla, CA 92037.

DC Comics, a Warner Bros. Entertainment Company.

Acknowledgements

Our thanks to those who helped this challenging project—among them Trevor Sands, Alberto Monteiro, Stefan Jones, Vince Gerardis, Joe Carroll, Joe Miller, Ruben Krasnopolsky, Dustin Laurence and David Clark. Nothing could have happened without John Nee, Scott Dunbier and Paul Levitz of DC and WildStorm. Or Gregory Benford, who dared me to write the original novelette "Thor Meets Captain America," or the voters who kindly nominated it for a Hugo Award. Of course it was an honor working on a "mini-movie" with the brilliant Scott Hampton and legendary Todd Klein. Special appreciation goes to animation maestro Steve Gold, who first stirred an ambition to extend that story to epic length, and Jeff Mariotte who helped make it reality.

David Brin

For help and inspiration—first and foremost Karen Hankala, puppeteer and pal! Also to her boy toy, Durwin Talon. In the inspiration zone, a large *gracias* to my brothers-in-arms—Dave, Chris, and Ray, for keeping that bar raised high. George, John, Mark—I know you're probably getting tired of being dragged through my acknowledgements, but you're just going to have to deal. (Beverly rocks!) To Letitia, of course! Duh! To Meredith and Sherri for untold kindnesses. And one more mammoth thank you to my family, Dave Elliott, Mark Kneece, Bob Pendarvis, the baristas at Caffe Driade, Stephen King, Stanley Kubrick, Nick Drake, Tom Petty, Yousaf Islam, Will Patton, and 5,000 others.

Scott Hampton

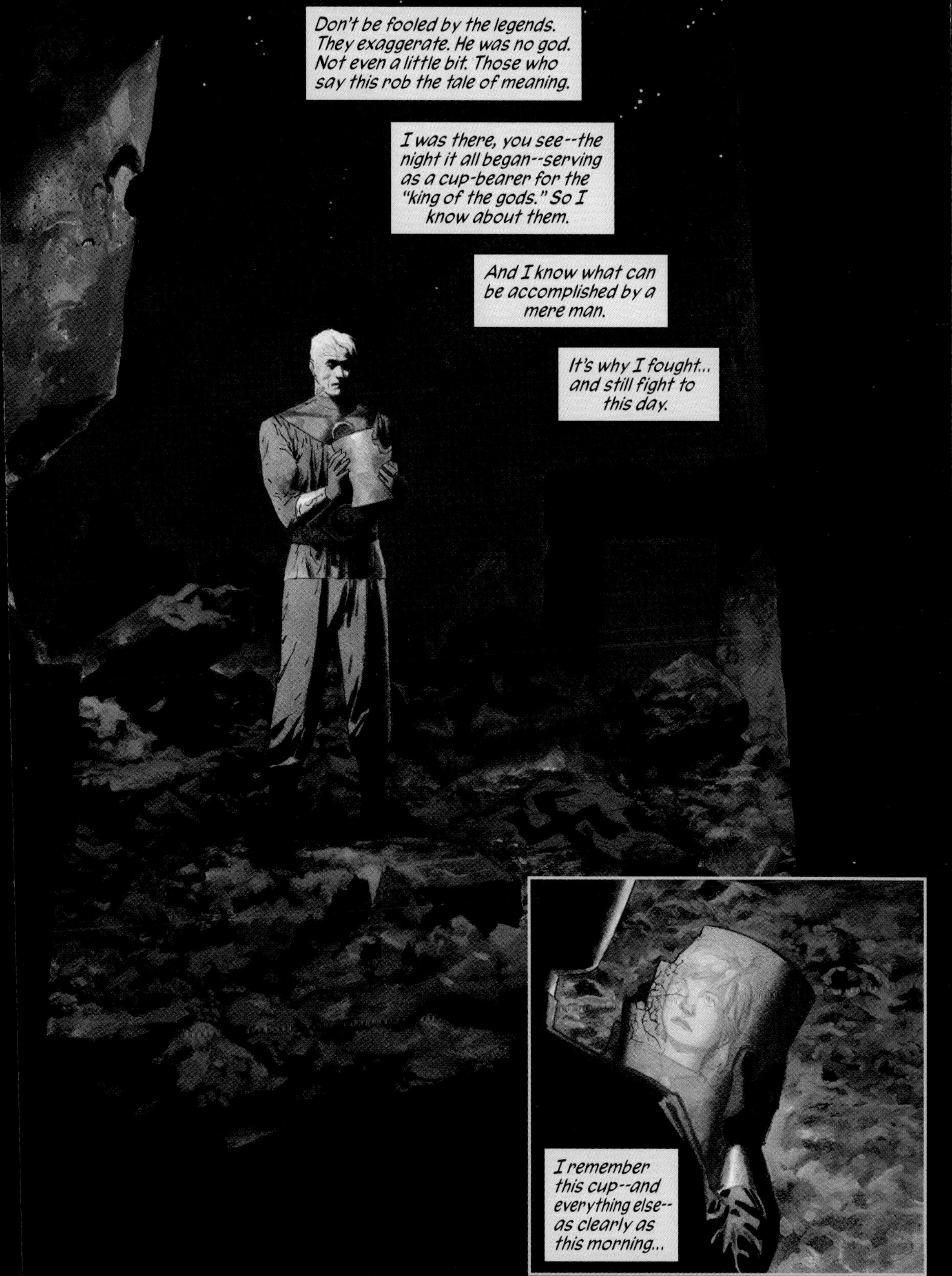

Don't be fooled by the legends. They exaggerate. He was no god. Not even a little bit. Those who say this rob the tale of meaning.
I was there, you see--the night it all began--serving as a cup-bearer for the "king of the gods." So I know about them.
And I know what can be accomplished by a mere man.
It's why I fought... and still fight to this day.
I remember this cup--and everything else--as clearly as this morning...

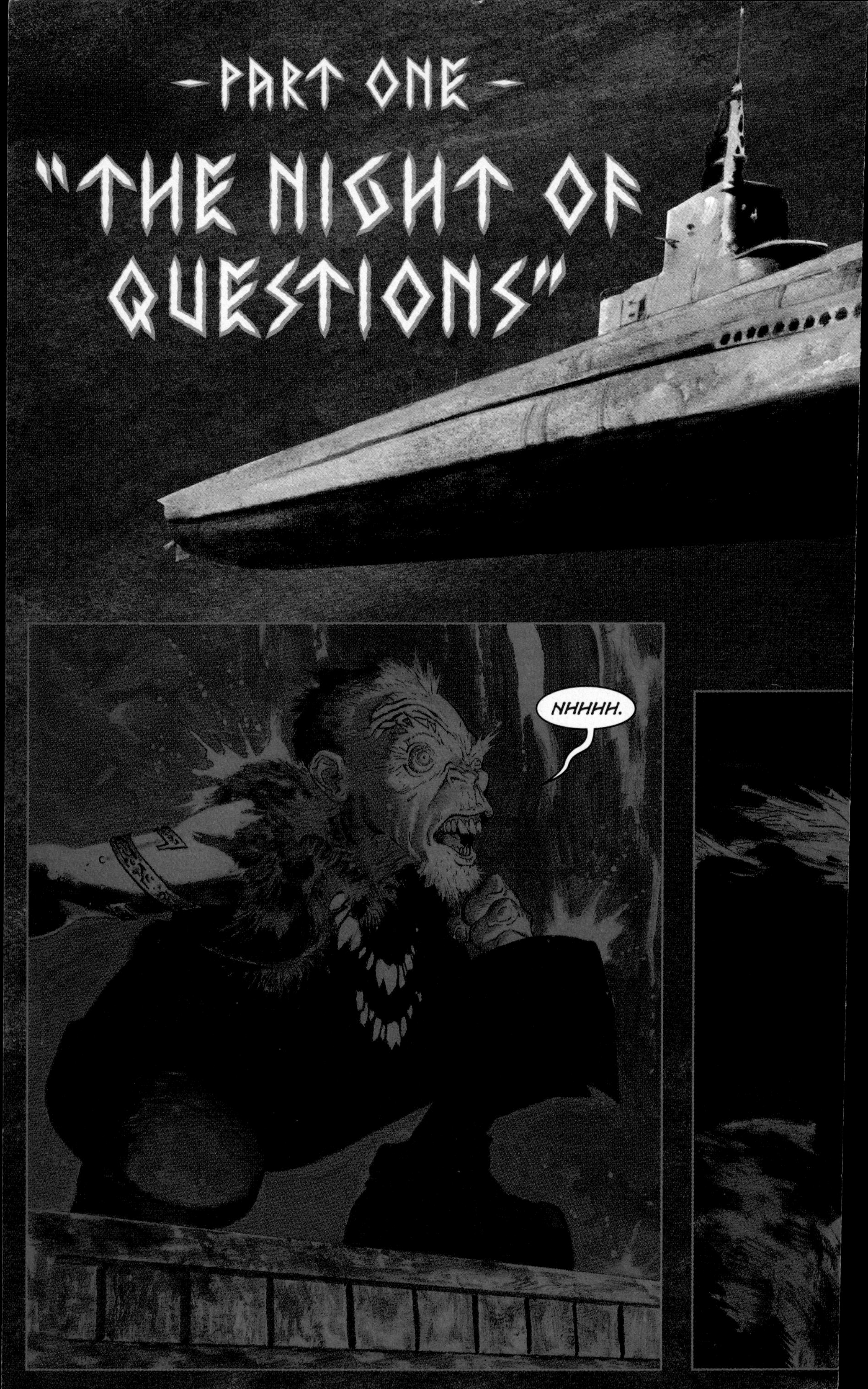

-PART ONE-
"THE NIGHT OF QUESTIONS"
NHHHH.

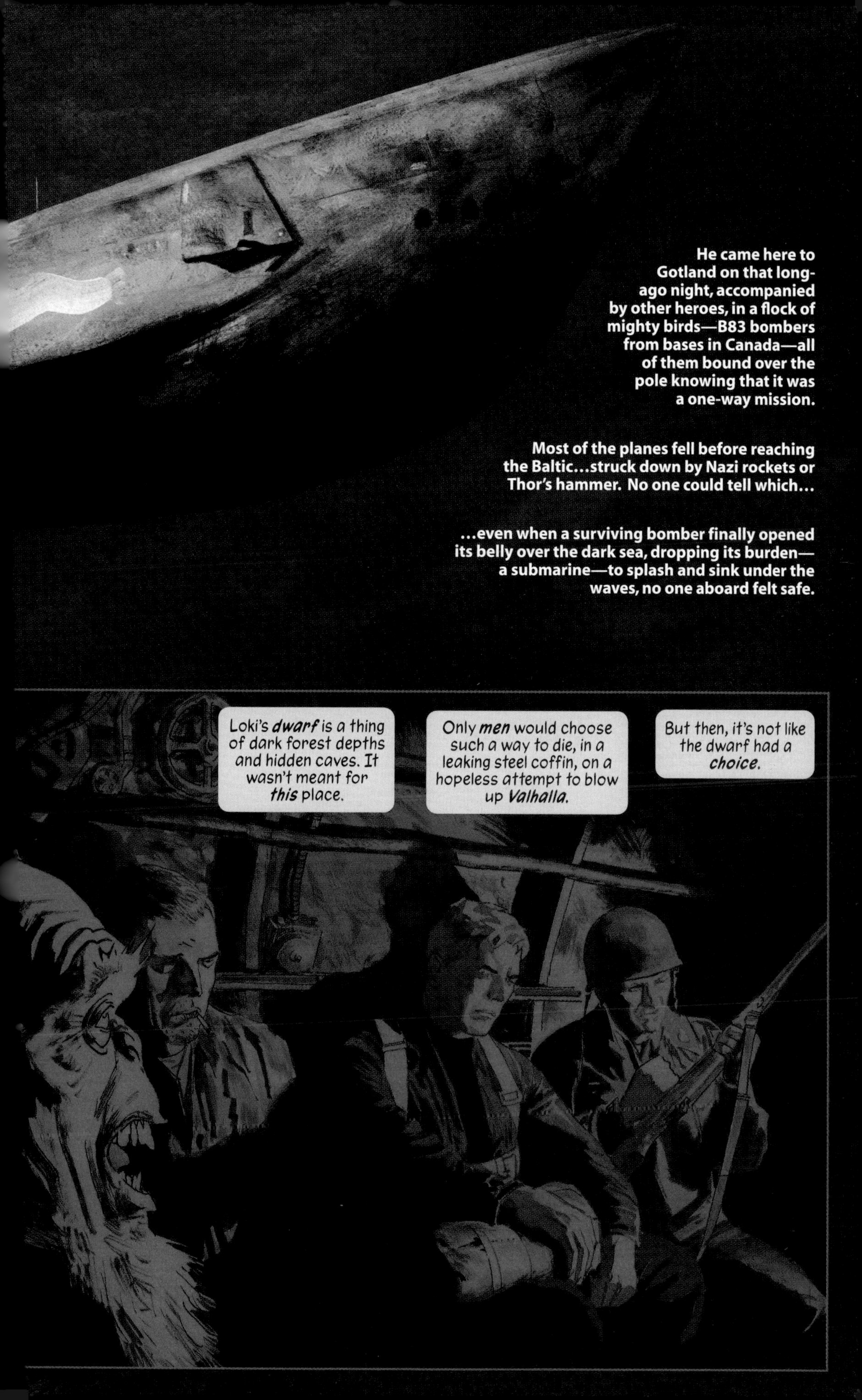
He came here to Gotland on that long-ago night, accompanied by other heroes, in a flock of mighty birds—B83 bombers from bases in Canada—all of them bound over the pole knowing that it was a one-way mission.
Most of the planes fell before reaching the Baltic...struck down by Nazi rockets or Thor's hammer. No one could tell which...
...even when a surviving bomber finally opened its belly over the dark sea, dropping its burden—a submarine—to splash and sink under the waves, no one aboard felt safe.
Loki's *dwarf* is a thing of dark forest depths and hidden caves. It wasn't meant for *this* place.
Only *men* would choose such a way to die, in a leaking steel coffin, on a hopeless attempt to blow up *Valhalla.*
But then, it's not like the dwarf had a *choice.*

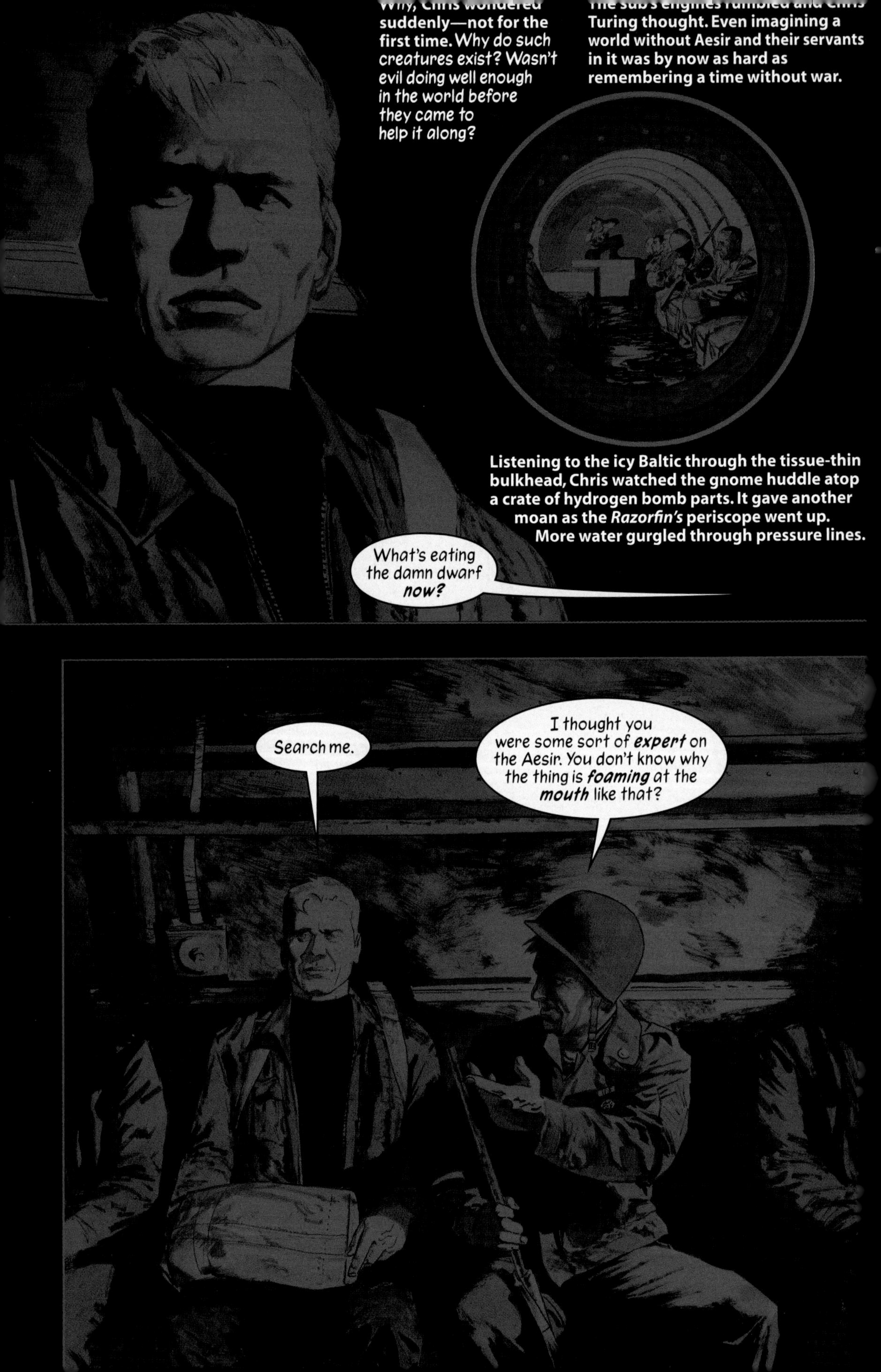
Why, Chris wondered suddenly—not for the first time. Why do such creatures exist? Wasn't evil doing well enough in the world before they came to help it along?
The sub's engines rumbled and Chris Turing thought. Even imagining a world without Aesir and their servants in it was by now as hard as remembering a time without war.
Listening to the icy Baltic through the tissue-thin bulkhead, Chris watched the gnome huddle atop a crate of hydrogen bomb parts. It gave another moan as the *Razorfin's* periscope went up. More water gurgled through pressure lines.
What's eating the damn dwarf *now?*
Search me.
I thought you were some sort of *expert* on the Aesir. You don't know why the thing is *foaming* at the *mouth* like that?

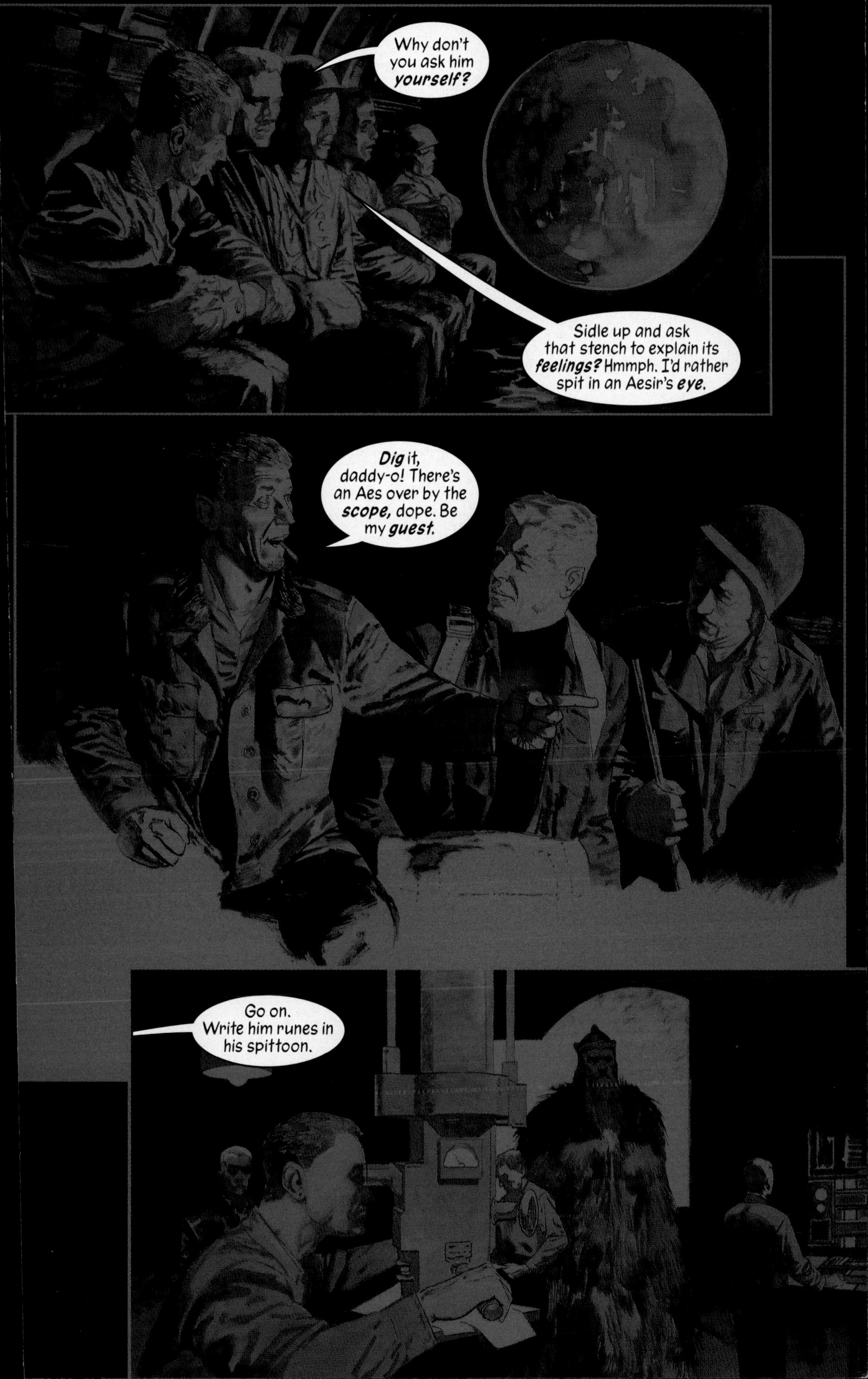
Why don't you ask him *yourself?*
Sidle up and ask that stench to explain its *feelings?* Hmmph. I'd rather spit in an Aesir's *eye*.
Dig it, daddy-o! There's an Aes over by the *scope,* dope. Be my *guest*.
Go on. Write him runes in his spittoon.

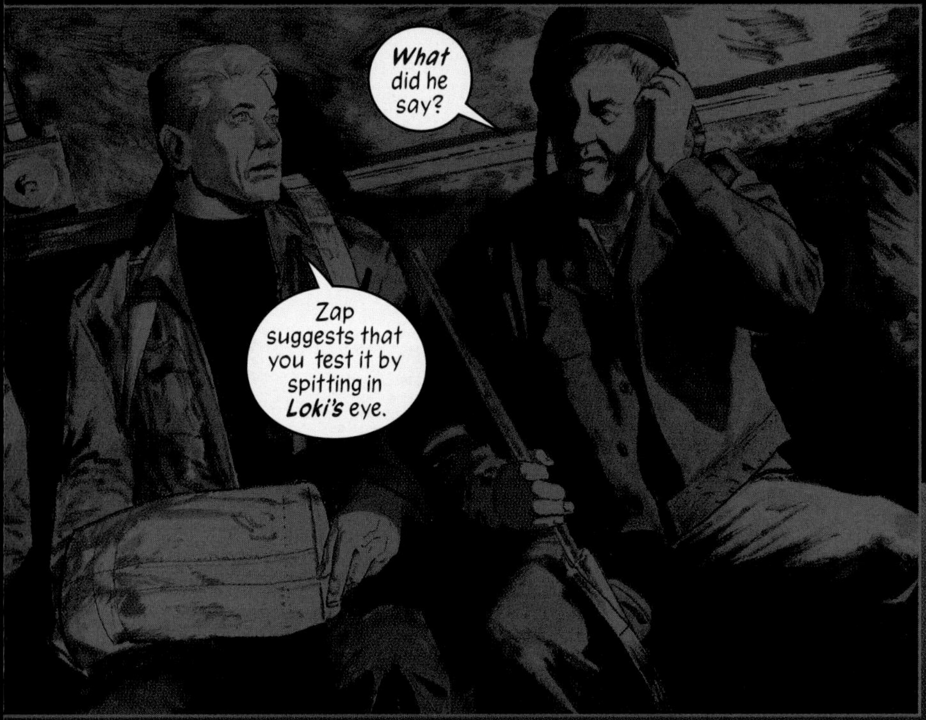
What did he say?
Zap suggests that you test it by spitting in *Loki's* eye.

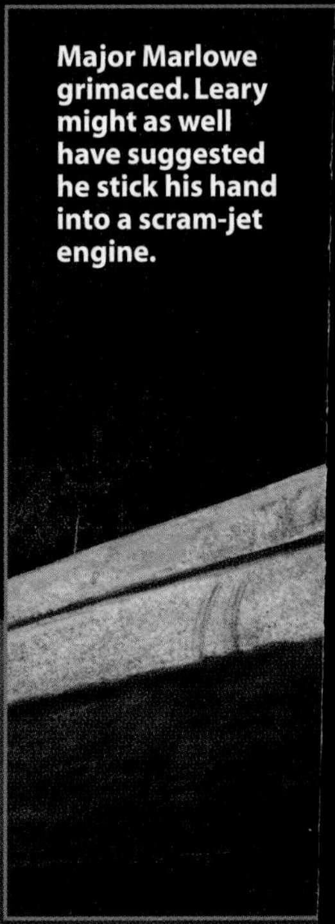
Major Marlowe grimaced. Leary might as well have suggested he stick his hand into a scram-jet engine.

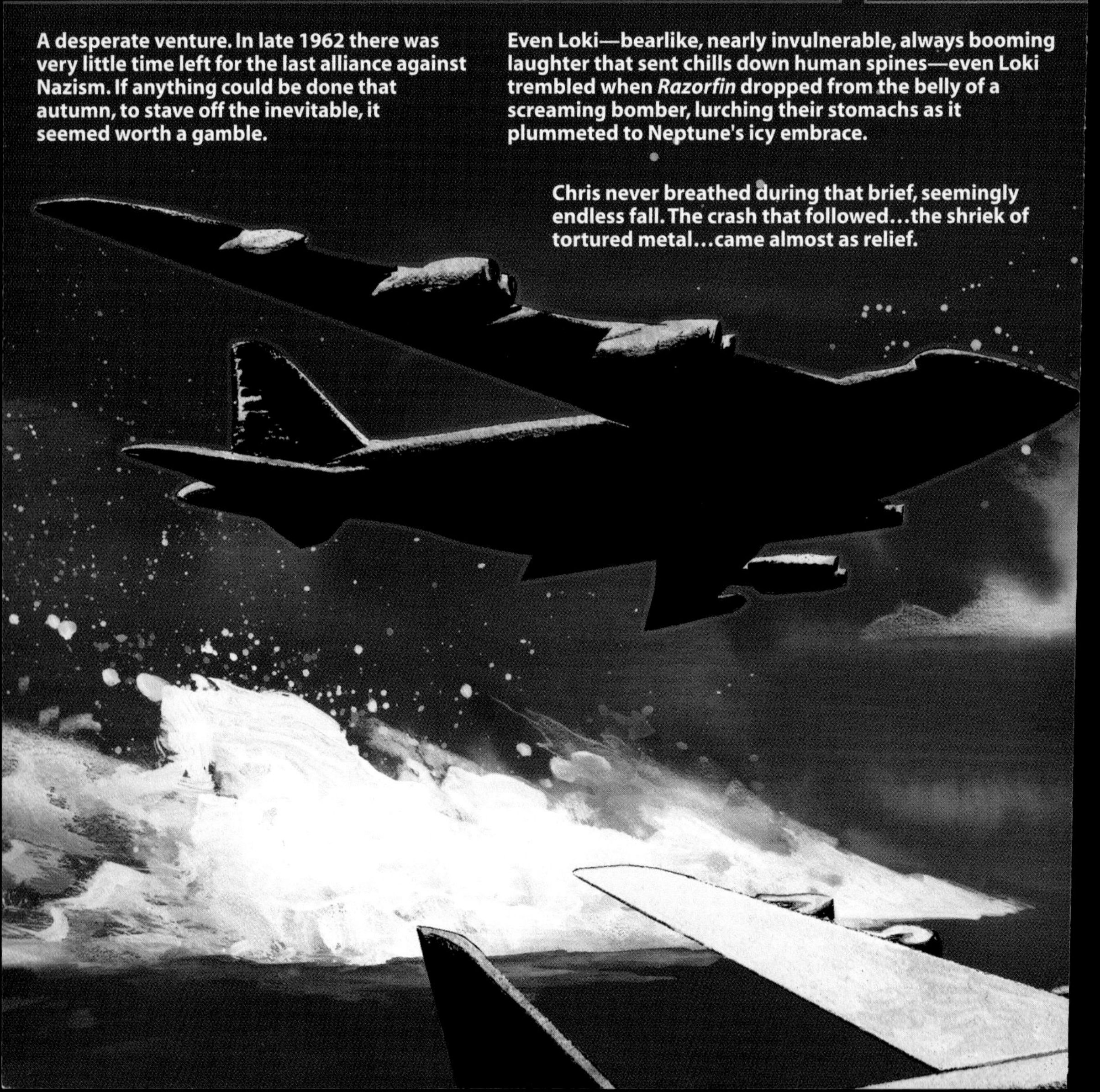
A desperate venture. In late 1962 there was very little time left for the last alliance against Nazism. If anything could be done that autumn, to stave off the inevitable, it seemed worth a gamble.
Even Loki—bearlike, nearly invulnerable, always booming laughter that sent chills down human spines—even Loki trembled when *Razorfin* dropped from the belly of a screaming bomber, lurching their stomachs as it plummeted to Neptune's icy embrace.
Chris never breathed during that brief, seemingly endless fall. The crash that followed…the shriek of tortured metal…came almost as relief.

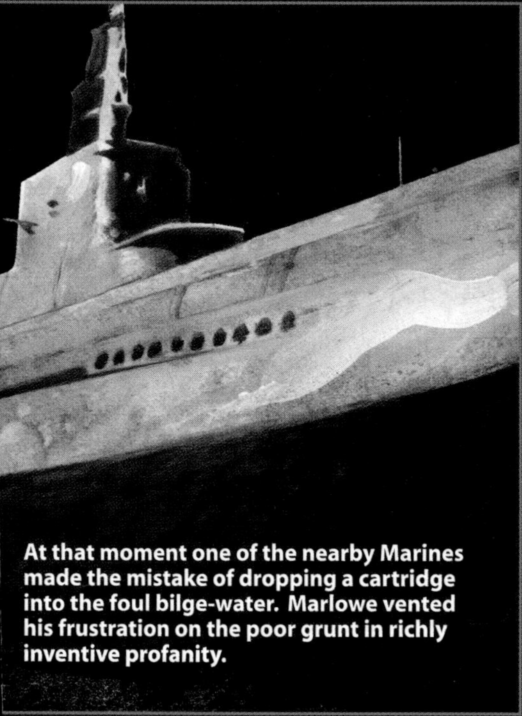
At that moment one of the nearby Marines made the mistake of dropping a cartridge into the foul bilge-water. Marlowe vented his frustration on the poor grunt in richly inventive profanity.

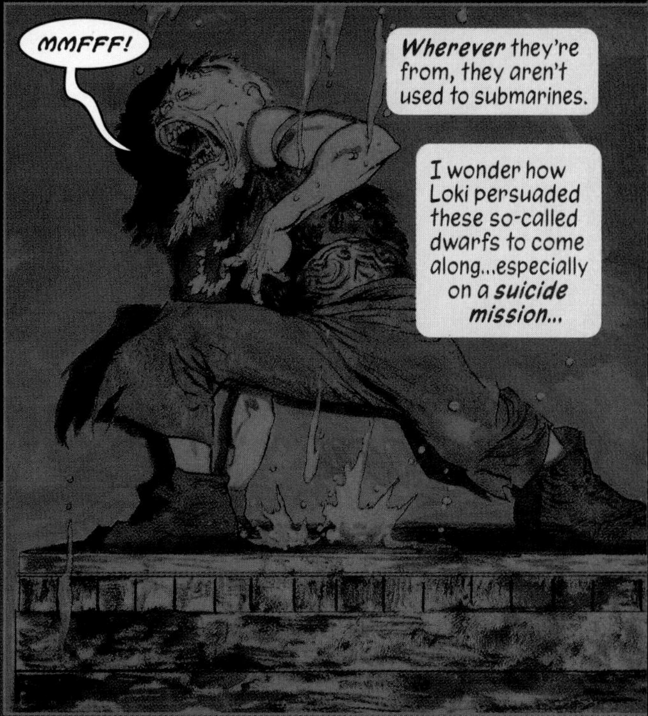
MMFFF!
Wherever they're from, they aren't used to submarines.
I wonder how Loki persuaded these so-called dwarfs to come along...especially on a suicide mission...

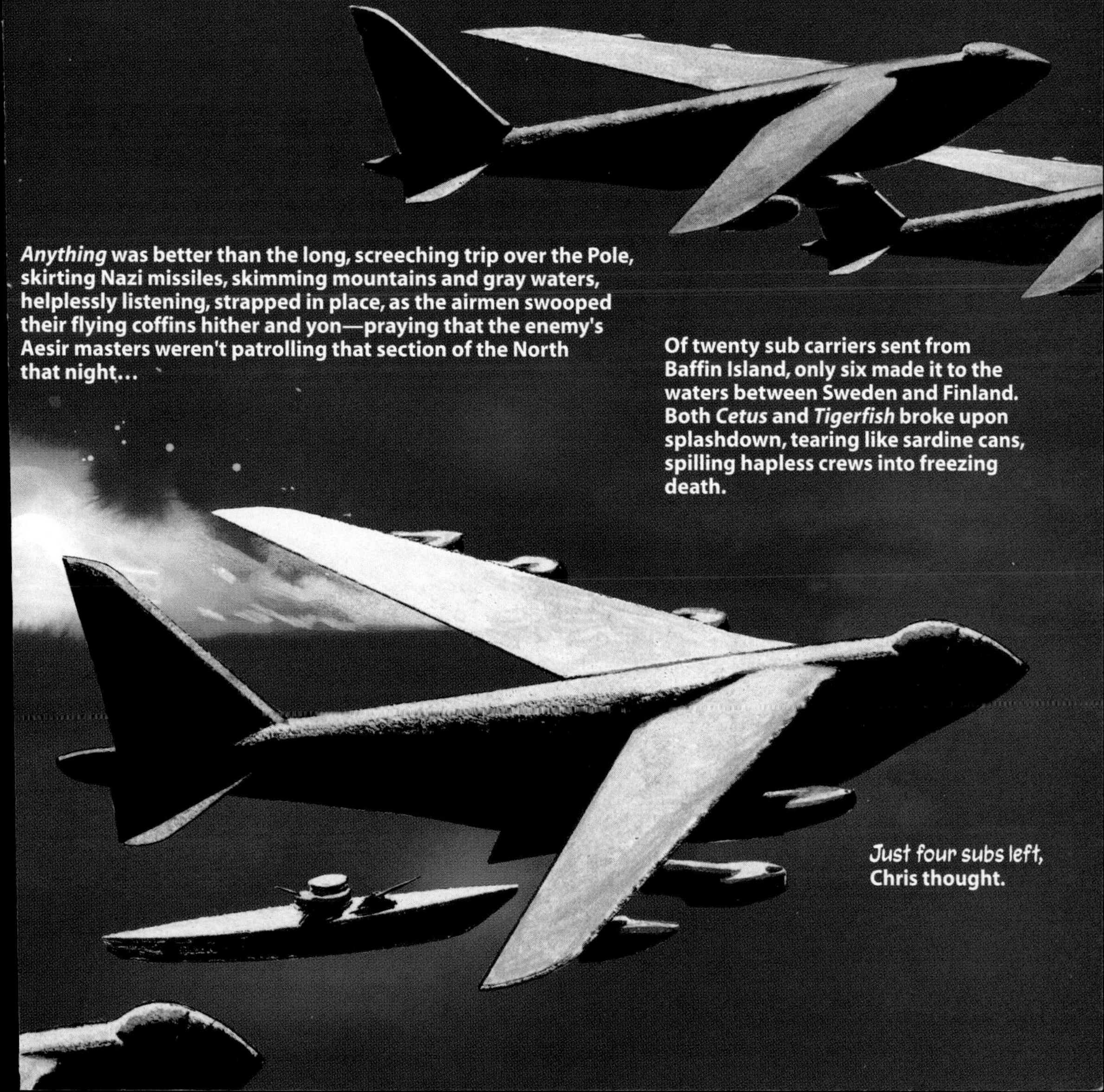
Anything was better than the long, screeching trip over the Pole, skirting Nazi missiles, skimming mountains and gray waters, helplessly listening, strapped in place, as the airmen swooped their flying coffins hither and yon—praying that the enemy's Aesir masters weren't patrolling that section of the North that night…
Of twenty sub carriers sent from Baffin Island, only six made it to the waters between Sweden and Finland. Both Cetus and Tigerfish broke upon splashdown, tearing like sardine cans, spilling hapless crews into freezing death.
Just four subs left, Chris thought.

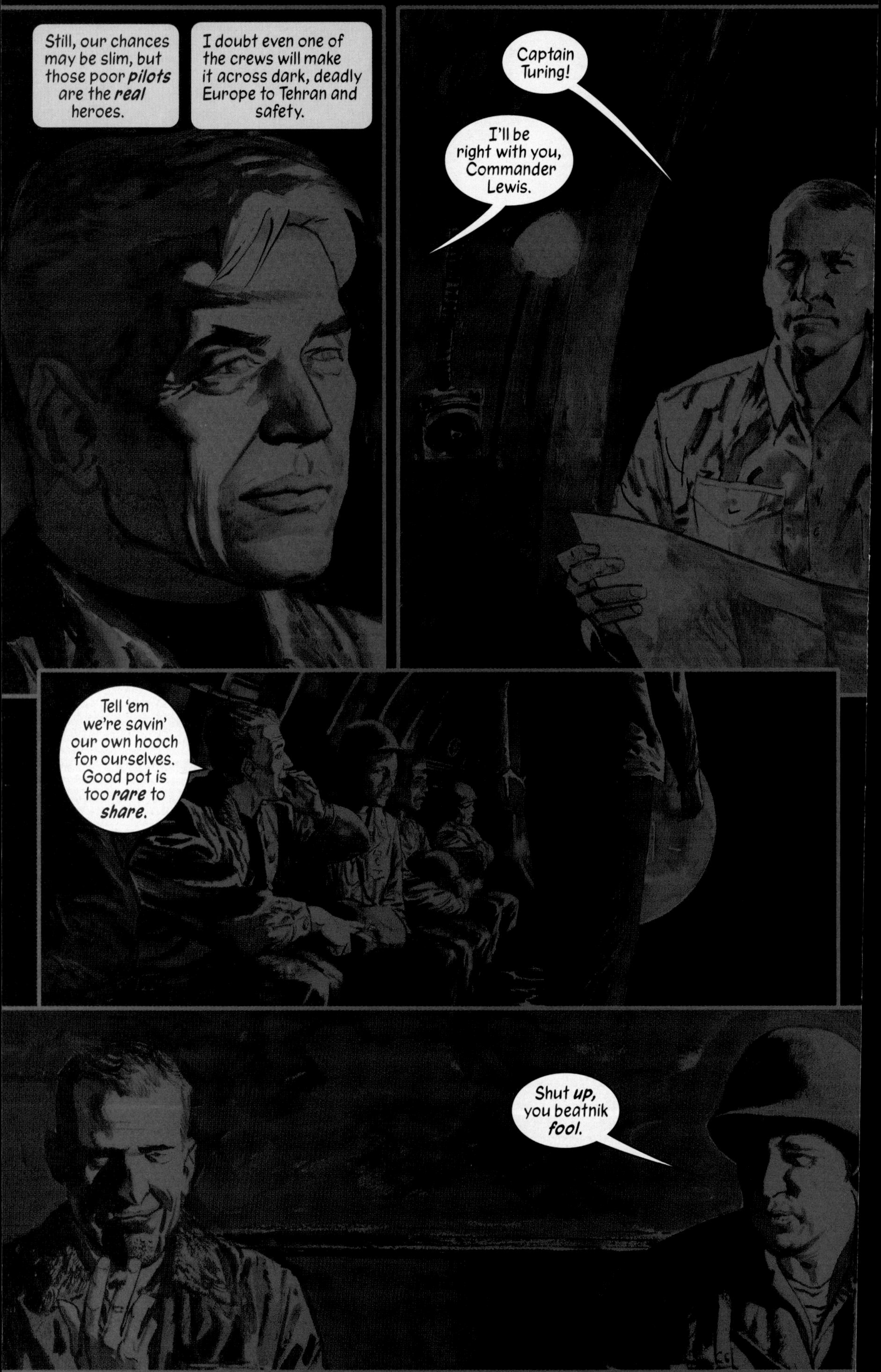

Still, our chances may be slim, but those poor *pilots* are the *real* heroes.
I doubt even one of the crews will make it across dark, deadly Europe to Tehran and safety.
Captain Turing!
I'll be right with you, Commander Lewis.
Tell 'em we're savin' our own hooch for ourselves. Good pot is too *rare* to *share*.
Shut *up*, you beatnik *fool*.

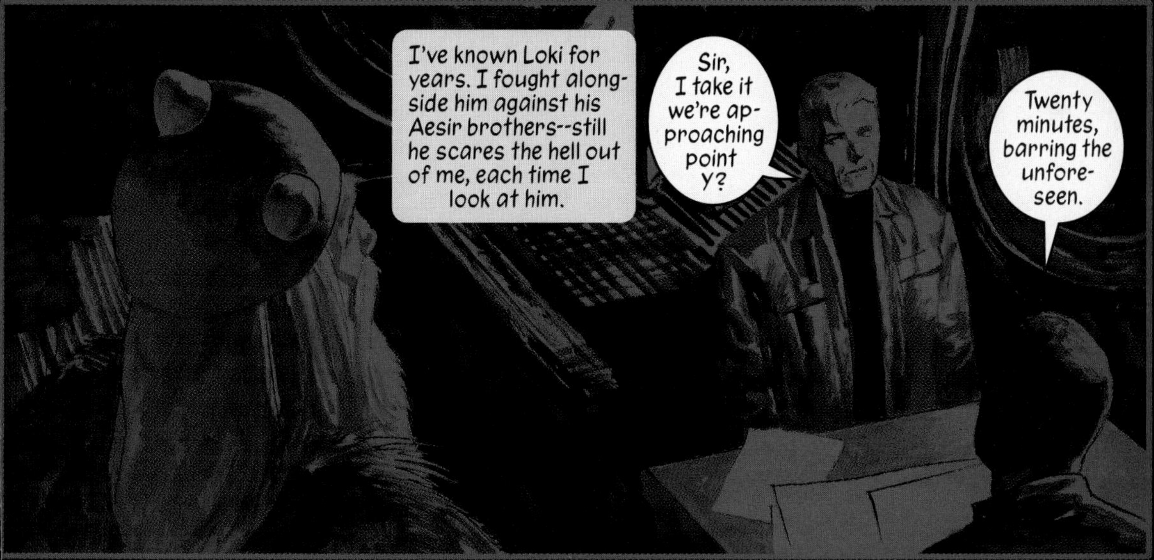
I've known Loki for years. I fought alongside him against his Aesir brothers--still he scares the hell out of me, each time I look at him.
Sir, I take it we're approaching point Y?
Twenty minutes, barring the unforeseen.

In the dim light, Chris thought Lewis seemed to have aged over the last twenty hours. The young sub commander knew his squadron wasn't the only thing considered expendable in this operation. Several thousand miles to the west, what remained of the North American Surface Navy was engaged hopelessly for one reason only—to distract the Kriegsmarine and the SS, and especially a certain "god of the sea"—away from the Baltic and Operation Ragnarok. Loki's cousin Tyr wasn't very potent against submarines, but unless his attention was drawn elsewhere, he could make life Hell for them when their tiny force tried to land.

So tonight, instead, he would be making Hell for American and Canadian and Mexican sailors, far away.

Chris shied from thinking about how many boys would die off Labrador, just to keep one alien creature occupied, while four surviving subs tried to sneak in through the back door…

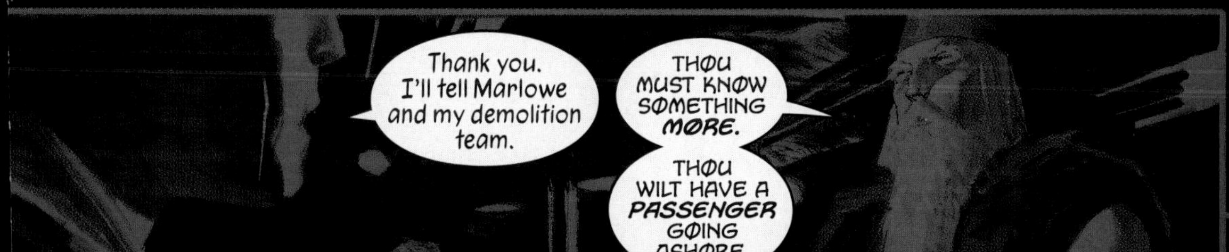
Thank you. I'll tell Marlowe and my demolition team.
THOU MUST KNOW SOMETHING *MORE*.
THOU WILT HAVE A *PASSENGER* GOING ASHORE.

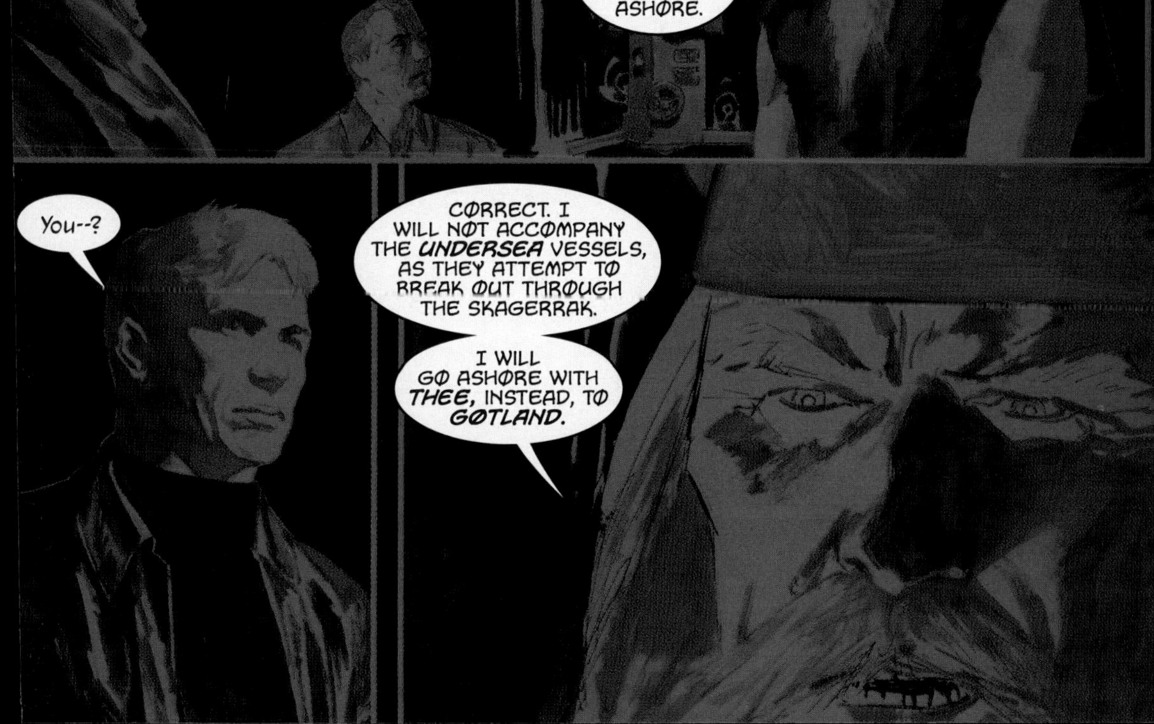
You--?
CORRECT. I WILL NOT ACCOMPANY THE *UNDERSEA* VESSELS, AS THEY ATTEMPT TO BREAK OUT THROUGH THE SKAGERRAK.
I WILL GO ASHORE WITH *THEE*, INSTEAD, TO *GOTLAND*.

Chris kept his face blank. There was no way he or Lewis or anybody else could stop this creature from doing whatever it wanted. One way or another, the Allies were about to lose their only Aesir friend in the long war against the Nazi plague.

If the word "friend" ever really described Loki—who had appeared one day on the tarmac of a Scottish airfield during the final evacuation of Britain, accompanied by eight small, bearded beings carrying boxes. He had led them up to the nearest amazed officer and imperiously commandeered the Prime Minister's personal plane to take him the rest of the way to America.

Perhaps an armored battalion might have stopped him. Battle reports told that Aesir *could* be killed, if you were very lucky, pounding one hard and fast enough. But the local commander decided to take a chance.

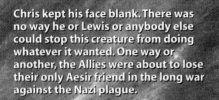

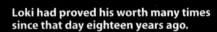

Loki had proved his worth many times since that day eighteen years ago.

Until now, that is.

If you insist.

I *DO.* IT IS MY *WILL.*

Then I'll explain to Major Marlowe. Excuse me, please.

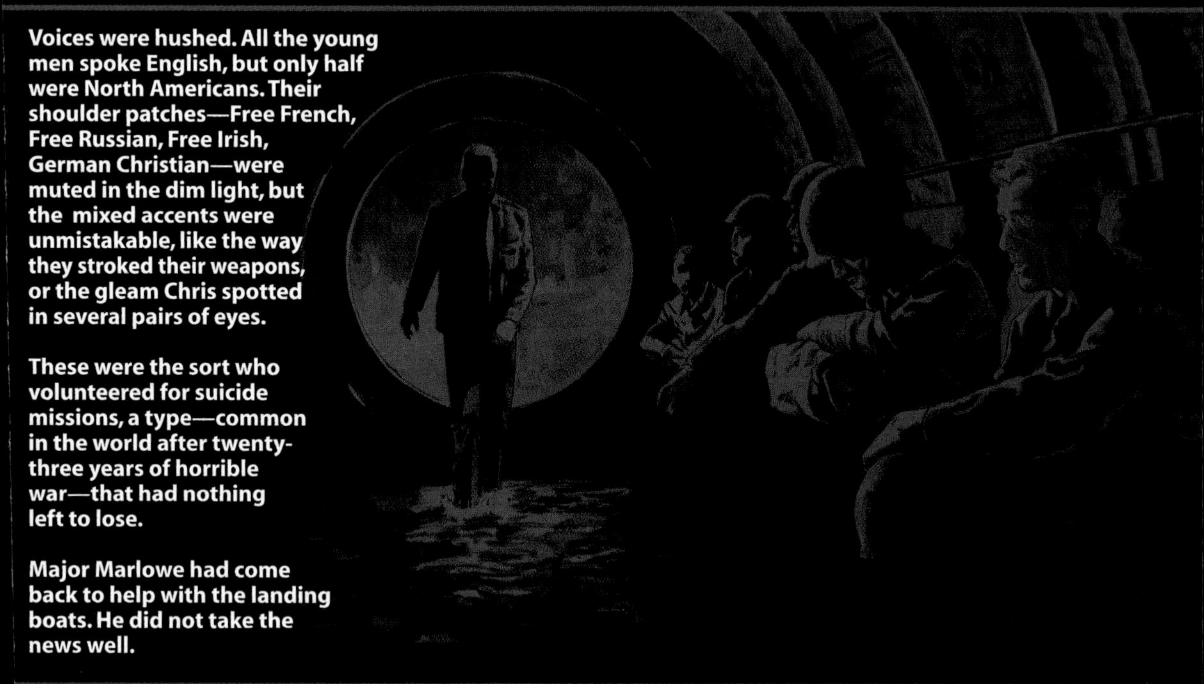
Voices were hushed. All the young men spoke English, but only half were North Americans. Their shoulder patches—Free French, Free Russian, Free Irish, German Christian—were muted in the dim light, but the mixed accents were unmistakable, like the way they stroked their weapons, or the gleam Chris spotted in several pairs of eyes.
These were the sort who volunteered for suicide missions, a type—common in the world after twenty-three years of horrible war—that had nothing left to lose.
Major Marlowe had come back to help with the landing boats. He did not take the news well.

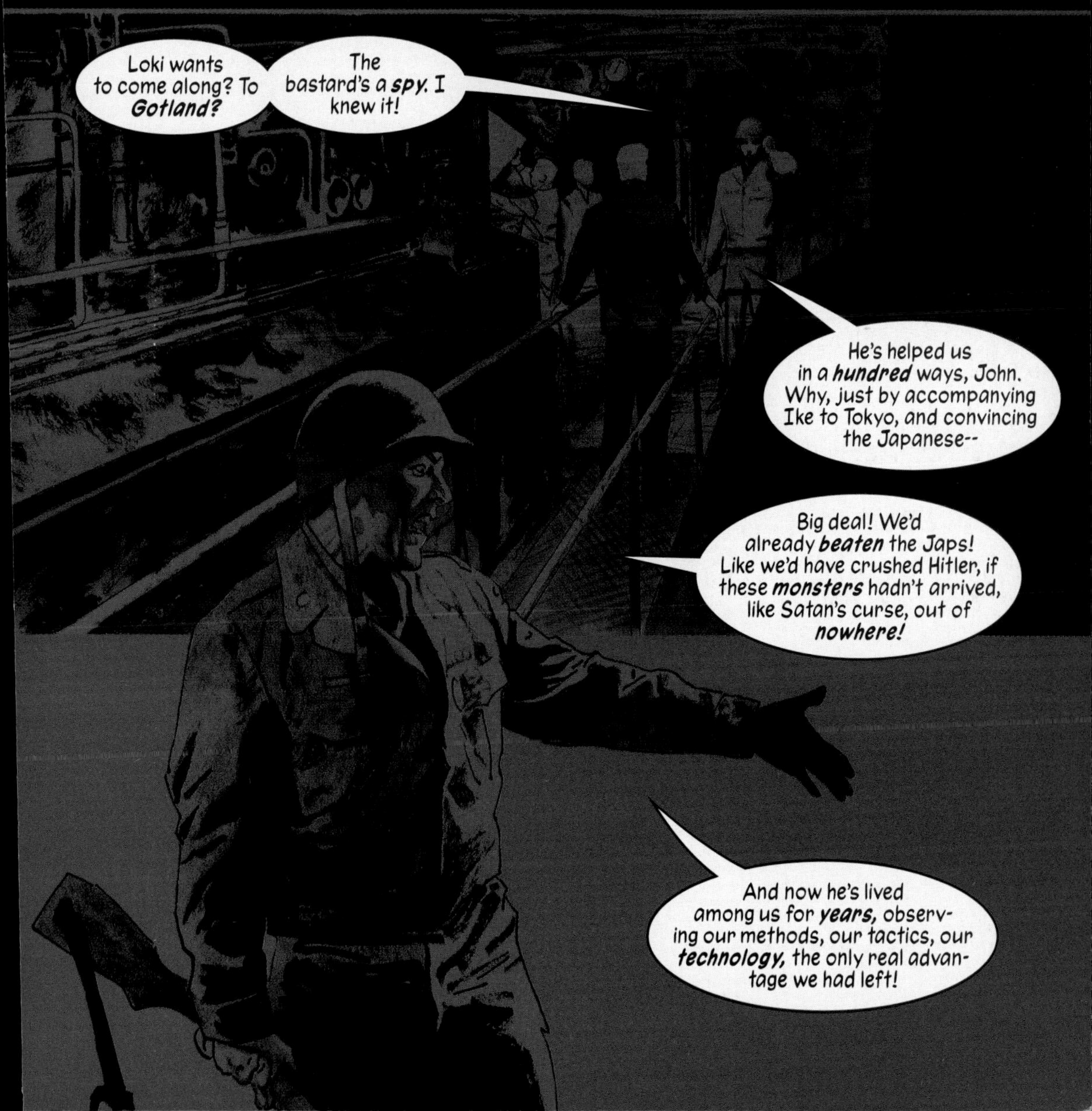
Loki wants to come along? To *Gotland?*
The bastard's a *spy.* I knew it!
He's helped us in a *hundred* ways, John. Why, just by accompanying Ike to Tokyo, and convincing the Japanese--
Big deal! We'd already *beaten* the Japs! Like we'd have crushed Hitler, if these *monsters* hadn't arrived, like Satan's curse, out of *nowhere!*
And now he's lived among us for *years,* observing our methods, our tactics, our *technology,* the only real advantage we had left!

Chris grimaced. How could he explain to Marlowe? The Marine officer had never been to Tehran, as Chris had, only last year. Marlowe had never seen the capital city of Israel-Iran, America's greatest and most stalwart ally, bulwark of the East.

There, in dozens of armed settlements along the east bank of the Euphrates, Chris had met fierce men and women who bore on their arms tattooed numbers from Treblinka, Dachau, Auschwitz. He heard their story of how, one hopeless night under barbed wire and the stench of chimneys, the starving, doomed masses looked up to see a strange vapor fall from the sky. Unbelieving, death-starkened eyes stared in wonderment as the mists gathered and coalesced into something that seemed almost solid.

Out of that eerie fog, a *bridge* of many colors formed—a rainbow arch climbing apparently without end, out of the places of horror into a moonless night. And from the heights, each doomed man and woman saw a dark-eyed figure on a flying horse ride down. They felt him whisper to them *inside* their minds.

COME, CHILDREN, WHILE YOUR TORMENTERS BLINK UNBELIEVINGLY IN MY WEB OF THE MIND. COME ALL, OVER MY BRIDGE TO SAFETY, BEFORE MY COUSINS DESCRY MY TREASON.

When they sank to their knees, or rocked in thankful prayer, the figure only snorted derision. His voice hissed within their heads.

DO NOT MISTAKE ME FOR YOUR GOD, WHO LEFT YOU HERE TO DIE! I CANNOT EXPLAIN THAT ONE'S ABSENCE TO YOU, OR HIS PLAN IN ALL THIS. THE ALL-FATHER IS A MYSTERY EVEN TO GREAT ODIN!

KNOW ONLY THAT I WILL TAKE YOU TO SAFETY NOW, SUCH AS THERE MAY BE IN THIS WORLD. BUT ONLY IF YOU HURRY! COME, AND BE GRATE-FUL LATER, IF YOU MUST!

Down to the camps, to bleak ghettoes, to a city under siege—the bridges formed in a single night, and with dawn were gone like vapor or a dream. Two million people, the old, the lame, women, children, the slaves of Hitler's war factories, climbed those paths—for there was no other choice—and found themselves transported to a desert land, by the banks of an ancient river.

They arrived just in time to take up hasty arms and save a British Army fleeing the wreckage of Egypt and Palestine. They fused with the astonished Persians, with refugees from crippled Russia, building a new nation out of chaos.

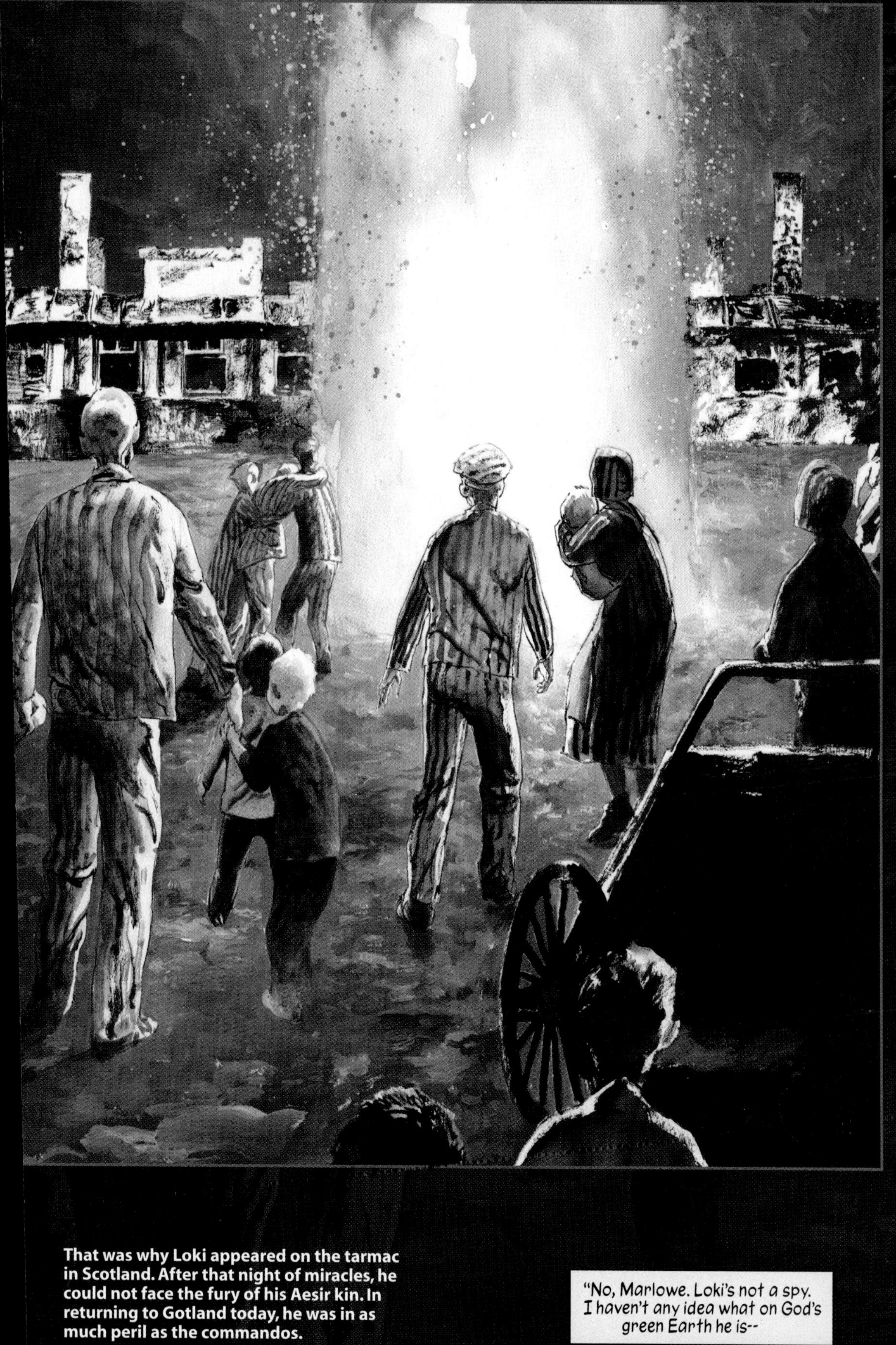
That was why Loki appeared on the tarmac in Scotland. After that night of miracles, he could not face the fury of his Aesir kin. In returning to Gotland today, he was in as much peril as the commandos.
"No, Marlowe. Loki's not a spy. I haven't any idea what on God's green Earth he is--

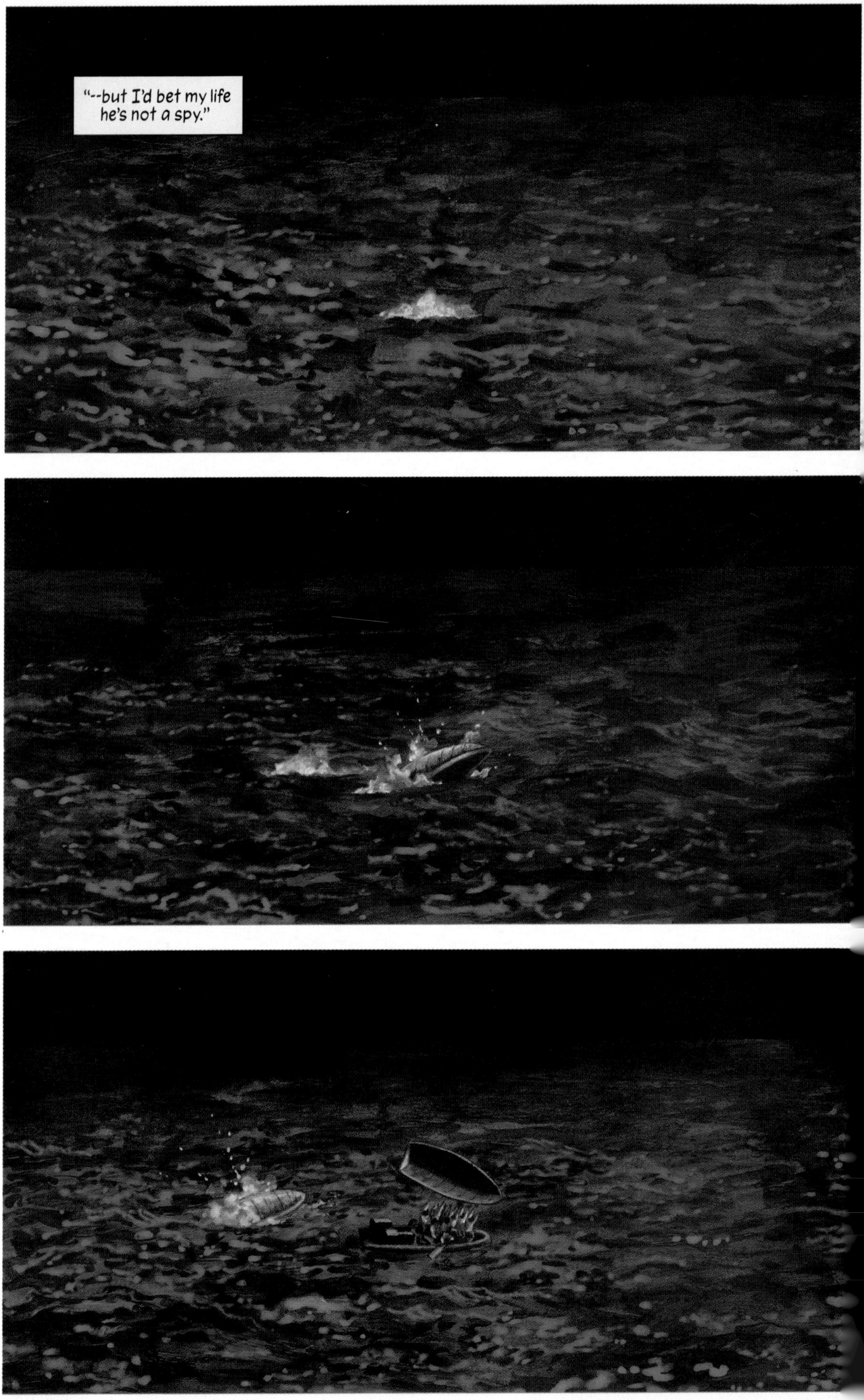
"--but I'd bet my life he's not a spy."

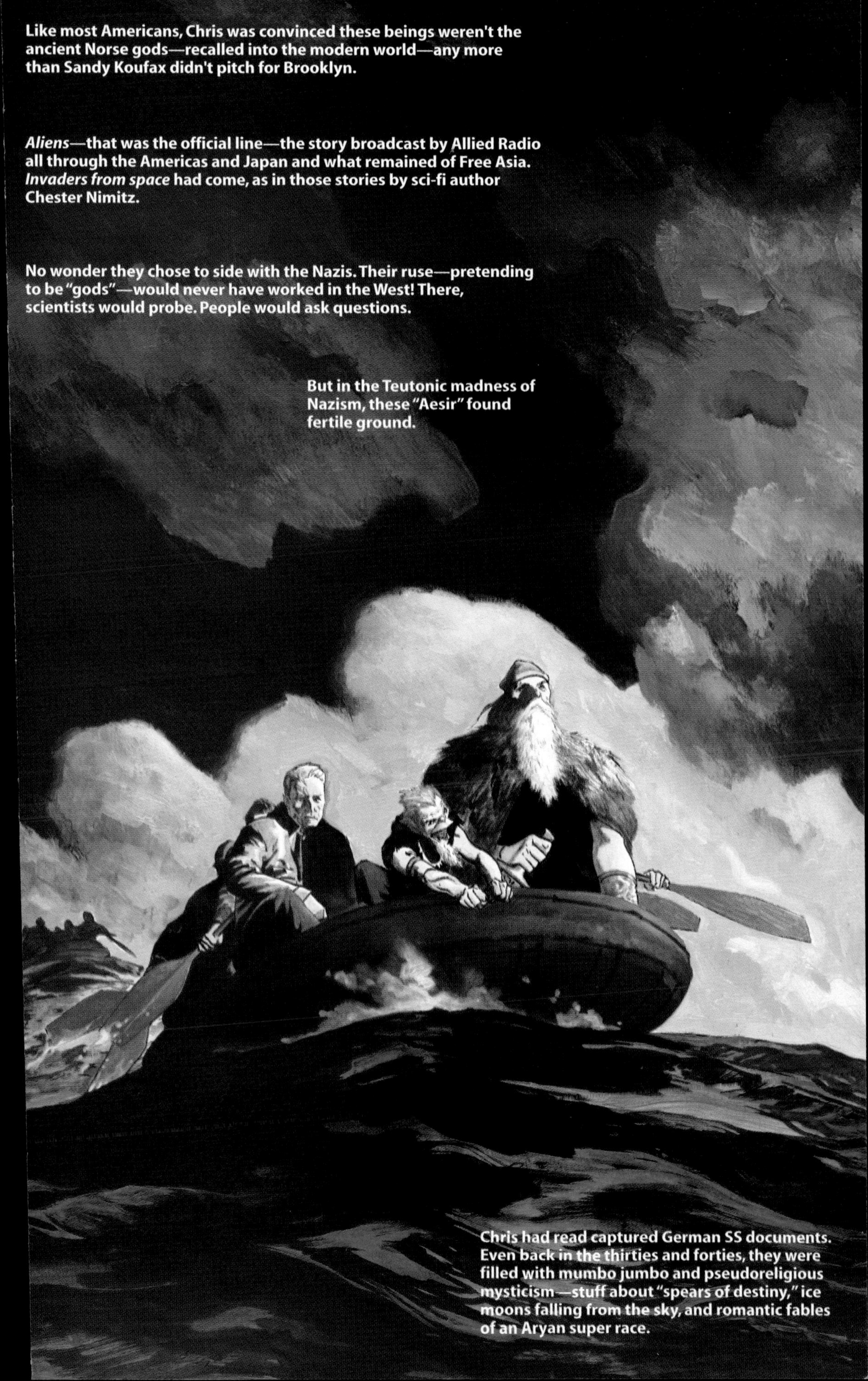
Like most Americans, Chris was convinced these beings weren't the ancient Norse gods—recalled into the modern world—any more than Sandy Koufax didn't pitch for Brooklyn.
Aliens—that was the official line—the story broadcast by Allied Radio all through the Americas and Japan and what remained of Free Asia. *Invaders from space* had come, as in those stories by sci-fi author Chester Nimitz.
No wonder they chose to side with the Nazis. Their ruse—pretending to be "gods"—would never have worked in the West! There, scientists would probe. People would ask questions.
But in the Teutonic madness of Nazism, these "Aesir" found fertile ground.
Chris had read captured German SS documents. Even back in the thirties and forties, they were filled with mumbo jumbo and pseudoreligious mysticism—stuff about "spears of destiny," ice moons falling from the sky, and romantic fables of an Aryan super race.

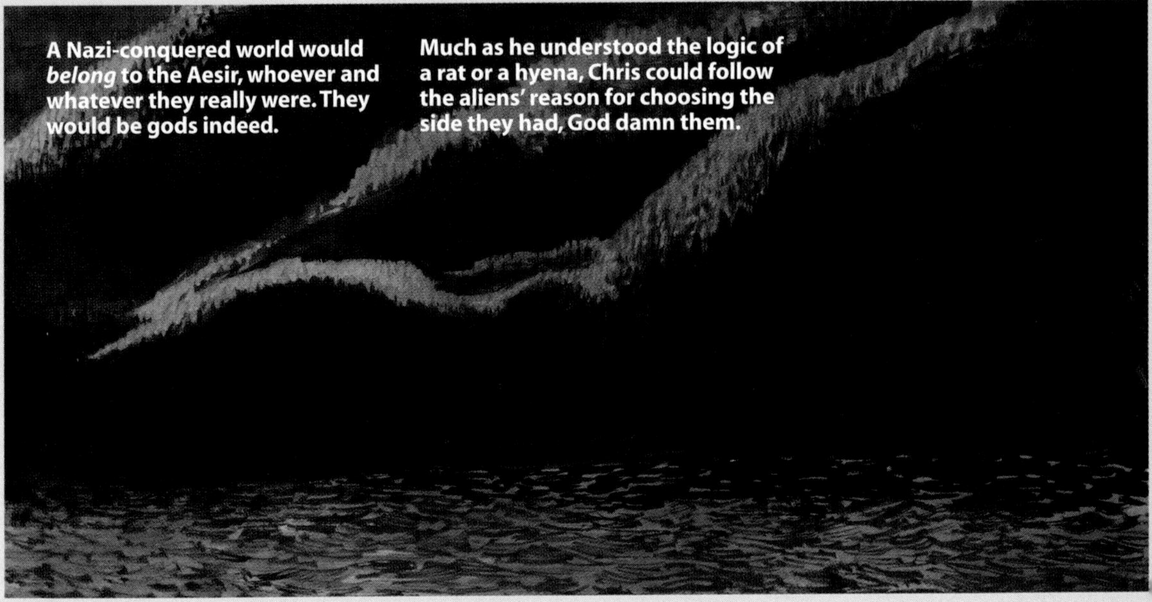
A Nazi-conquered world would *belong* to the Aesir, whoever and whatever they really were. They would be gods indeed.
Much as he understood the logic of a rat or a hyena, Chris could follow the aliens' reason for choosing the side they had, God damn them.

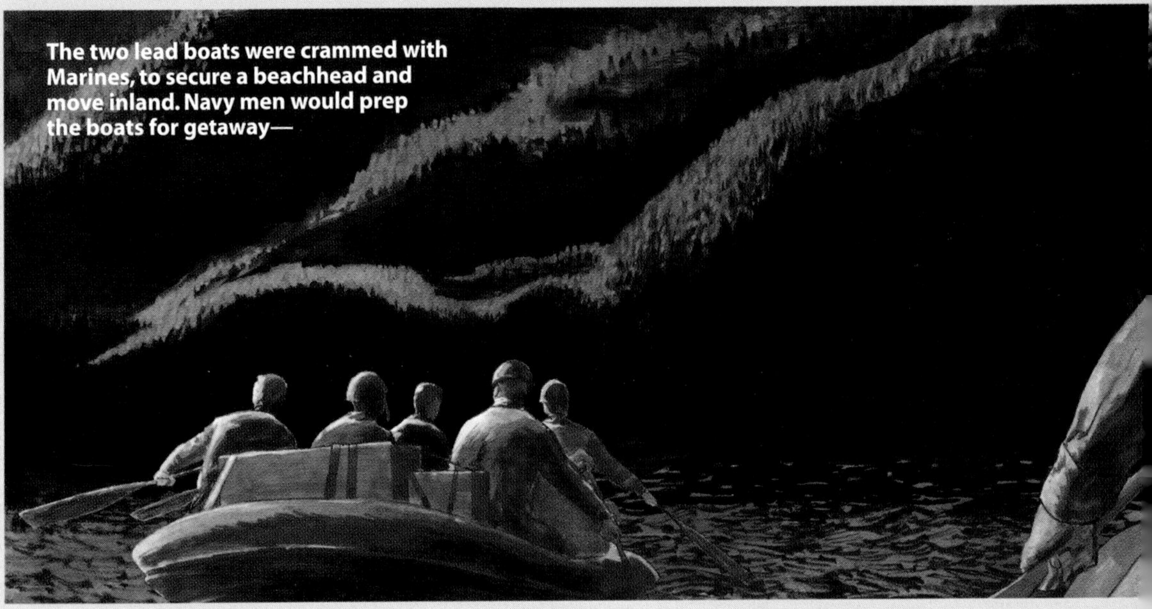
The two lead boats were crammed with Marines, to secure a beachhead and move inland. Navy men would prep the boats for getaway—

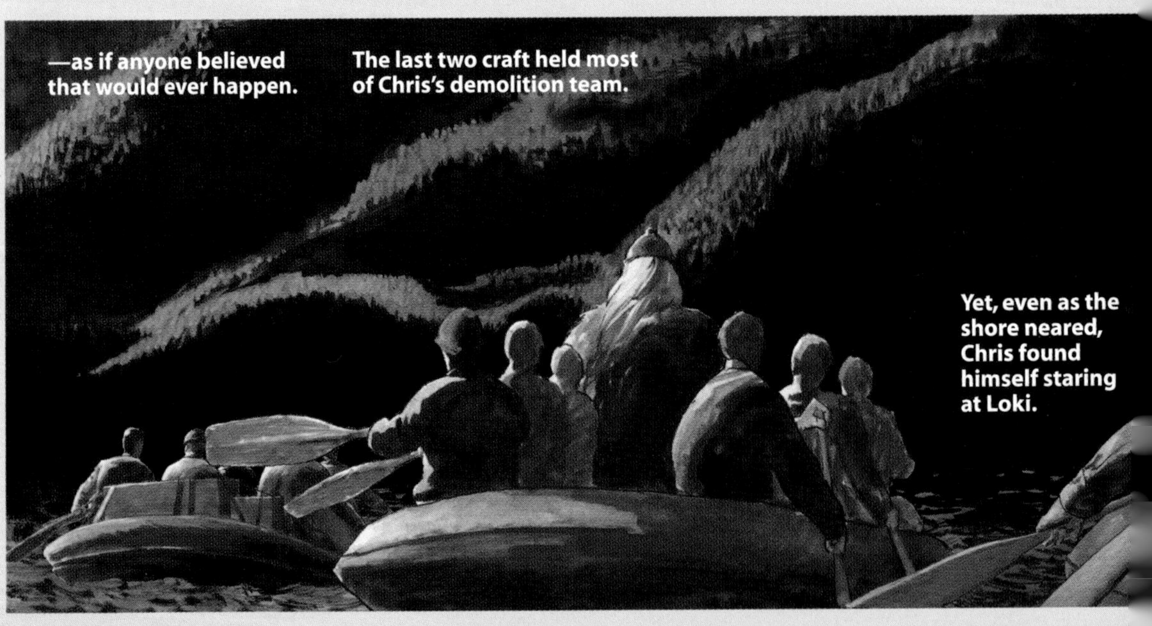
—as if anyone believed that would ever happen.
The last two craft held most of Chris's demolition team.
Yet, even as the shore neared, Chris found himself staring at Loki.

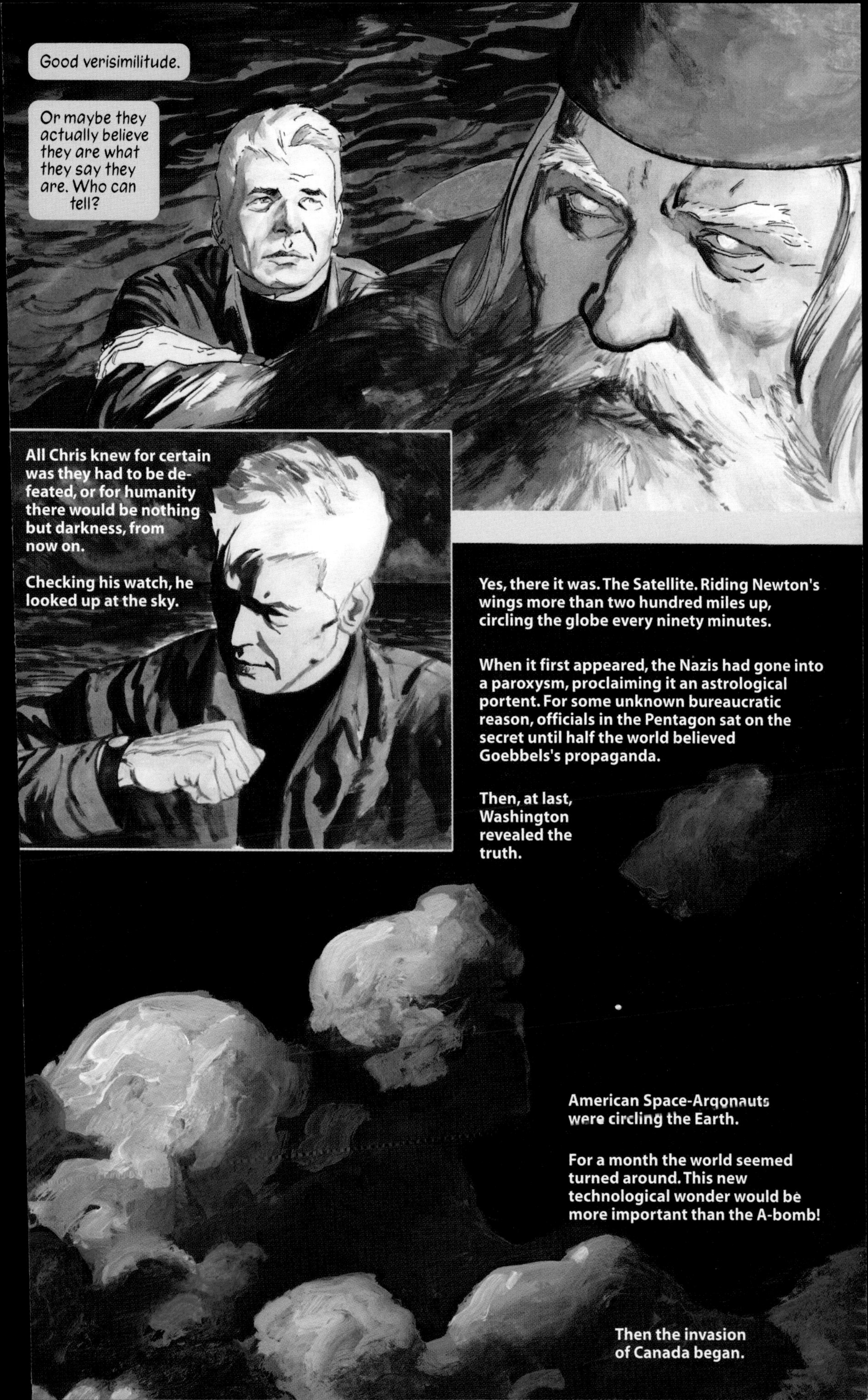

Good verisimilitude.
Or maybe they actually believe they are what they say they are. Who can tell?
All Chris knew for certain was they had to be de-feated, or for humanity there would be nothing but darkness, from now on.
Checking his watch, he looked up at the sky.
Yes, there it was. The Satellite. Riding Newton's wings more than two hundred miles up, circling the globe every ninety minutes.
When it first appeared, the Nazis had gone into a paroxysm, proclaiming it an astrological portent. For some unknown bureaucratic reason, officials in the Pentagon sat on the secret until half the world believed Goebbels's propaganda.
Then, at last, Washington revealed the truth.
American Space-Argonauts were circling the Earth.
For a month the world seemed turned around. This new technological wonder would be more important than the A-bomb!
Then the invasion of Canada began.

Chris turned his mind away from what was happening now, in the Atlantic. He wished he had one of those new "laser" communicators, so he could tell the men in the Satellite how things were progressing down here. But the light amplification devices were so secret, the Chiefs refused to let any be taken into the enemy's heartland.

Were the Nazis working on a way to shoot down the Satellite? How, with the aliens to help them, could the enemy let their early lead in rocketry slip so badly?

Perhaps they can't operate in space anymore-- as they haven't been able to crush our submarine force.

But how could aliens be unable to destroy such a crude spacecraft?

Chris shook his head.

Not that it matters. Tonight the Atlantic Fleet is dying. This winter we'll be forced to use big bombs--wrecking the continent even if we slow them down.

He looked at the figure in the boat's prow.

How can cleverness or industry prevail against such power?

Those fur-covered shoulders were passive now. But Chris had seen Loki tear down buildings with his hands. And Loki admitted to being one of the *weakest* of these "gods."

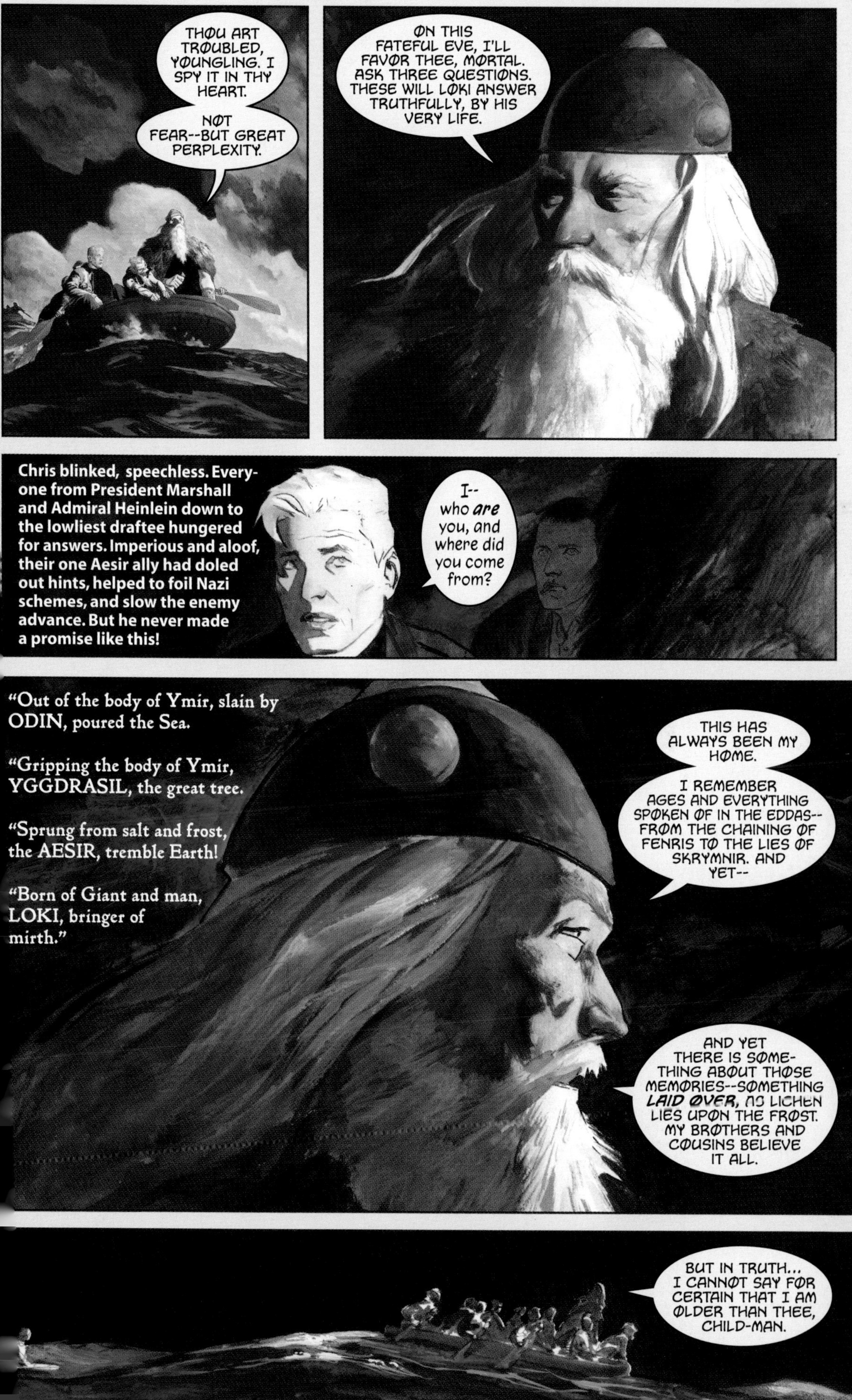
THOU ART TROUBLED, YOUNGLING. I SPY IT IN THY HEART.
NOT FEAR--BUT GREAT PERPLEXITY.
ON THIS FATEFUL EVE, I'LL FAVOR THEE, MORTAL. ASK THREE QUESTIONS. THESE WILL LOKI ANSWER TRUTHFULLY, BY HIS VERY LIFE.
Chris blinked, speechless. Everyone from President Marshall and Admiral Heinlein down to the lowliest draftee hungered for answers. Imperious and aloof, their one Aesir ally had doled out hints, helped to foil Nazi schemes, and slow the enemy advance. But he never made a promise like this!
I-- who *are* you, and where did you come from?
"Out of the body of Ymir, slain by ODIN, poured the Sea.
"Gripping the body of Ymir, YGGDRASIL, the great tree.
"Sprung from salt and frost, the AESIR, tremble Earth!
"Born of Giant and man, LOKI, bringer of mirth."
THIS HAS ALWAYS BEEN MY HOME.
I REMEMBER AGES AND EVERYTHING SPOKEN OF IN THE EDDAS--FROM THE CHAINING OF FENRIS TO THE LIES OF SKRYMNIR. AND YET--
AND YET THERE IS SOMETHING ABOUT THOSE MEMORIES--SOMETHING *LAID OVER*, AS LICHEN LIES UPON THE FROST. MY BROTHERS AND COUSINS BELIEVE IT ALL.
BUT IN TRUTH... I CANNOT SAY FOR CERTAIN THAT I AM OLDER THAN THEE, CHILD-MAN.

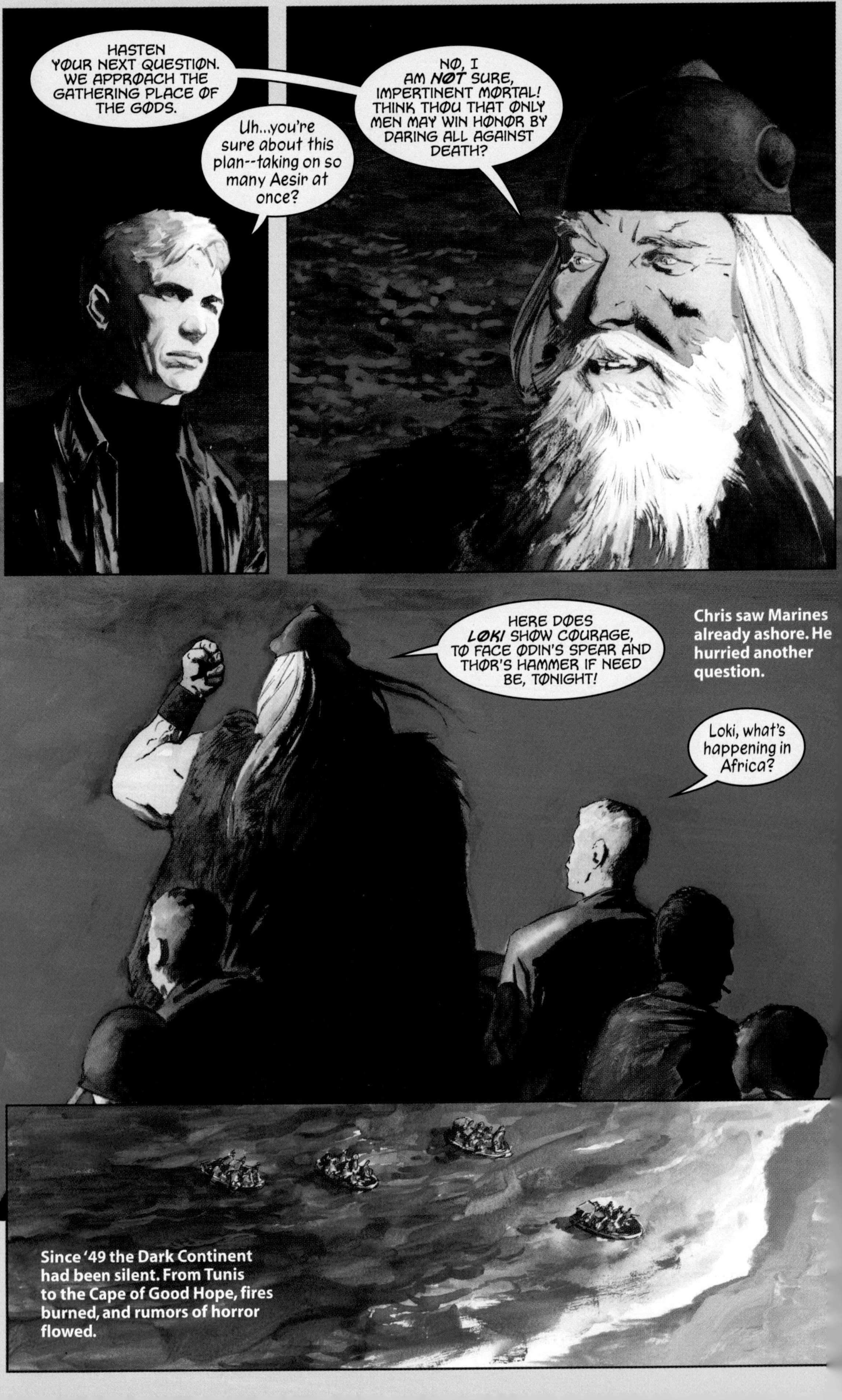
HASTEN YOUR NEXT QUESTION. WE APPROACH THE GATHERING PLACE OF THE GODS.
Uh...you're sure about this plan--taking on so many Aesir at once?
NO, I AM NOT SURE, IMPERTINENT MORTAL! THINK THOU THAT ONLY MEN MAY WIN HONOR BY DARING ALL AGAINST DEATH?
HERE DOES LOKI SHOW COURAGE, TO FACE ODIN'S SPEAR AND THOR'S HAMMER IF NEED BE, TONIGHT!
Chris saw Marines already ashore. He hurried another question.
Loki, what's happening in Africa?
Since '49 the Dark Continent had been silent. From Tunis to the Cape of Good Hope, fires burned, and rumors of horror flowed.

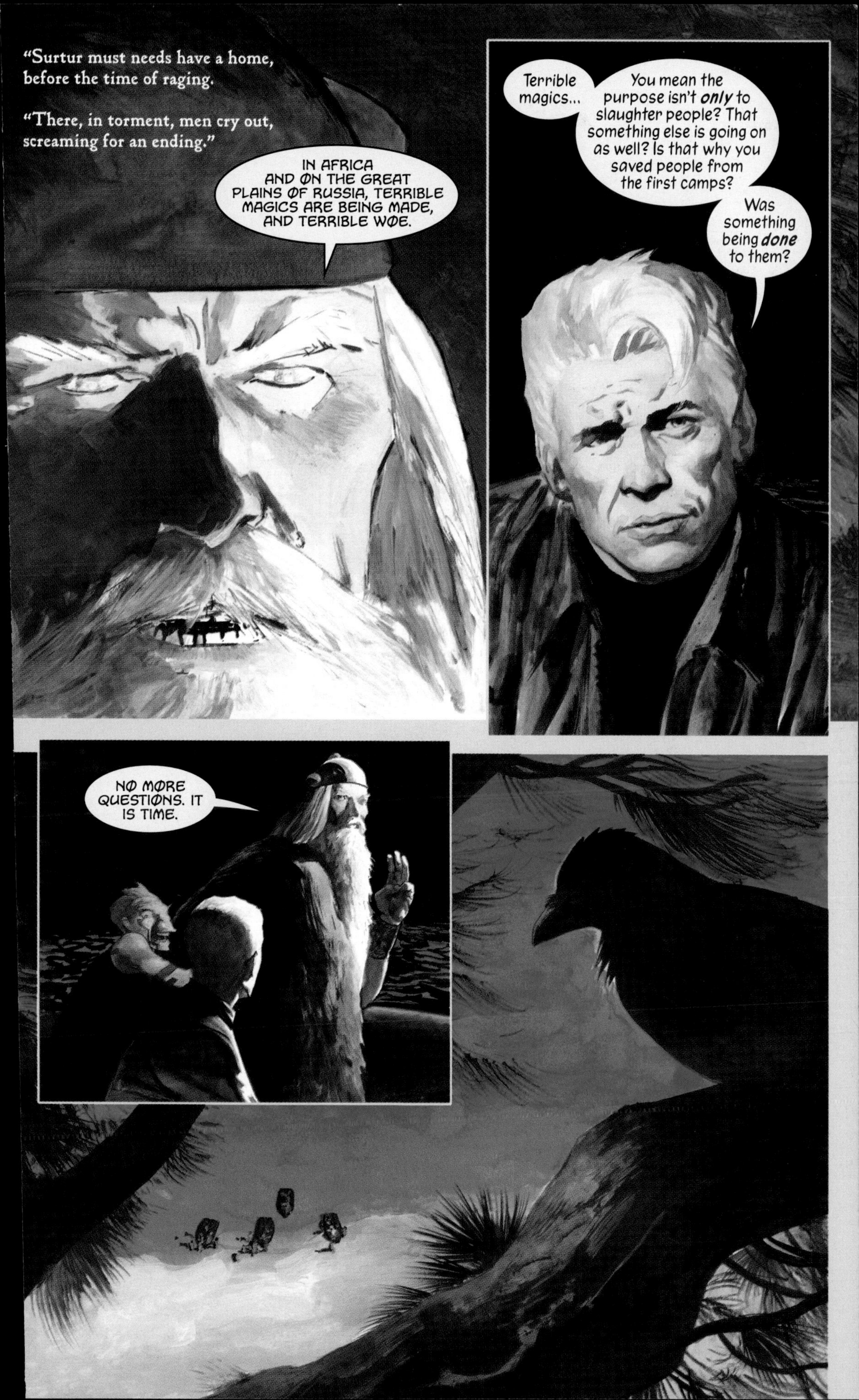
"Surtur must needs have a home,
before the time of raging.
"There, in torment, men cry out,
screaming for an ending."
IN AFRICA AND ON THE GREAT PLAINS OF RUSSIA, TERRIBLE MAGICS ARE BEING MADE, AND TERRIBLE WOE.
Terrible magics...
You mean the purpose isn't *only* to slaughter people? That something else is going on as well? Is that why you saved people from the first camps?
Was something being *done* to them?
NO MORE QUESTIONS. IT IS TIME.

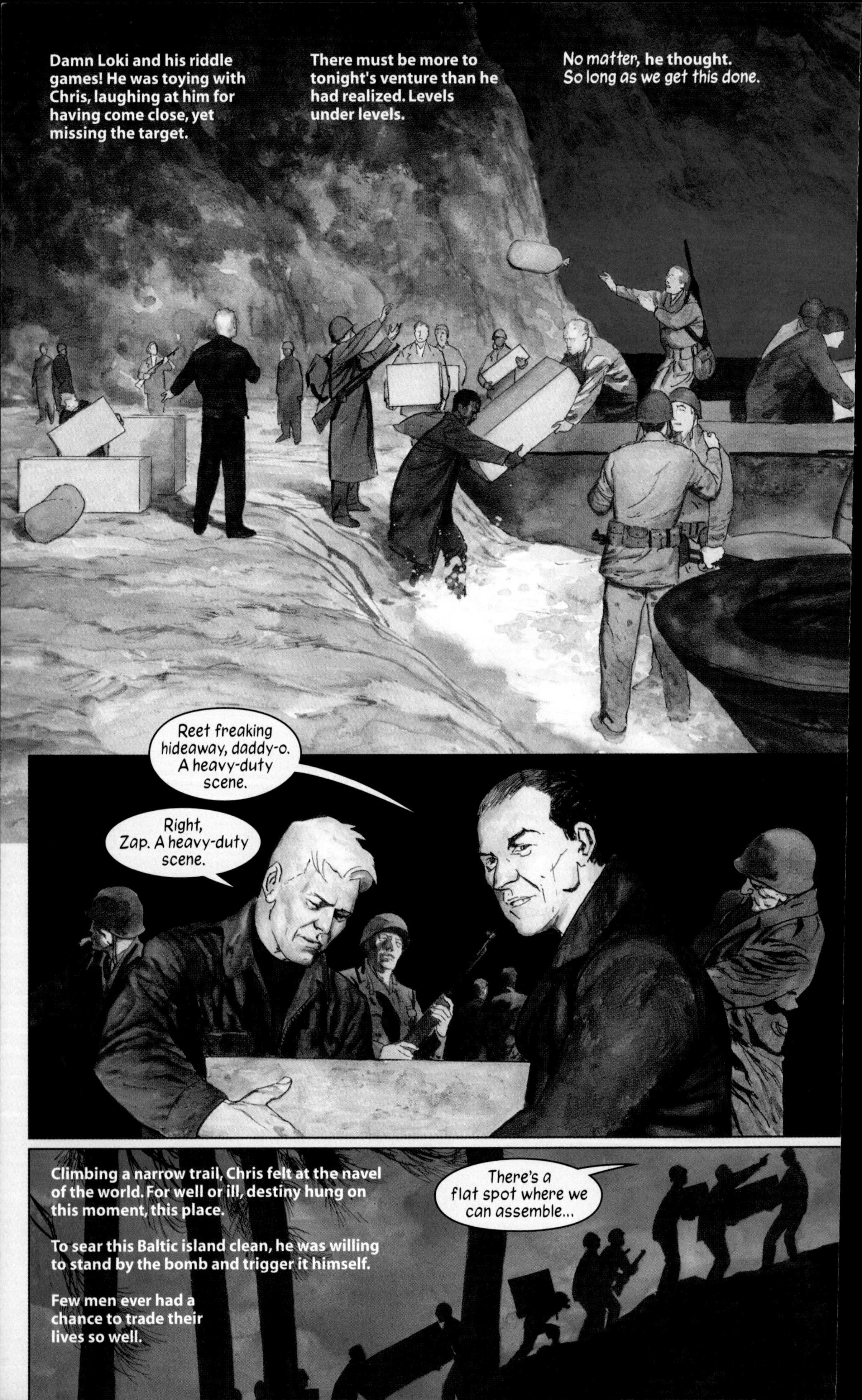
Damn Loki and his riddle games! He was toying with Chris, laughing at him for having come close, yet missing the target.
There must be more to tonight's venture than he had realized. Levels under levels.
No matter, he thought. So long as we get this done.
Reet freaking hideaway, daddy-o. A heavy-duty scene.
Right, Zap. A heavy-duty scene.
Climbing a narrow trail, Chris felt at the navel of the world. For well or ill, destiny hung on this moment, this place.
To sear this Baltic island clean, he was willing to stand by the bomb and trigger it himself.
Few men ever had a chance to trade their lives so well.
There's a flat spot where we can assemble...

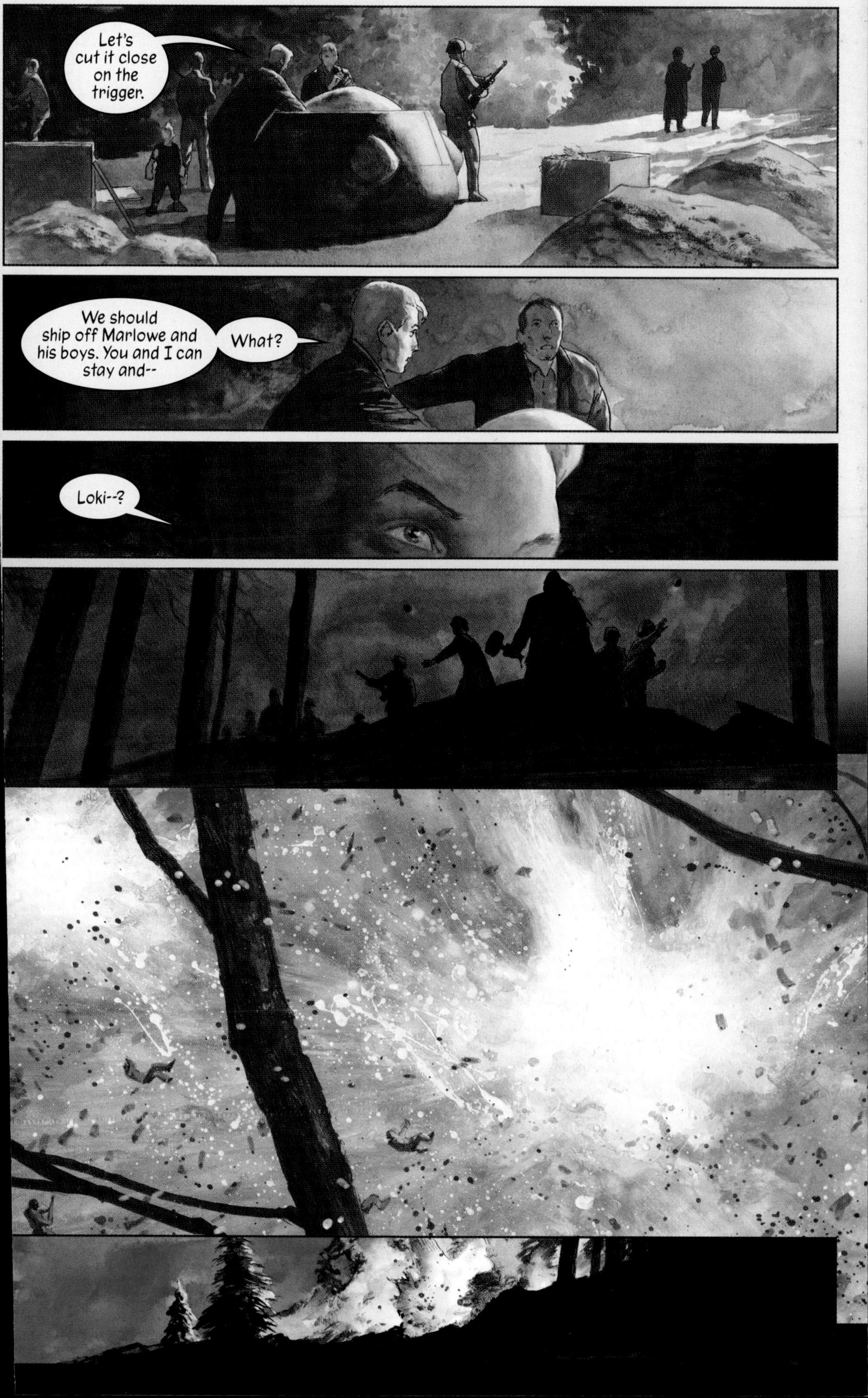
Let's cut it close on the trigger.
We should ship off Marlowe and his boys. You and I can stay and--
What?
Loki--?

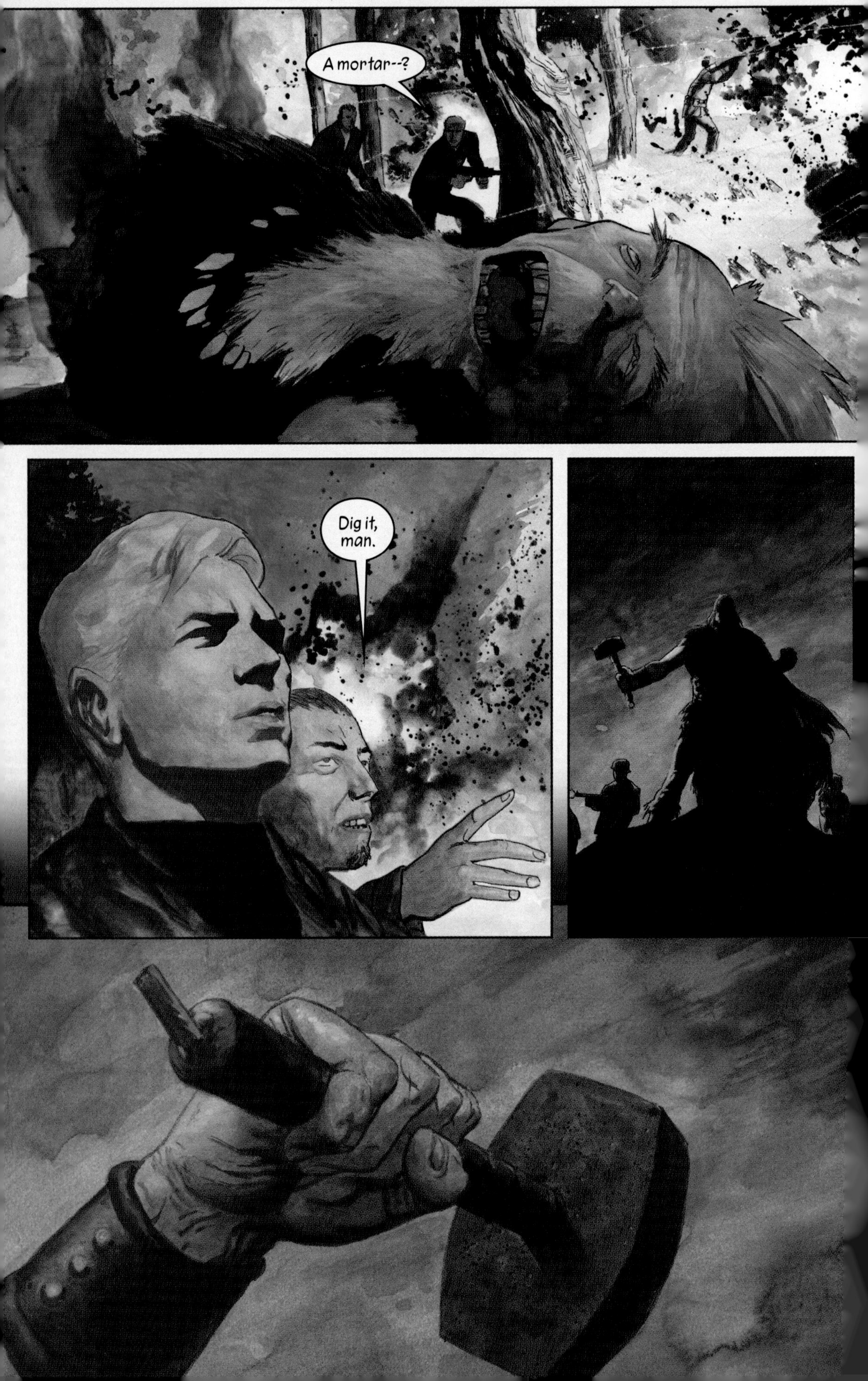
A mortar--?
Dig it, man.

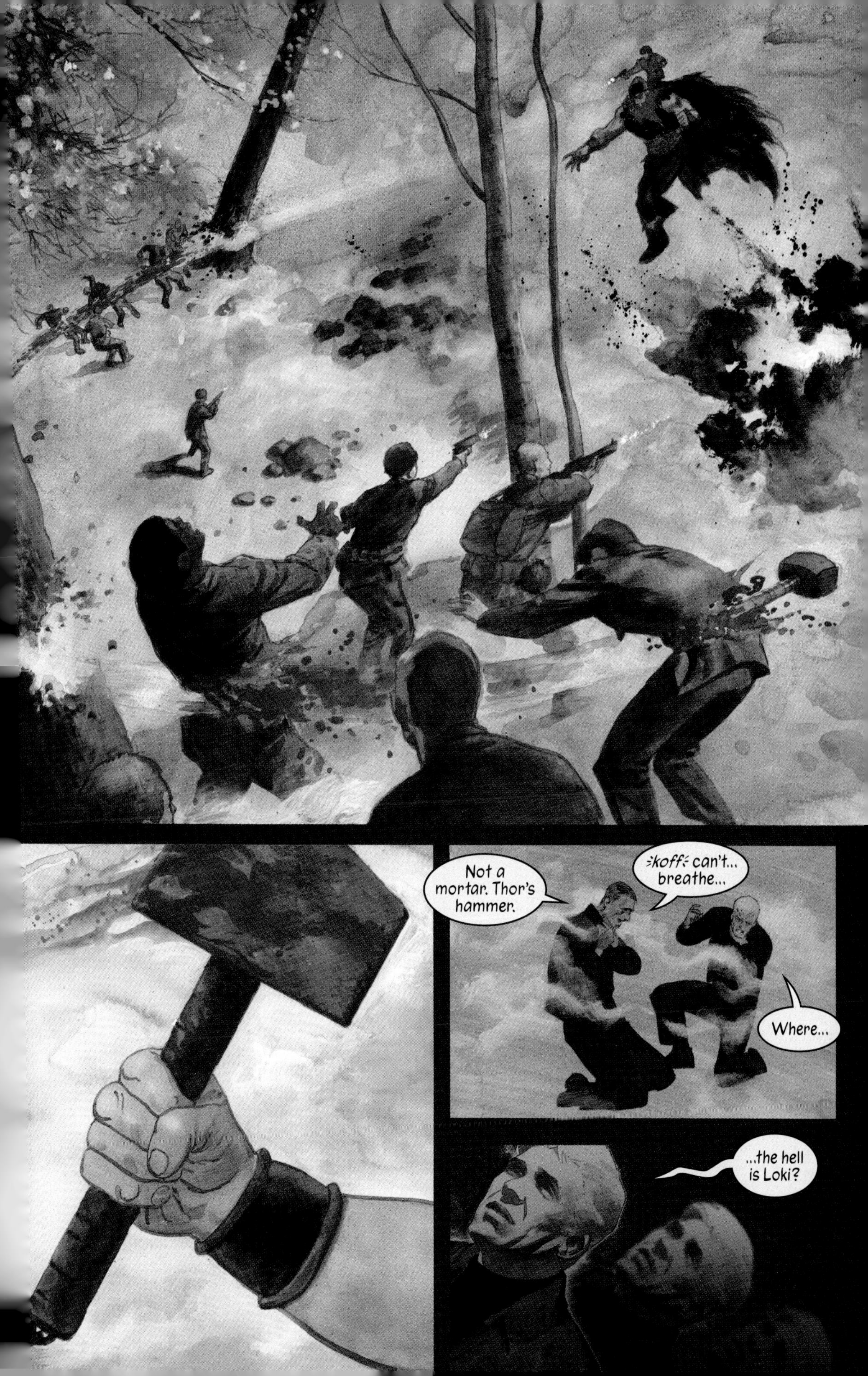
Not a mortar. Thor's hammer.
koff can't... breathe...
Where...
...the hell is Loki?

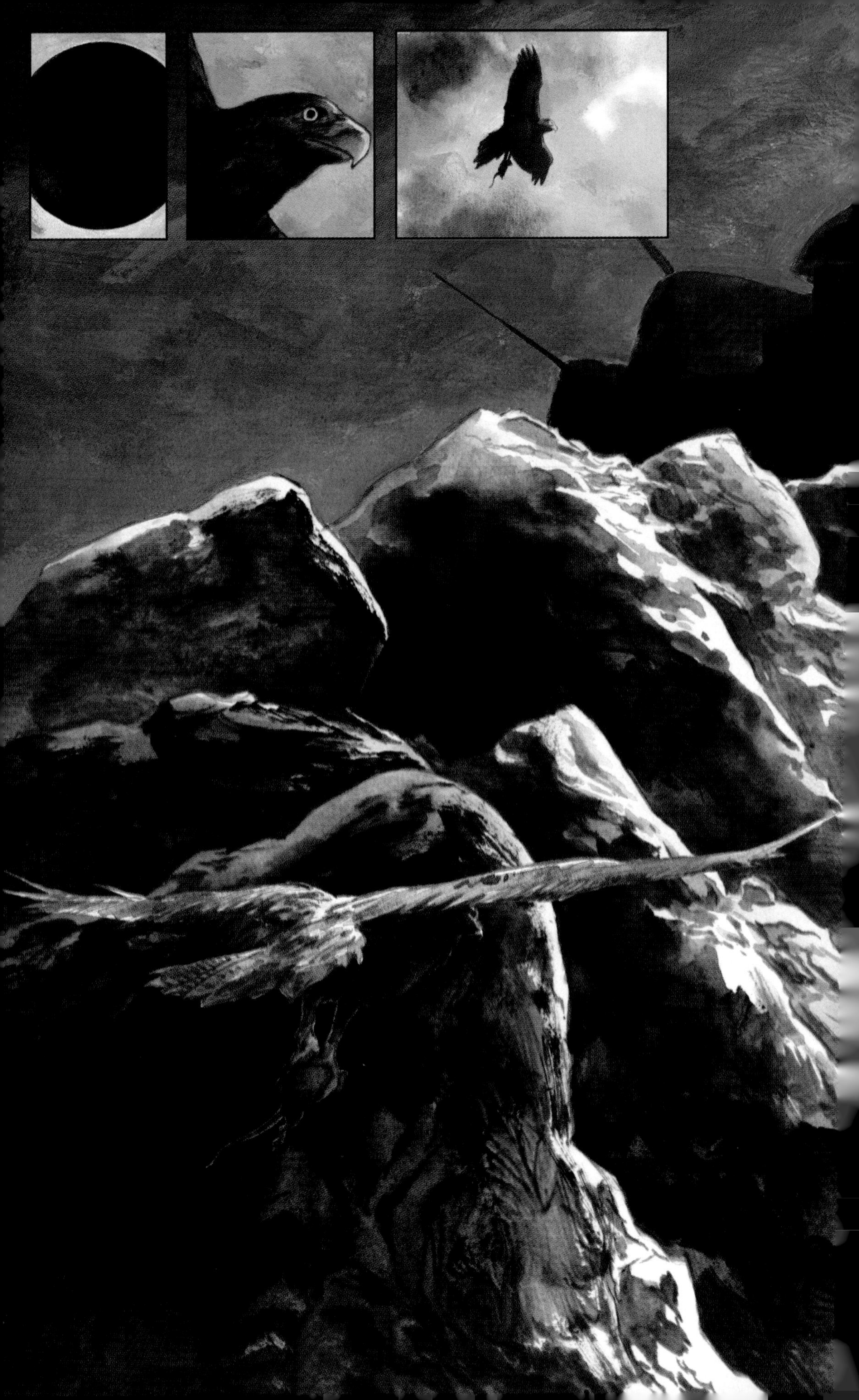

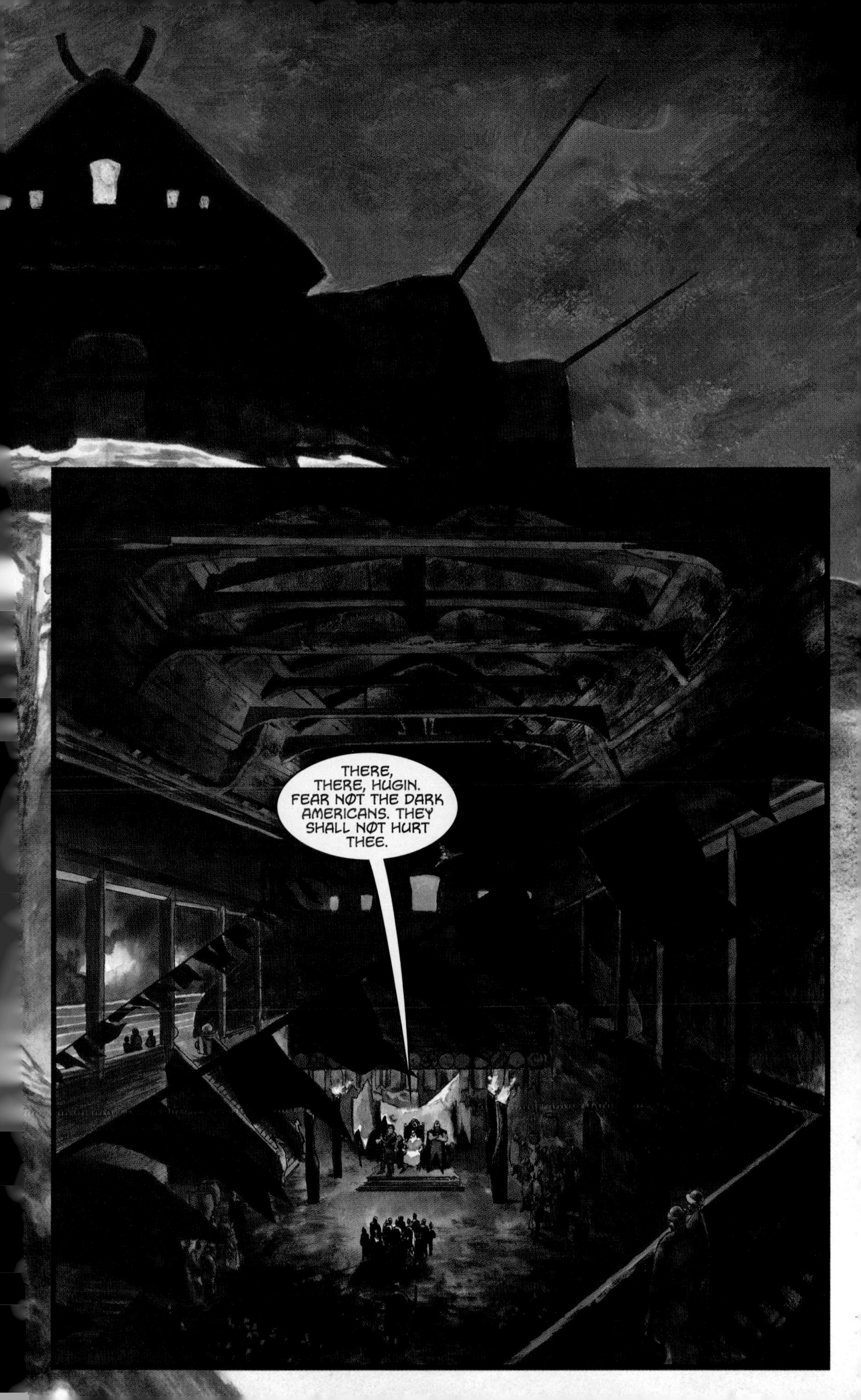
THERE, THERE, HUGIN. FEAR NØT THE DARK AMERICANS. THEY SHALL NØT HURT THEE.

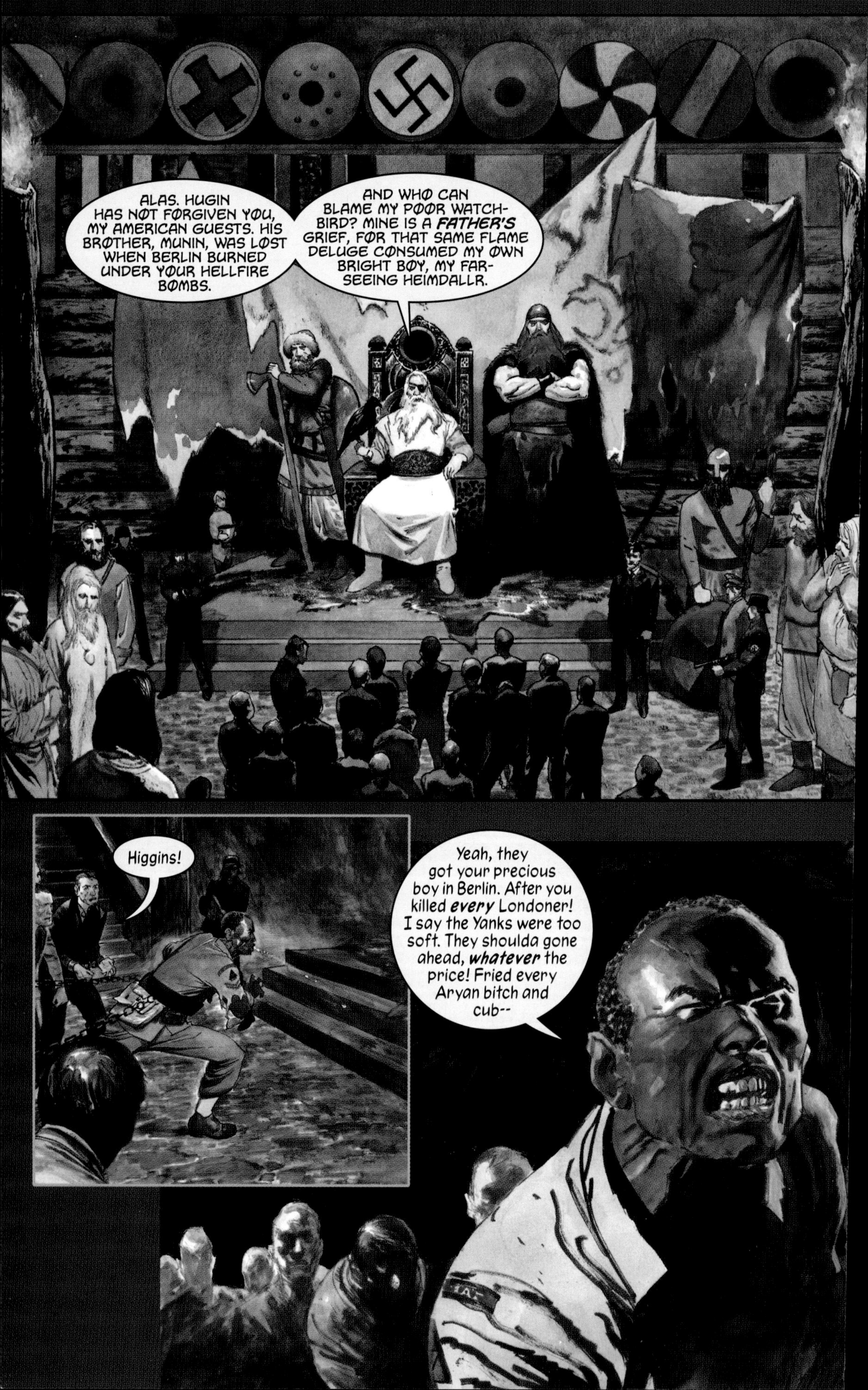
ALAS. HUGIN HAS NØT FØRGIVEN YØU, MY AMERICAN GUESTS. HIS BRØTHER, MUNIN, WAS LØST WHEN BERLIN BURNED UNDER YØUR HELLFIRE BØMBS.
AND WHØ CAN BLAME MY PØØR WATCH-BIRD? MINE IS A **FATHER'S** GRIEF, FØR THAT SAME FLAME DELUGE CØNSUMED MY ØWN BRIGHT BØY, MY FAR-SEEING HEIMDALLR.
Higgins!
Yeah, they got your precious boy in Berlin. After you killed **every** Londoner! I say the Yanks were too soft. They shoulda gone ahead, **whatever** the price! Fried every Aryan bitch and cub--

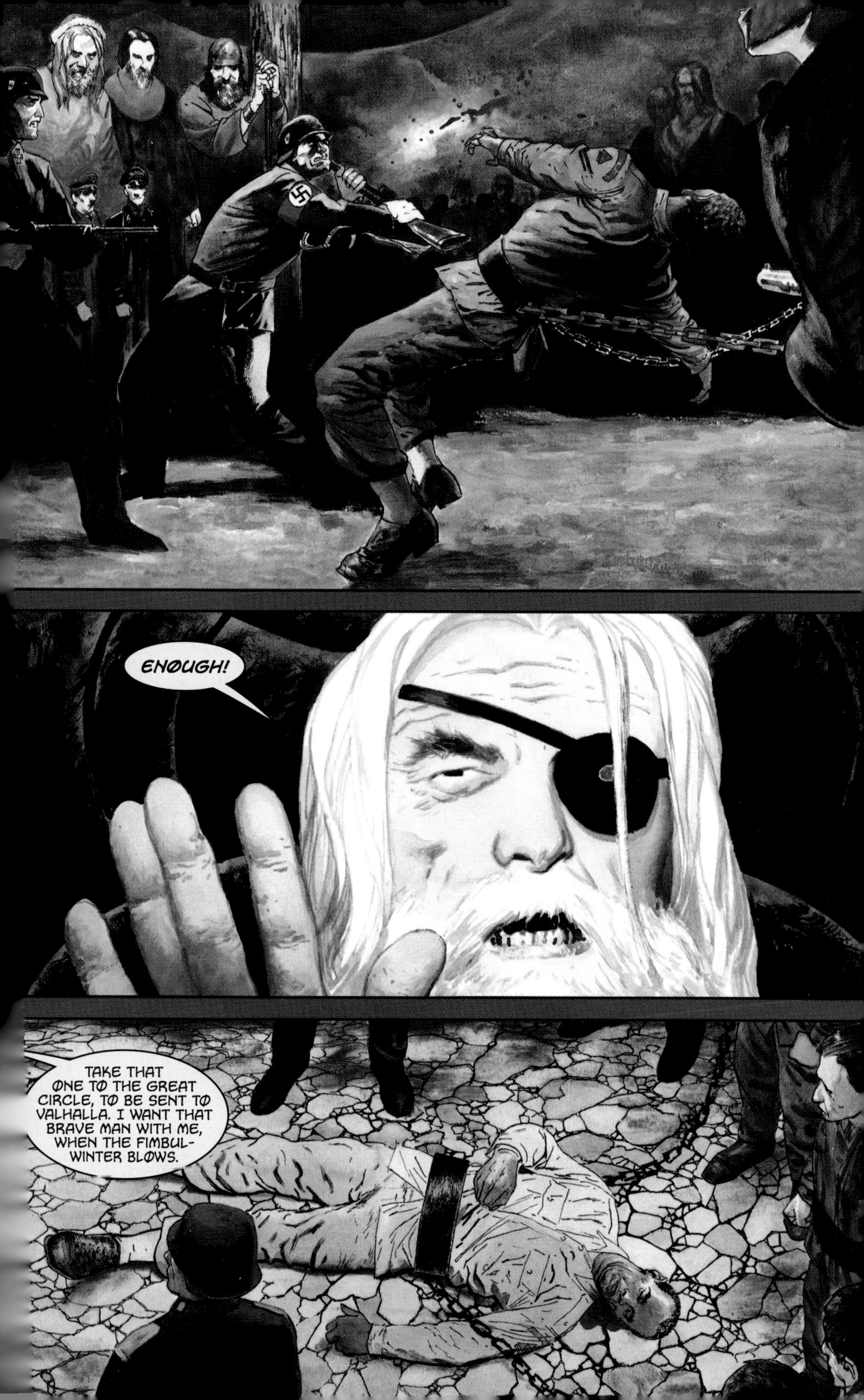
ENØUGH!
TAKE THAT ØNE TØ THE GREAT CIRCLE, TØ BE SENT TØ VALHALLA. I WANT THAT BRAVE MAN WITH ME, WHEN THE FIMBUL-WINTER BLØWS.

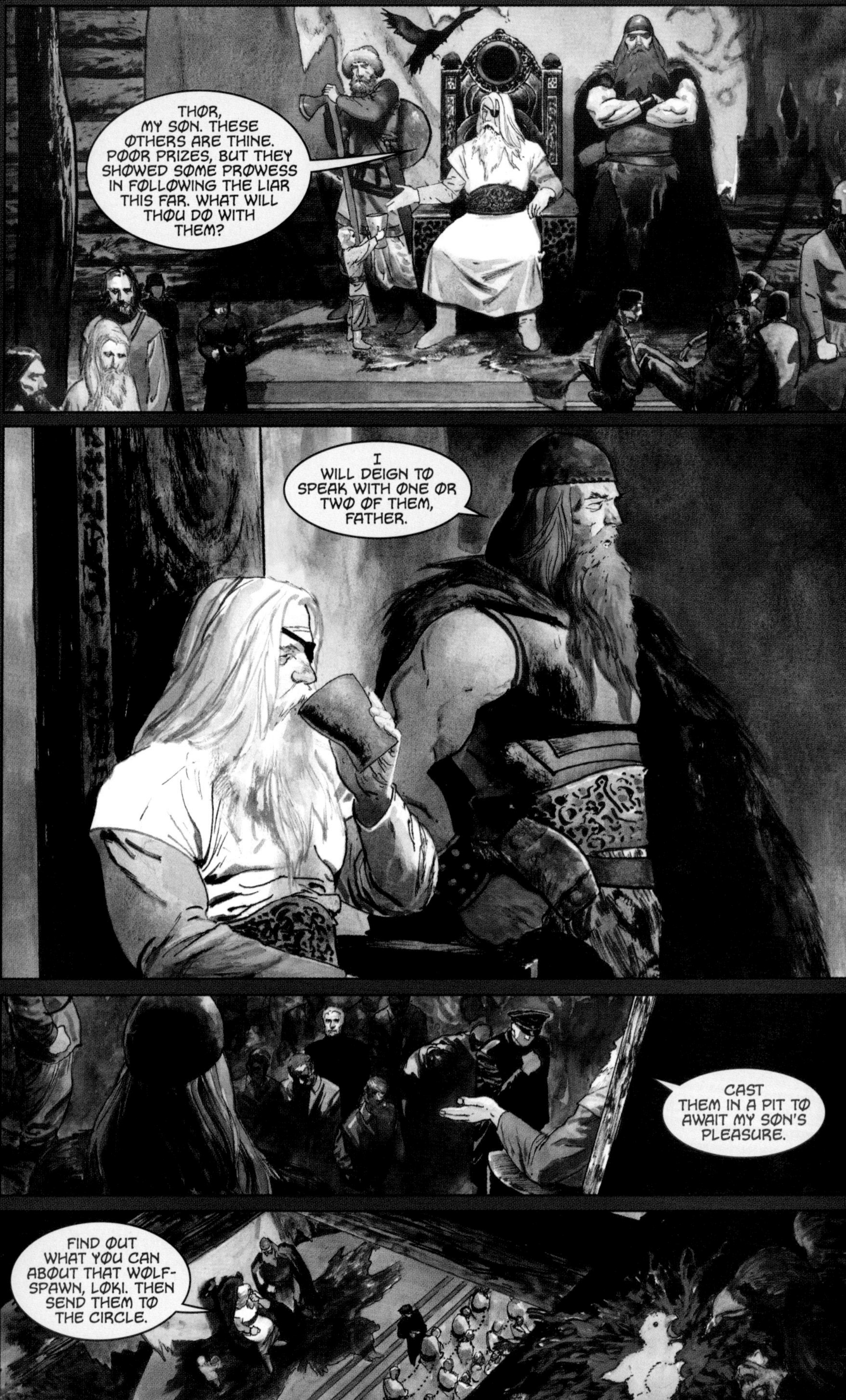
THOR, MY SON. THESE OTHERS ARE THINE. POOR PRIZES, BUT THEY SHOWED SOME PROWESS IN FOLLOWING THE LIAR THIS FAR. WHAT WILL THOU DO WITH THEM?
I WILL DEIGN TO SPEAK WITH ONE OR TWO OF THEM, FATHER.
CAST THEM IN A PIT TO AWAIT MY SON'S PLEASURE.
FIND OUT WHAT YOU CAN ABOUT THAT WOLF-SPAWN, LOKI. THEN SEND THEM TO THE CIRCLE.

For hours, Chris sat in the dungeon, with his thoughts. With unwanted memories. Major Marlowe had been right about one thing. The Nazis would never have won without the Aesir, or something like them. Hitler and his gang must have believed from the start that they could somehow call forth ancient "gods," or they surely wouldn't have dared wage such a war, certain to bring in America.

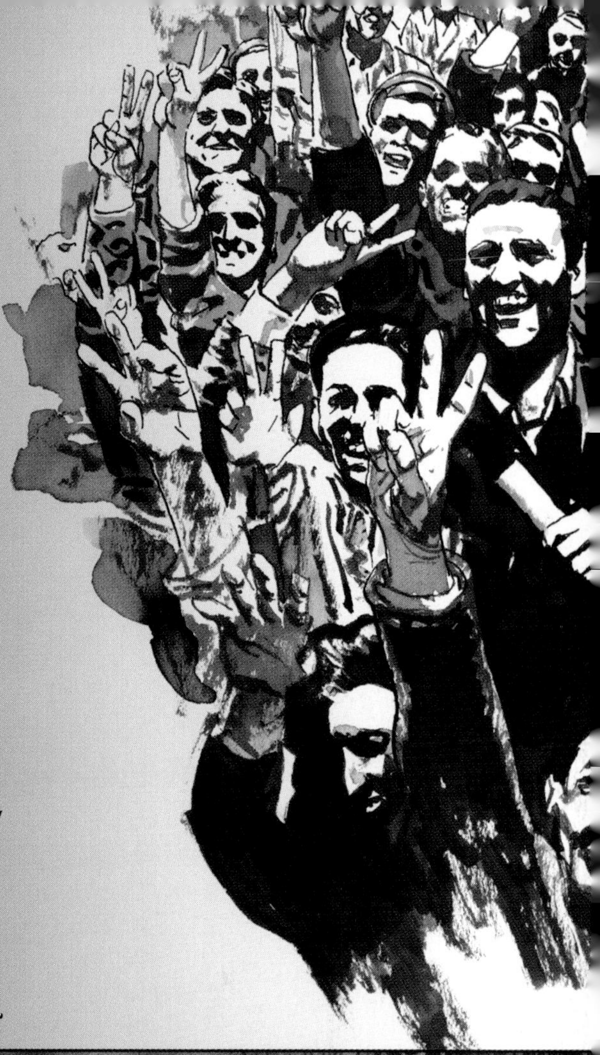

Indeed, by early 1944 it seemed all but over. There was still Hell to pay, of course, but nobody back home feared defeat anymore. The Russians were pushing from the East. Rome would soon fall and the Mediterranean was an Allied lake. The Japanese Empire crumbled—driven back or bottled in island after island—while the greatest armada of all time gathered in England, preparing to cross the Channel and lance the Nazi boil for good and all.

In factories and shipyards, the Arsenal of Democracy poured forth more materiel per month than the Third Reich produced in its best year. Ships rolled off the ways at intervals of hours. Planes every few minutes…

…while a rabble of farmers and city boys in soldier suits became tempered warriors in a great army, on a par with their experienced foe, and outnumbering the enemy as well.

Already there was talk of postwar recovery, rebuilding, and a "United Nations" to keep the peace forever.

Chris had been a child in knee pants, back in '44, devouring Chet Nimitz novels and praying that there would be something half as glorious to do in his adulthood as what his uncles were then achieving overseas. Maybe adventures in space! For after this, the horror of war would surely never be allowed again.

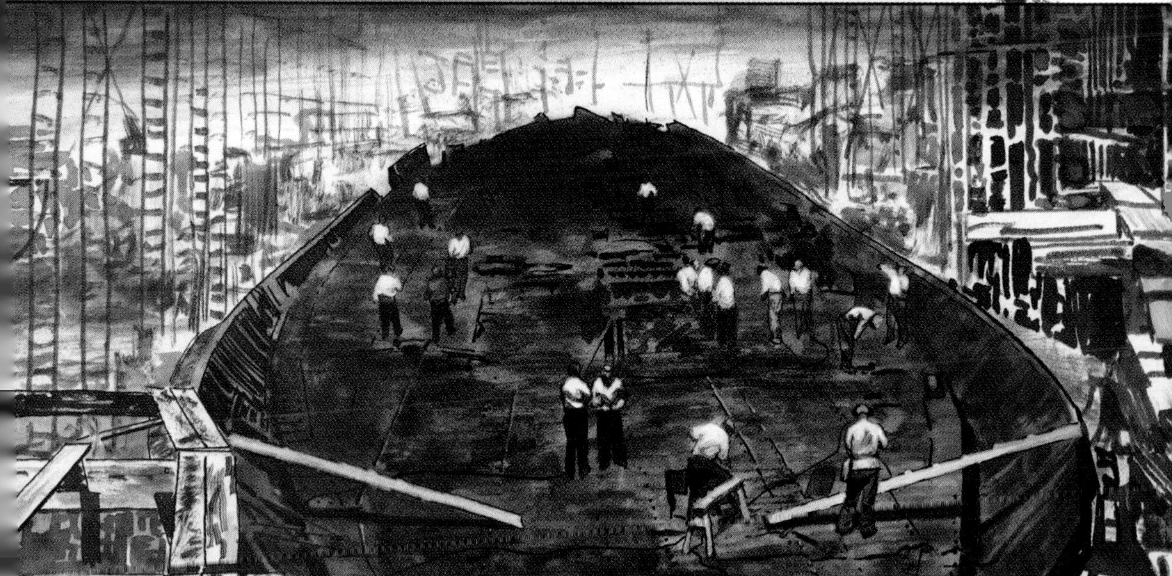

Then came rumors—tales of setbacks on the Eastern Front—of reeling Soviet armies sent into sudden and unexpected retreat. The reasons were unclear—mostly, what came back were superstitious rumblings, beyond belief.

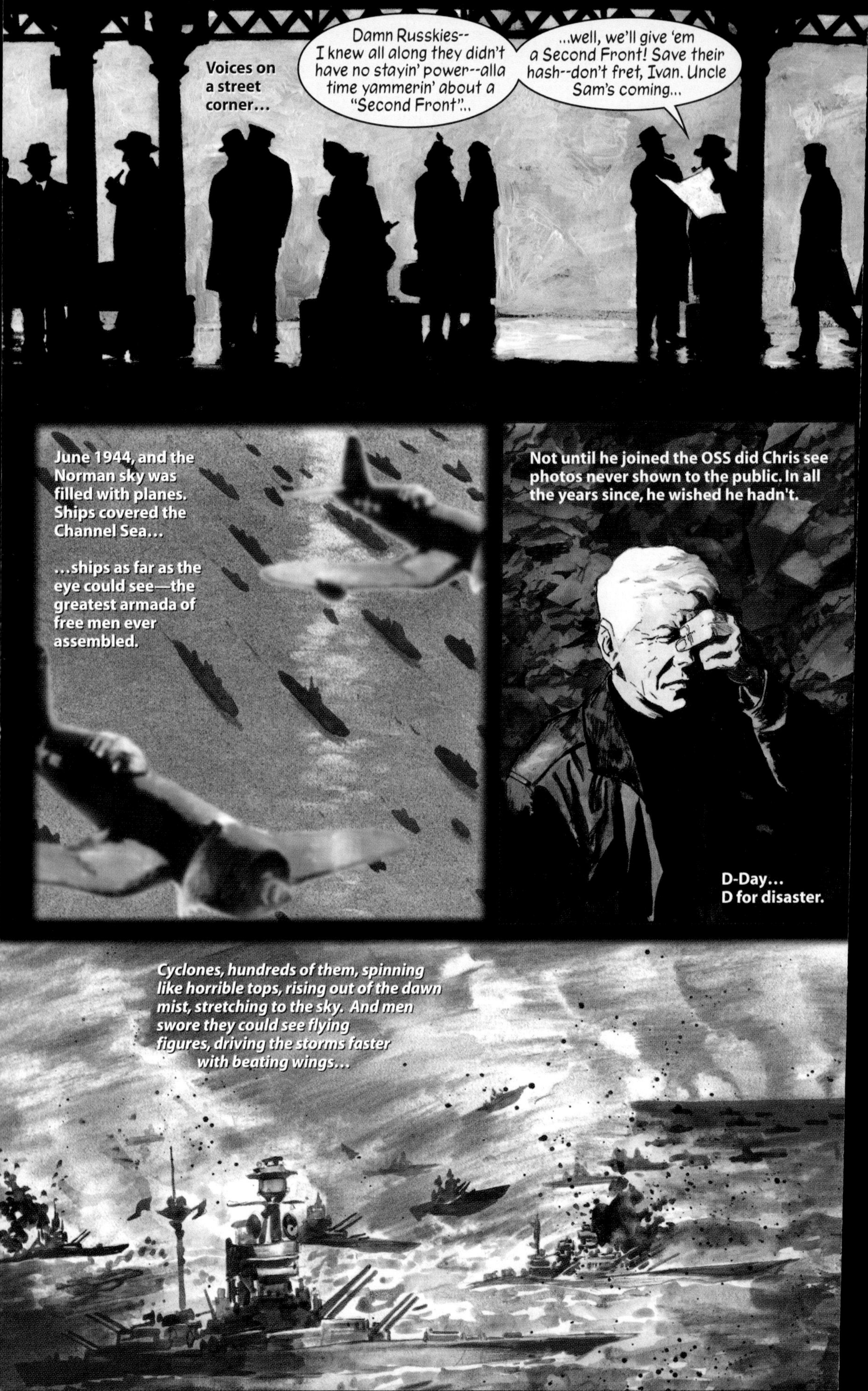
Voices on a street corner...
Damn Russkies-- I knew all along they didn't have no stayin' power--alla time yammerin' about a "Second Front"...
...well, we'll give 'em a Second Front! Save their hash--don't fret, Ivan. Uncle Sam's coming...
June 1944, and the Norman sky was filled with planes. Ships covered the Channel Sea...
...ships as far as the eye could see—the greatest armada of free men ever assembled.
Not until he joined the OSS did Chris see photos never shown to the public. In all the years since, he wished he hadn't.
D-Day... D for disaster.
Cyclones, hundreds of them, spinning like horrible tops, rising out of the dawn mist, stretching to the sky. And men swore they could see flying figures, driving the storms faster with beating wings...

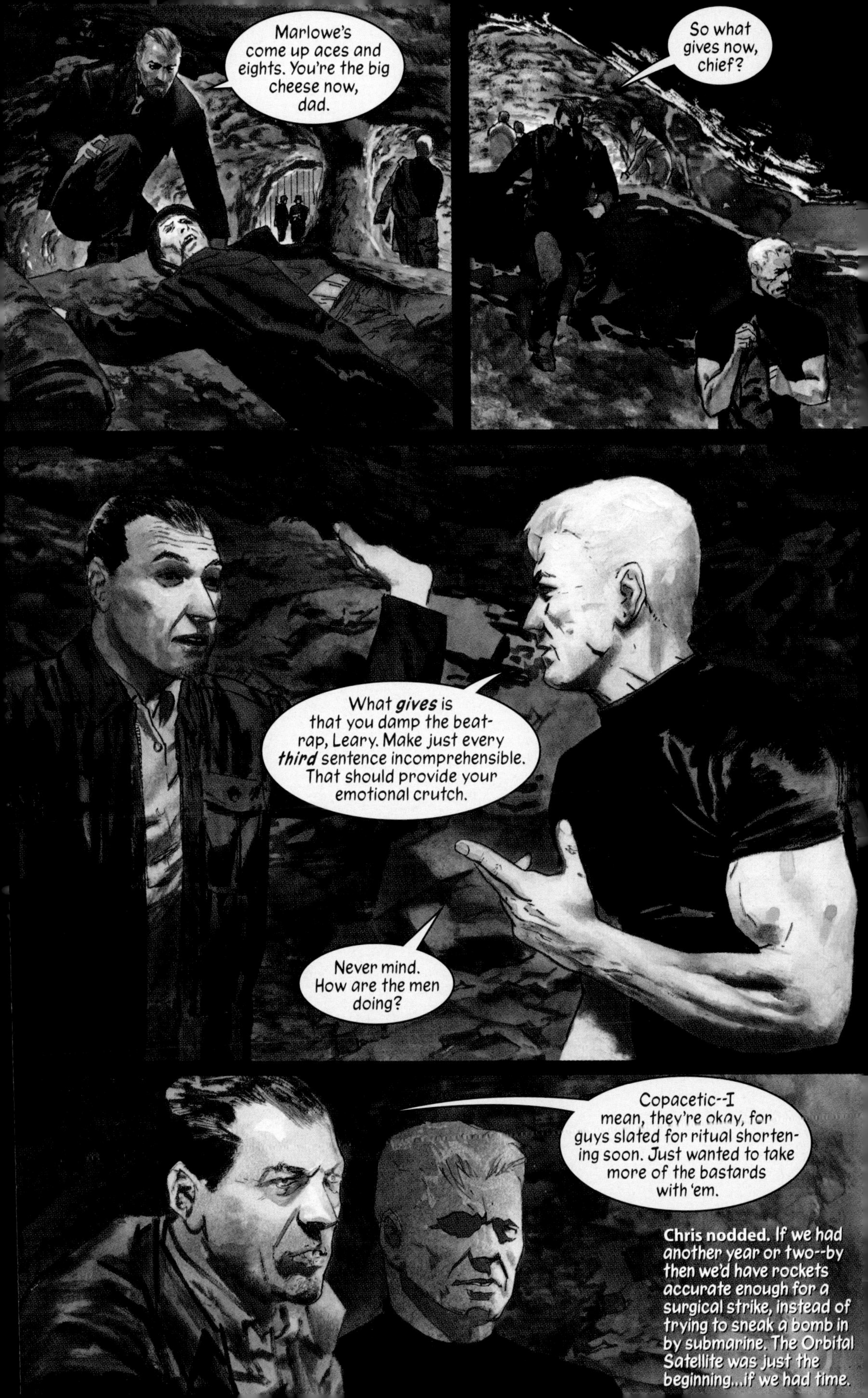
Marlowe's come up aces and eights. You're the big cheese now, dad.
So what gives now, chief?
What *gives* is that you damp the beat-rap, Leary. Make just every *third* sentence incomprehensible. That should provide your emotional crutch.
Never mind. How are the men doing?
Copacetic--I mean, they're okay, for guys slated for ritual shortening soon. Just wanted to take more of the bastards with 'em.
Chris nodded. If we had another year or two--by then we'd have rockets accurate enough for a surgical strike, instead of trying to sneak a bomb in by submarine. The Orbital Satellite was just the beginning...if we had time.

Higgins was right, man. We shoulda pasted them with everything we had. Melted Europe to slag, if that's what it took.

By the time we had enough bombs to do much, they had atomic weapons, too.

So? After we fried Peenemunde, their delivery systems stagnated. And they haven't got a clue how to go thermonuclear! Even if they did manage to disassemble the bomb we brought--

God forbid!

I scoped--I mean I checked the destruct triggers myself, Chris.

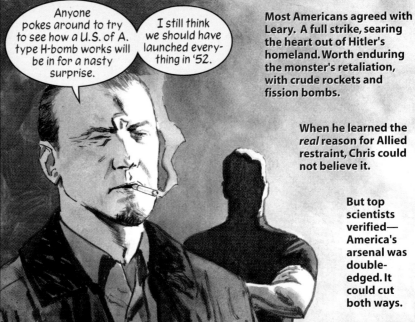

Anyone pokes around to try to see how a U.S. of A. type H-bomb works will be in for a nasty surprise.

I still think we should have launched everything in '52.

Most Americans agreed with Leary. A full strike, searing the heart out of Hitler's homeland. Worth enduring the monster's retaliation, with crude rockets and fission bombs.

When he learned the *real* reason for Allied restraint, Chris could not believe it.

But top scientists verified— America's arsenal was double-edged. It could cut both ways.

The great Thor would deign to speak vit' your leader.

This one. This strayed sheep. Our lord asked for him.

Cool as glass, daddy-o. Drive 'em crazy, baby.

You too, Leary. Stay...hip, man.

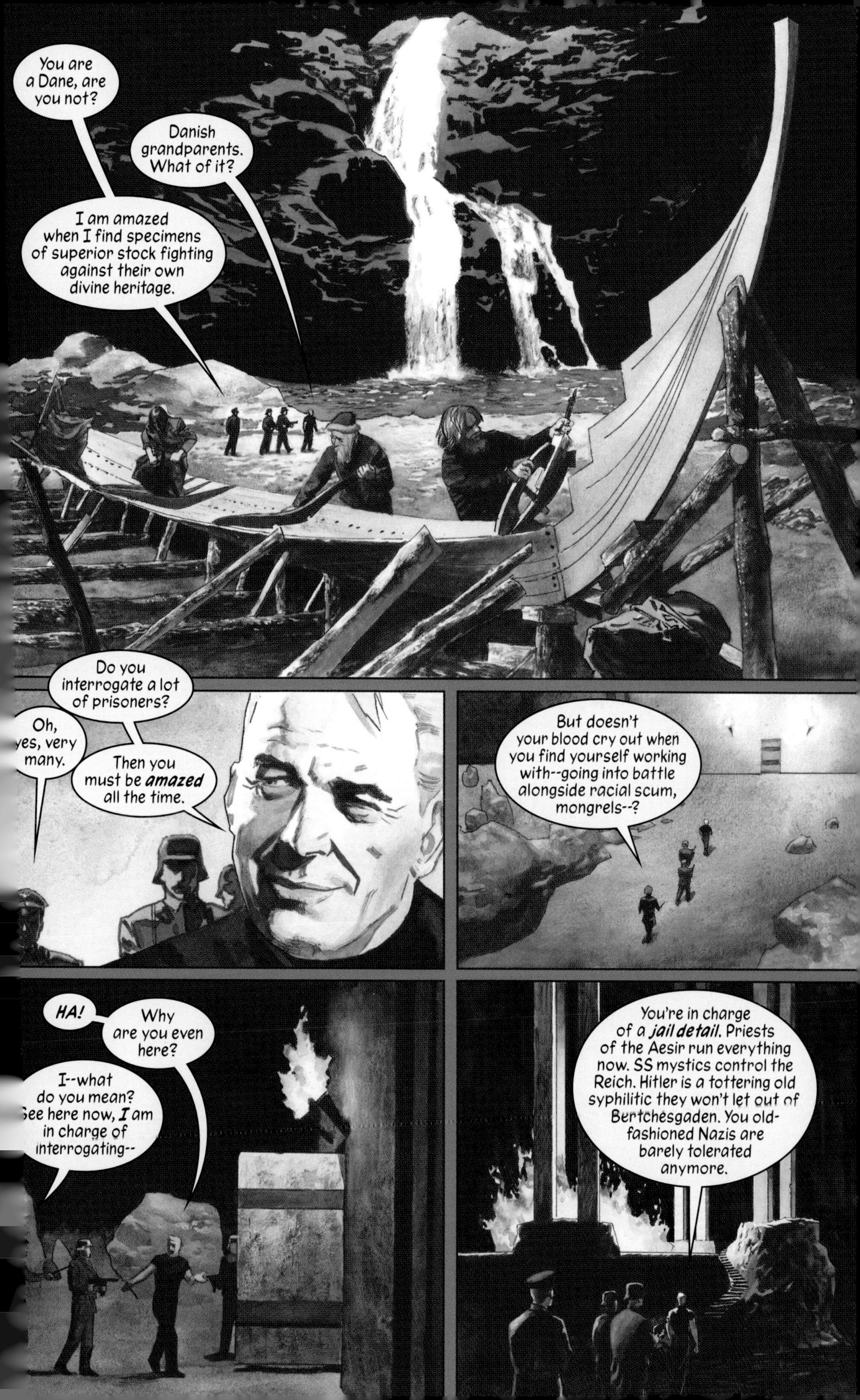
You are a Dane, are you not?
Danish grandparents. What of it?
I am amazed when I find specimens of superior stock fighting against their own divine heritage.
Do you interrogate a lot of prisoners?
Oh, yes, very many.
Then you must be *amazed* all the time.
But doesn't your blood cry out when you find yourself working with--going into battle alongside racial scum, mongrels--?
HA!
Why are you even here?
I--what do you mean? See here now, *I* am in charge of interrogating--
You're in charge of a *jail detail*. Priests of the Aesir run everything now. SS mystics control the Reich. Hitler is a tottering old syphilitic they won't let out of Bertchesgaden. You old-fashioned Nazis are barely tolerated anymore.

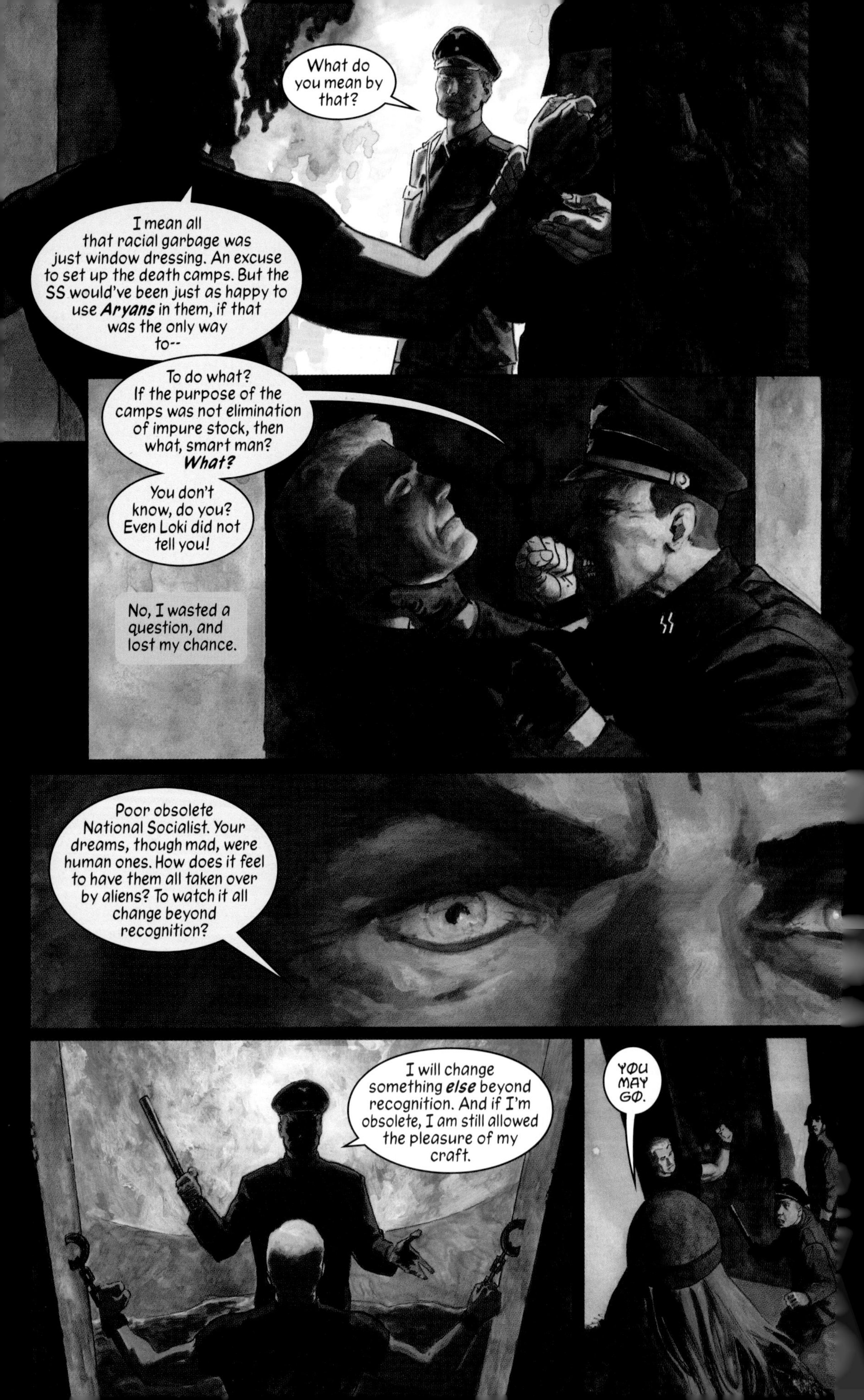
What do you mean by that?
I mean all that racial garbage was just window dressing. An excuse to set up the death camps. But the SS would've been just as happy to use **Aryans** in them, if that was the only way to--
To do what? If the purpose of the camps was not elimination of impure stock, then what, smart man? **What?**
You don't know, do you? Even Loki did not tell you!
No, I wasted a question, and lost my chance.
Poor obsolete National Socialist. Your dreams, though mad, were human ones. How does it feel to have them all taken over by aliens? To watch it all change beyond recognition?
I will change something **else** beyond recognition. And if I'm obsolete, I am still allowed the pleasure of my craft.
YOU MAY GO.

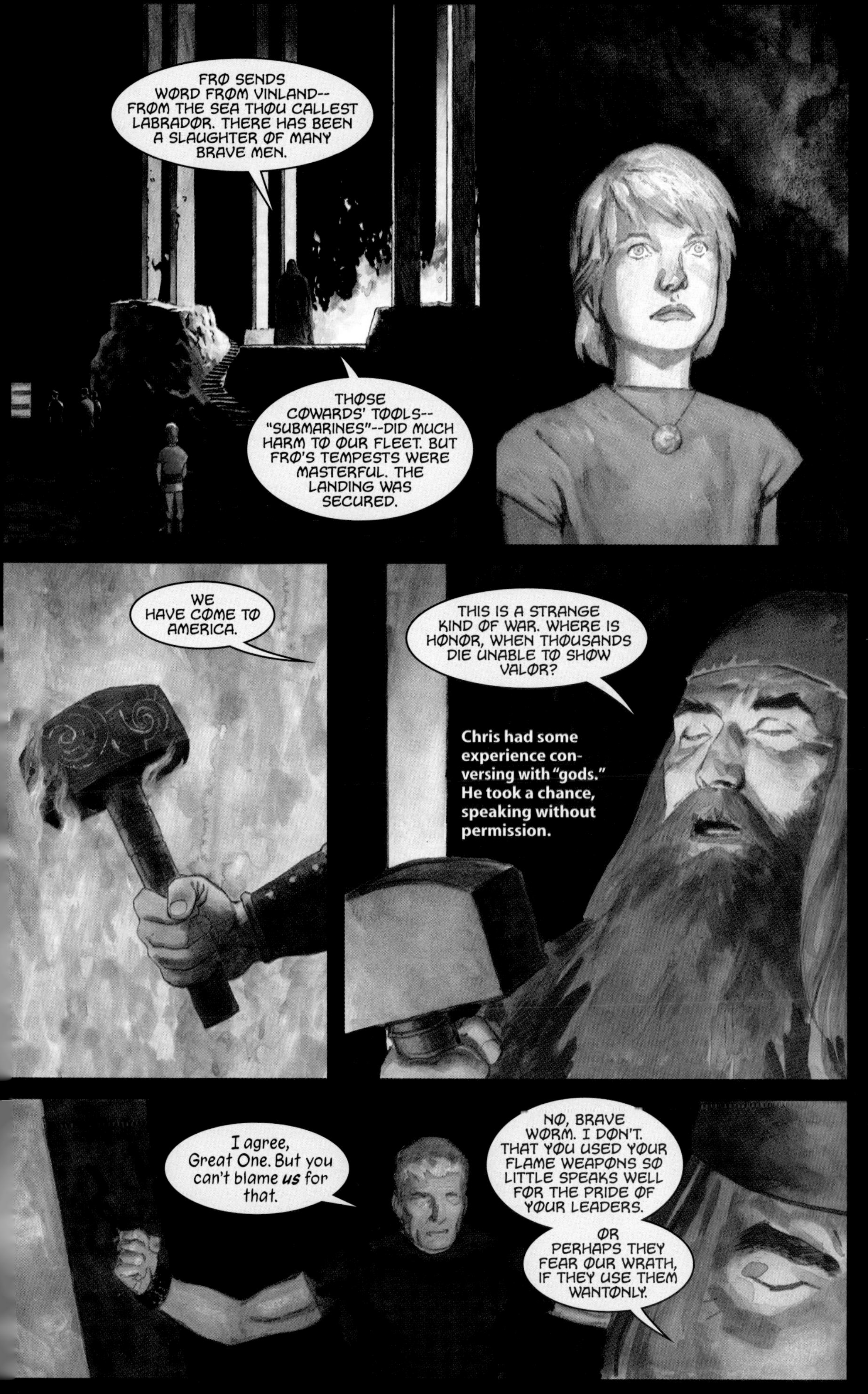
FRØ SENDS WØRD FRØM VINLAND-- FRØM THE SEA THØU CALLEST LABRADØR. THERE HAS BEEN A SLAUGHTER ØF MANY BRAVE MEN.
THØSE CØWARDS' TØØLS-- "SUBMARINES"--DID MUCH HARM TØ ØUR FLEET. BUT FRØ'S TEMPESTS WERE MASTERFUL. THE LANDING WAS SECURED.
WE HAVE CØME TØ AMERICA.
THIS IS A STRANGE KIND ØF WAR. WHERE IS HØNØR, WHEN THØUSANDS DIE UNABLE TØ SHØW VALØR?
Chris had some experience conversing with "gods." He took a chance, speaking without permission.
I agree, Great One. But you can't blame *us* for that.
NØ, BRAVE WØRM. I DØN'T. THAT YØU USED YØUR FLAME WEAPØNS SØ LITTLE SPEAKS WELL FØR THE PRIDE ØF YØUR LEADERS.
ØR PERHAPS THEY FEAR ØUR WRATH, IF THEY USE THEM WANTØNLY.

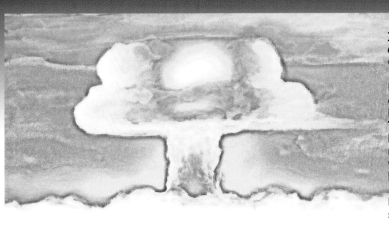

I never should have been allowed on this mission. I know too much, Chris realized.

Loki had been the one to overrule High Command and insist that Chris come along. That made him the only one here who knew the secret reason—the real reason—why the H-bombs were kept leashed.

Dust from atom blasts, and soot from burning cities. Allied Command feared those more than radiation or Nazi retaliation.

We too prefer a more personal approach. No man wishes to be killed by powers beyond his understanding, impossible to resist.

HA! WELL SAID. THOU DOST CHASTIZE LIKE FREYR--WORDS THAT REAP, AS THEY SOW.

BUT NOW, SPEAK TO ME OF LOKI.

YOU WILL EARN MERIT, SMALL ONE, IF YOU TELL ME HOW TO FIND THE BROTHER OF LIES.

Those gray eyes were like ice. Reality wavered as Chris looked into them.

With all his will, he tore his gaze away, shutting his eyes.

Chris spoke with a dry mouth.

I--don't know what you're talking about.

LOKI, YOUNGLING. SAY WHERE THE TRICKSTER CAN BE FOUND, AND YOU MAY ESCAPE YOUR DOOM. IN THE COMING WORLD, THERE WILL BE NO GREATER PLACE FOR A MAN THAN BY MY SIDE.

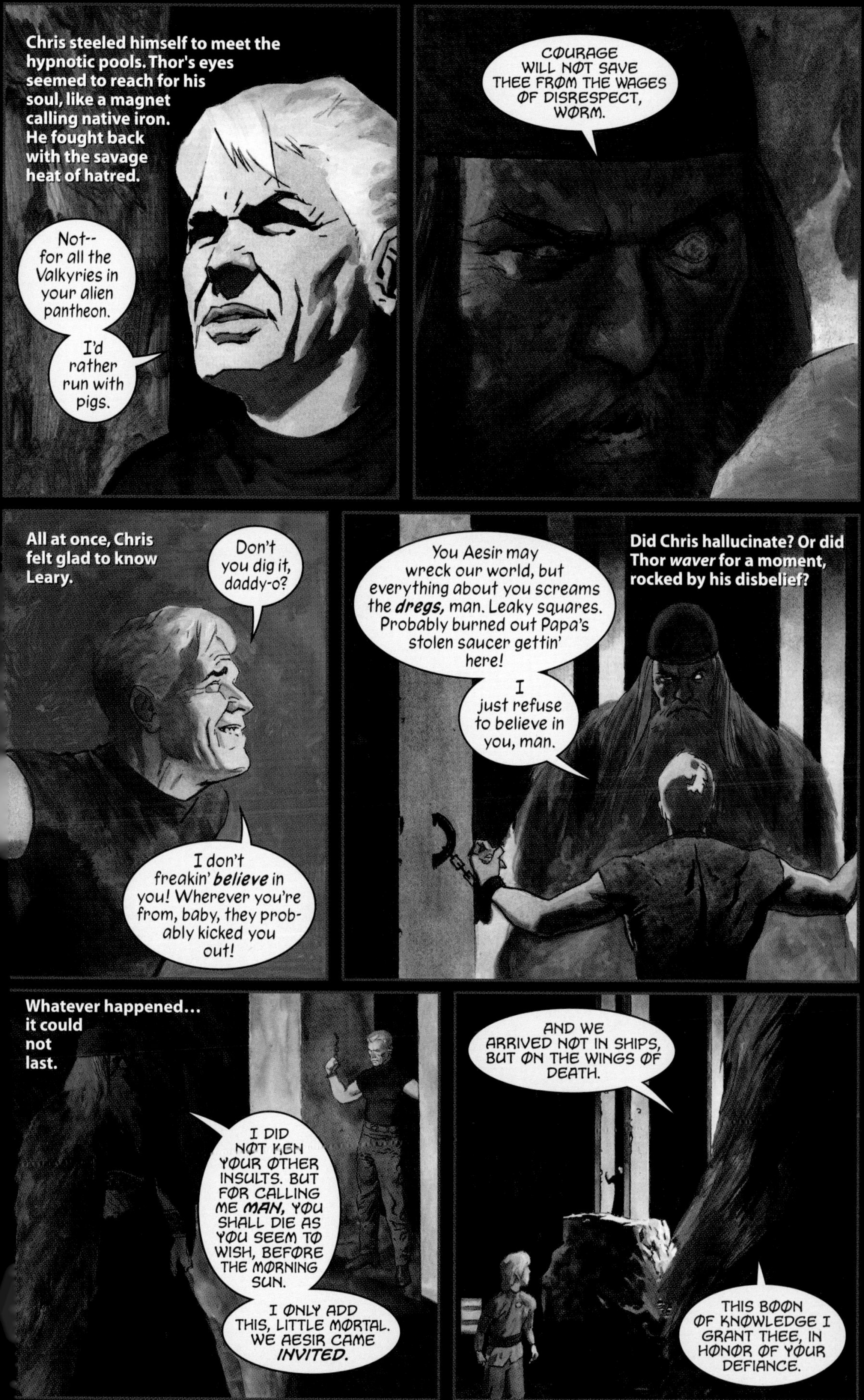

Chris steeled himself to meet the hypnotic pools. Thor's eyes seemed to reach for his soul, like a magnet calling native iron. He fought back with the savage heat of hatred.
Not--for all the Valkyries in your alien pantheon.
I'd rather run with pigs.
COURAGE WILL NOT SAVE THEE FROM THE WAGES OF DISRESPECT, WORM.
All at once, Chris felt glad to know Leary.
Don't you dig it, daddy-o?
I don't freakin' *believe* in you! Wherever you're from, baby, they probably kicked you out!
Did Chris hallucinate? Or did Thor *waver* for a moment, rocked by his disbelief?
You Aesir may wreck our world, but everything about you screams the *dregs,* man. Leaky squares. Probably burned out Papa's stolen saucer gettin' here!
I just refuse to believe in you, man.
Whatever happened… it could not last.
I DID NOT KEN YOUR OTHER INSULTS. BUT FOR CALLING ME *MAN,* YOU SHALL DIE AS YOU SEEM TO WISH, BEFORE THE MORNING SUN.
I ONLY ADD THIS, LITTLE MORTAL. WE AESIR CAME *INVITED.*
AND WE ARRIVED NOT IN SHIPS, BUT ON THE WINGS OF DEATH.
THIS BOON OF KNOWLEDGE I GRANT THEE, IN HONOR OF YOUR DEFIANCE.

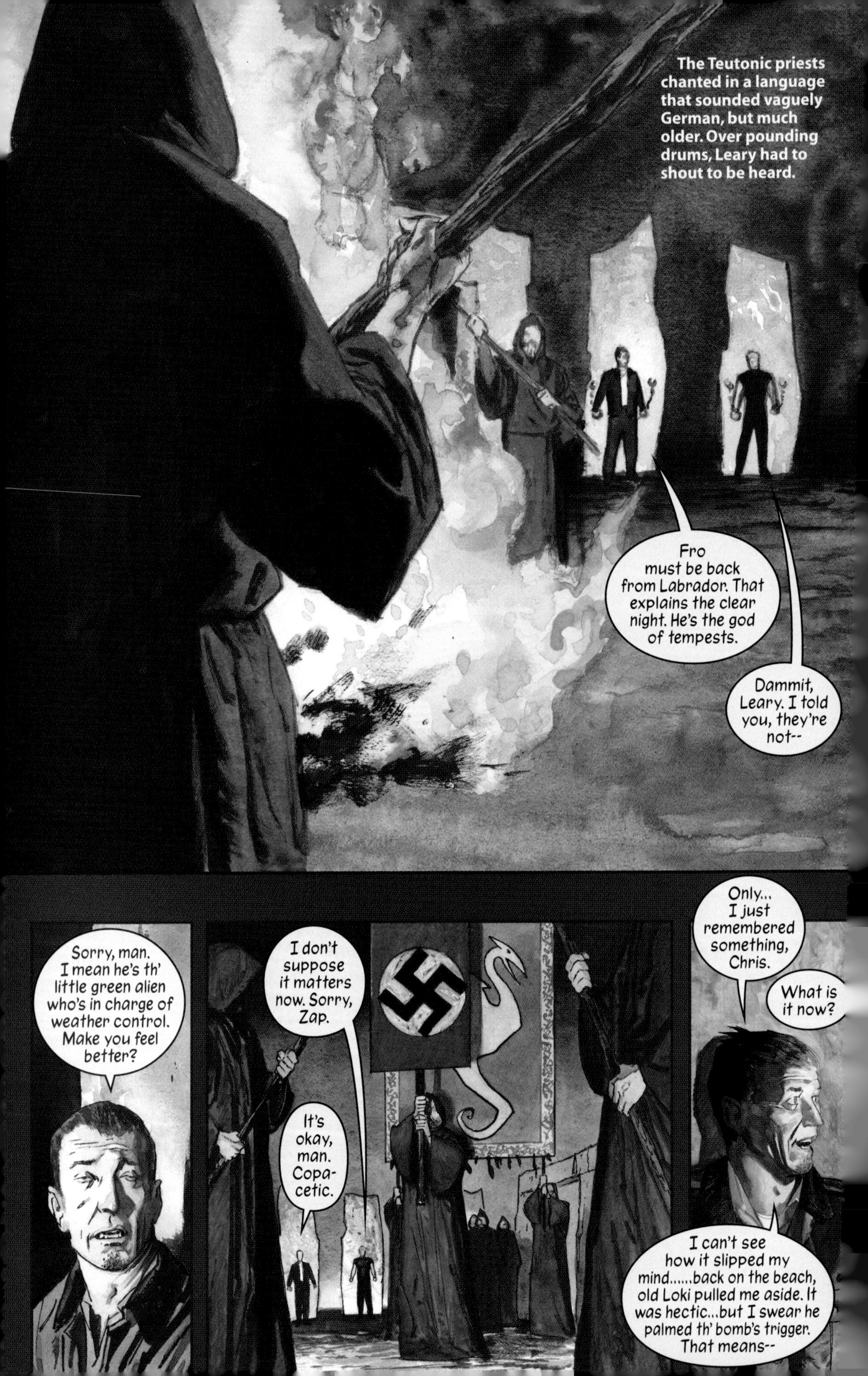

The Teutonic priests chanted in a language that sounded vaguely German, but much older. Over pounding drums, Leary had to shout to be heard.
Fro must be back from Labrador. That explains the clear night. He's the god of tempests.
Dammit, Leary. I told you, they're not--
Sorry, man. I mean he's th' little green alien who's in charge of weather control. Make you feel better?
I don't suppose it matters now. Sorry, Zap.
It's okay, man. Copa-cetic.
Only... I just remembered something, Chris.
What is it now?
I can't see how it slipped my mind......back on the beach, old Loki pulled me aside. It was hectic...but I swear he palmed th' bomb's trigger. That means--

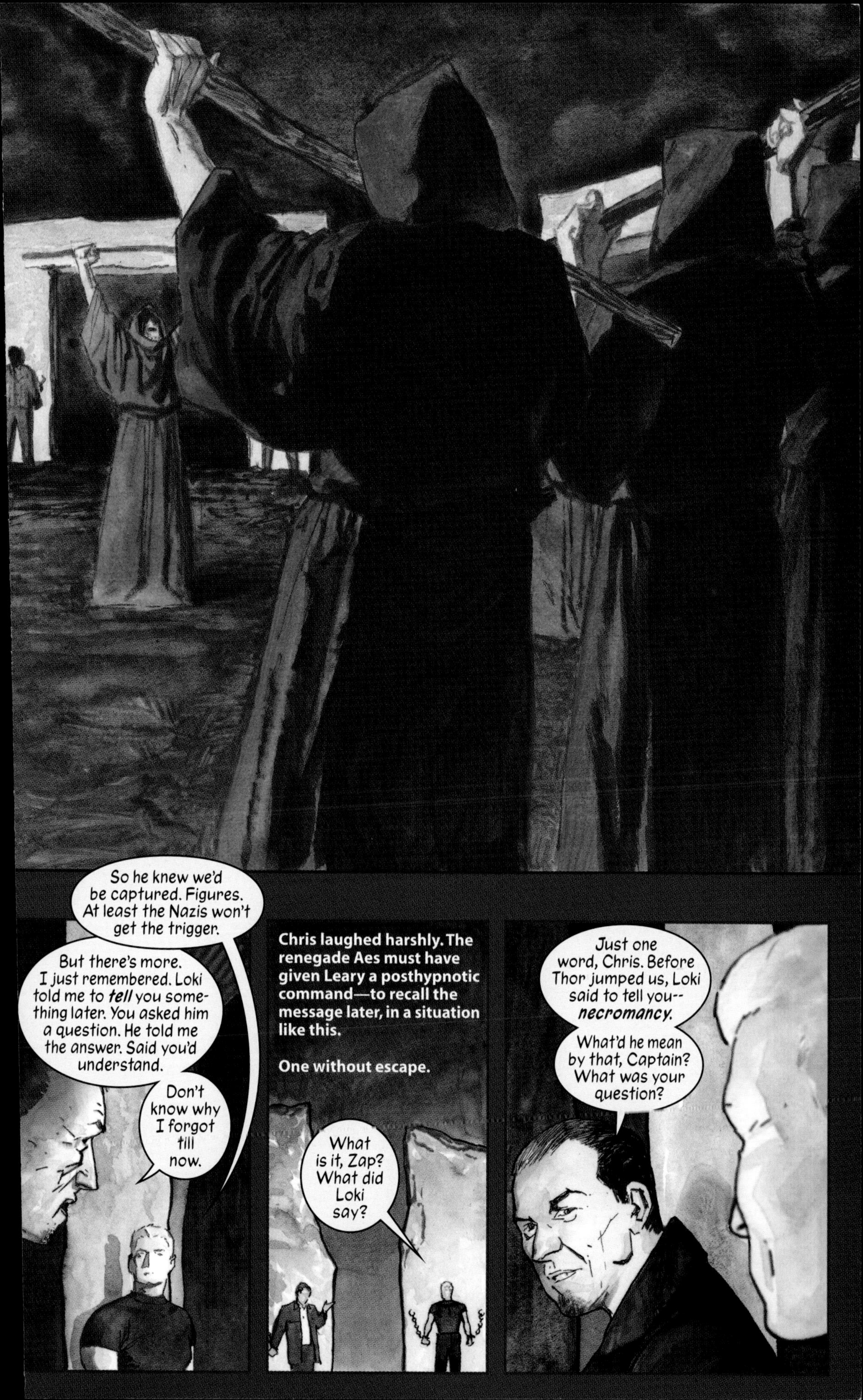
So he knew we'd be captured. Figures. At least the Nazis won't get the trigger.
But there's more. I just remembered. Loki told me to *tell* you something later. You asked him a question. He told me the answer. Said you'd understand.
Don't know why I forgot till now.
Chris laughed harshly. The renegade Aes must have given Leary a posthypnotic command—to recall the message later, in a situation like this.
One without escape.
What is it, Zap? What did Loki say?
Just one word, Chris. Before Thor jumped us, Loki said to tell you-- *necromancy*.
What'd he mean by that, Captain? What was your question?

Chris stared at a funnel of sparks climbing toward the Moon.

With his last question he had asked Loki about the camps—about the awesome, horrible, concentrated effort of death that had been perpetrated, first in Europe, then Russia and Africa. What were they *for*? So systematic. Industrialized. There had to be more to it than eliminating bothersome minorities.

Moreover, why had Loki, who normally seemed oblivious to human life, acted to rescue so many from the death factories, at great risk to himself?

Necromancy. That was Loki's delayed reply, told in such a way that Chris might have his answer, but never tell anyone who mattered...

Necromancy—

The word stood for the performance of magic, but magic of a special, terrible kind. In legend, a necromancer used the death agony of human beings to drive his spells. A majority of old human cultures had dabbled in the notion, some of them passionately.

But that was superstitious nonsense!

Wasn't it?

Light-headed under the persistent chanting, Chris looked across the sand at the hulking Aesir, seated on their gilded thrones, wishing he could dismiss the idea.

Was *that* why the Nazis had dared to wage such a war? Because they believed they could *industrialize* magic? Perform human sacrifice in vast, controlled batches? Create such distilled horror that the ancient spells would actually work?

It explained so much. Across history, other nations had gone insane. Other movements had been evil or tried awful wizardries. But none perpetrated murder with such dedicated efficiency. The horror must have been directed not so much at death itself, but at some hideous goal *beyond* death!

Chris murmured half-aloud, in shock.

"They...*made*...the Aesir! That's what Loki meant when he said his own memories might be false--that he might be no older than I am..."

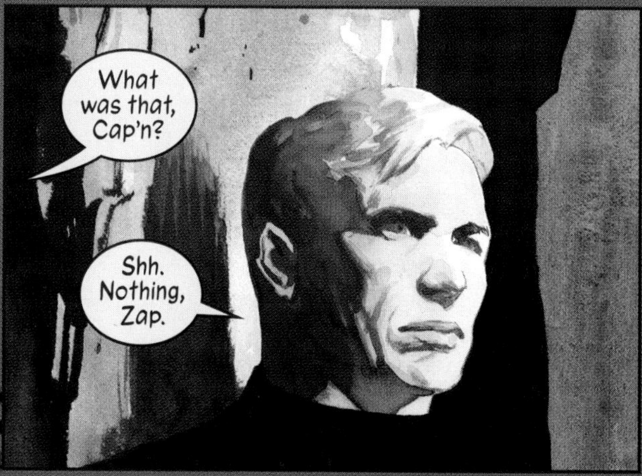
What was that, Cap'n?
Shh. Nothing, Zap.

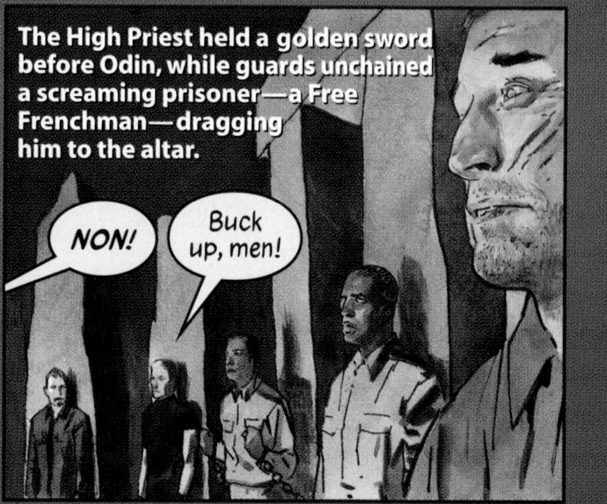
The High Priest held a golden sword before Odin, while guards unchained a screaming prisoner—a Free Frenchman—dragging him to the altar.
NON!
Buck up, men!

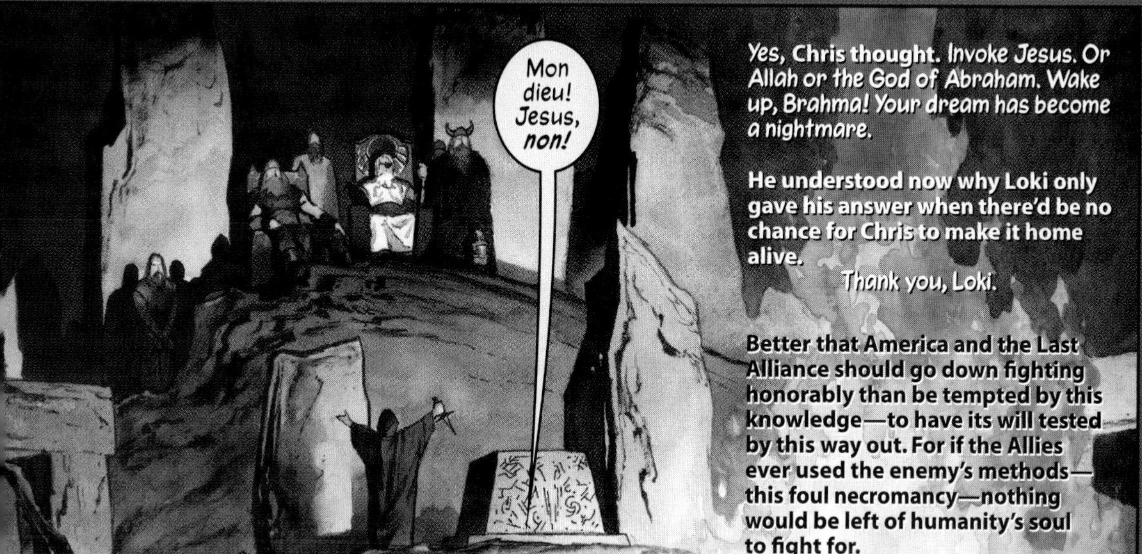
Mon dieu! Jesus, non!
Yes, Chris thought. Invoke Jesus. Or Allah or the God of Abraham. Wake up, Brahma! Your dream has become a nightmare.
He understood now why Loki only gave his answer when there'd be no chance for Chris to make it home alive.
Thank you, Loki.
Better that America and the Last Alliance should go down fighting honorably than be tempted by this knowledge—to have its will tested by this way out. For if the Allies ever used the enemy's methods—this foul necromancy—nothing would be left of humanity's soul to fight for.

Vho would we Americans conjure, Chris wondered, we used those spells? Superman? Captain Marvel?)h, they'd be more than a match for the Aesir! Our ıyths were boundless.

le laughed, and the sound turned into a sob as nother scream of agony pierced the night.

hank you, Loki, for sparing us that test of our souls.

e had no idea where the renegade "trickster god" ent, or if this debacle was only a cloak for some eeper, more secret mission. Could that be? Chris ondered. President Marshall wouldn't tell an OSS aptain everything. This mission could be a feint, minor piece in a greater plan.

ısers and satellites--they could be just part of it. ıere may be a silver bullet--a thorn of mistletoe, ll.

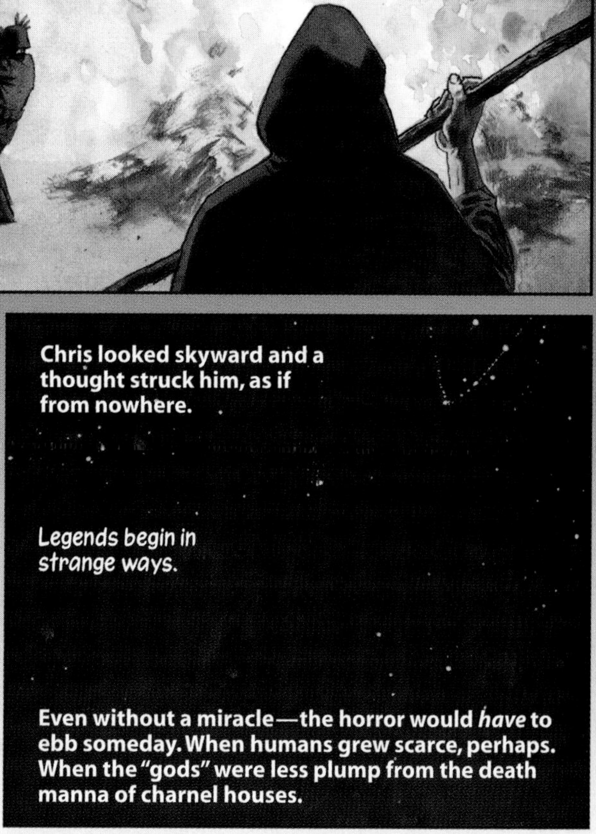
Chris looked skyward and a thought struck him, as if from nowhere.
Legends begin in strange ways.
Even without a miracle—the horror would have to ebb someday. When humans grew scarce, perhaps. When the "gods" were less plump from the death manna of charnel houses.

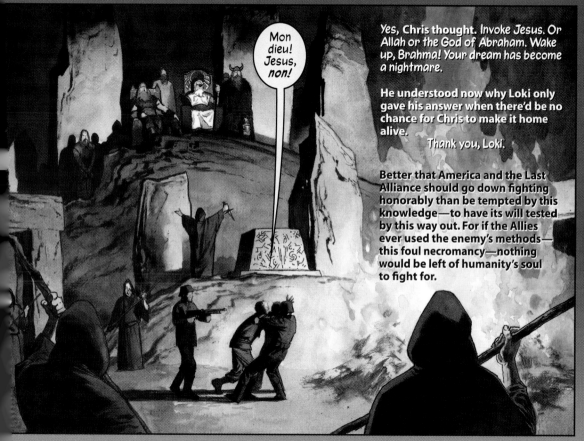

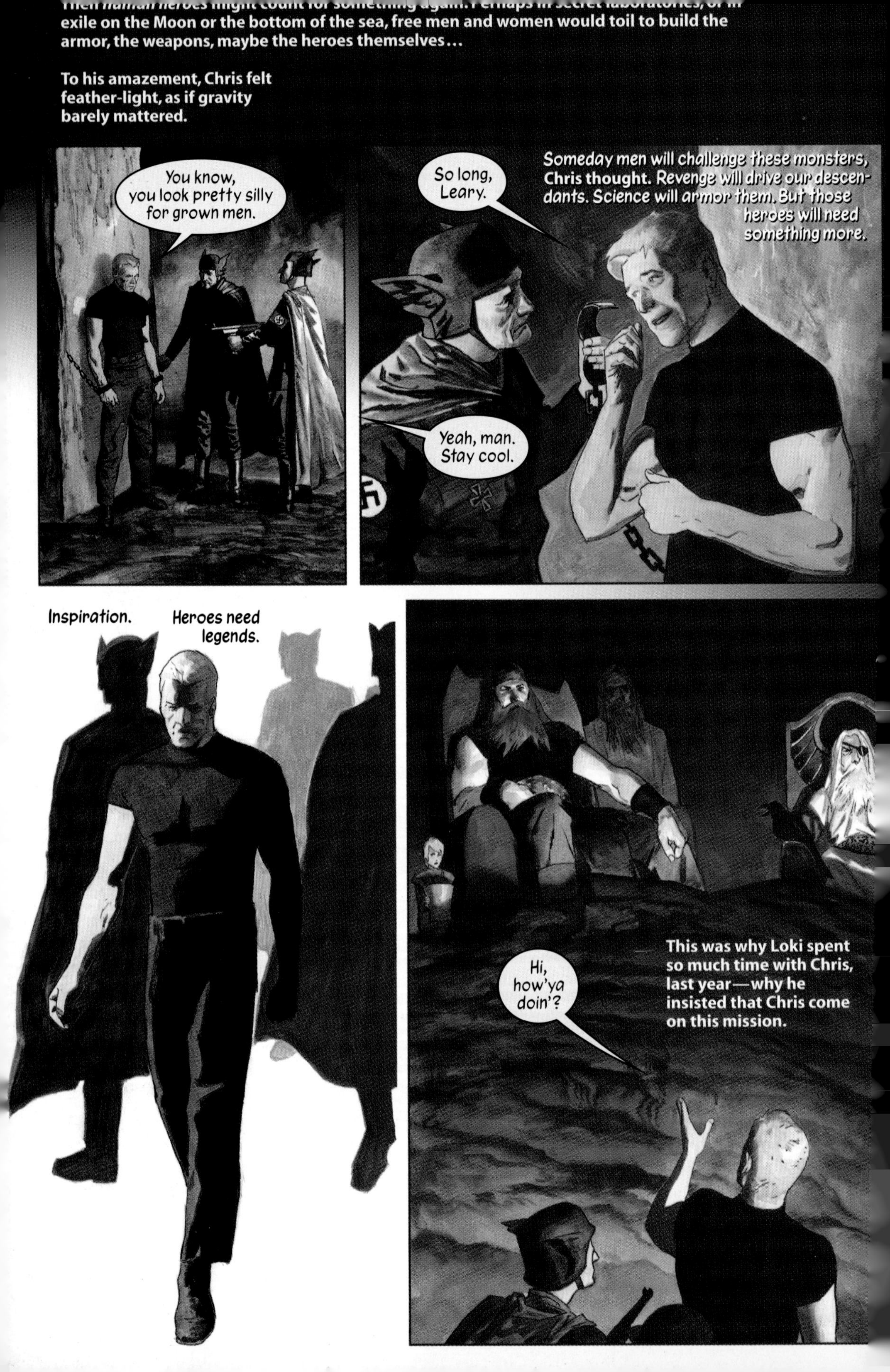
Then human heroes might count for something again. Perhaps in secret laboratories, or in exile on the Moon or the bottom of the sea, free men and women would toil to build the armor, the weapons, maybe the heroes themselves…
To his amazement, Chris felt feather-light, as if gravity barely mattered.
You know, you look pretty silly for grown men.
So long, Leary.
Someday men will challenge these monsters, Chris thought. Revenge will drive our descendants. Science will armor them. But those heroes will need something more.
Yeah, man. Stay cool.
Inspiration.
Heroes need legends.
Hi, how'ya doin'?
This was why Loki spent so much time with Chris, last year—why he insisted that Chris come on this mission.

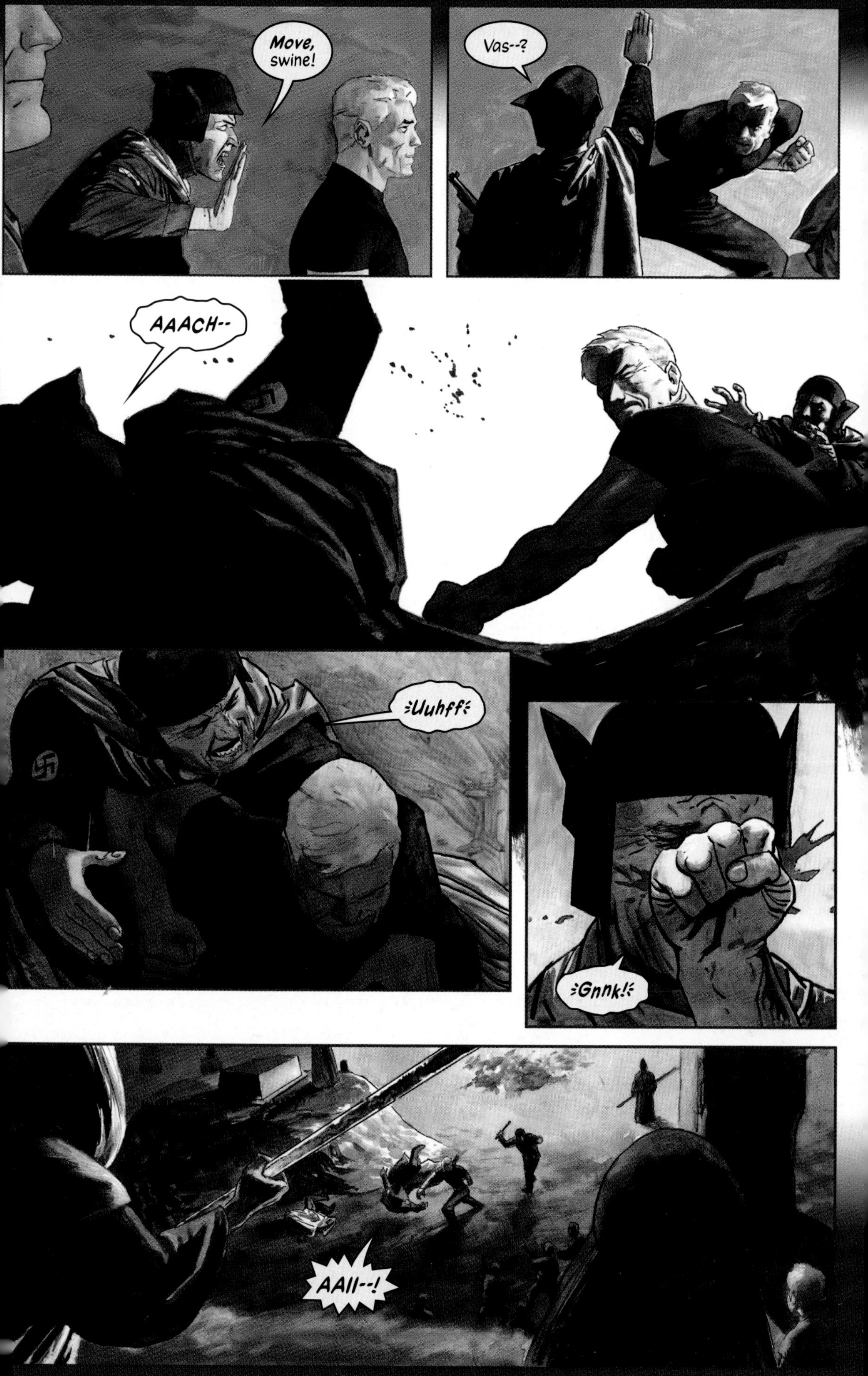
Move, swine!
Vas--?
AAACH--
Uuhff
Gnnk!
AAII--!

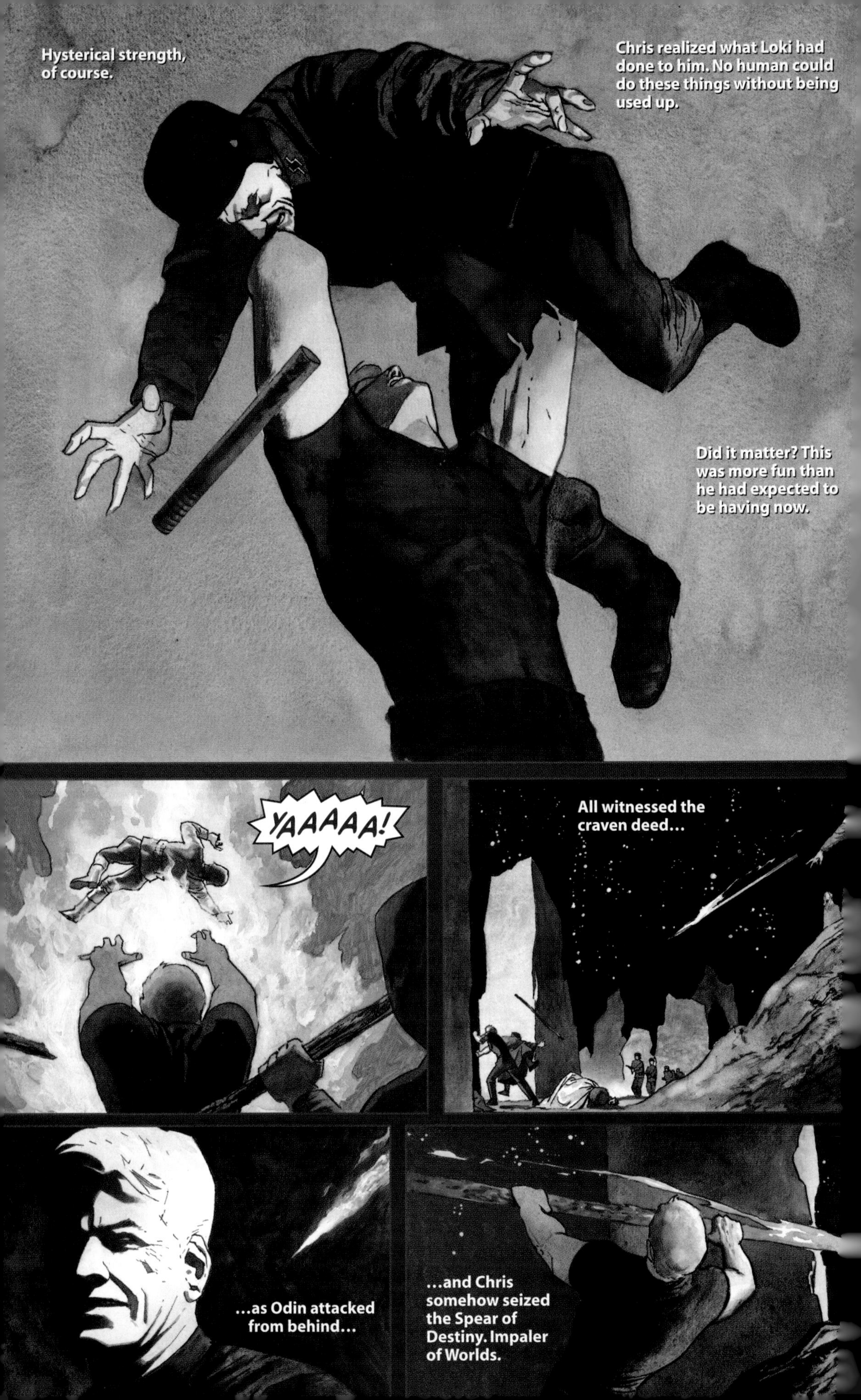
Hysterical strength, of course.
Chris realized what Loki had done to him. No human could do these things without being used up.
Did it matter? This was more fun than he had expected to be having now.
YAAAAA!
All witnessed the craven deed…
…as Odin attacked from behind…
…and Chris somehow seized the Spear of Destiny. Impaler of Worlds.

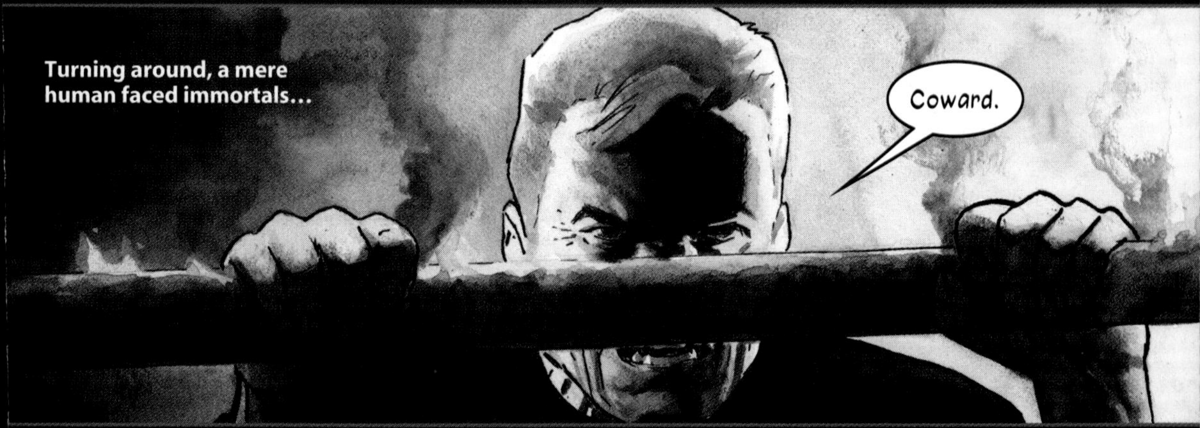
Turning around, a mere human faced immortals…
Coward.

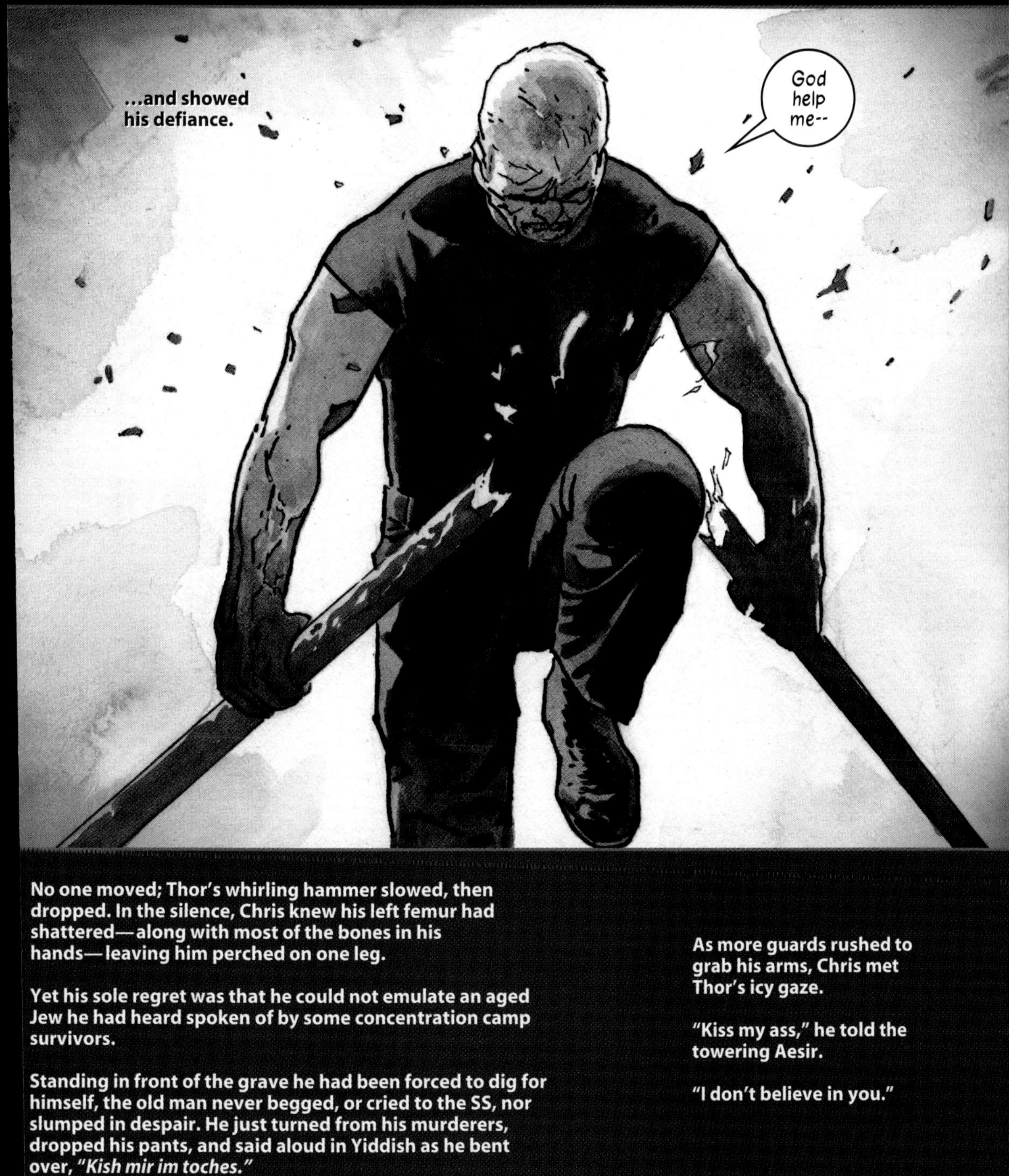
…and showed his defiance.
God help me--

No one moved; Thor's whirling hammer slowed, then dropped. In the silence, Chris knew his left femur had shattered—along with most of the bones in his hands—leaving him perched on one leg.

Yet his sole regret was that he could not emulate an aged Jew he had heard spoken of by some concentration camp survivors.

Standing in front of the grave he had been forced to dig for himself, the old man never begged, or cried to the SS, nor slumped in despair. He just turned from his murderers, dropped his pants, and said aloud in Yiddish as he bent over, *"Kish mir im toches."*

As more guards rushed to grab his arms, Chris met Thor's icy gaze.

"Kiss my ass," he told the towering Aesir.

"I don't believe in you."

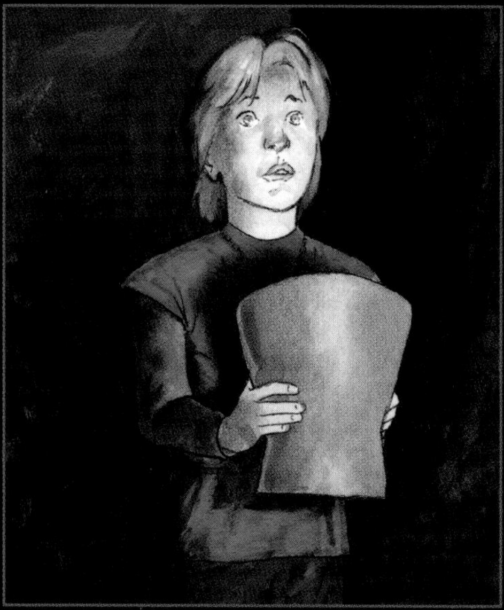

Quaking with fear, the Nordic Priests bound Chris to the altar. All that time he kept his gaze on Thor.

Then we all saw IT happen. Something mortals would remember.

Thor blinked first. The giant shivered… and looked away.

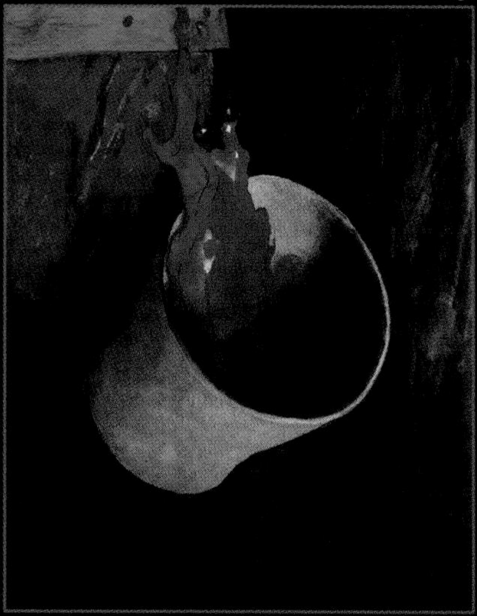

Chris laughed out loud then, knowing that nothing in the world could stop this story.

Loki, you bastard. You used me, and I guess I should thank you.

But rest assured, Loki, someday we'll get you, too.

He laughed again as the dismayed High Priest fumbled the knife. A trembling acolyte dropped his swastika banner and Chris roared.

Then came Leary's high-pitched giggle. Another prisoner barked a hoarse guffaw, and another.

Across the chilly Baltic, where all had been still, an uncertain wind now rose, unbidden, blowing from the West.

And overhead, a swift new glimmer sailed, where older stars merely drifted across the sky.

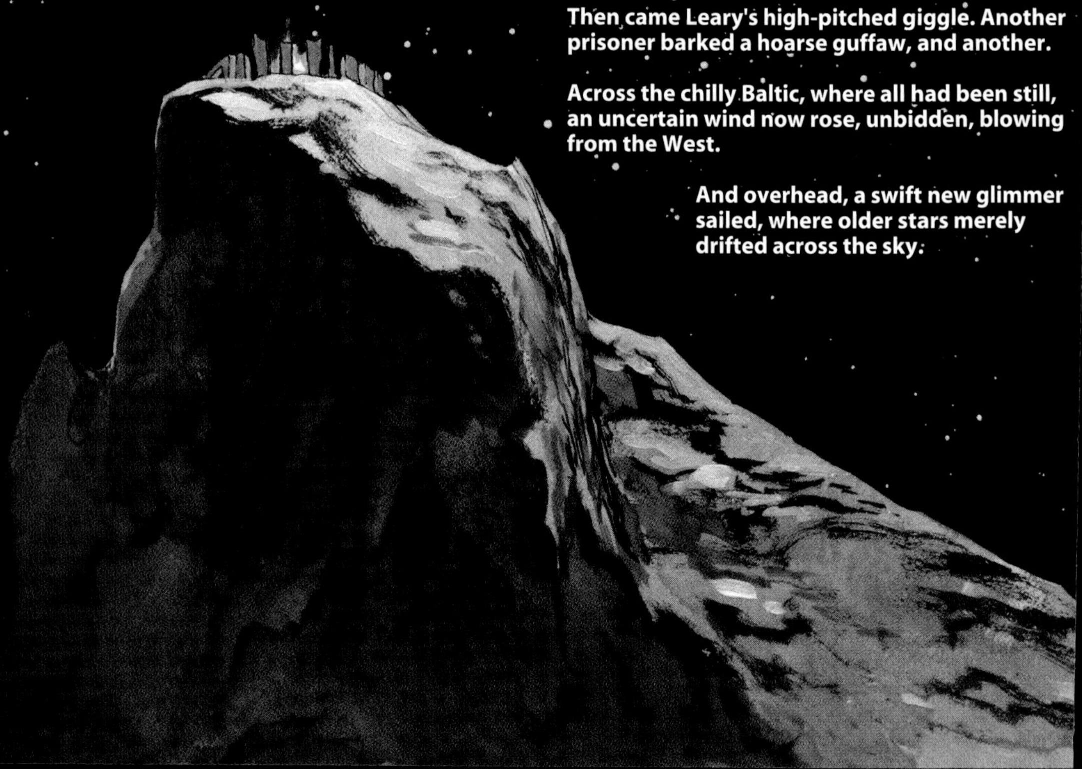

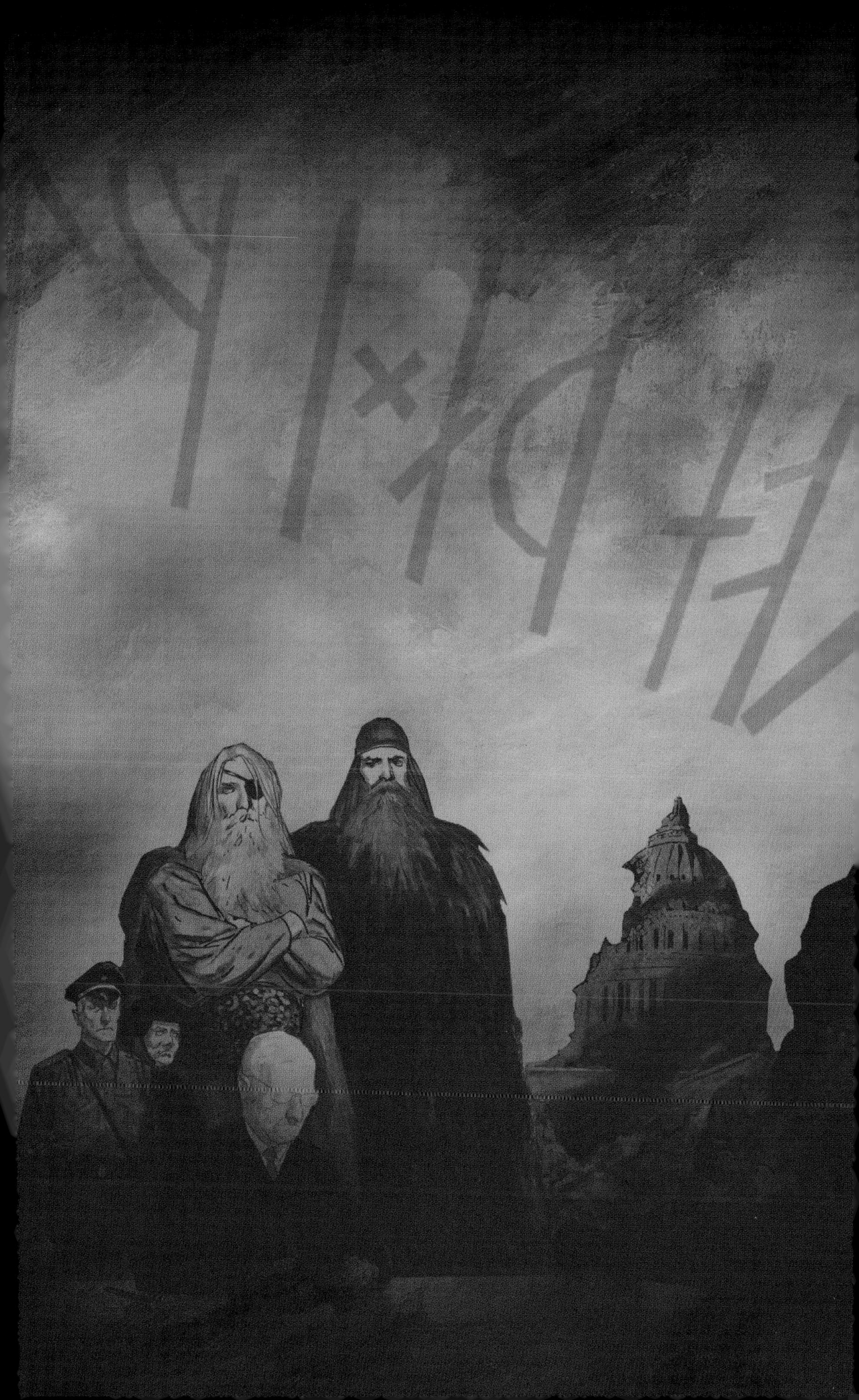

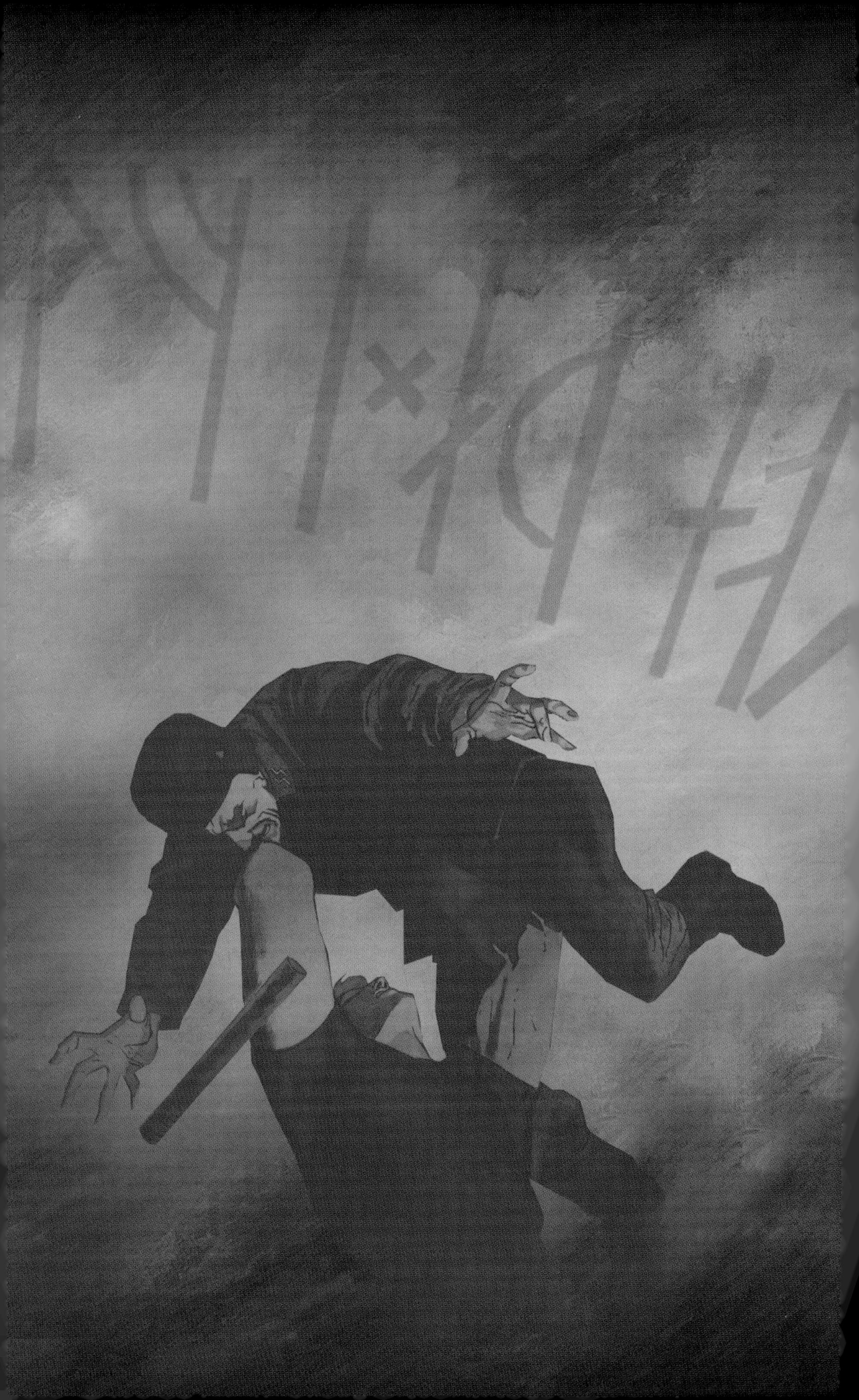

— PART TWO —

"WEATHERMEN"

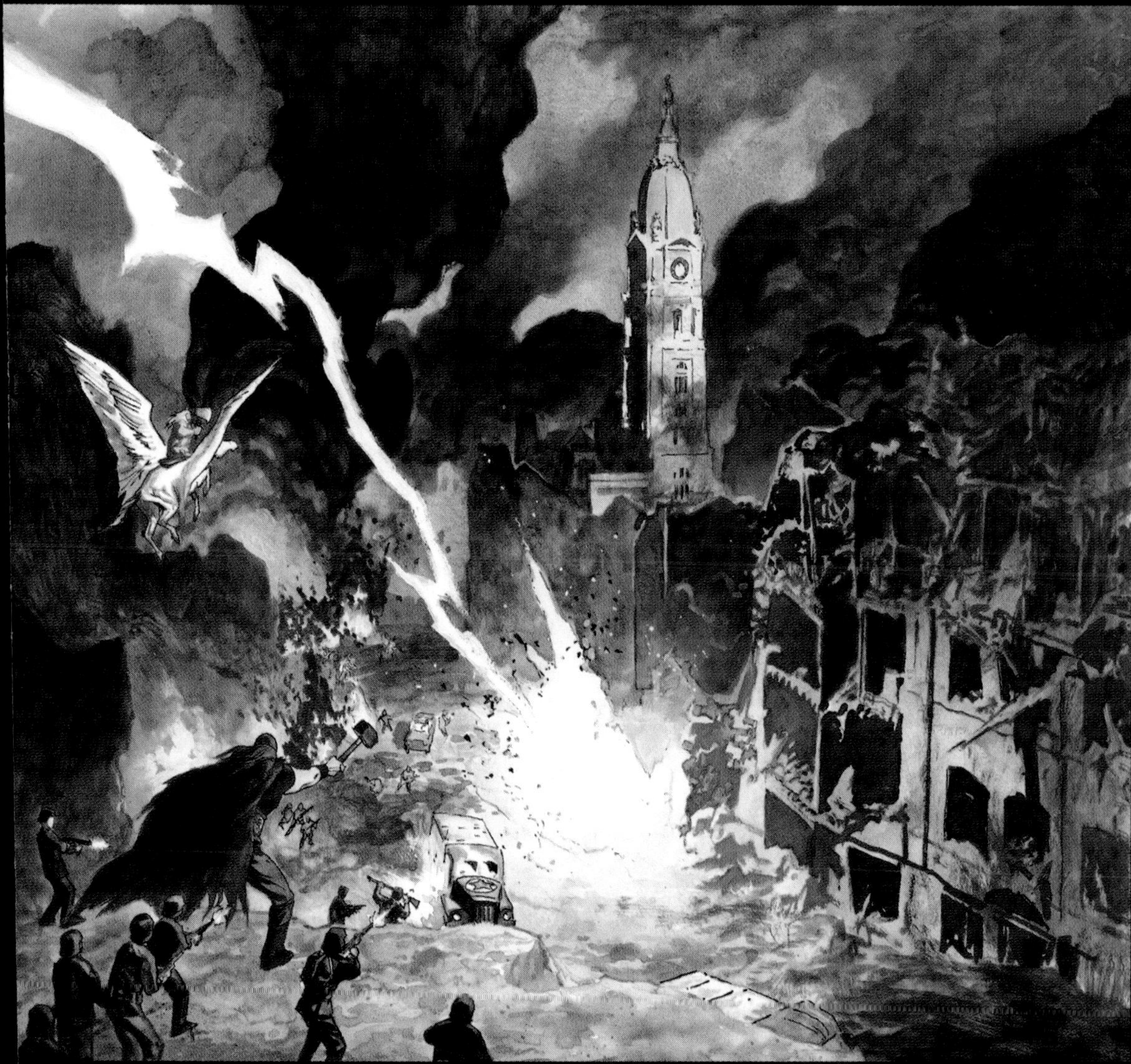

Was this a face to be oppos'd
against the warring winds?
To stand against the deep
dread-bolted thunder?

—William Shakespeare,
King Lear

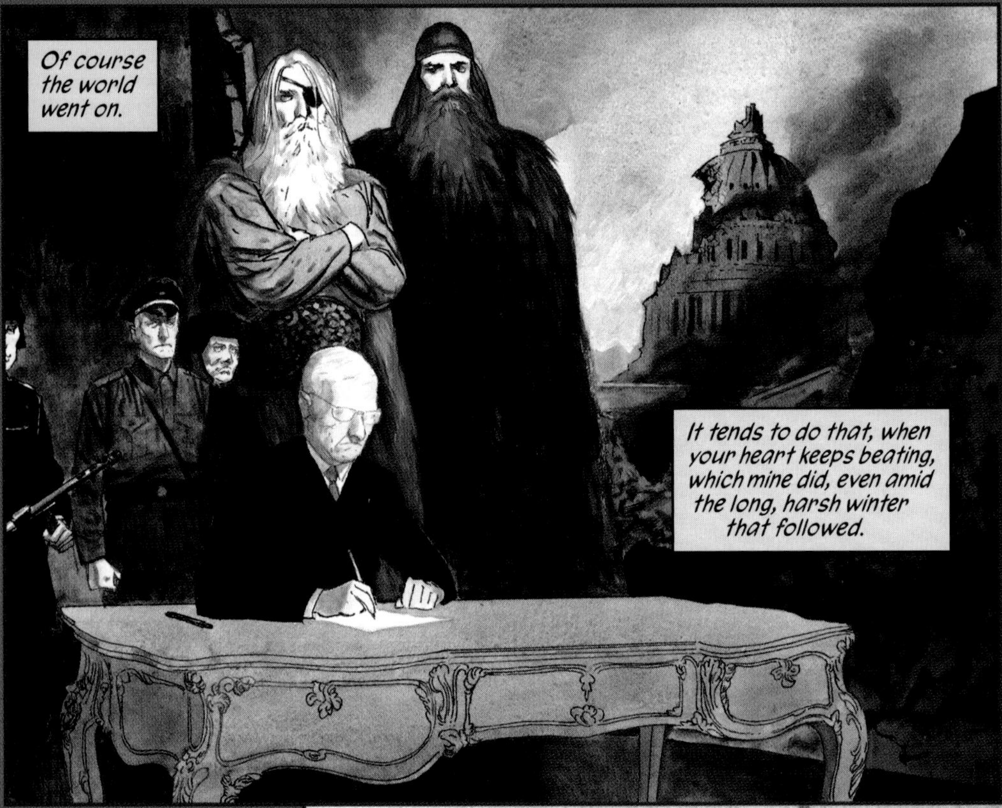
Of course the world went on.
It tends to do that, when your heart keeps beating, which mine did, even amid the long, harsh winter that followed.

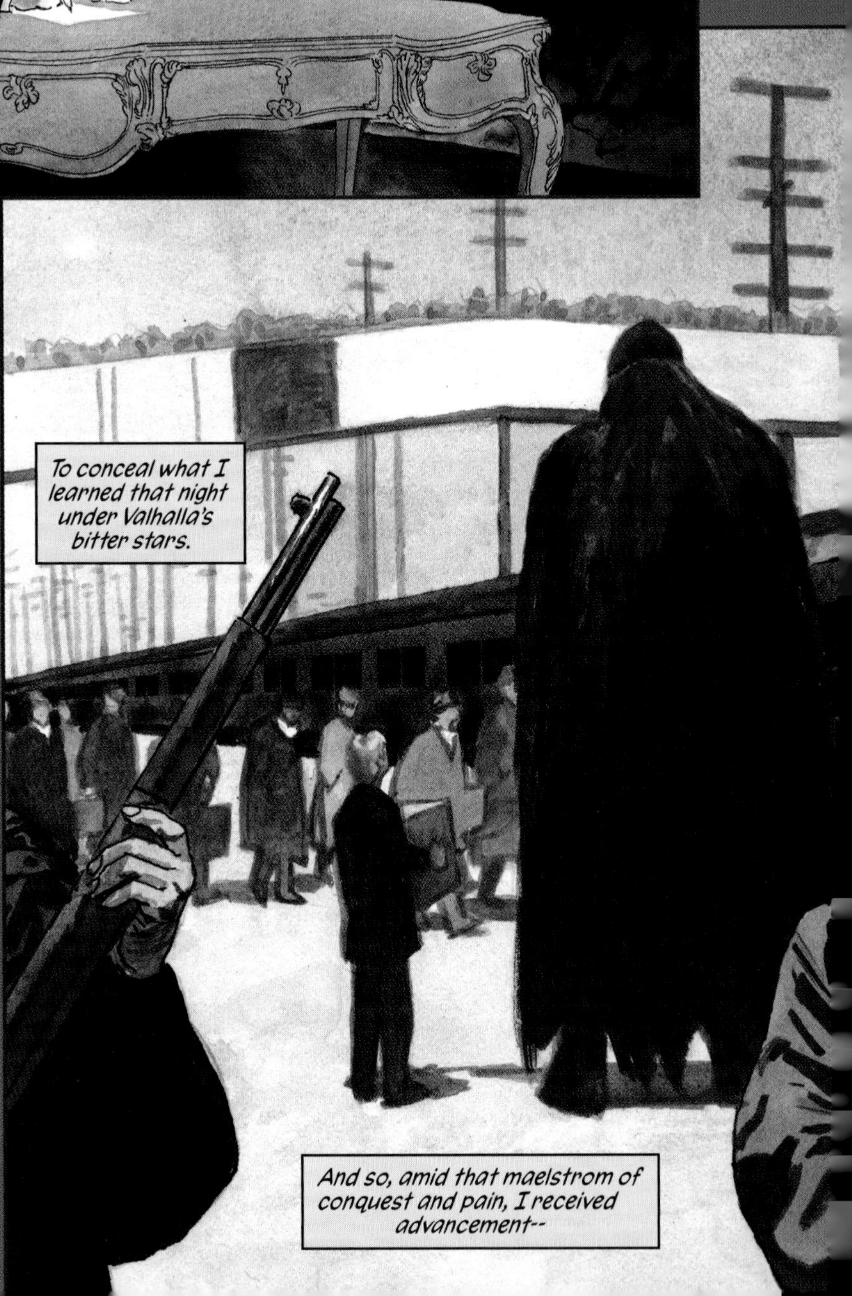
To conceal what I learned that night under Valhalla's bitter stars.
And so, amid that maelstrom of conquest and pain, I received advancement--

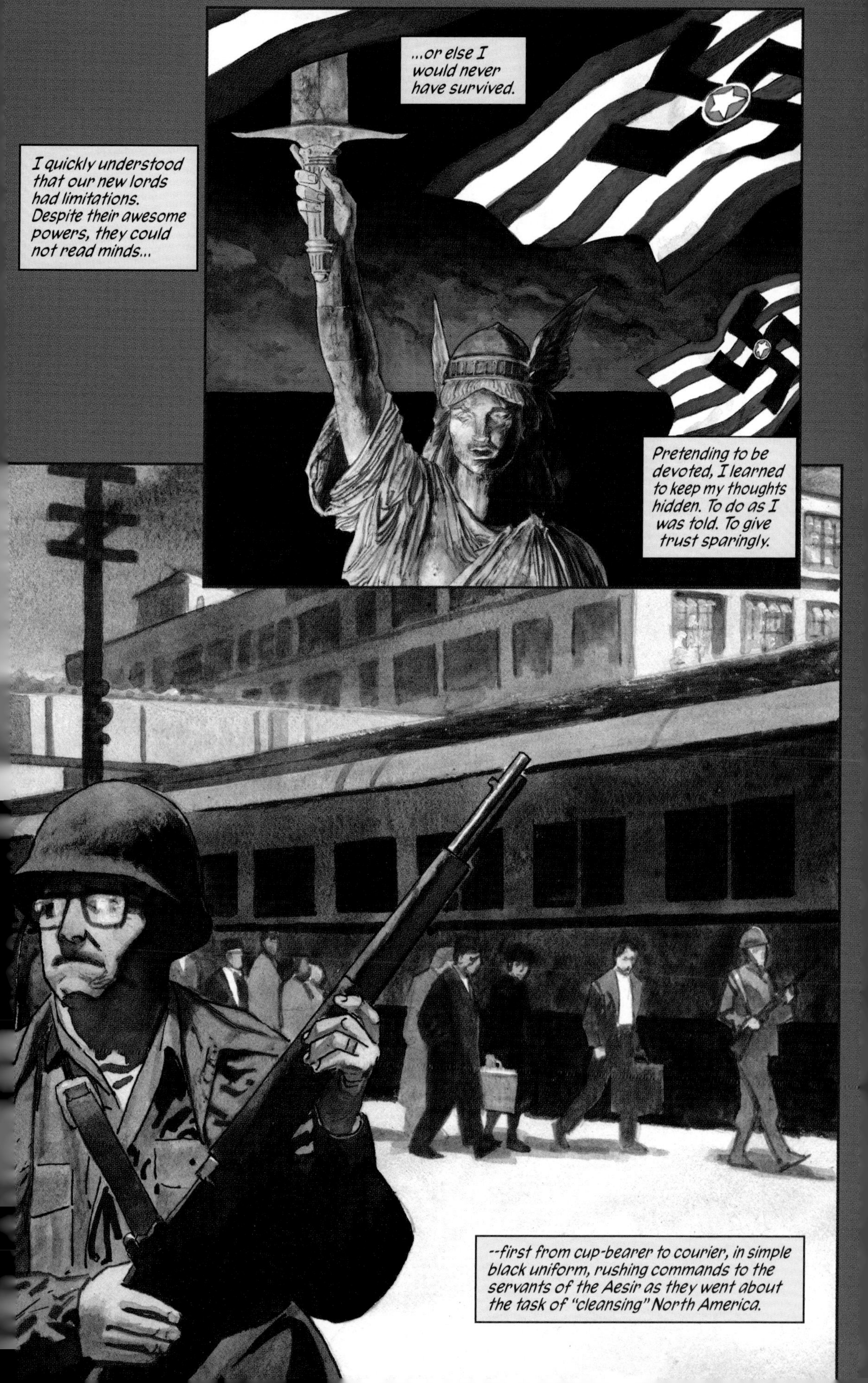
I quickly understood that our new lords had limitations. Despite their awesome powers, they could not read minds...
...or else I would never have survived.
Pretending to be devoted, I learned to keep my thoughts hidden. To do as I was told. To give trust sparingly.
--first from cup-bearer to courier, in simple black uniform, rushing commands to the servants of the Aesir as they went about the task of "cleansing" North America.

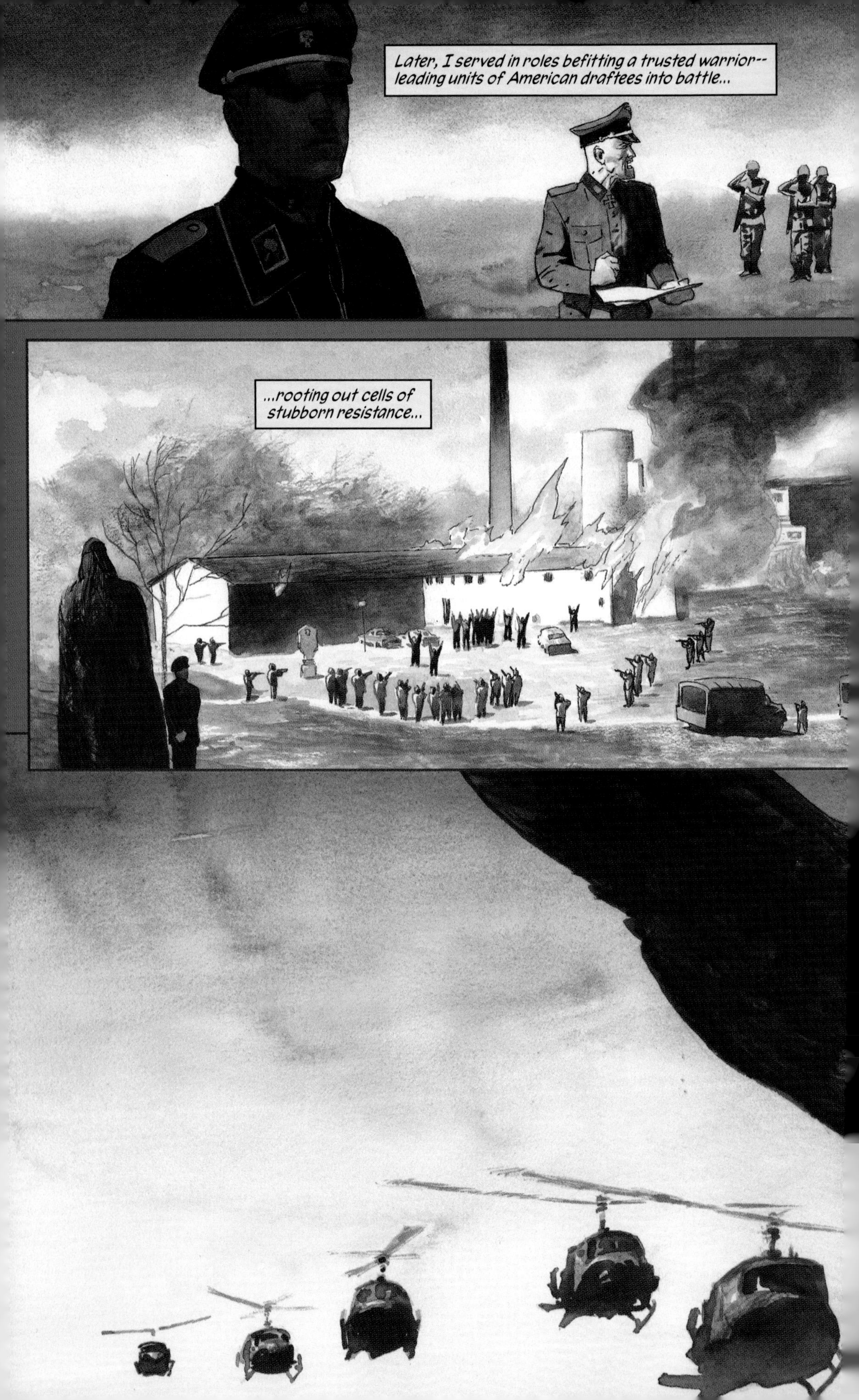
Later, I served in roles befitting a trusted warrior-- leading units of American draftees into battle...
...rooting out cells of stubborn resistance...

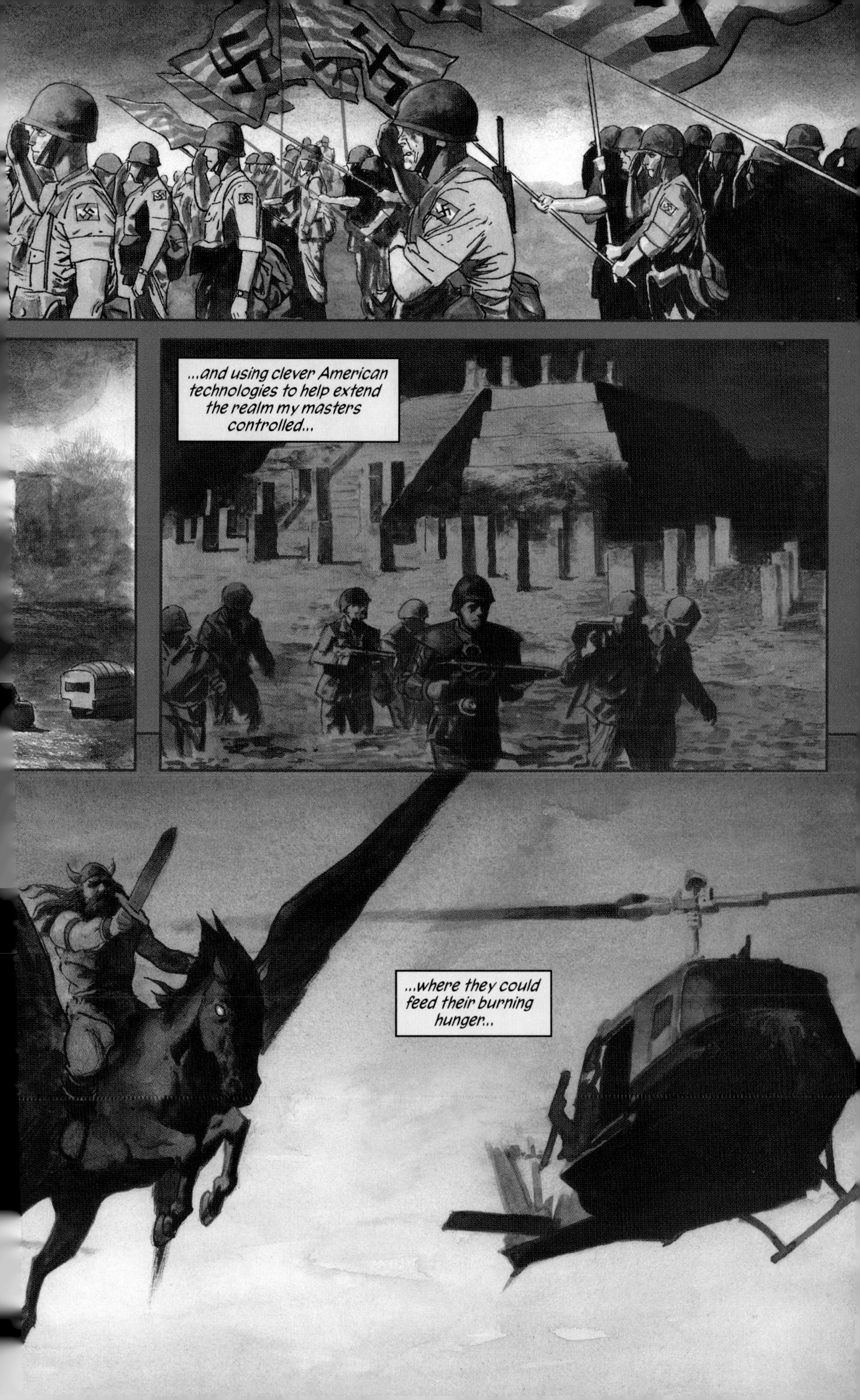
...and using clever American technologies to help extend the realm my masters controlled...
...where they could feed their burning hunger...

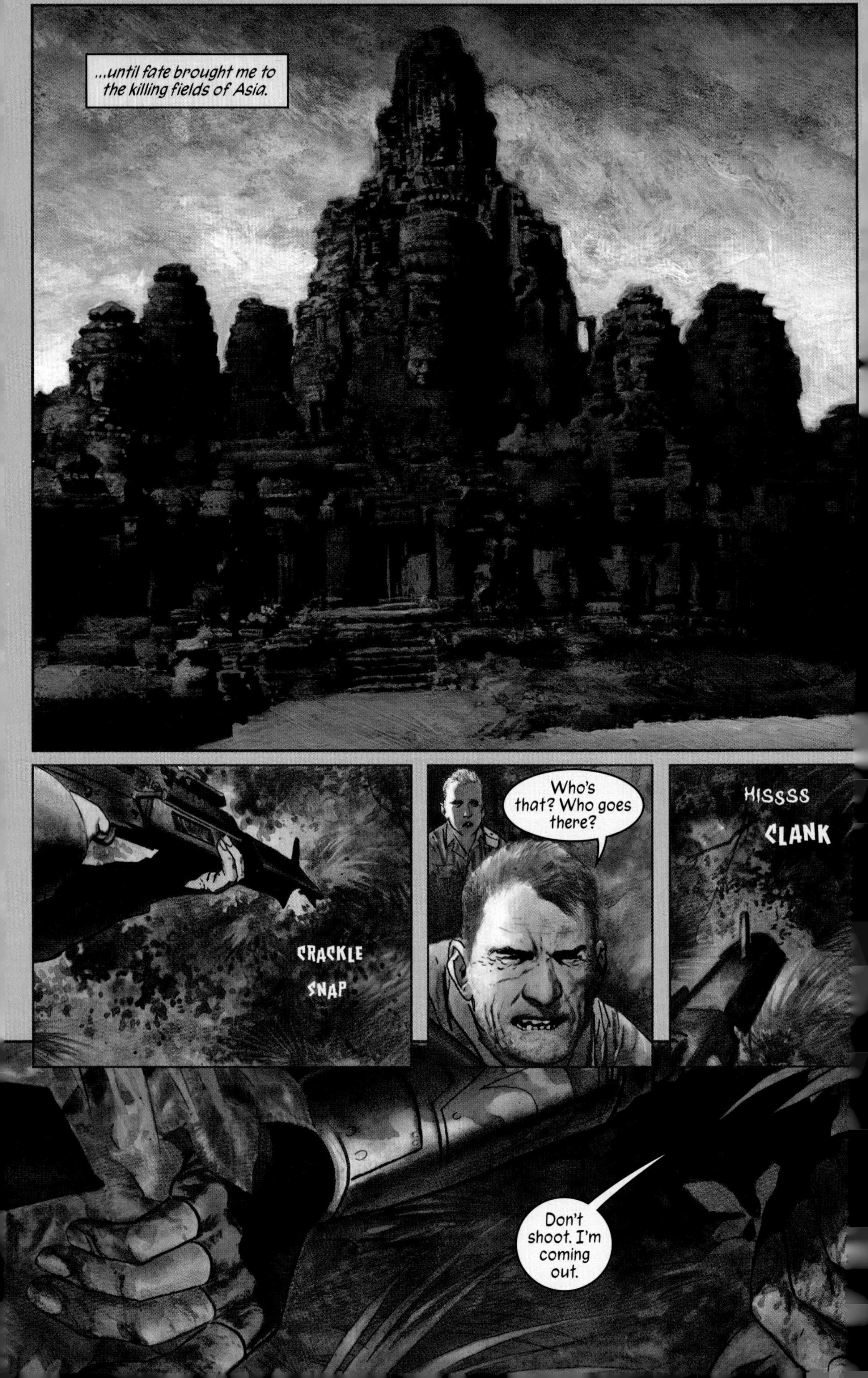
...until fate brought me to the killing fields of Asia.
CRACKLE
SNAP
Who's that? Who goes there?
HISSSS
CLANK
Don't shoot. I'm coming out.

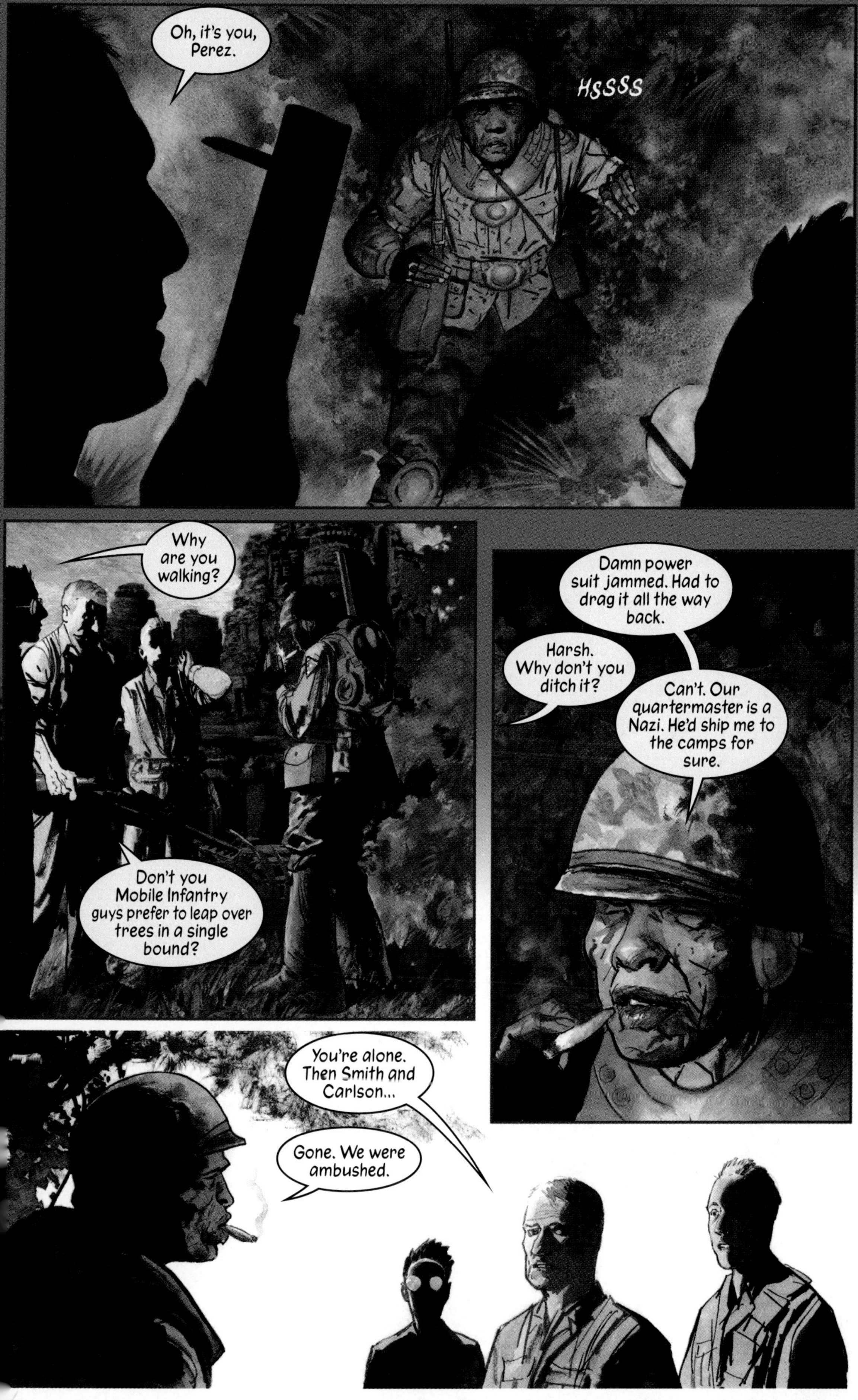
Oh, it's you, Perez.
HSSSS
Why are you walking?
Don't you Mobile Infantry guys prefer to leap over trees in a single bound?
Damn power suit jammed. Had to drag it all the way back.
Harsh. Why don't you ditch it?
Can't. Our quartermaster is a Nazi. He'd ship me to the camps for sure.
You're alone. Then Smith and Carlson...
Gone. We were ambushed.

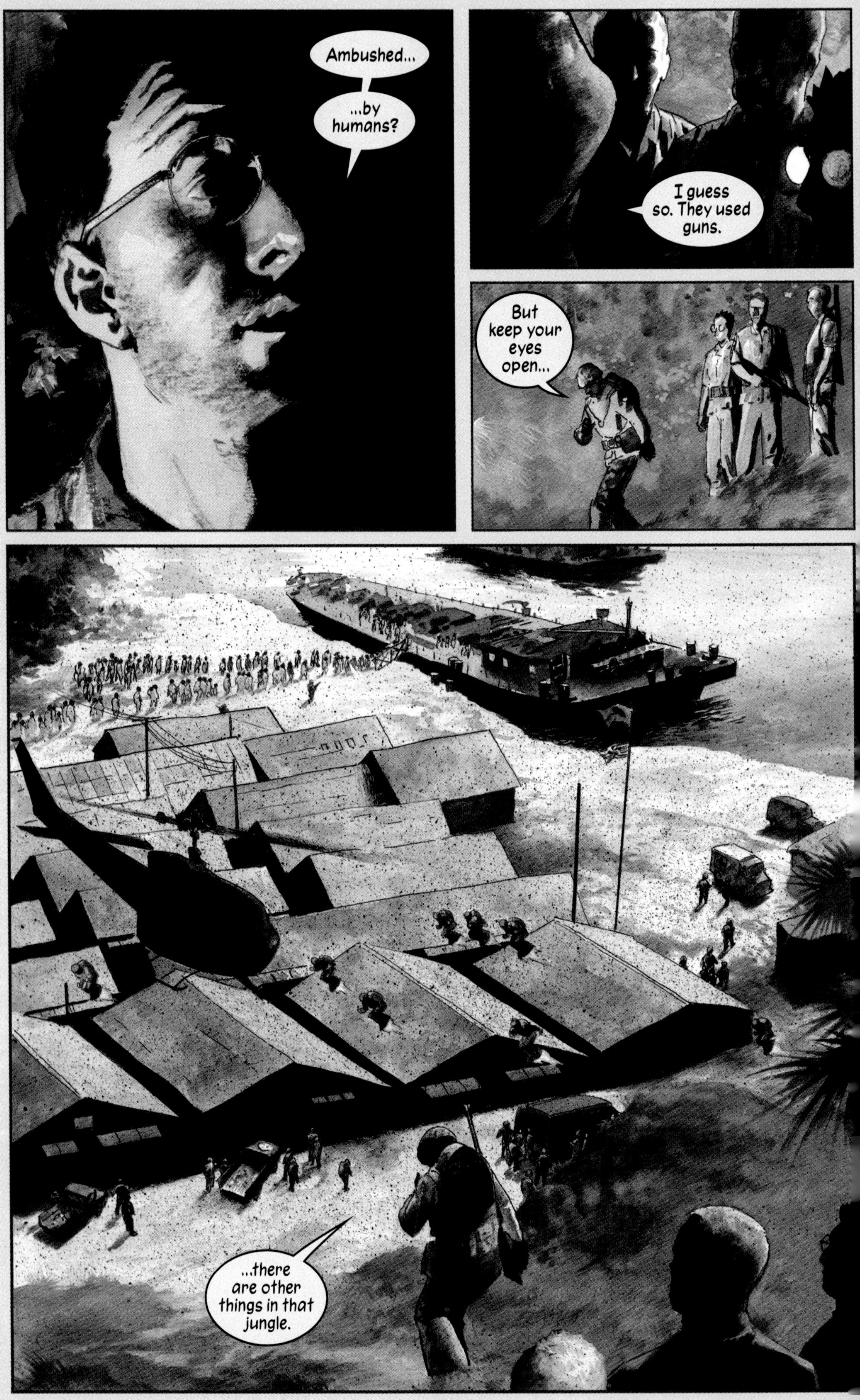
Ambushed...
...by humans?
I guess so. They used guns.
But keep your eyes open...
...there are other things in that jungle.

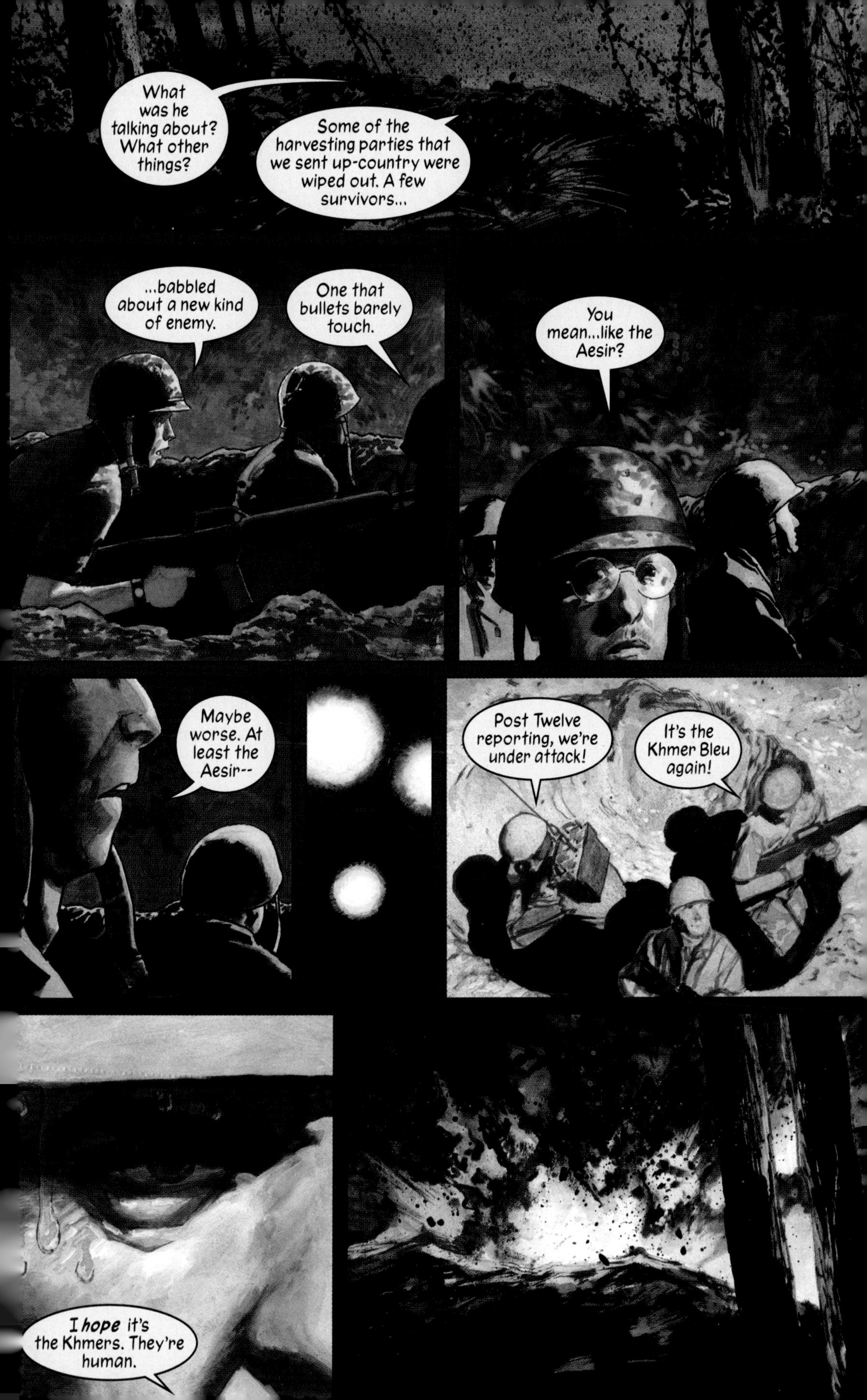
What was he talking about? What other things?
Some of the harvesting parties that we sent up-country were wiped out. A few survivors...
...babbled about a new kind of enemy.
One that bullets barely touch.
You mean...like the Aesir?
Maybe worse. At least the Aesir--
Post Twelve reporting, we're under attack!
It's the Khmer Bleu again!
I *hope* it's the Khmers. They're human.

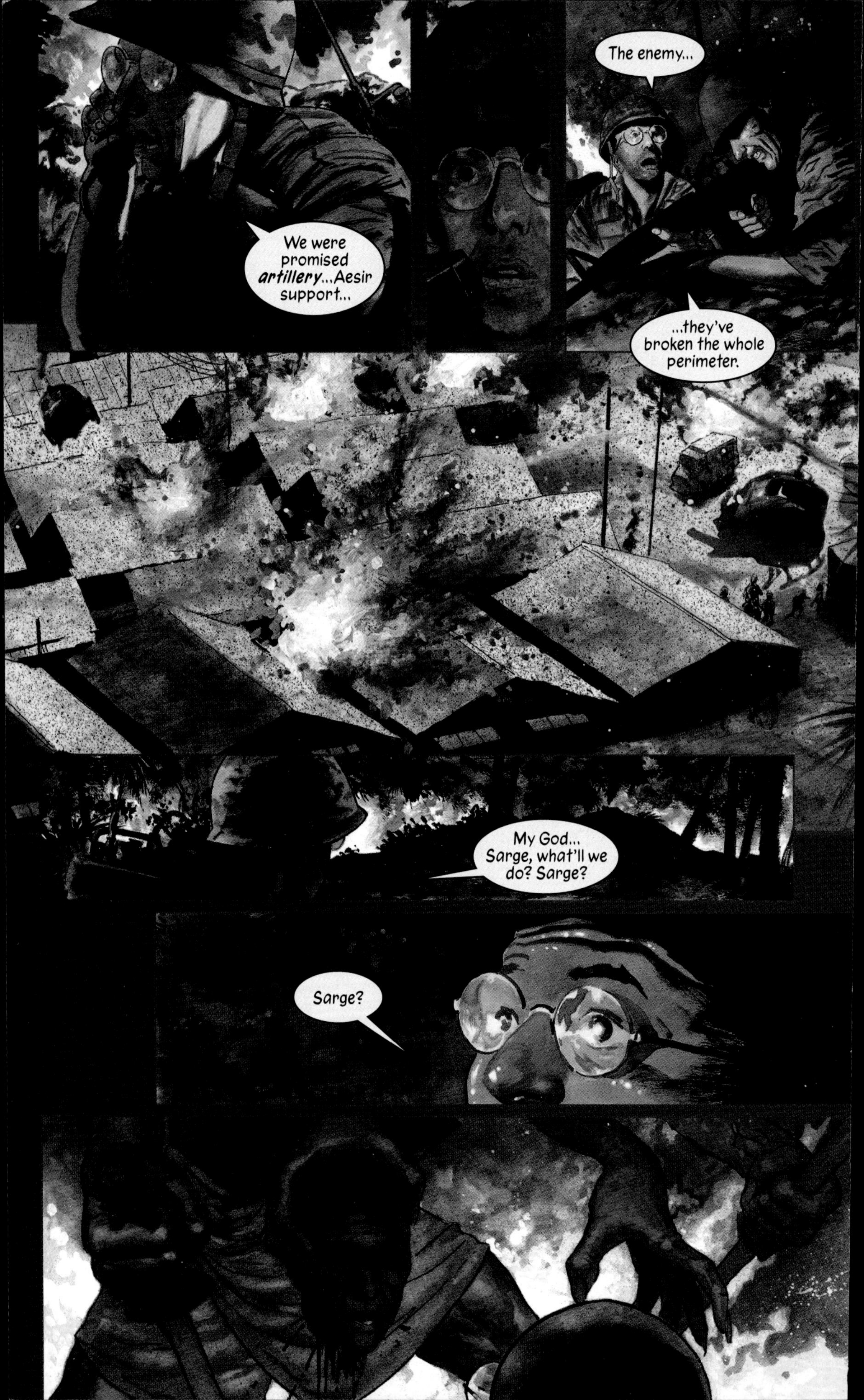
We were promised artillery...Aesir support...
The enemy...
...they've broken the whole perimeter.
My God... Sarge, what'll we do? Sarge?
Sarge?

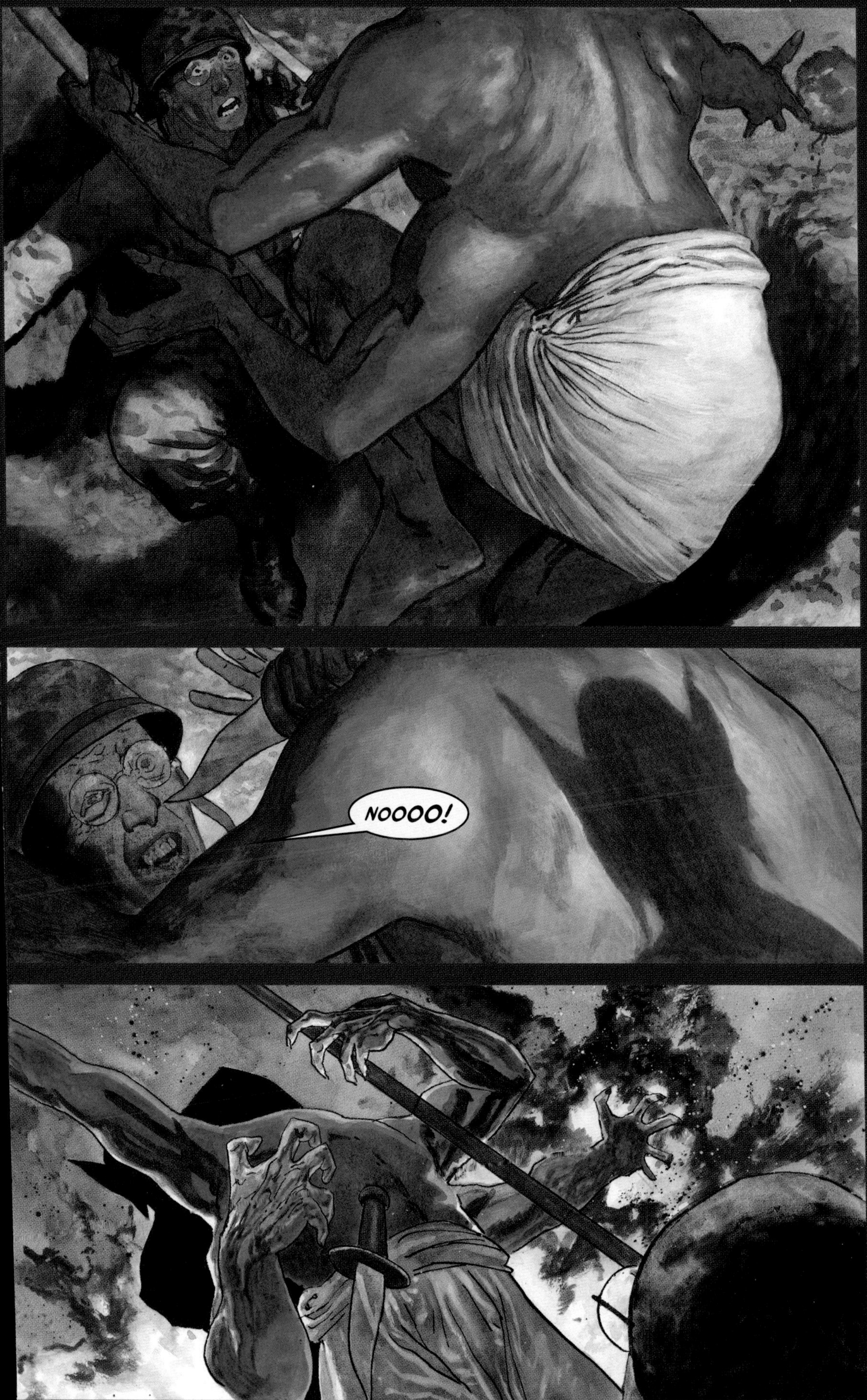
NOOOO!

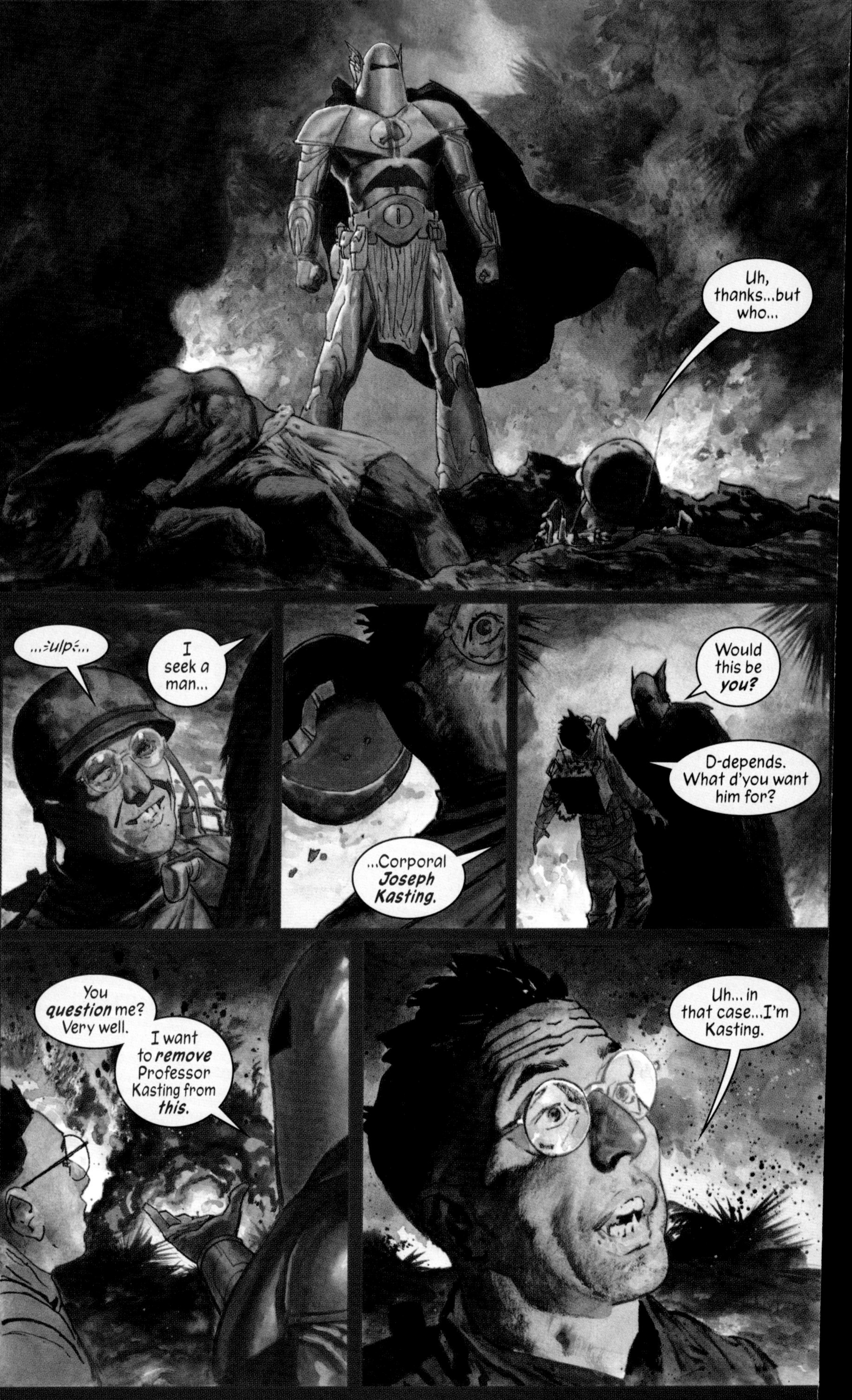
Uh, thanks...but who...
...ulp...
I seek a man...
...Corporal Joseph Kasting.
Would this be you?
D-depends. What d'you want him for?
You question me? Very well.
I want to remove Professor Kasting from this.
Uh... in that case...I'm Kasting.

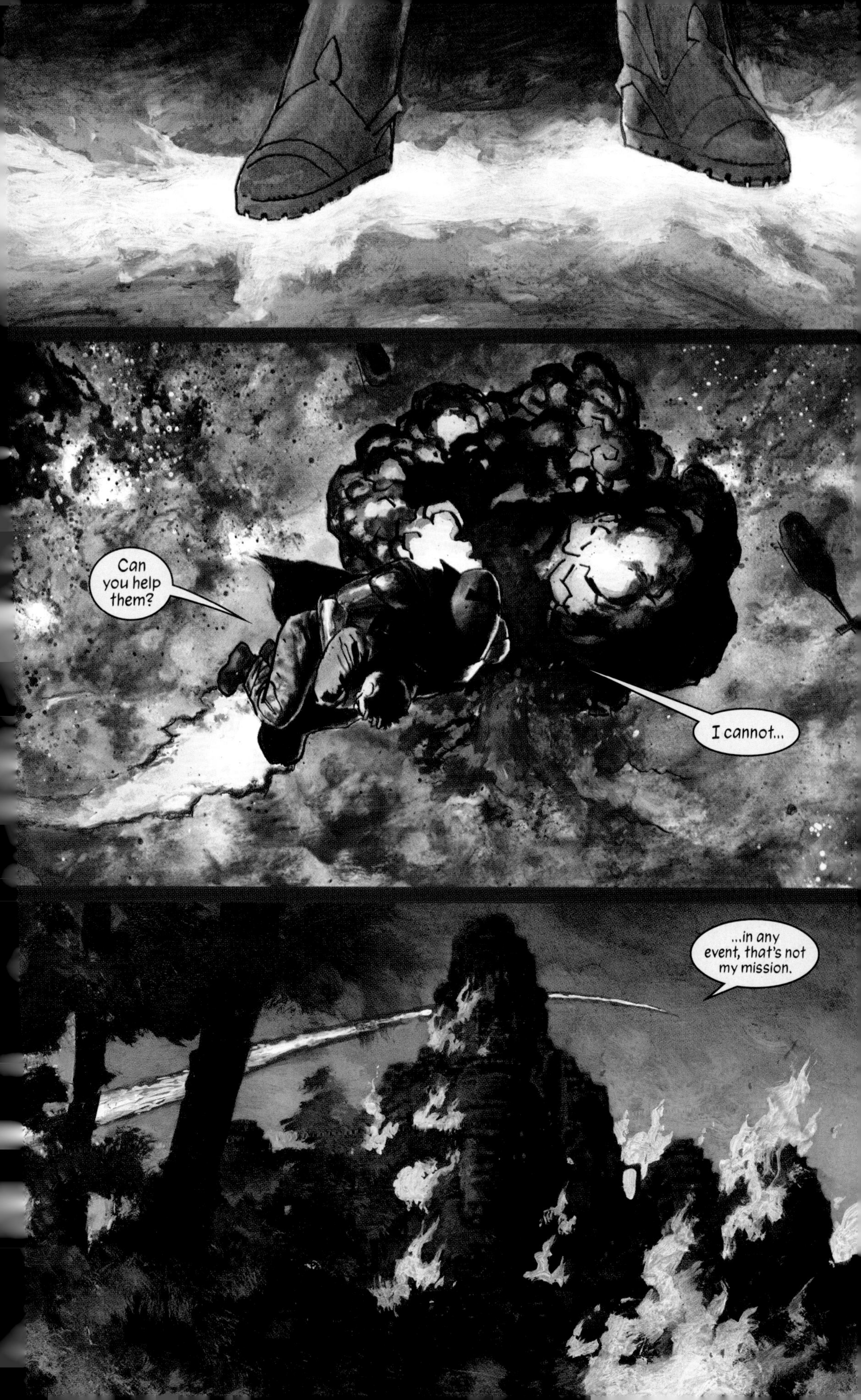
Can you help them?
I cannot...
...in any event, that's not my mission.

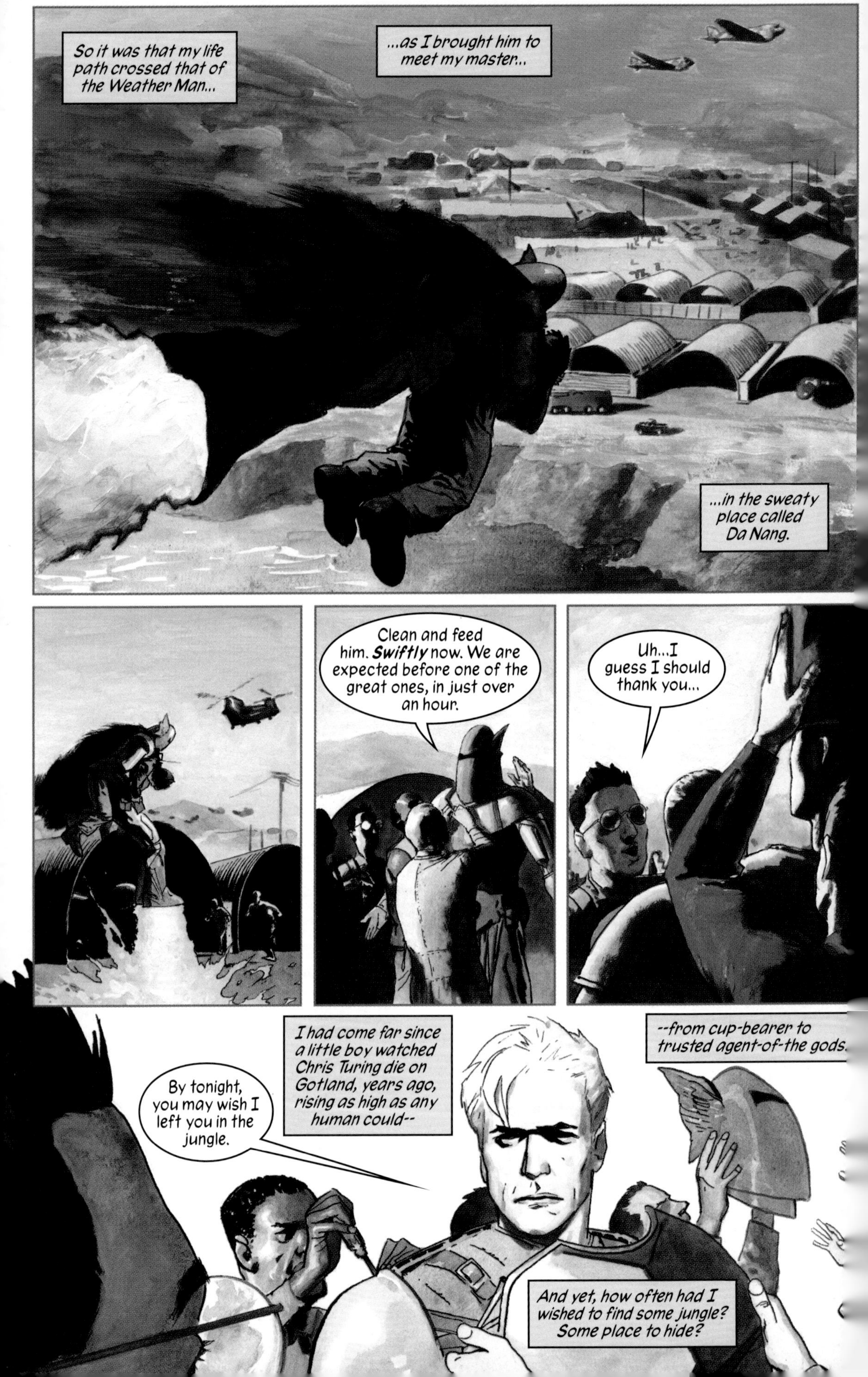

So it was that my life path crossed that of the Weather Man...
...as I brought him to meet my master...
...in the sweaty place called Da Nang.
Clean and feed him. *Swiftly* now. We are expected before one of the great ones, in just over an hour.
Uh...I guess I should thank you...
By tonight, you may wish I left you in the jungle.
I had come far since a little boy watched Chris Turing die on Gotland, years ago, rising as high as any human could--
--from cup-bearer to trusted agent-of-the gods.
And yet, how often had I wished to find some jungle? Some place to hide?

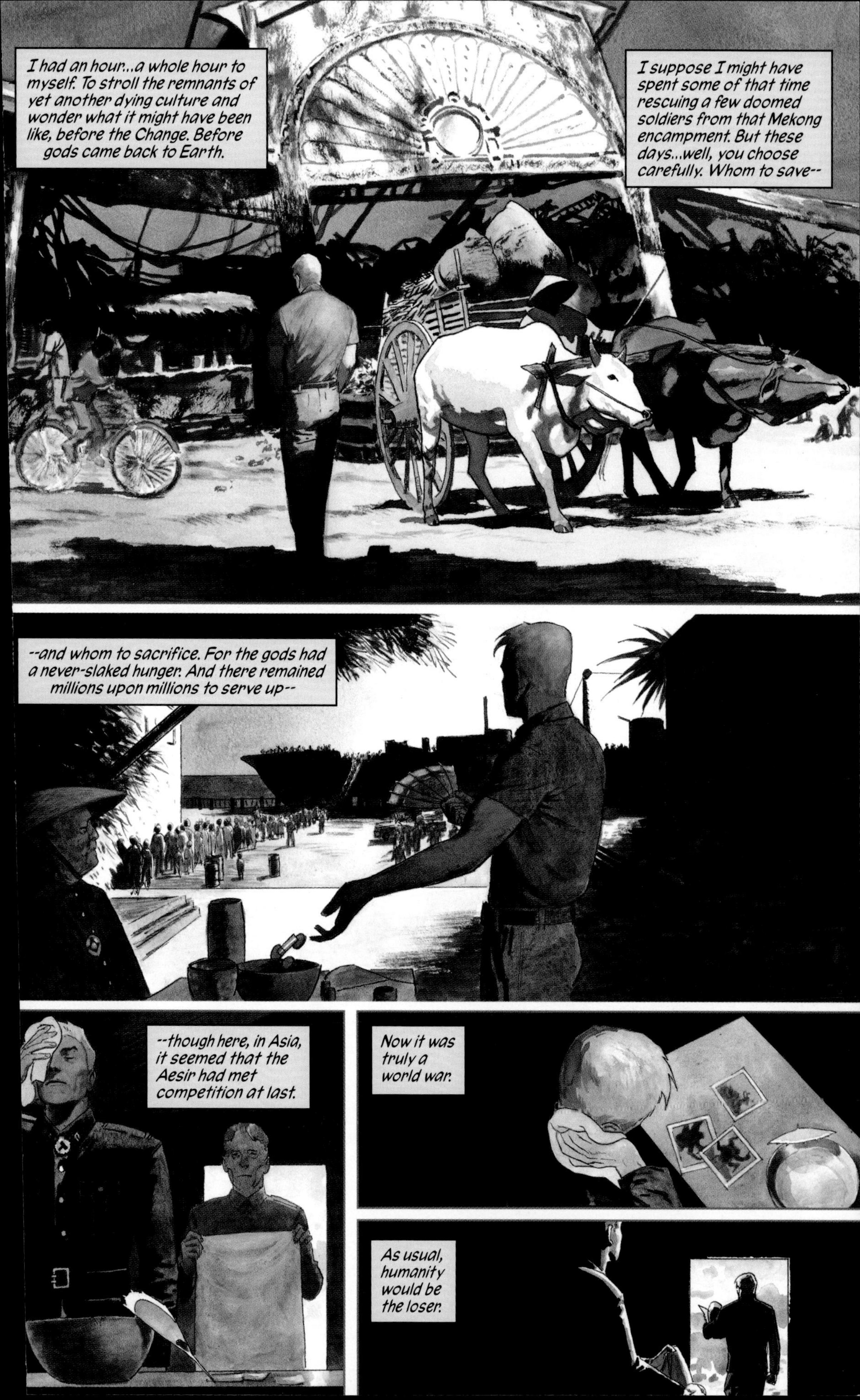
I had an hour...a whole hour to myself. To stroll the remnants of yet another dying culture and wonder what it might have been like, before the Change. Before gods came back to Earth.
I suppose I might have spent some of that time rescuing a few doomed soldiers from that Mekong encampment. But these days...well, you choose carefully. Whom to save--
--and whom to sacrifice. For the gods had a never-slaked hunger. And there remained millions upon millions to serve up--
--though here, in Asia, it seemed that the Aesir had met competition at last.
Now it was truly a world war.
As usual, humanity would be the loser.

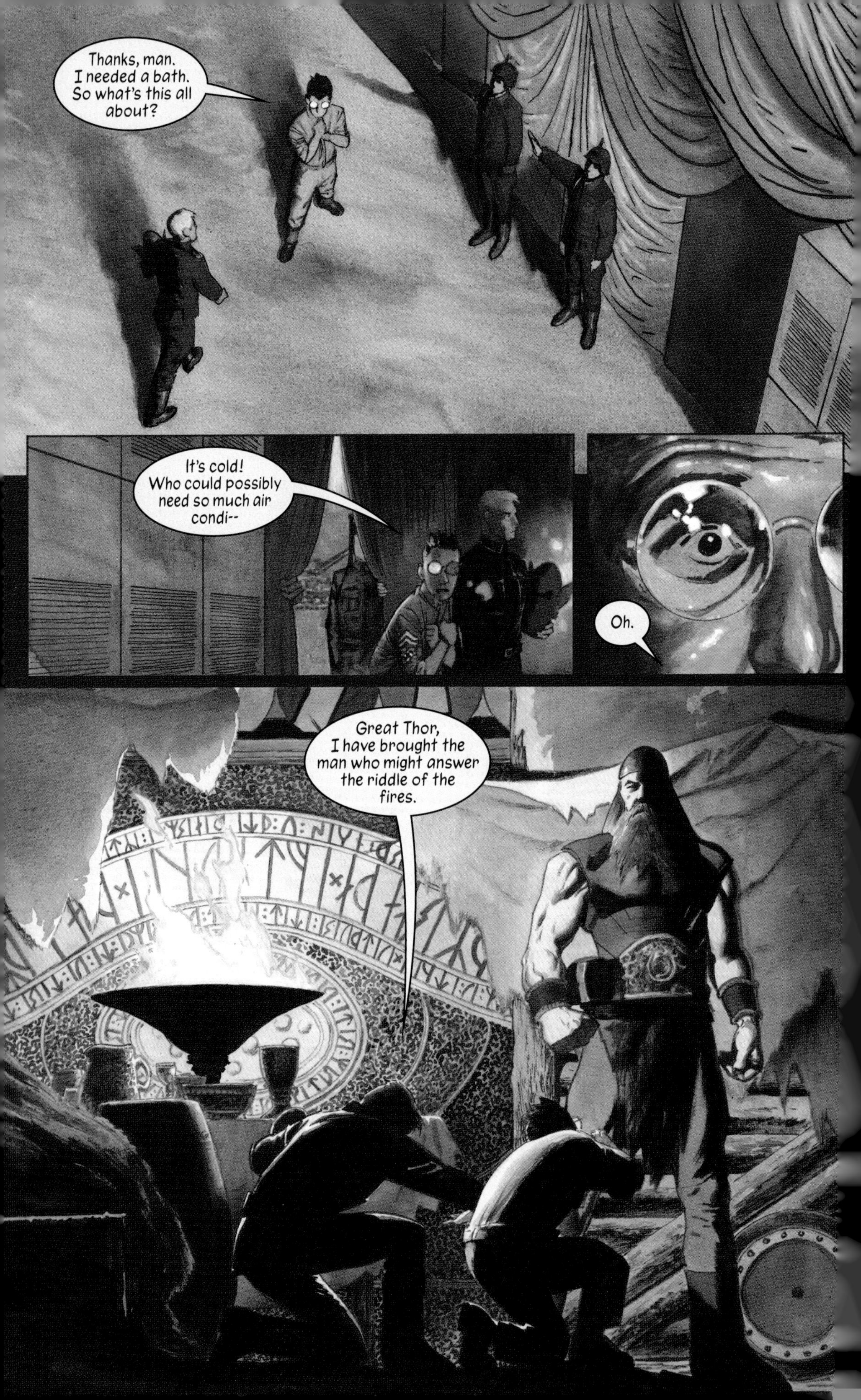
Thanks, man. I needed a bath. So what's this all about?
It's cold! Who could possibly need so much air condi--
Oh.
Great Thor, I have brought the man who might answer the riddle of the fires.

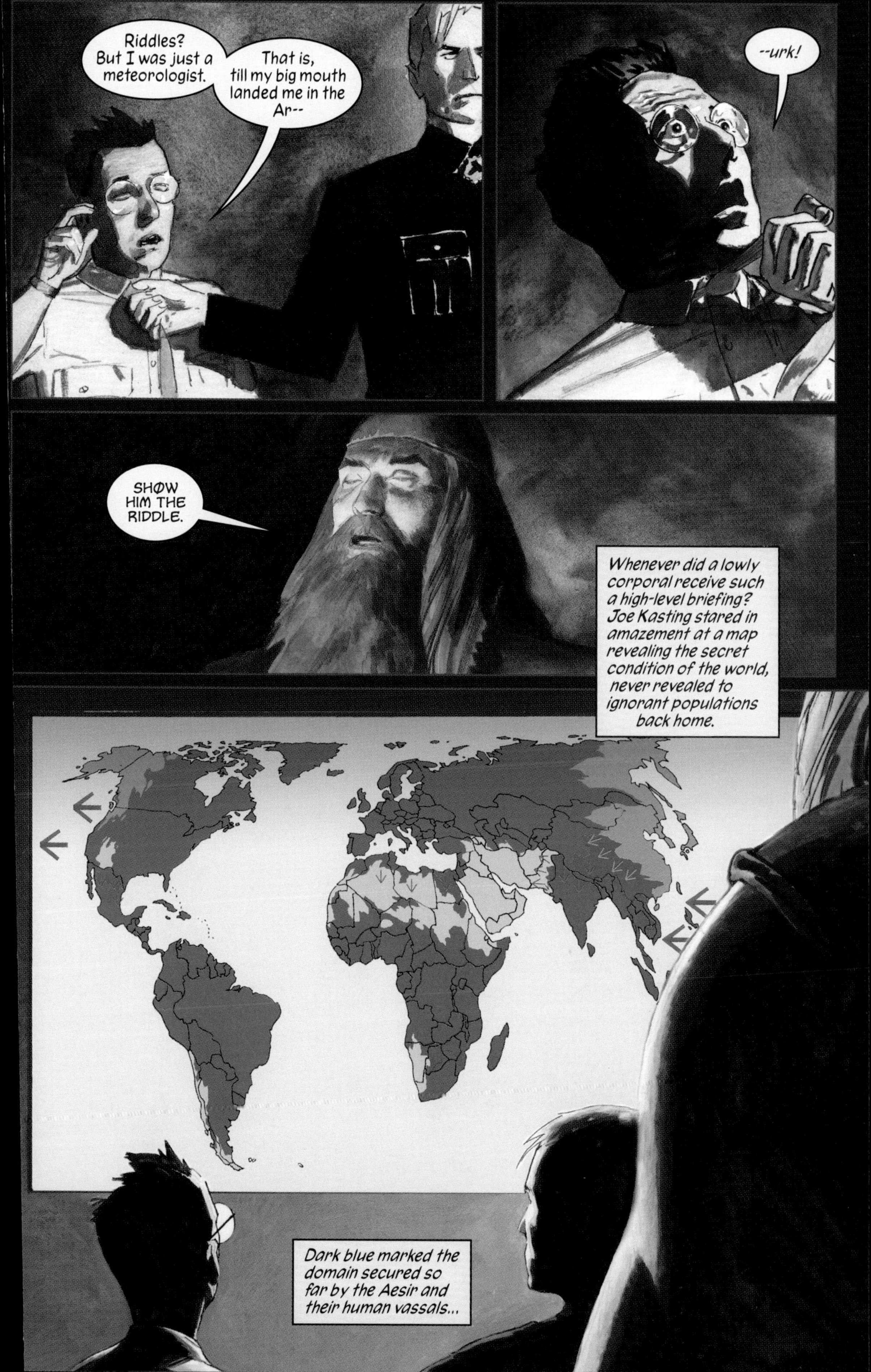

Riddles? But I was just a meteorologist.
That is, till my big mouth landed me in the Ar--
--urk!
SHOW HIM THE RIDDLE.
Whenever did a lowly corporal receive such a high-level briefing? Joe Kasting stared in amazement at a map revealing the secret condition of the world, never revealed to ignorant populations back home.
Dark blue marked the domain secured so far by the Aesir and their human vassals...

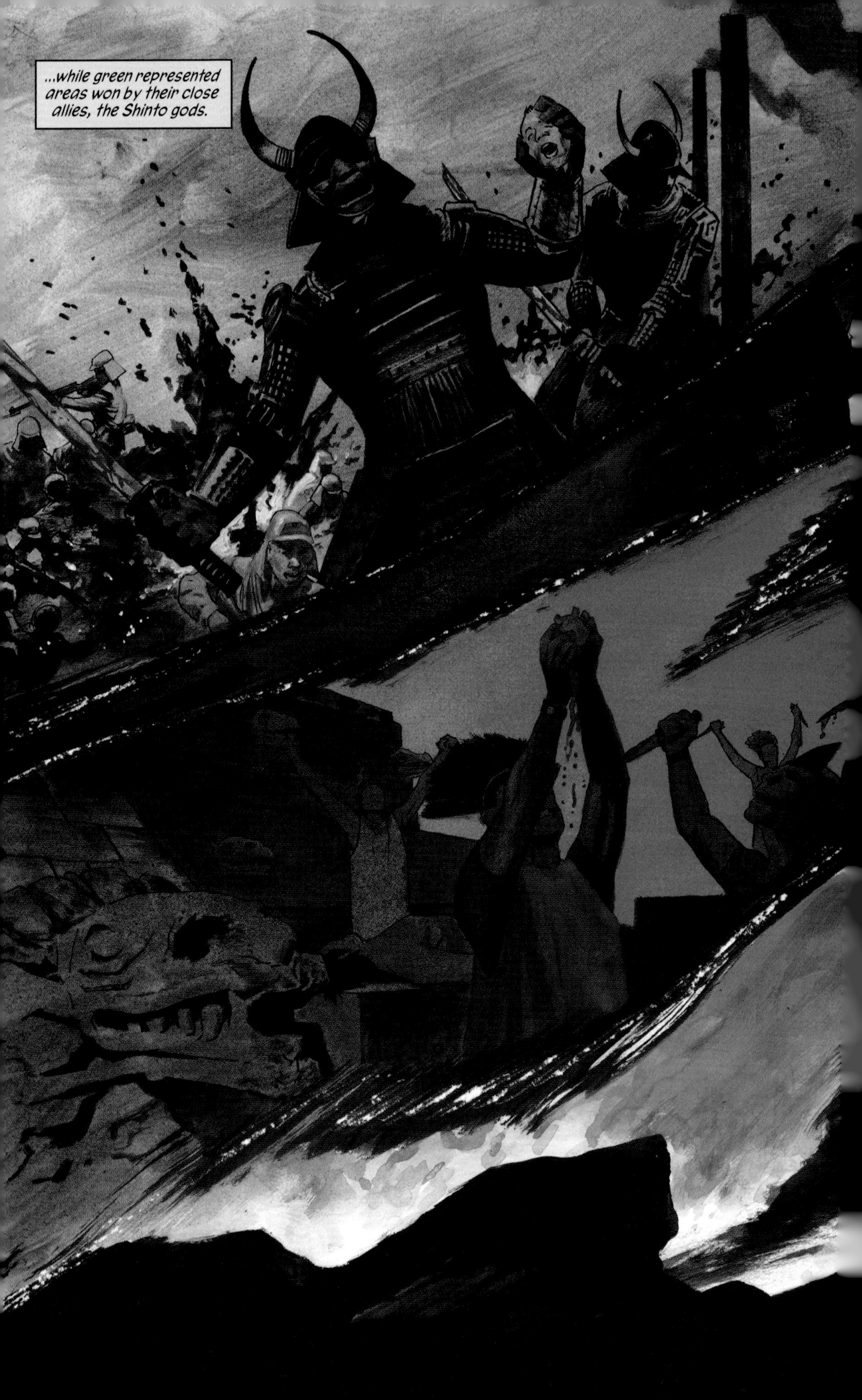
...while green represented areas won by their close allies, the Shinto gods.

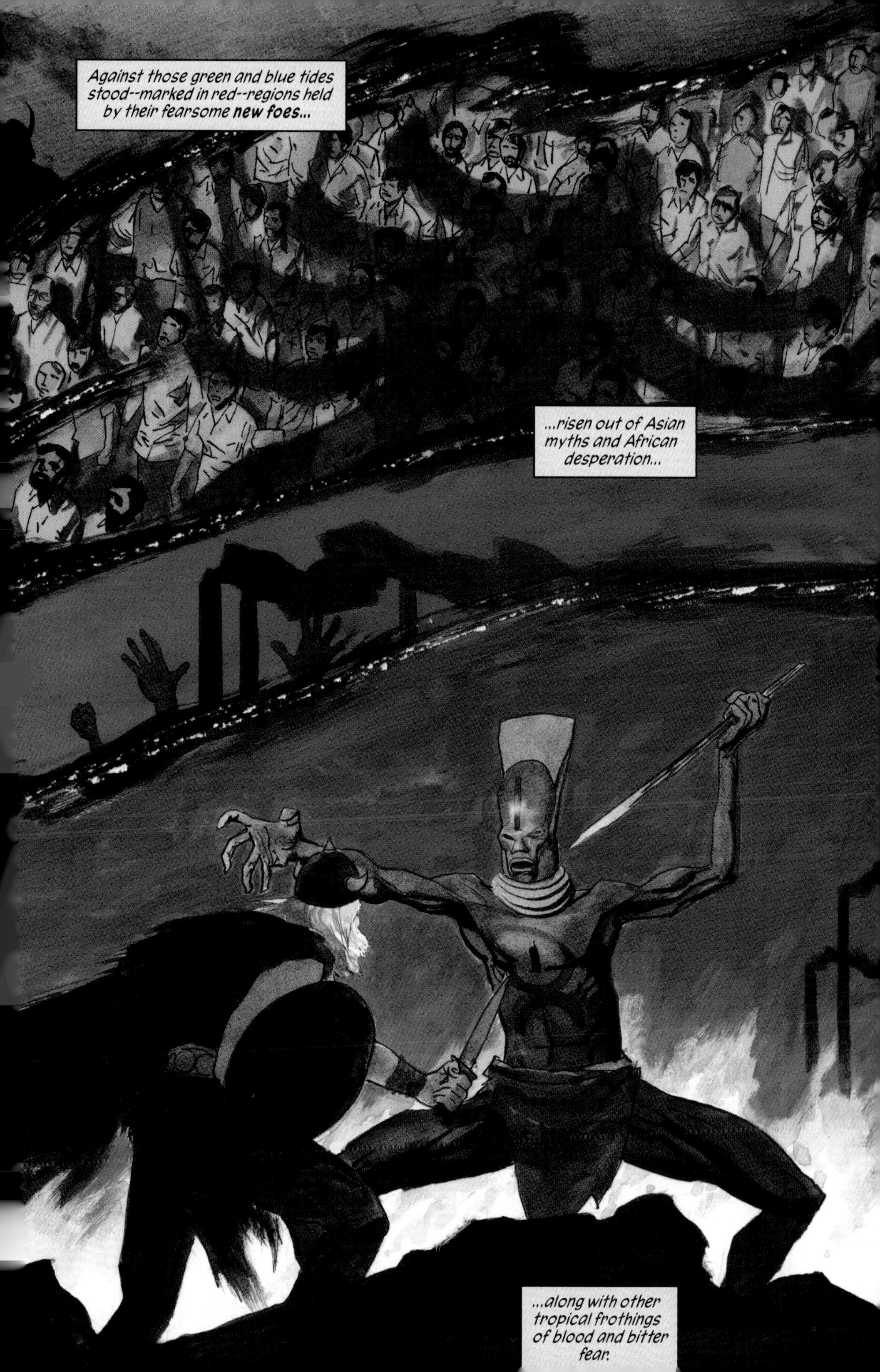
Against those green and blue tides stood--marked in red--regions held by their fearsome **new foes...**
...risen out of Asian myths and African desperation...
...along with other tropical frothings of blood and bitter fear.

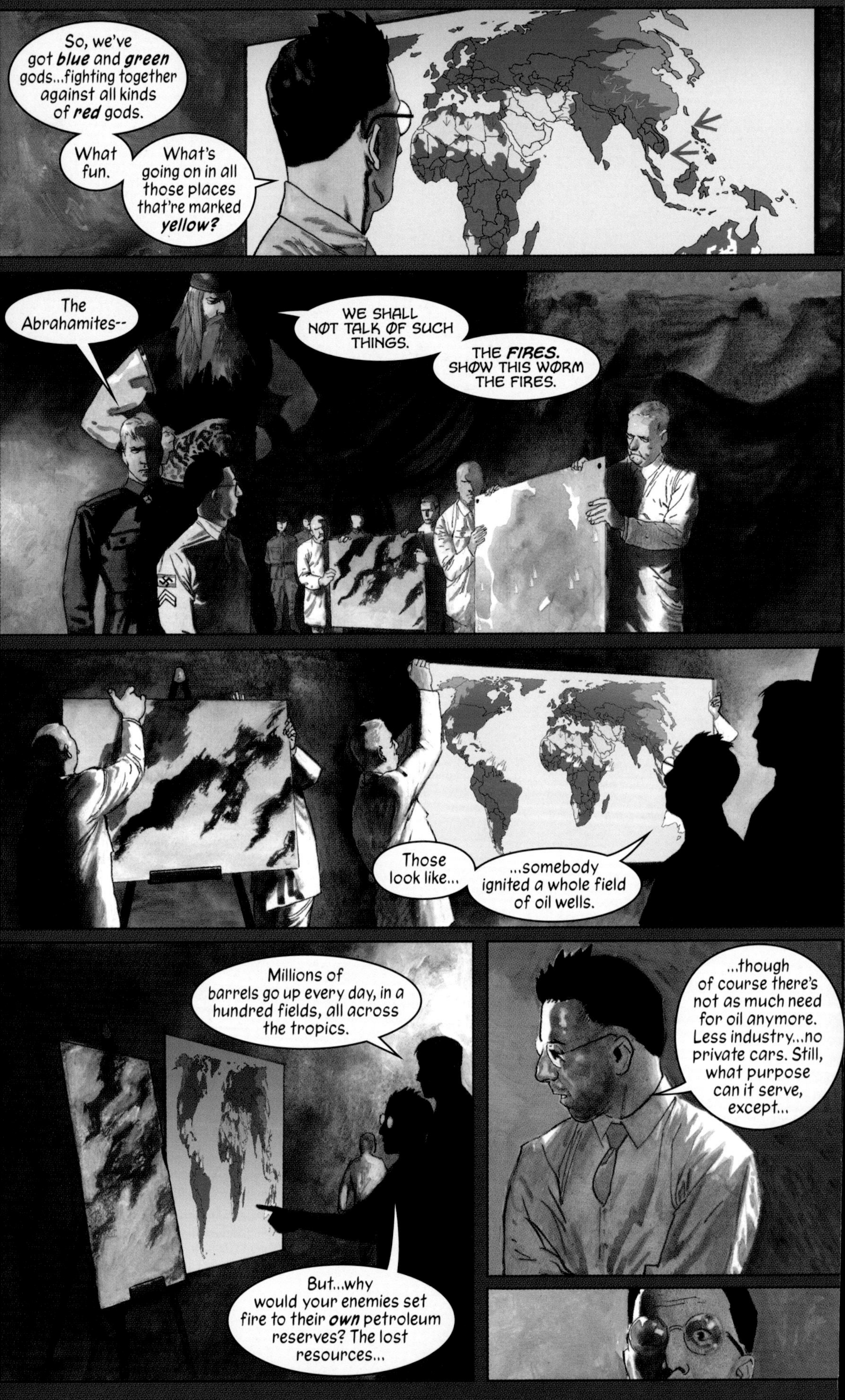
So, we've got *blue* and *green* gods...fighting together against all kinds of *red* gods.
What fun.
What's going on in all those places that're marked *yellow?*
The Abrahamites--
WE SHALL NOT TALK OF SUCH THINGS.
THE *FIRES.* SHOW THIS WORM THE FIRES.
Those look like...
...somebody ignited a whole field of oil wells.
Millions of barrels go up every day, in a hundred fields, all across the tropics.
But...why would your enemies set fire to their *own* petroleum reserves? The lost resources...
...though of course there's not as much need for oil anymore. Less industry...no private cars. Still, what purpose can it serve, except...

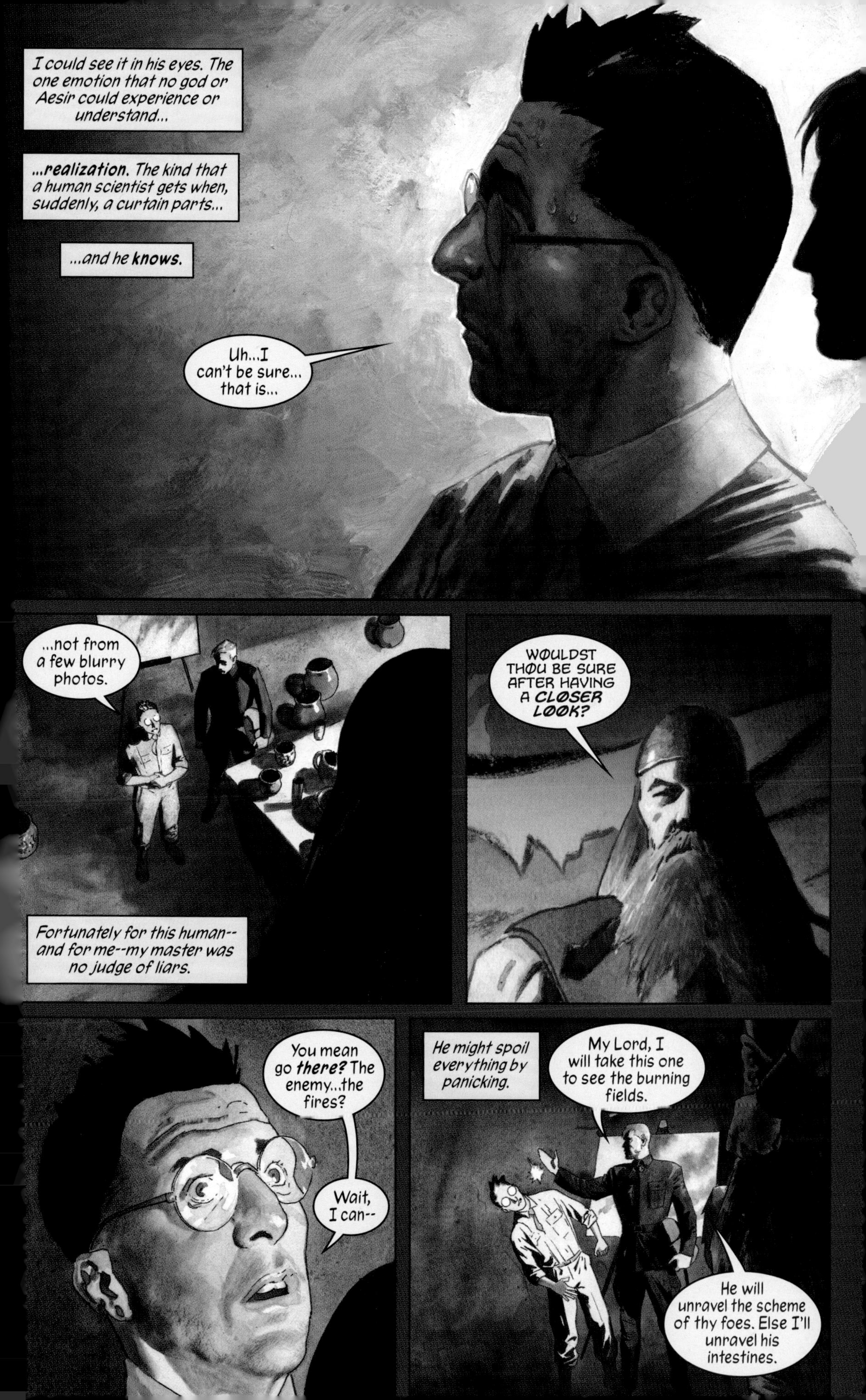

I could see it in his eyes. The one emotion that no god or Aesir could experience or understand...
...*realization*. The kind that a human scientist gets when, suddenly, a curtain parts...
...and he **knows**.
Uh...I can't be sure... that is...
...not from a few blurry photos.
Fortunately for this human--and for me--my master was no judge of liars.
WOULDST THOU BE SURE AFTER HAVING A *CLOSER LOOK?*
You mean go ***there?*** The enemy...the fires?
Wait, I can--
He might spoil everything by panicking.
My Lord, I will take this one to see the burning fields.
He will unravel the scheme of thy foes. Else I'll unravel his intestines.

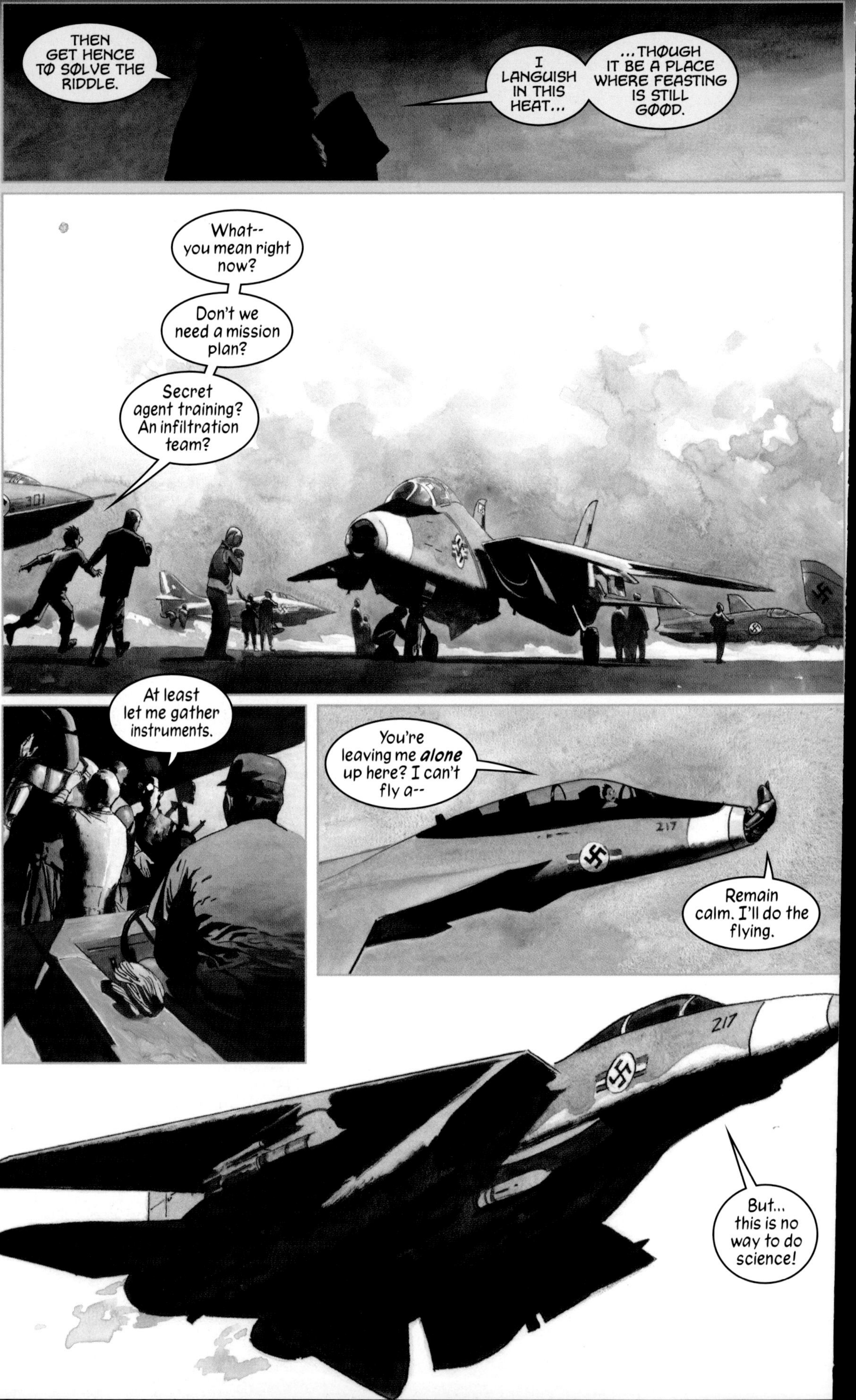
THEN GET HENCE TØ SØLVE THE RIDDLE.
I LANGUISH IN THIS HEAT...
...THØUGH IT BE A PLACE WHERE FEASTING IS STILL GØØD.
What-- you mean right now?
Don't we need a mission plan?
Secret agent training? An infiltration team?
At least let me gather instruments.
You're leaving me *alone* up here? I can't fly a--
Remain calm. I'll do the flying.
But... this is no way to do science!

I tried to ignore Kasting's nervous commentary about a war-ravaged coastline-- sunken vessels, burned-out towns and a slowly-poisoning sea. Becoming one with the plane, I flew. And flew, imagining that I was free.

The nearest fires were in Brunei...near what had been Indonesia...where once empires fought over rich resources. Spice and timber. Later, minerals and fuel.

Now, the world's **super**powers were battling over something even more valuable. Asia's rich trove of human lives.

And yet, it seemed that something had made **petroleum** important once again.

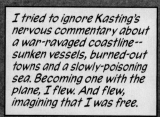

I don't know what you expect me to learn, just by looking.

I need a spectrograph...an air-sample analyzer and--

You don't fool me, Kasting. I can tell. You *already* know what's going on.

I don't know what you're...

...what the hell are *those*?!

That is our invitation to leave this place.

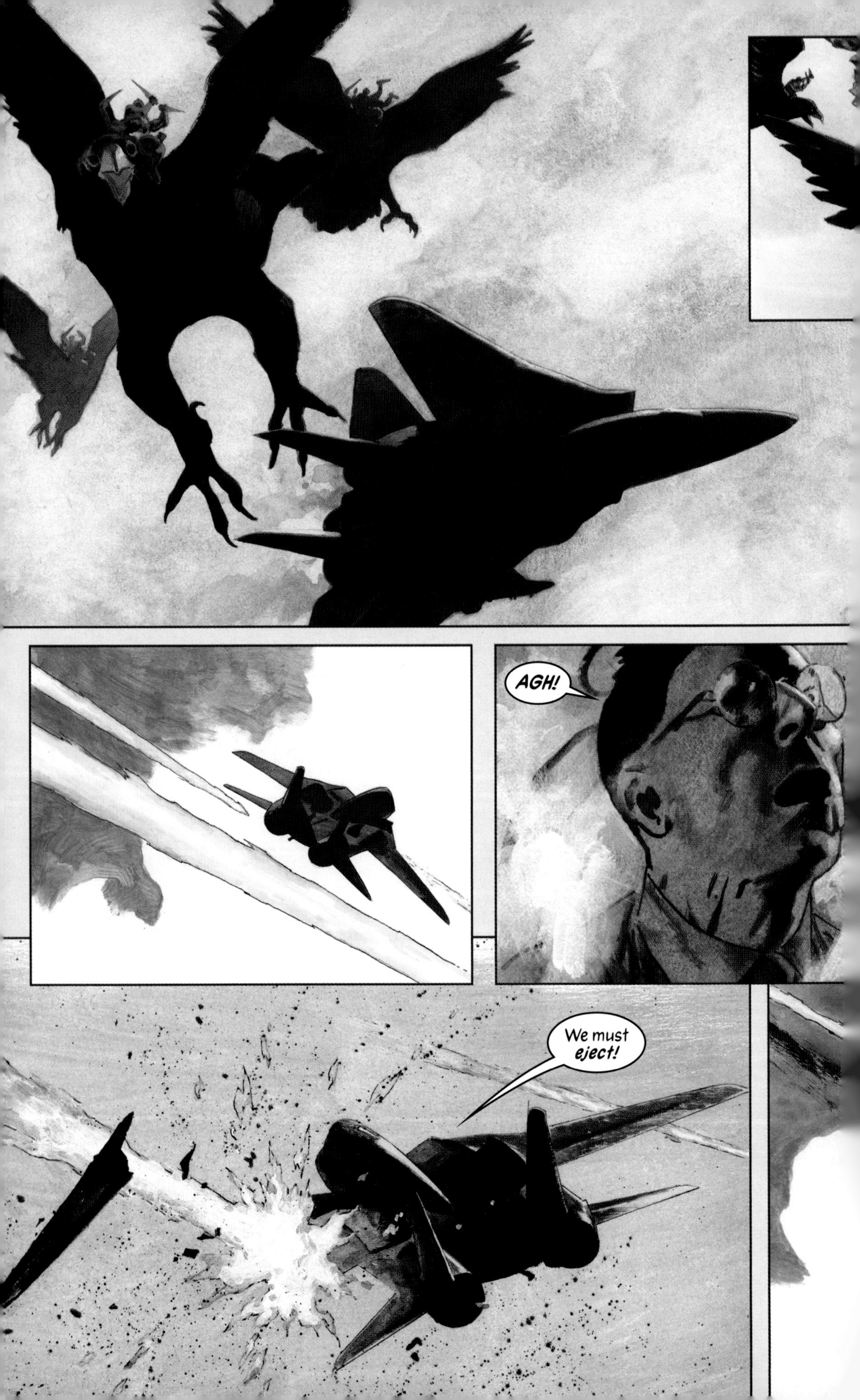
AGH!
We must eject!

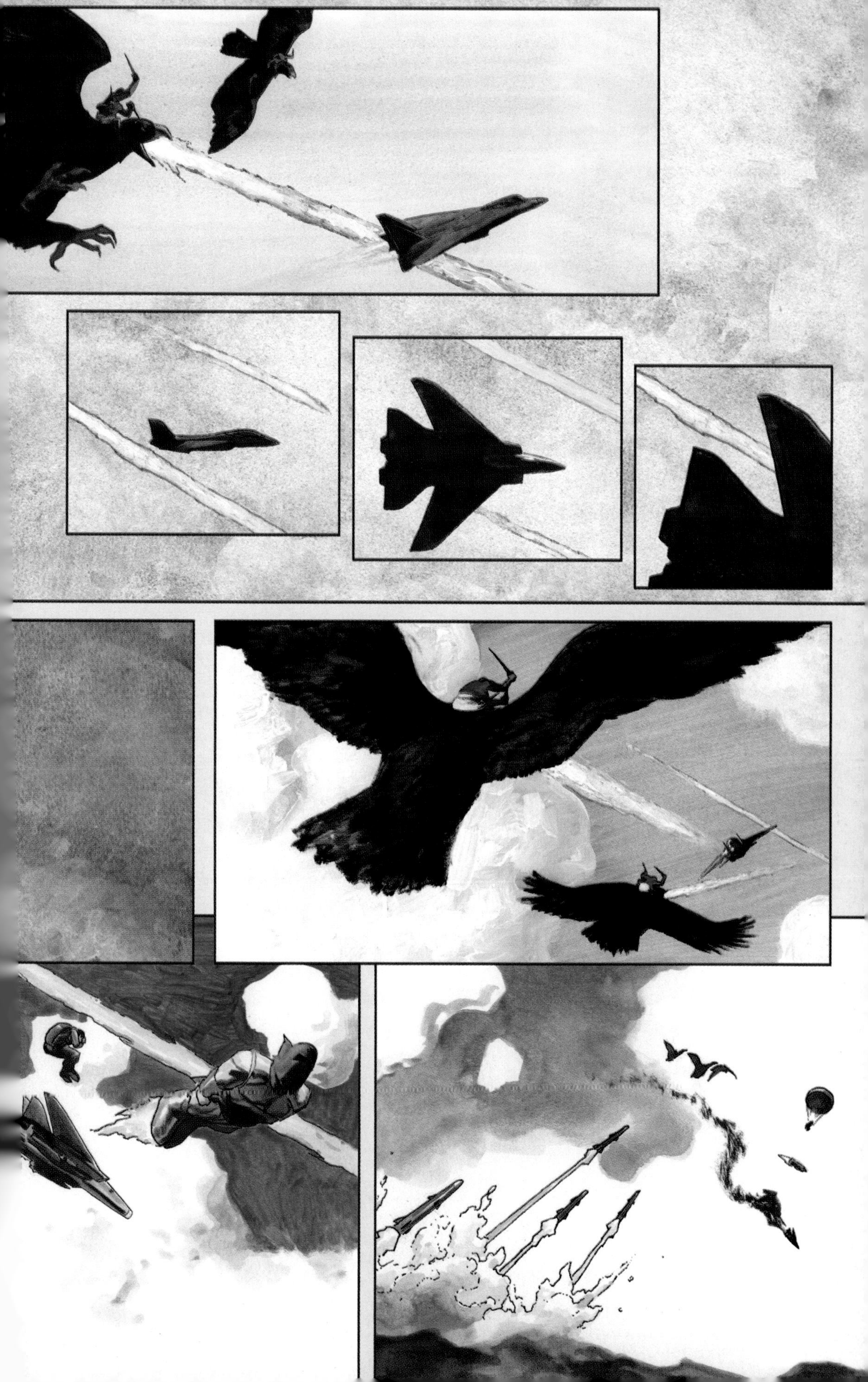

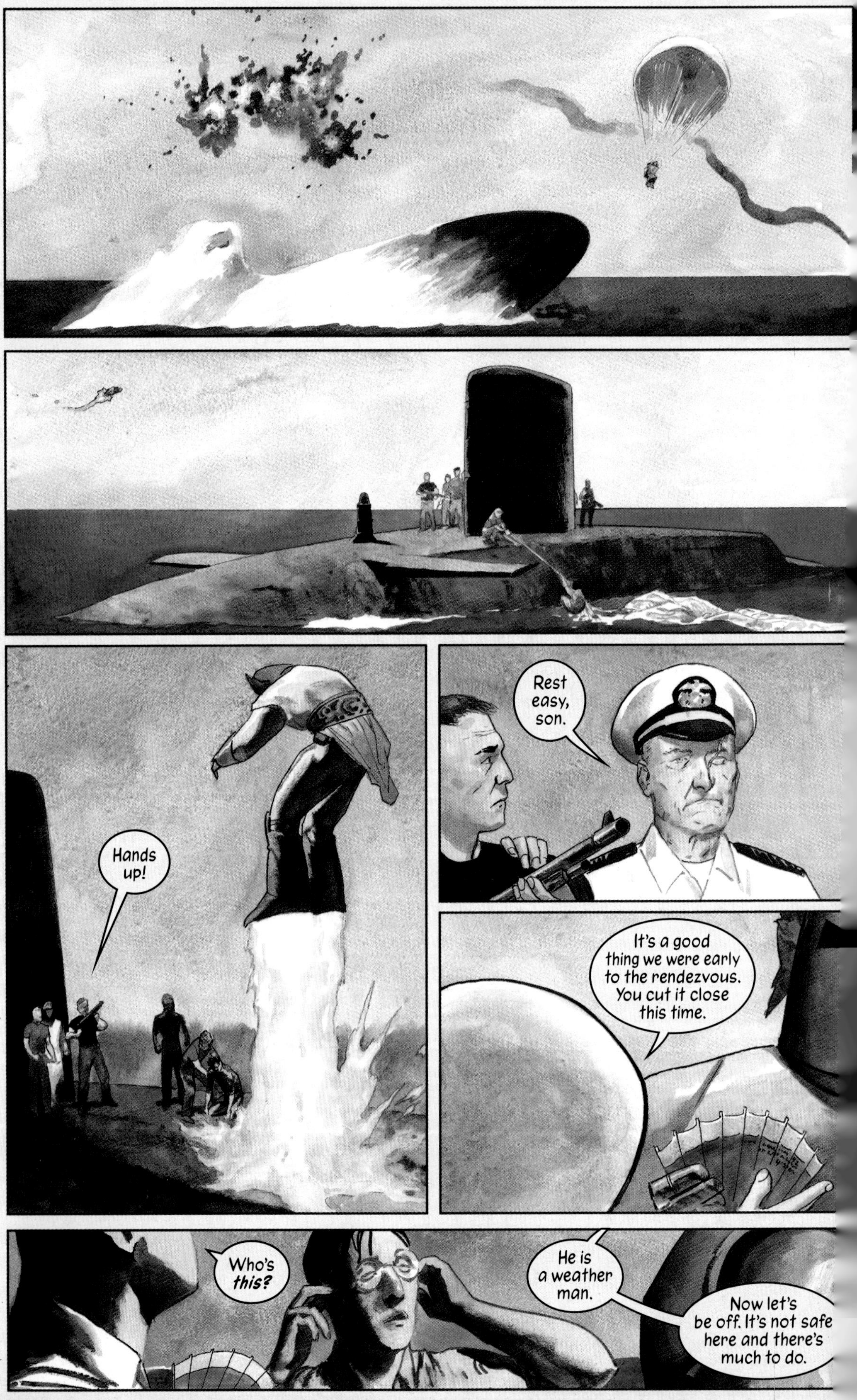
Hands up!
Rest easy, son.
It's a good thing we were early to the rendezvous. You cut it close this time.
Who's *this?*
He is a weather man.
Now let's be off. It's not safe here and there's much to do.

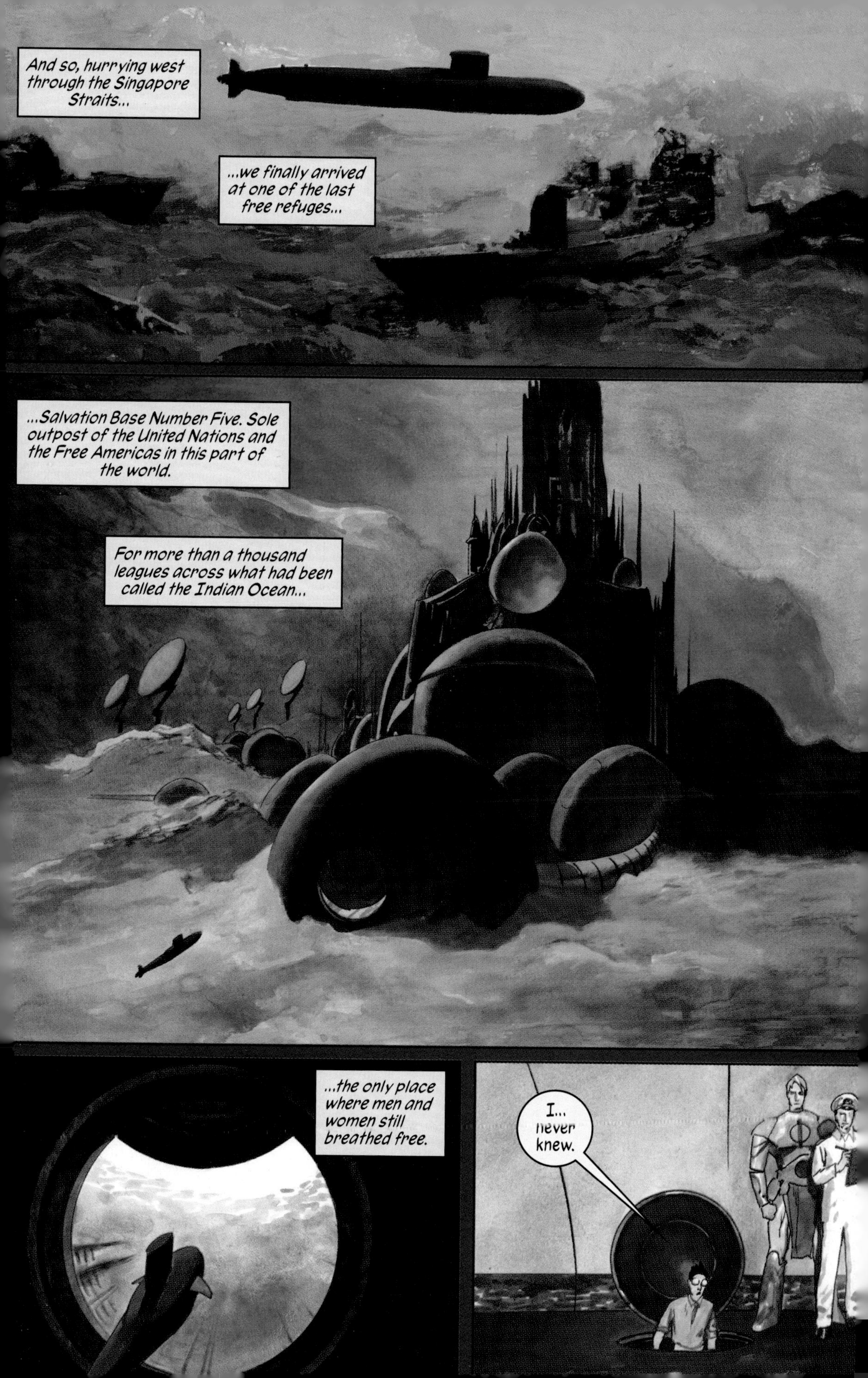

And so, hurrying west through the Singapore Straits...
...we finally arrived at one of the last free refuges...
...Salvation Base Number Five. Sole outpost of the United Nations and the Free Americas in this part of the world.
For more than a thousand leagues across what had been called the Indian Ocean...
...the only place where men and women still breathed free.
I... never knew.

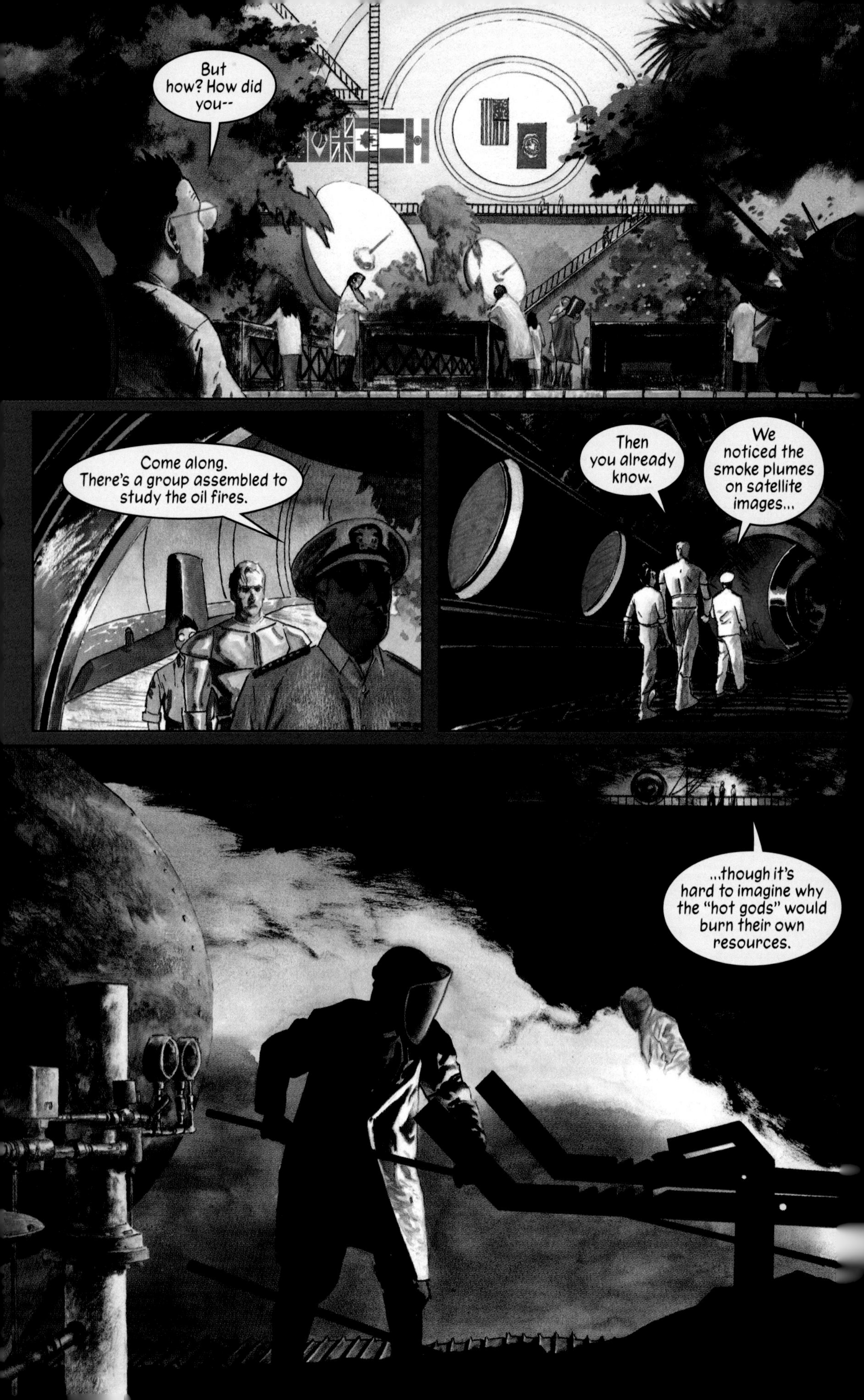
But how? How did you--
Come along. There's a group assembled to study the oil fires.
Then you already know.
We noticed the smoke plumes on satellite images...
...though it's hard to imagine why the "hot gods" would burn their own resources.

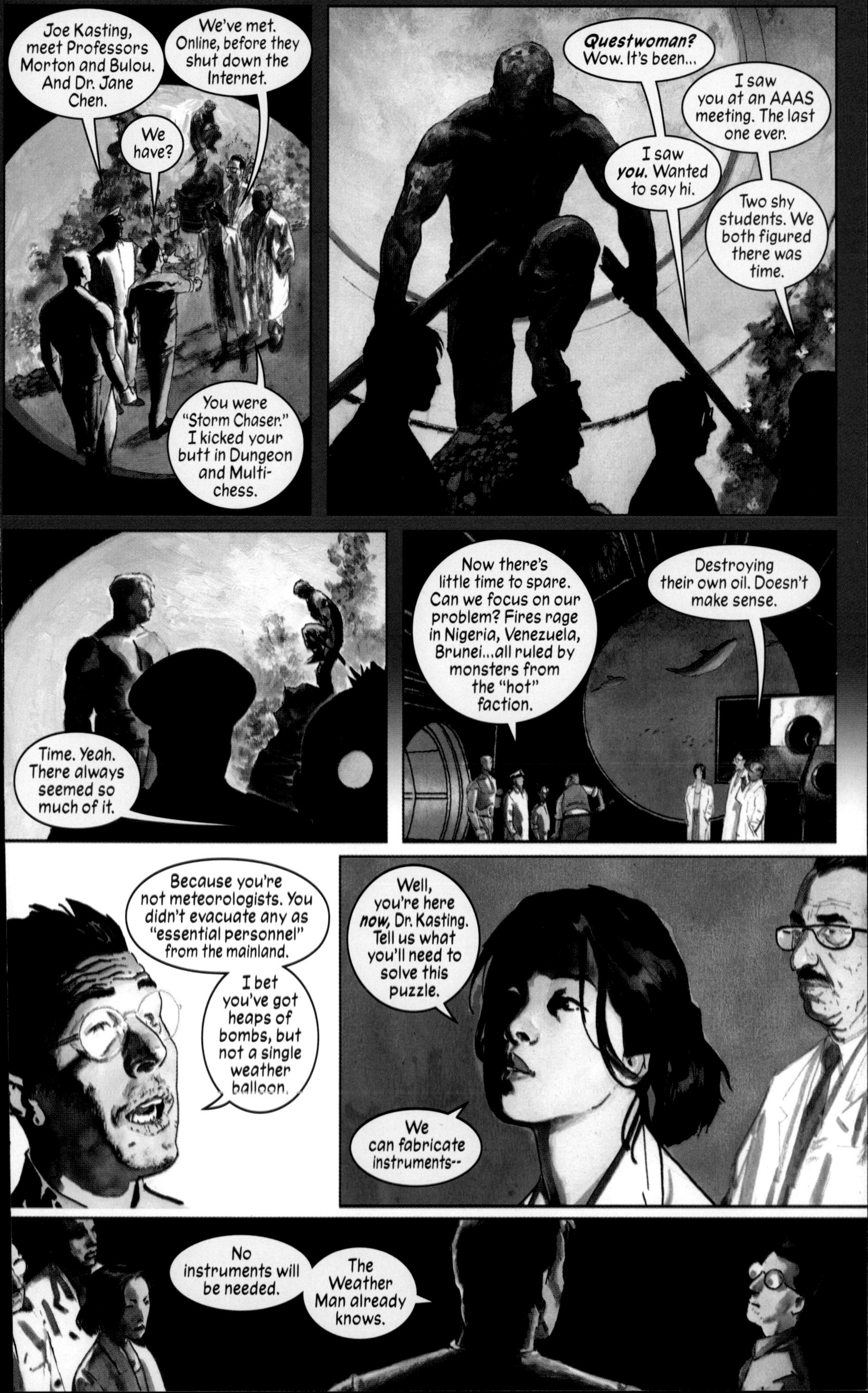
Joe Kasting, meet Professors Morton and Bulou. And Dr. Jane Chen.
We've met. Online, before they shut down the Internet.
We have?
You were "Storm Chaser." I kicked your butt in Dungeon and Multi-chess.
Questwoman? Wow. It's been...
I saw you at an AAAS meeting. The last one ever.
I saw you. Wanted to say hi.
Two shy students. We both figured there was time.
Time. Yeah. There always seemed so much of it.
Now there's little time to spare. Can we focus on our problem? Fires rage in Nigeria, Venezuela, Brunei...all ruled by monsters from the "hot" faction.
Destroying their own oil. Doesn't make sense.
Because you're not meteorologists. You didn't evacuate any as "essential personnel" from the mainland.
I bet you've got heaps of bombs, but not a single weather balloon.
Well, you're here now, Dr. Kasting. Tell us what you'll need to solve this puzzle.
We can fabricate instruments--
No instruments will be needed.
The Weather Man already knows.

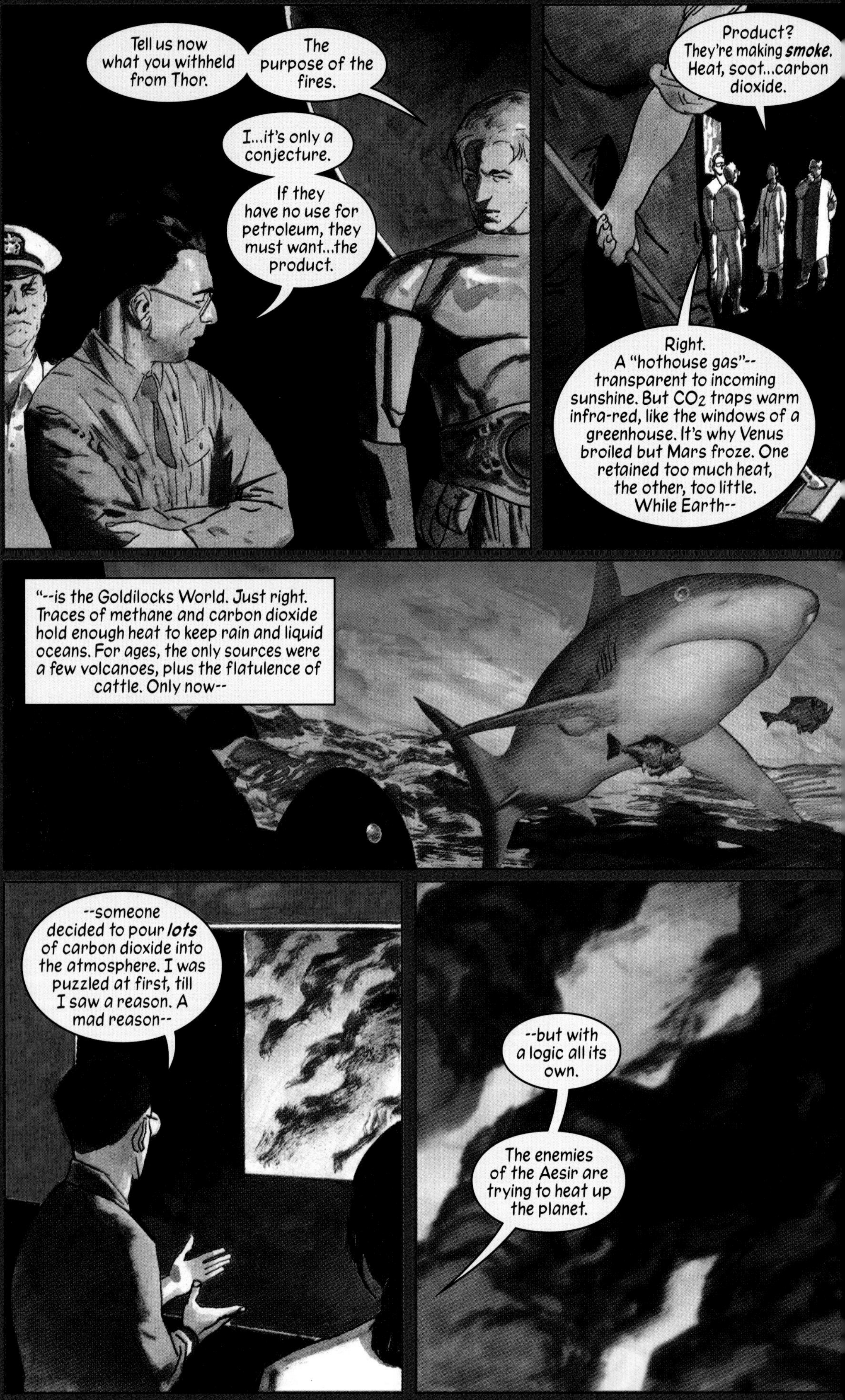

Tell us now what you withheld from Thor.
The purpose of the fires.
I...it's only a conjecture.
If they have no use for petroleum, they must want...the product.
Product? They're making **smoke.** Heat, soot...carbon dioxide.
Right. A "hothouse gas"--transparent to incoming sunshine. But CO_2 traps warm infra-red, like the windows of a greenhouse. It's why Venus broiled but Mars froze. One retained too much heat, the other, too little. While Earth--
"--is the Goldilocks World. Just right. Traces of methane and carbon dioxide hold enough heat to keep rain and liquid oceans. For ages, the only sources were a few volcanoes, plus the flatulence of cattle. Only now--
--someone decided to pour ***lots*** of carbon dioxide into the atmosphere. I was puzzled at first, till I saw a reason. A mad reason--
--but with a logic all its own.
The enemies of the Aesir are trying to heat up the planet.

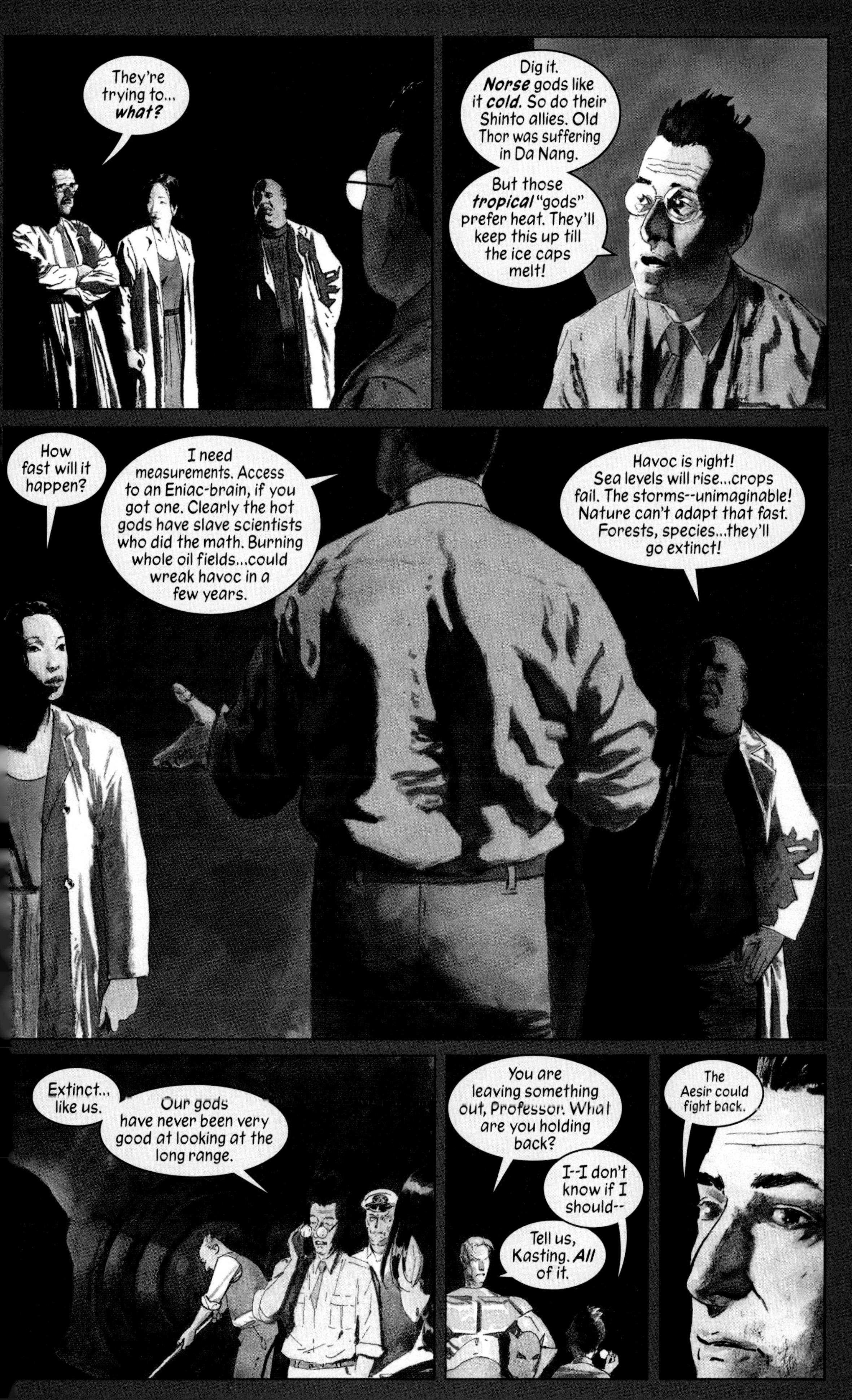

They're trying to... ***what?***
Dig it. ***Norse*** gods like it ***cold.*** So do their Shinto allies. Old Thor was suffering in Da Nang.
But those ***tropical*** "gods" prefer heat. They'll keep this up till the ice caps melt!
How fast will it happen?
I need measurements. Access to an Eniac-brain, if you got one. Clearly the hot gods have slave scientists who did the math. Burning whole oil fields...could wreak havoc in a few years.
Havoc is right! Sea levels will rise...crops fail. The storms--unimaginable! Nature can't adapt that fast. Forests, species...they'll go extinct!
Extinct... like us.
Our gods have never been very good at looking at the long range.
You are leaving something out, Professor. What are you holding back?
I--I don't know if I should--
Tell us, Kasting. ***All*** of it.
The Aesir could fight back.

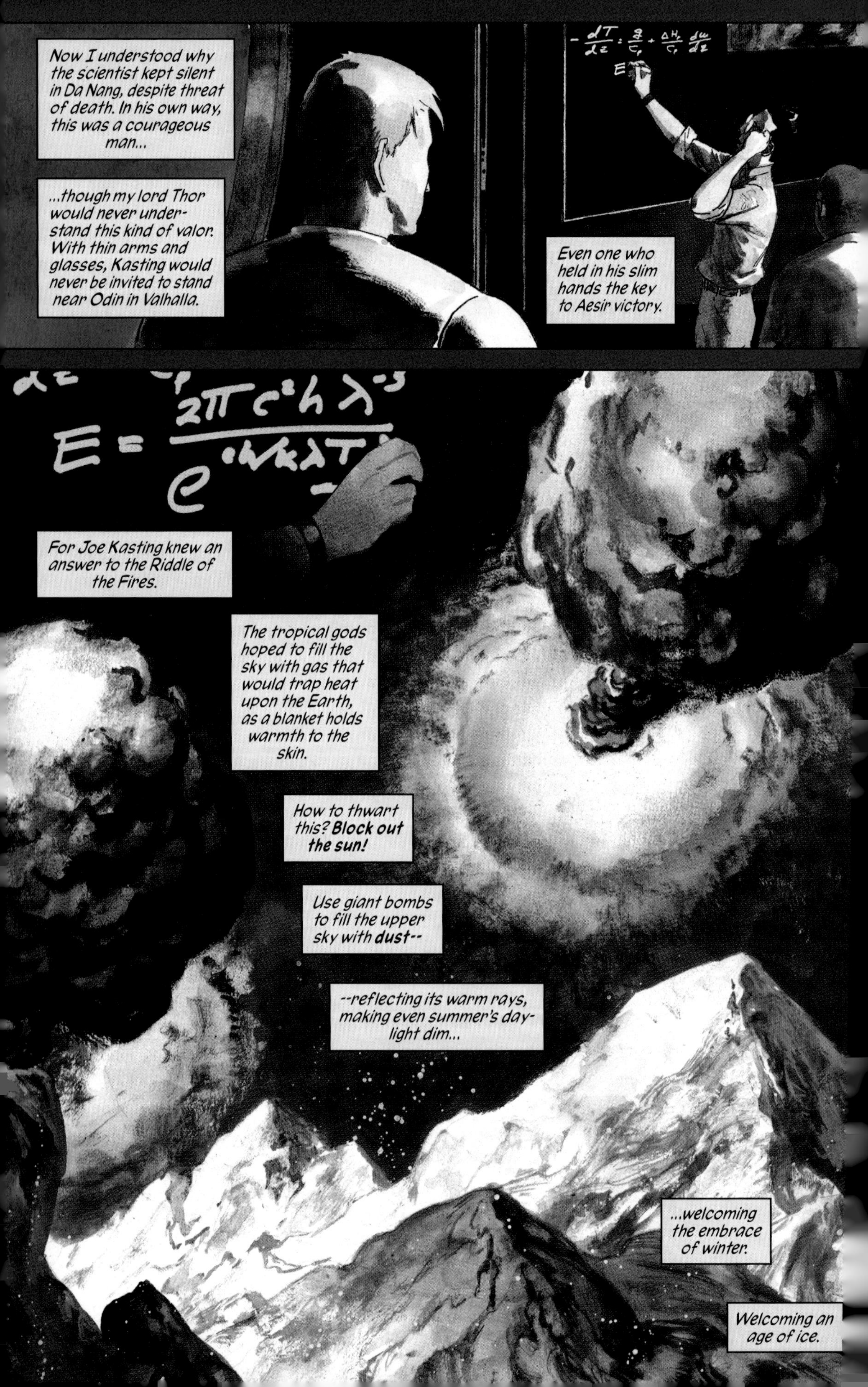
Now I understood why the scientist kept silent in Da Nang, despite threat of death. In his own way, this was a courageous man...
...though my lord Thor would never understand this kind of valor. With thin arms and glasses, Kasting would never be invited to stand near Odin in Valhalla.
Even one who held in his slim hands the key to Aesir victory.
For Joe Kasting knew an answer to the Riddle of the Fires.
The tropical gods hoped to fill the sky with gas that would trap heat upon the Earth, as a blanket holds warmth to the skin.
How to thwart this? **Block out the sun!**
Use giant bombs to fill the upper sky with **dust**--
--reflecting its warm rays, making even summer's daylight dim...
...welcoming the embrace of winter.
Welcoming an age of ice.

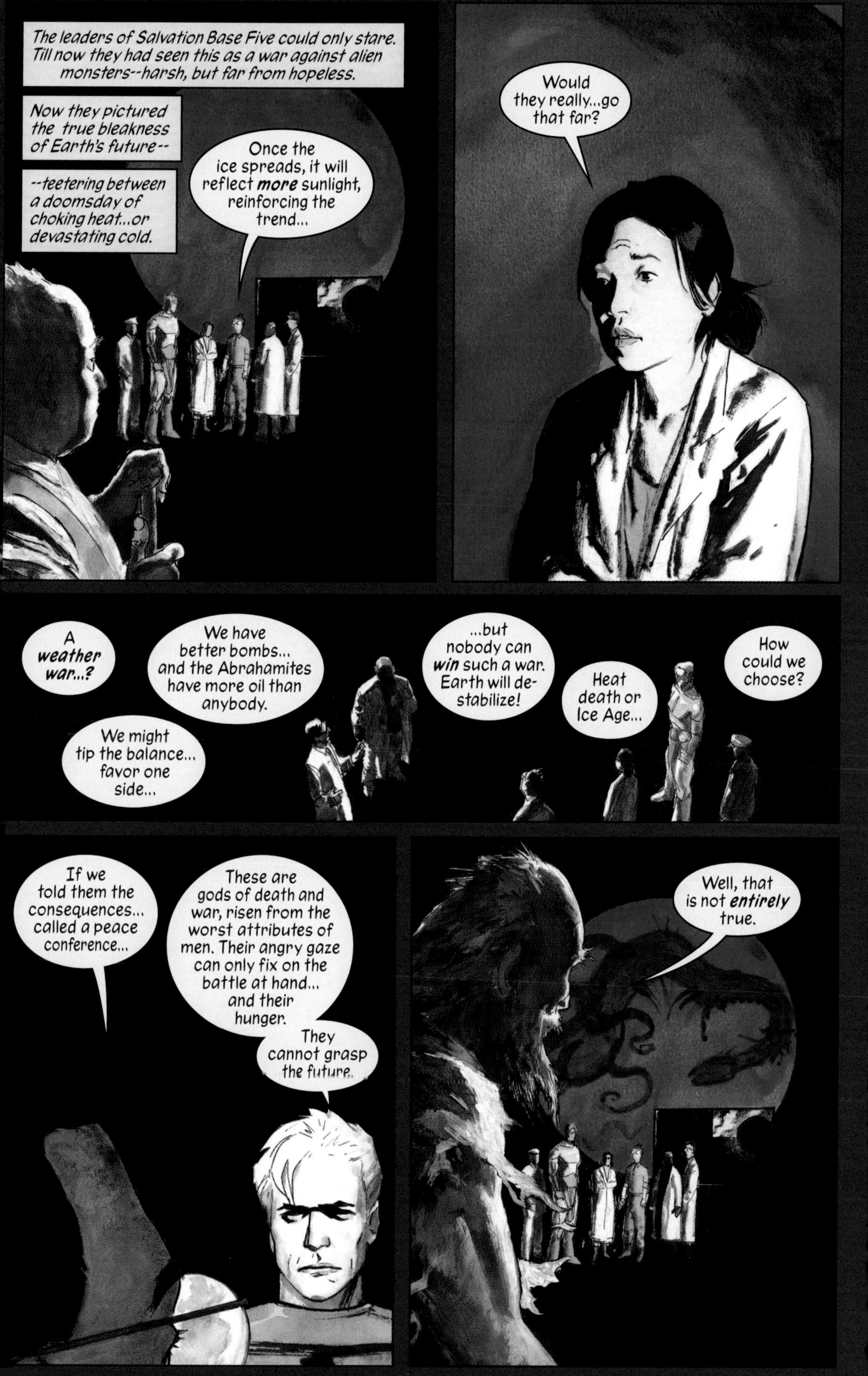
The leaders of Salvation Base Five could only stare. Till now they had seen this as a war against alien monsters--harsh, but far from hopeless.
Now they pictured the true bleakness of Earth's future--
--teetering between a doomsday of choking heat...or devastating cold.
Once the ice spreads, it will reflect more sunlight, reinforcing the trend...
Would they really...go that far?
A weather war...?
We have better bombs... and the Abrahamites have more oil than anybody.
We might tip the balance... favor one side...
...but nobody can win such a war. Earth will de-stabilize!
Heat death or Ice Age...
How could we choose?
If we told them the consequences... called a peace conference...
These are gods of death and war, risen from the worst attributes of men. Their angry gaze can only fix on the battle at hand... and their hunger.
They cannot grasp the future.
Well, that is not entirely true.

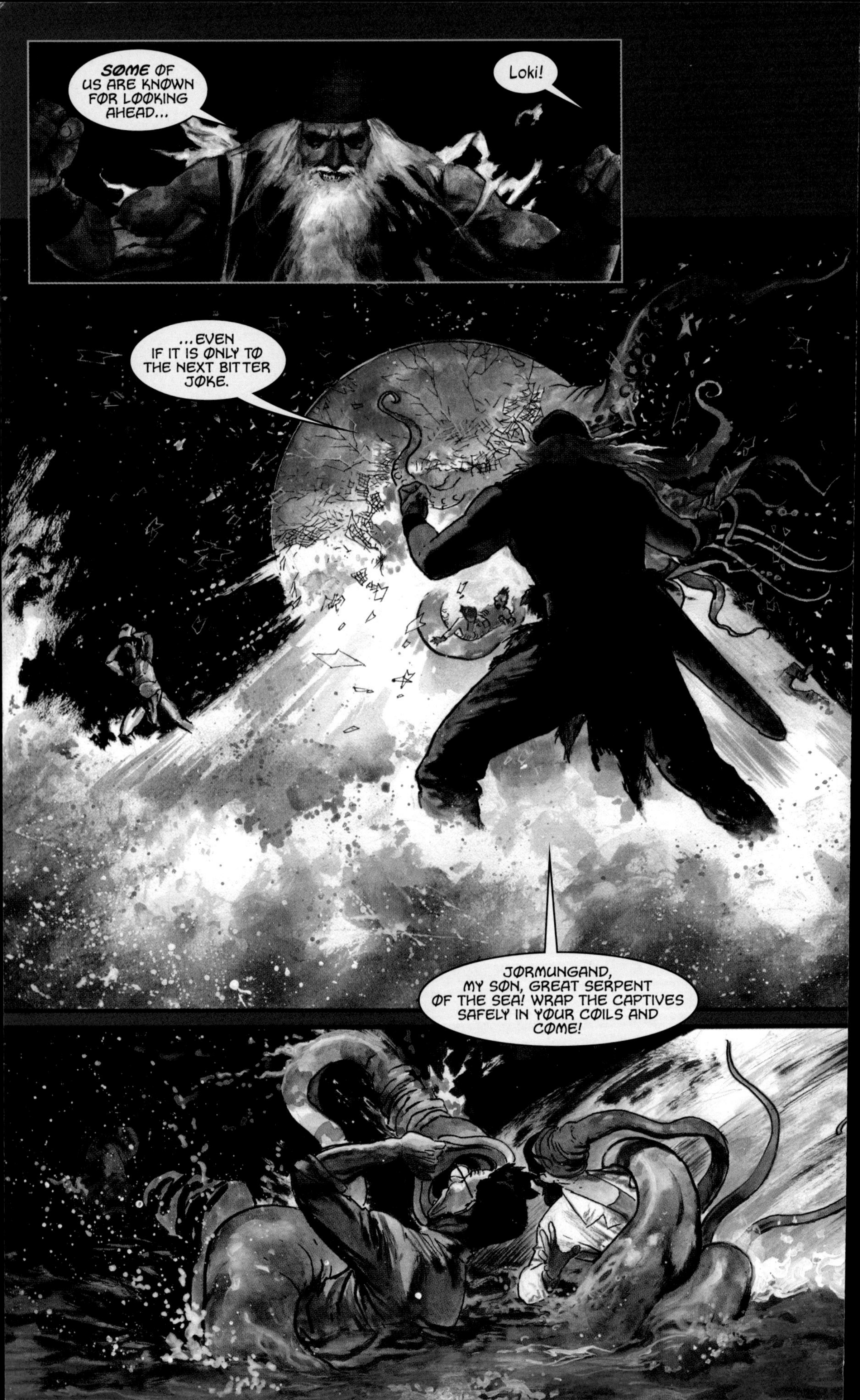
SOME OF US ARE KNOWN FOR LOOKING AHEAD...
Loki!
...EVEN IF IT IS ONLY TO THE NEXT BITTER JOKE.
JORMUNGAND, MY SON, GREAT SERPENT OF THE SEA! WRAP THE CAPTIVES SAFELY IN YOUR COILS AND COME!

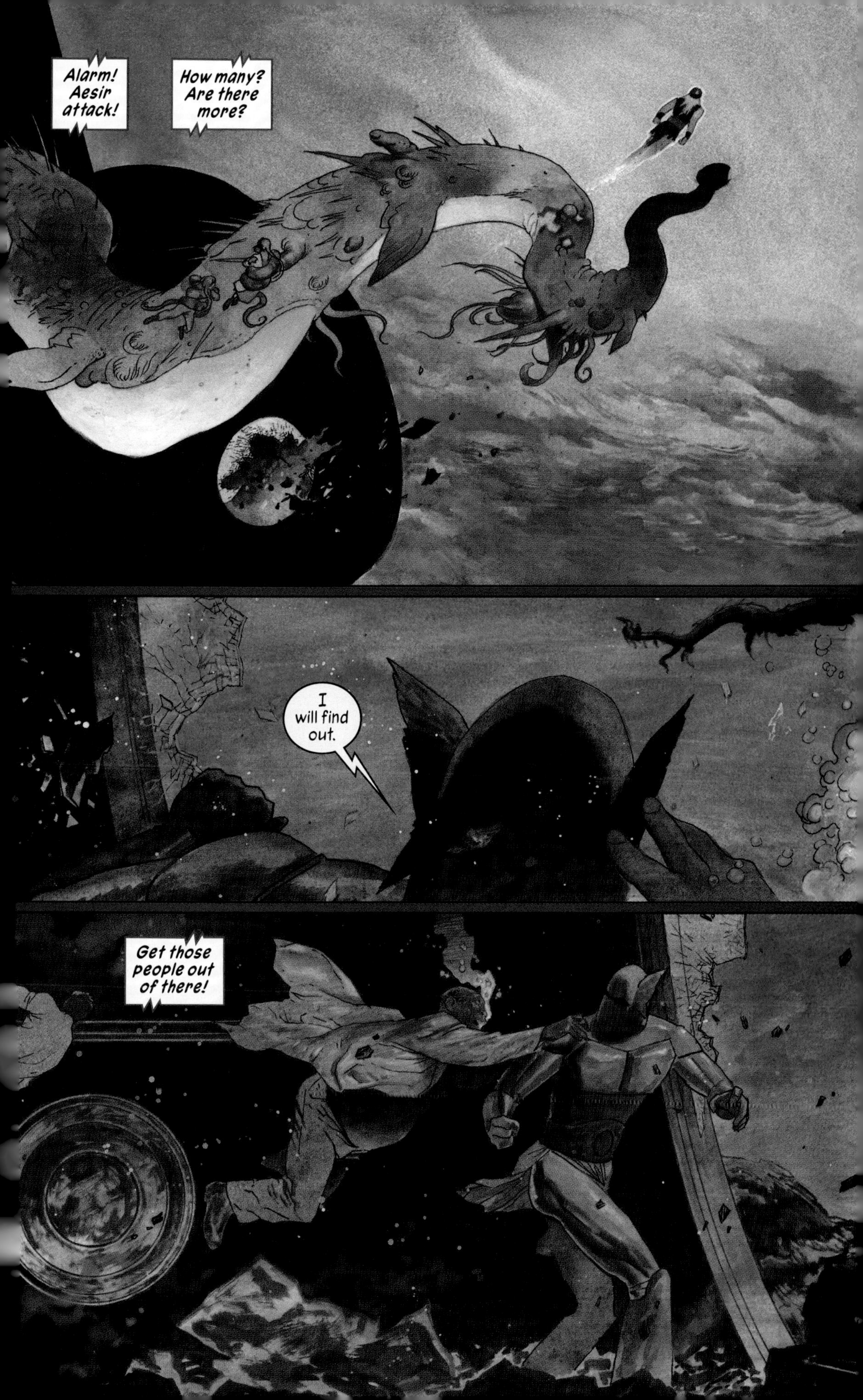
Alarm! Aesir attack!
How many? Are there more?
I will find out.
Get those people out of there!

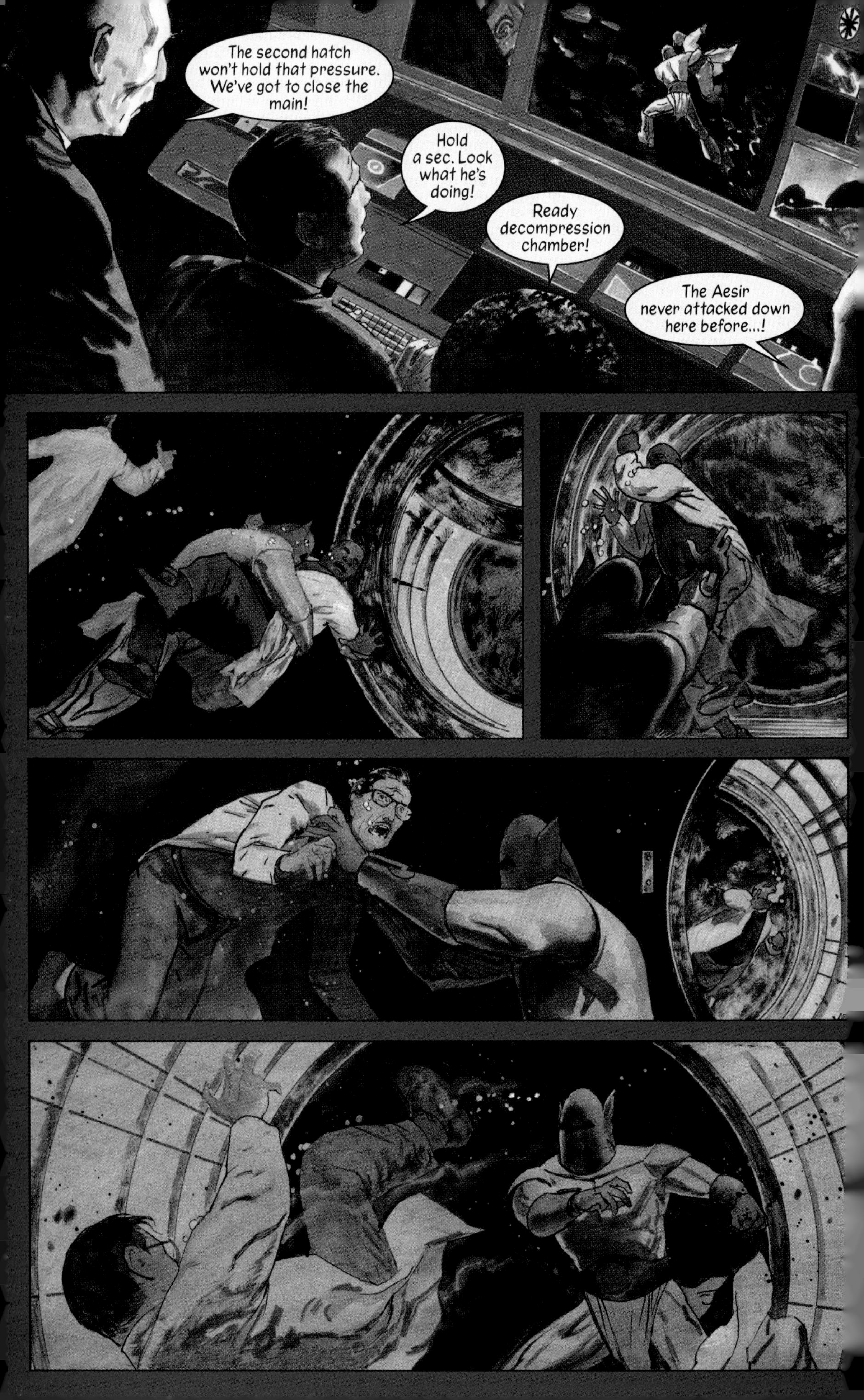
The second hatch won't hold that pressure. We've got to close the main!
Hold a sec. Look what he's doing!
Ready decompression chamber!
The Aesir never attacked down here before...!

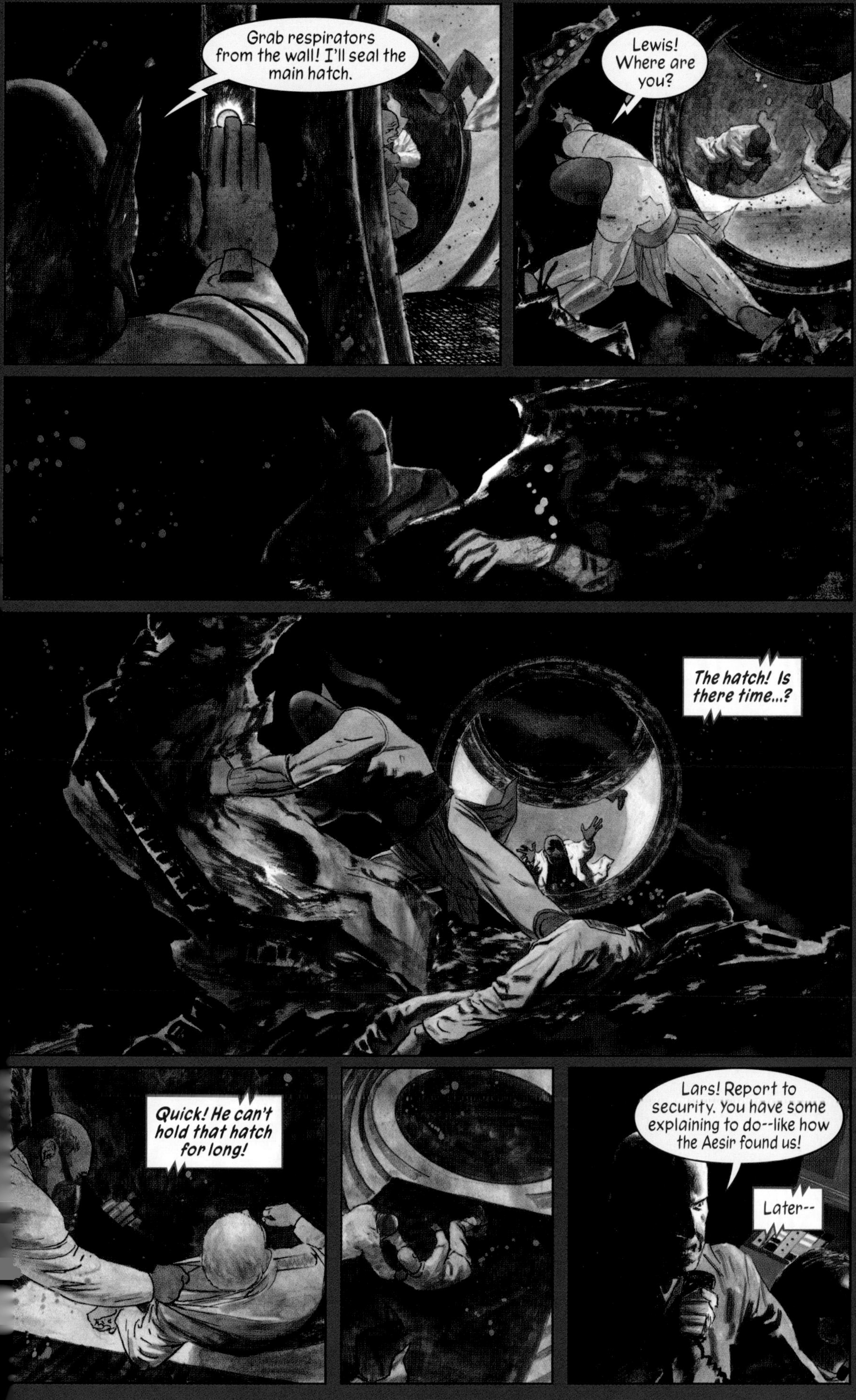
Grab respirators from the wall! I'll seal the main hatch.
Lewis! Where are you?
The hatch! Is there time...?
Quick! He can't hold that hatch for long!
Lars! Report to security. You have some explaining to do--like how the Aesir found us!
Later--

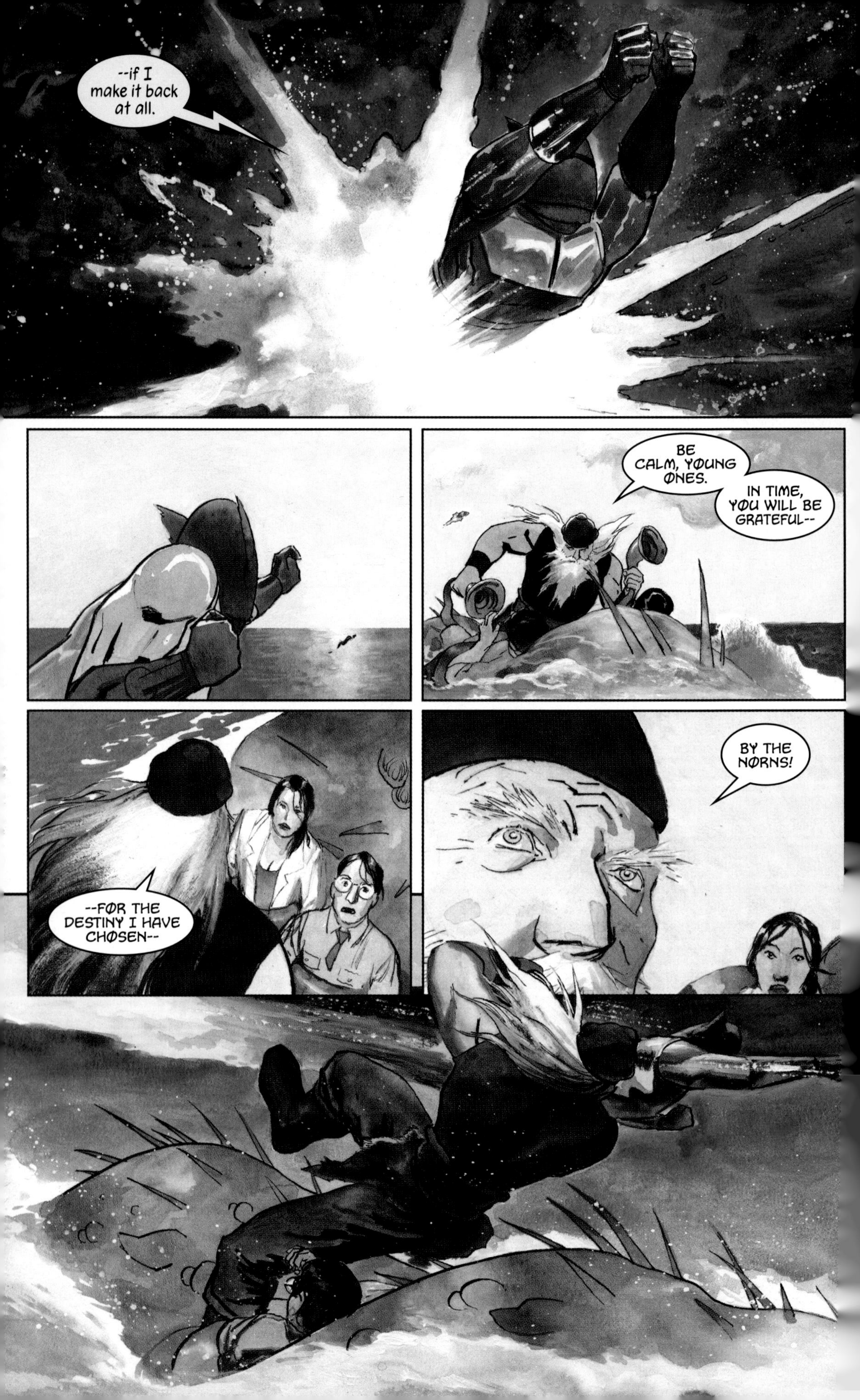
--if I make it back at all.
BE CALM, YØUNG ØNES.
IN TIME, YØU WILL BE GRATEFUL--
--FØR THE DESTINY I HAVE CHØSEN--
BY THE NØRNS!

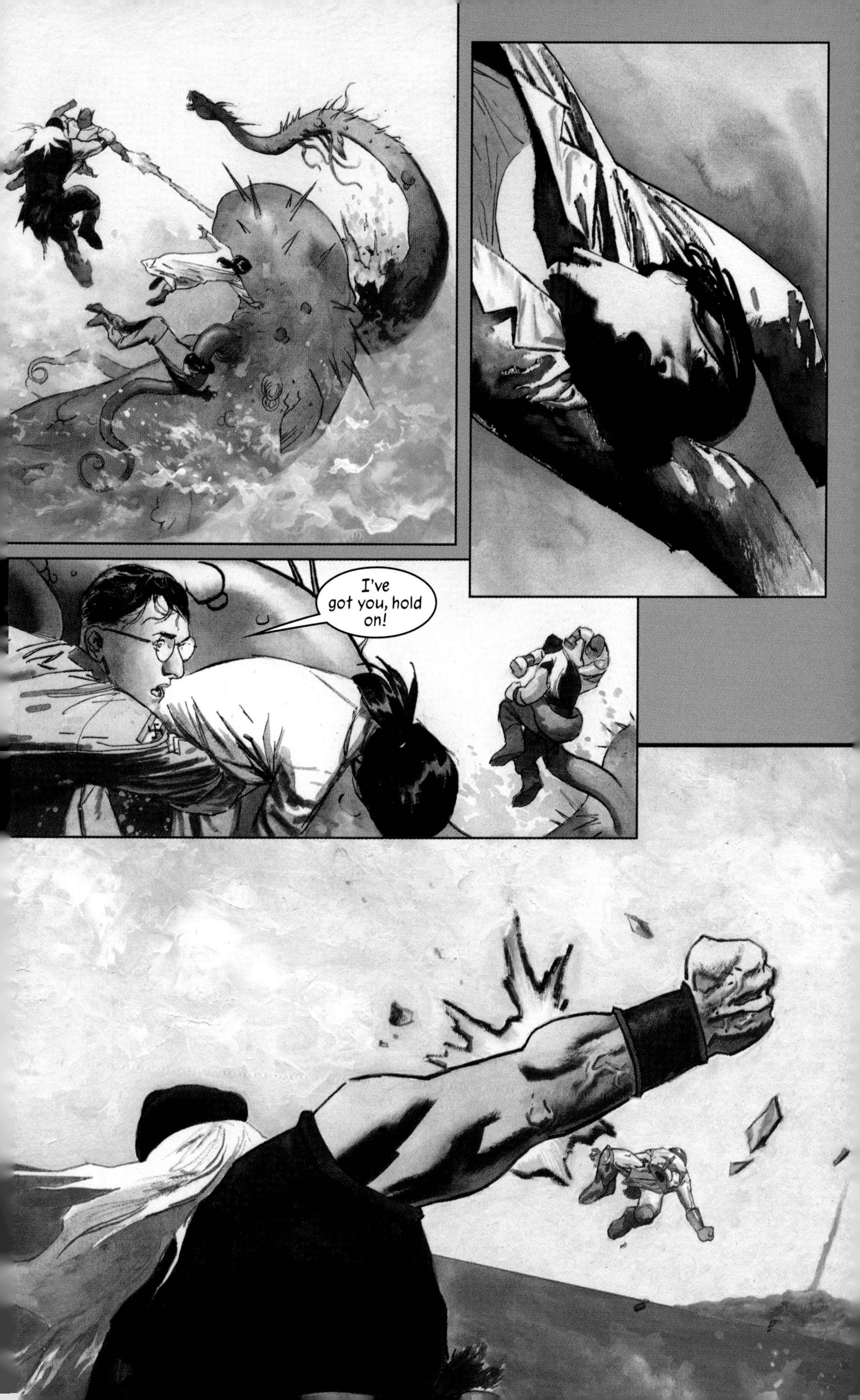
I've got you, hold on!

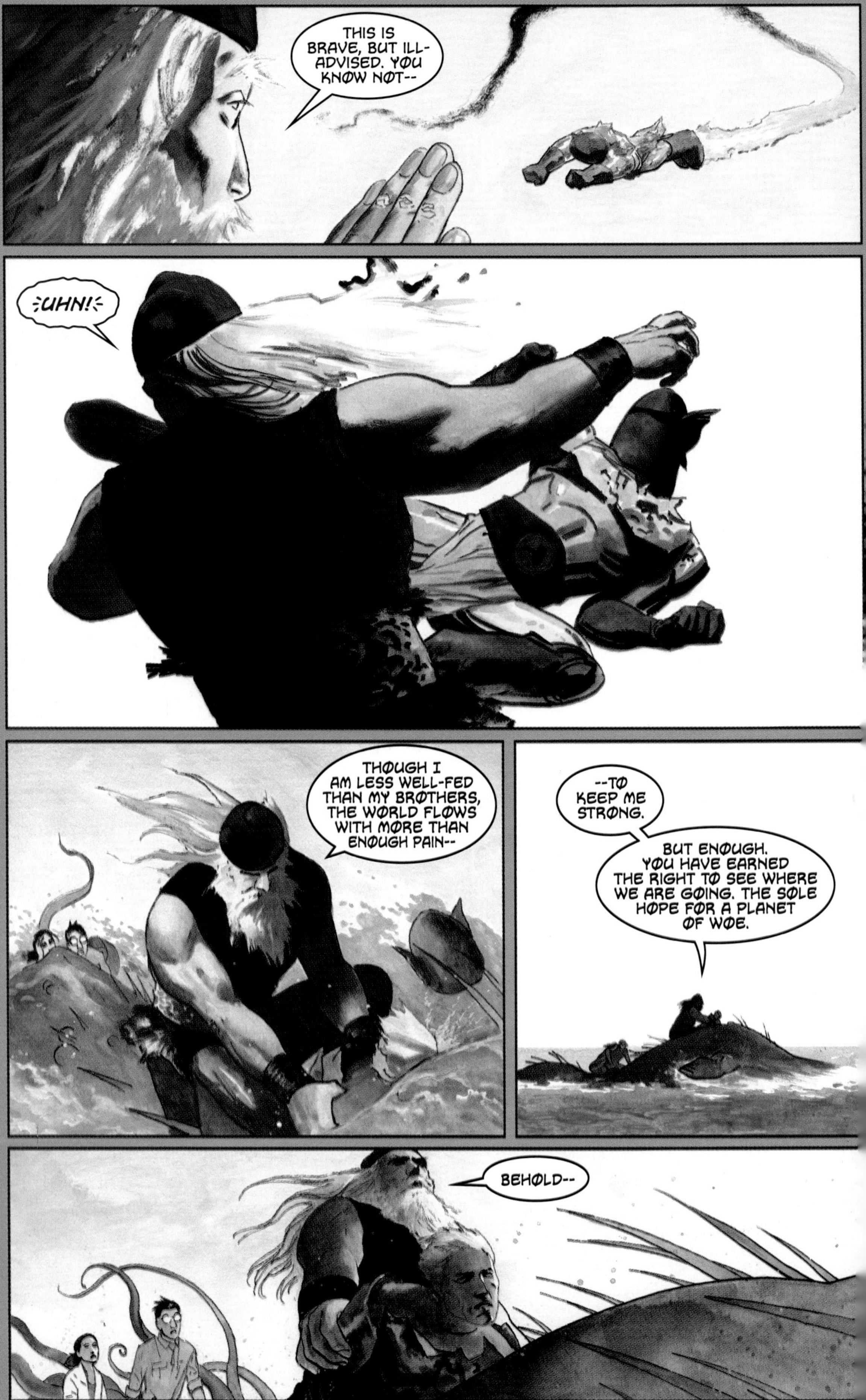
THIS IS BRAVE, BUT ILL-ADVISED. YOU KNOW NOT--
UHN!
THOUGH I AM LESS WELL-FED THAN MY BROTHERS, THE WORLD FLOWS WITH MORE THAN ENOUGH PAIN--
--TO KEEP ME STRONG.
BUT ENOUGH. YOU HAVE EARNED THE RIGHT TO SEE WHERE WE ARE GOING. THE SOLE HOPE FOR A PLANET OF WOE.
BEHOLD--

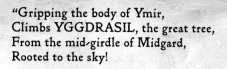

"Gripping the body of Ymir,
Climbs YGGDRASIL, the great tree,
From the mid-girdle of Midgard,
Rooted to the sky!

"As foretold long ago,
There will come Ragnarok!
Doomtime for gods and men—
Doom for all worlds!

"Doom...save for just a few.
Sheltered from fire and ice,
High in the branches of Yggdrasil."

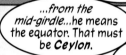
Ragnarok...

...from the mid-girdle...he means the equator. That must be Ceylon.

But how can a tree be rooted to the sky?

I...met a scientist at Base Nine. A refugee from the horror in Russia.

"He was mad. Babbled that a cable could...in theory...stretch up from the equator!

"Past low Earth orbit...

"...rooted to the sky by centrifugal force.

"He called it a space elevator."

A way to leave Earth without rockets.

YES, CHILD. TO LEAVE A RUINED WORLD, AS FORETOLD IN THE SAGAS.

ONLY, NO CABLE. A TREE.

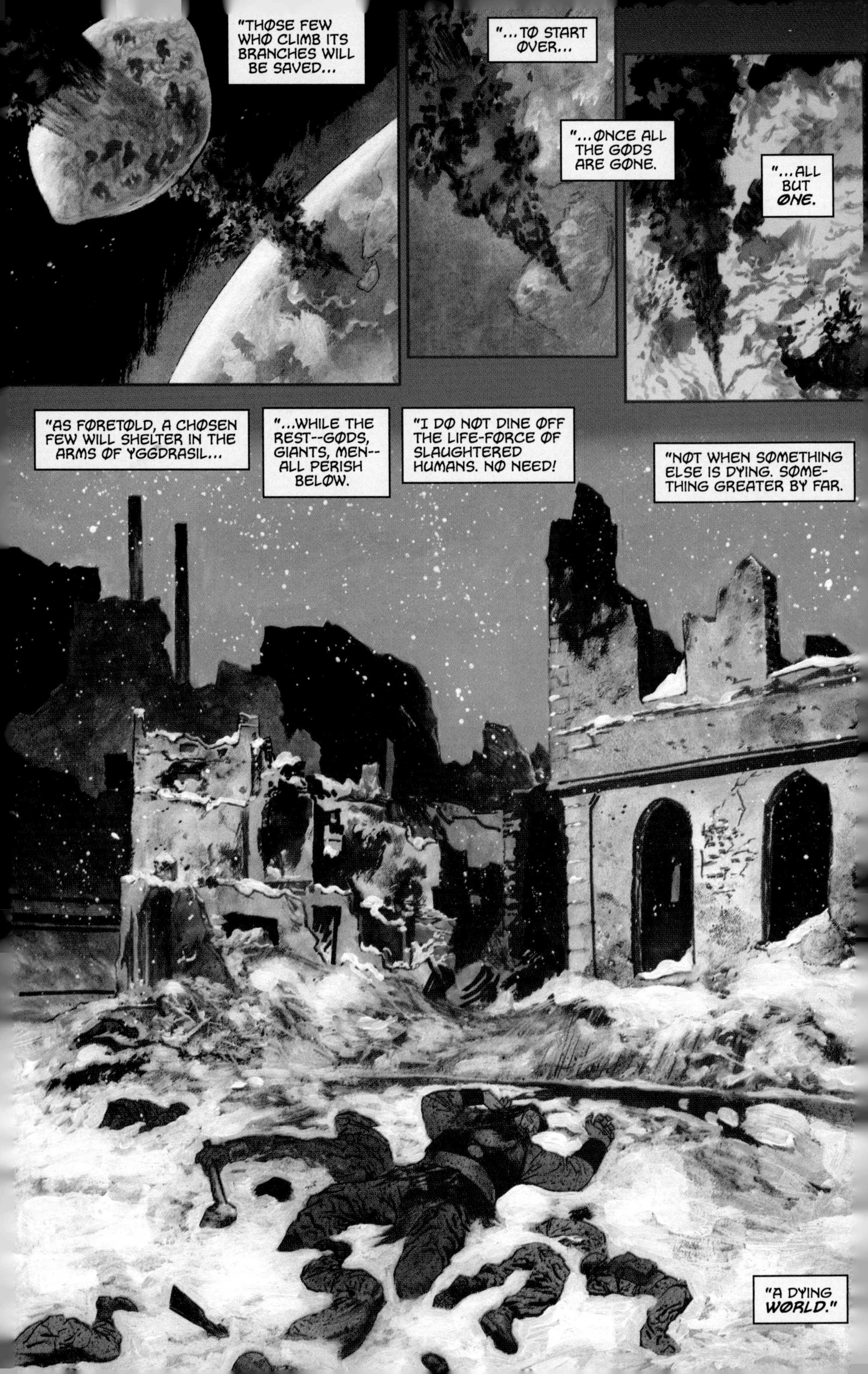
"THOSE FEW WHO CLIMB ITS BRANCHES WILL BE SAVED...
"...TO START OVER...
"...ONCE ALL THE GODS ARE GONE.
"...ALL BUT ONE.
"AS FORETOLD, A CHOSEN FEW WILL SHELTER IN THE ARMS OF YGGDRASIL...
"...WHILE THE REST--GODS, GIANTS, MEN--ALL PERISH BELOW.
"I DO NOT DINE OFF THE LIFE-FORCE OF SLAUGHTERED HUMANS. NO NEED!
"NOT WHEN SOMETHING ELSE IS DYING. SOMETHING GREATER BY FAR.
"A DYING WORLD."

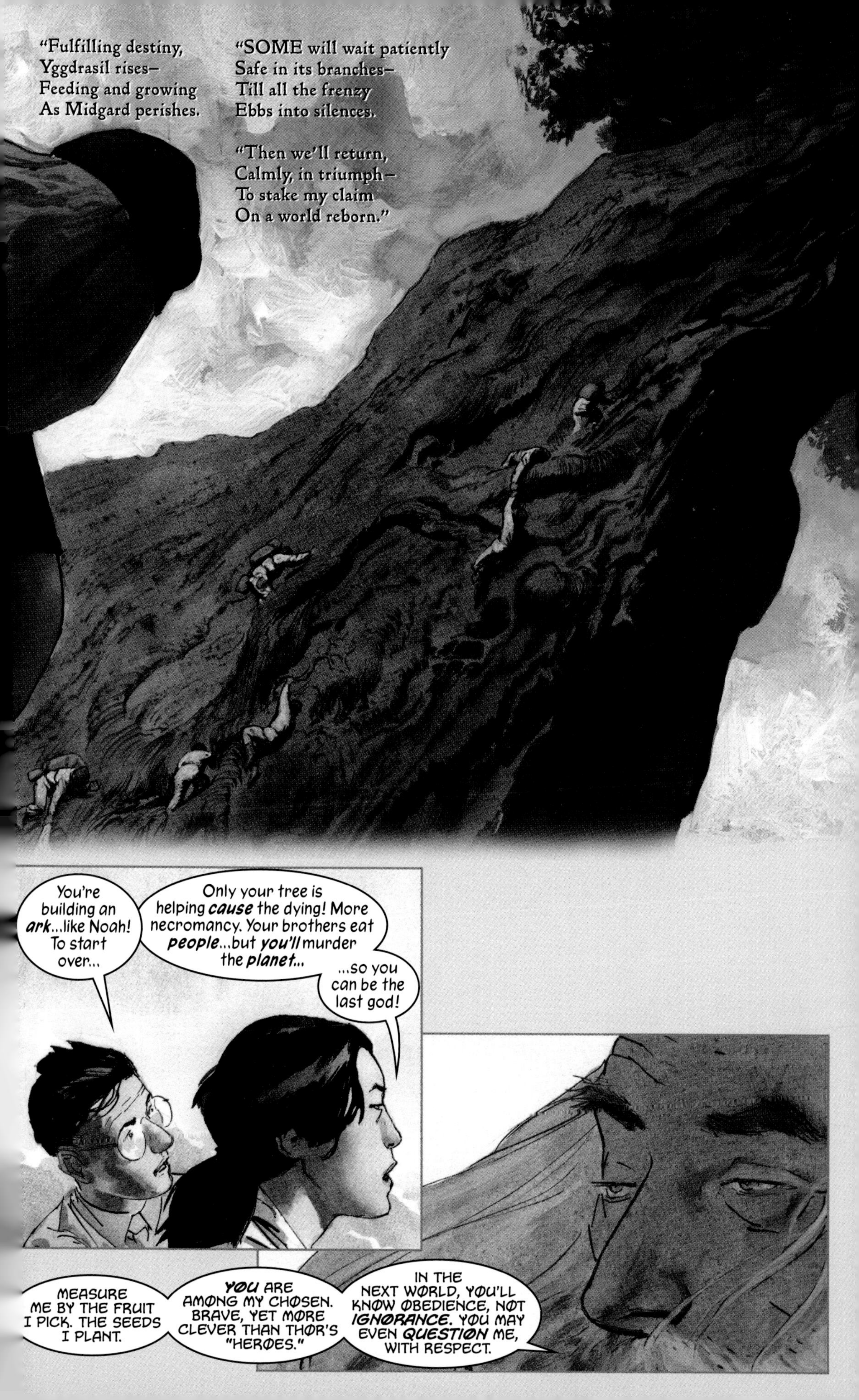
"Fulfilling destiny,
Yggdrasil rises–
Feeding and growing
As Midgard perishes.
"SOME will wait patiently
Safe in its branches–
Till all the frenzy
Ebbs into silences.
"Then we'll return,
Calmly, in triumph–
To stake my claim
On a world reborn."
You're building an ark...like Noah! To start over...
Only your tree is helping cause the dying! More necromancy. Your brothers eat people...but you'll murder the planet...
...so you can be the last god!
MEASURE ME BY THE FRUIT I PICK. THE SEEDS I PLANT.
YOU ARE AMONG MY CHOSEN. BRAVE, YET MORE CLEVER THAN THOR'S "HEROES."
IN THE NEXT WORLD, YOU'LL KNOW OBEDIENCE, NOT IGNORANCE. YOU MAY EVEN QUESTION ME, WITH RESPECT.

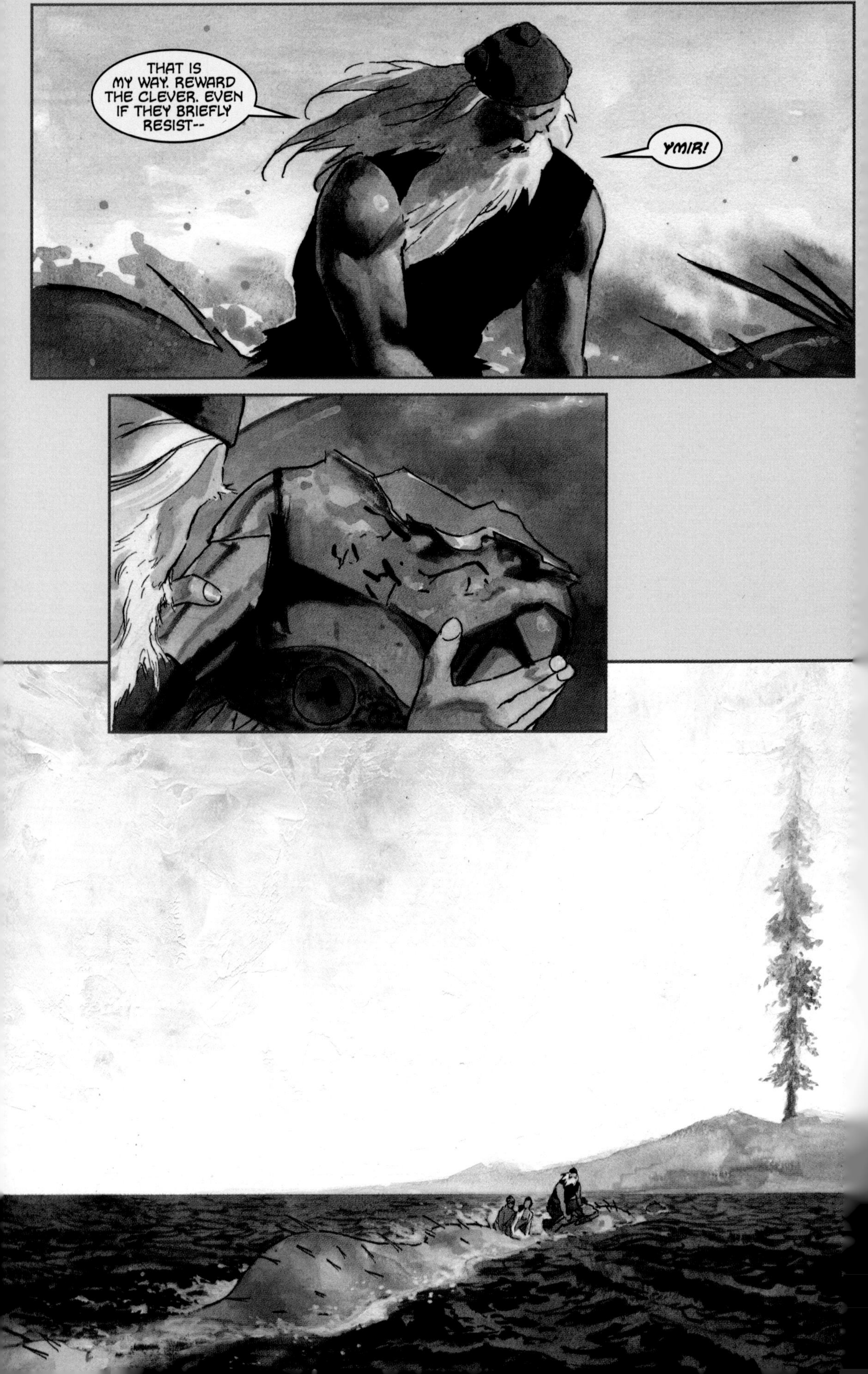
THAT IS MY WAY. REWARD THE CLEVER. EVEN IF THEY BRIEFLY RESIST--
YMIR!

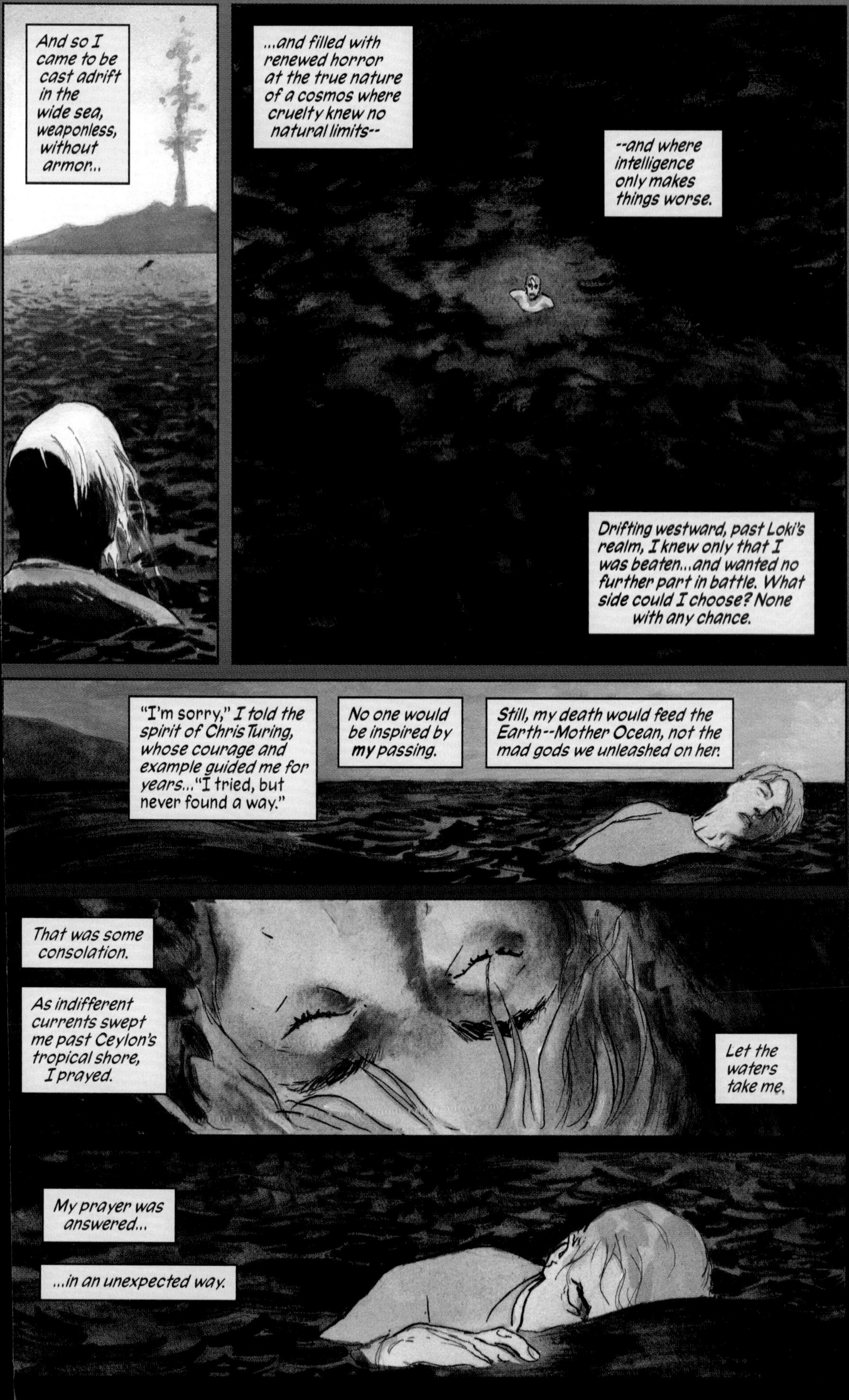
And so I came to be cast adrift in the wide sea, weaponless, without armor...
...and filled with renewed horror at the true nature of a cosmos where cruelty knew no natural limits--
--and where intelligence only makes things worse.
Drifting westward, past Loki's realm, I knew only that I was beaten...and wanted no further part in battle. What side could I choose? None with any chance.
"I'm sorry," I told the spirit of Chris Turing, whose courage and example guided me for years..."I tried, but never found a way."
No one would be inspired by my passing.
Still, my death would feed the Earth--Mother Ocean, not the mad gods we unleashed on her.
That was some consolation.
As indifferent currents swept me past Ceylon's tropical shore, I prayed.
Let the waters take me.
My prayer was answered...
...in an unexpected way.

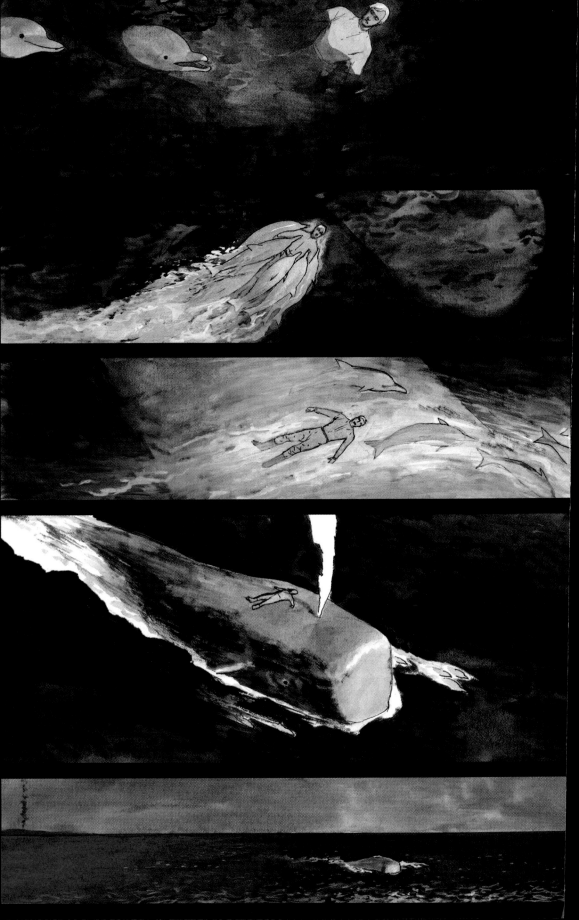

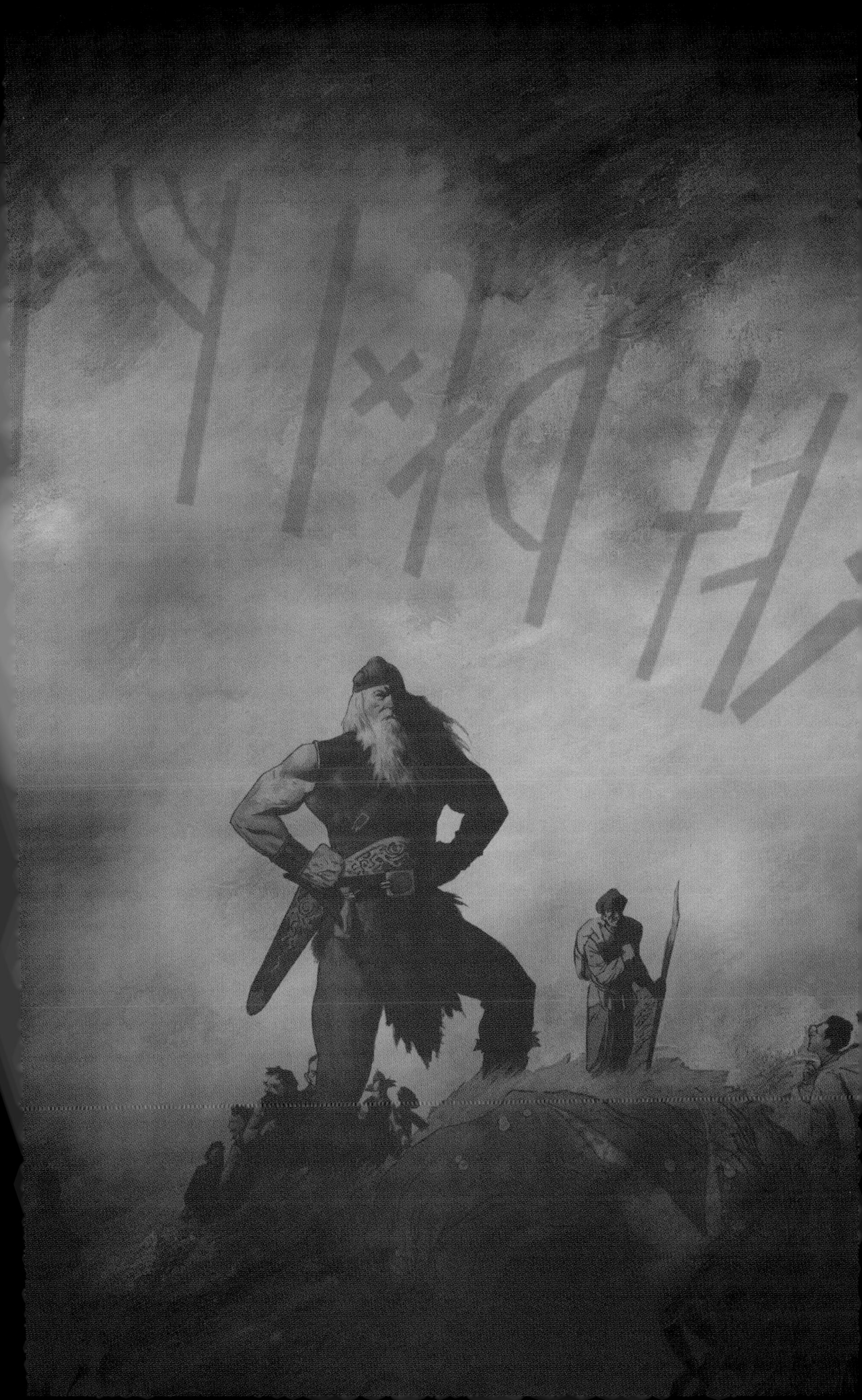

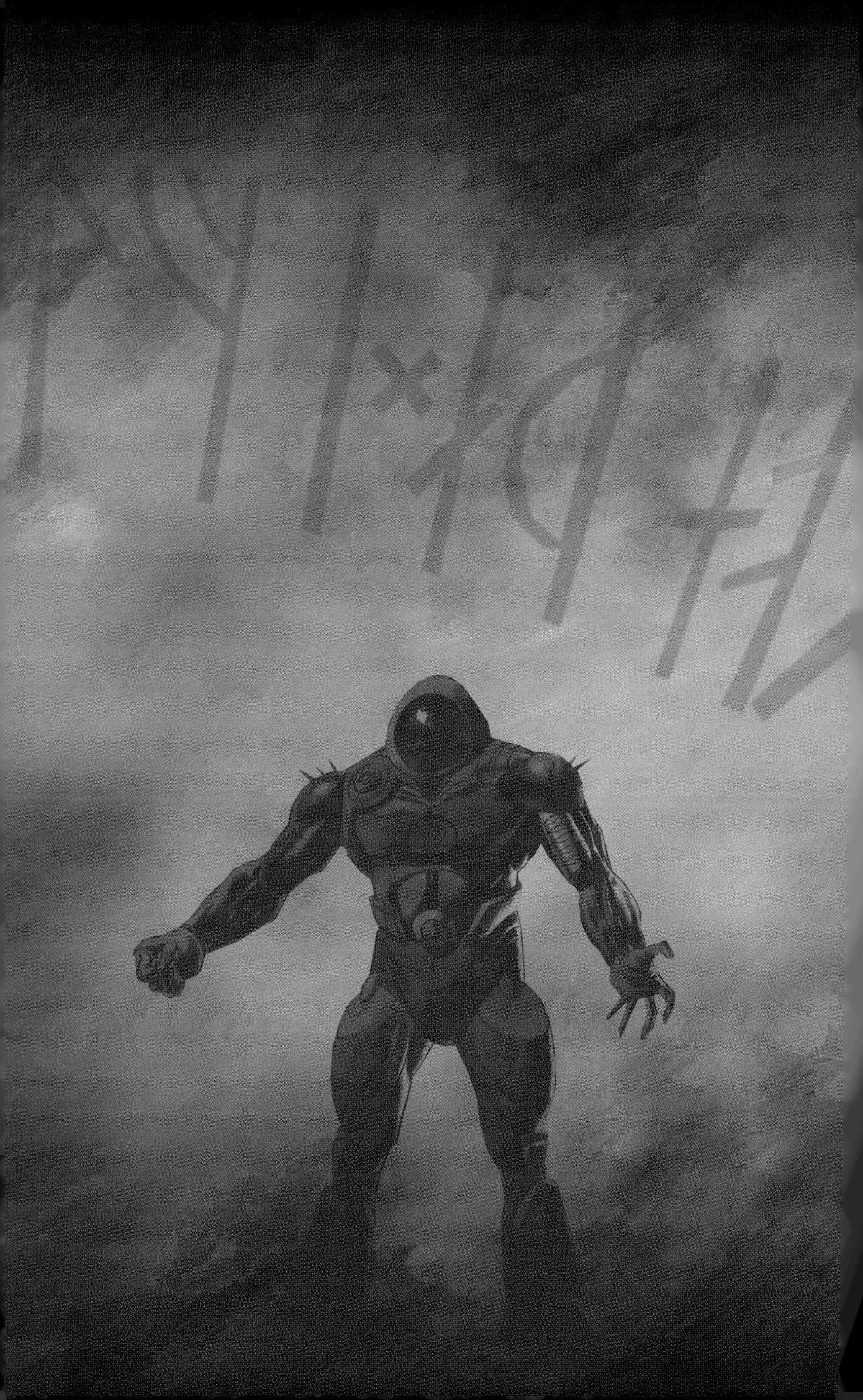

— PART THREE —
"SACRIFICE"

Bring in a wagon the sacred idols.
Hang a man from a tree,
Wound him by a lance.
Send smoke curling to Valhalla.
Thus is the sacrifice holy to Woden,
Called Odin by the Norse,
and God of the Middle Day.

— The Norse Sagas

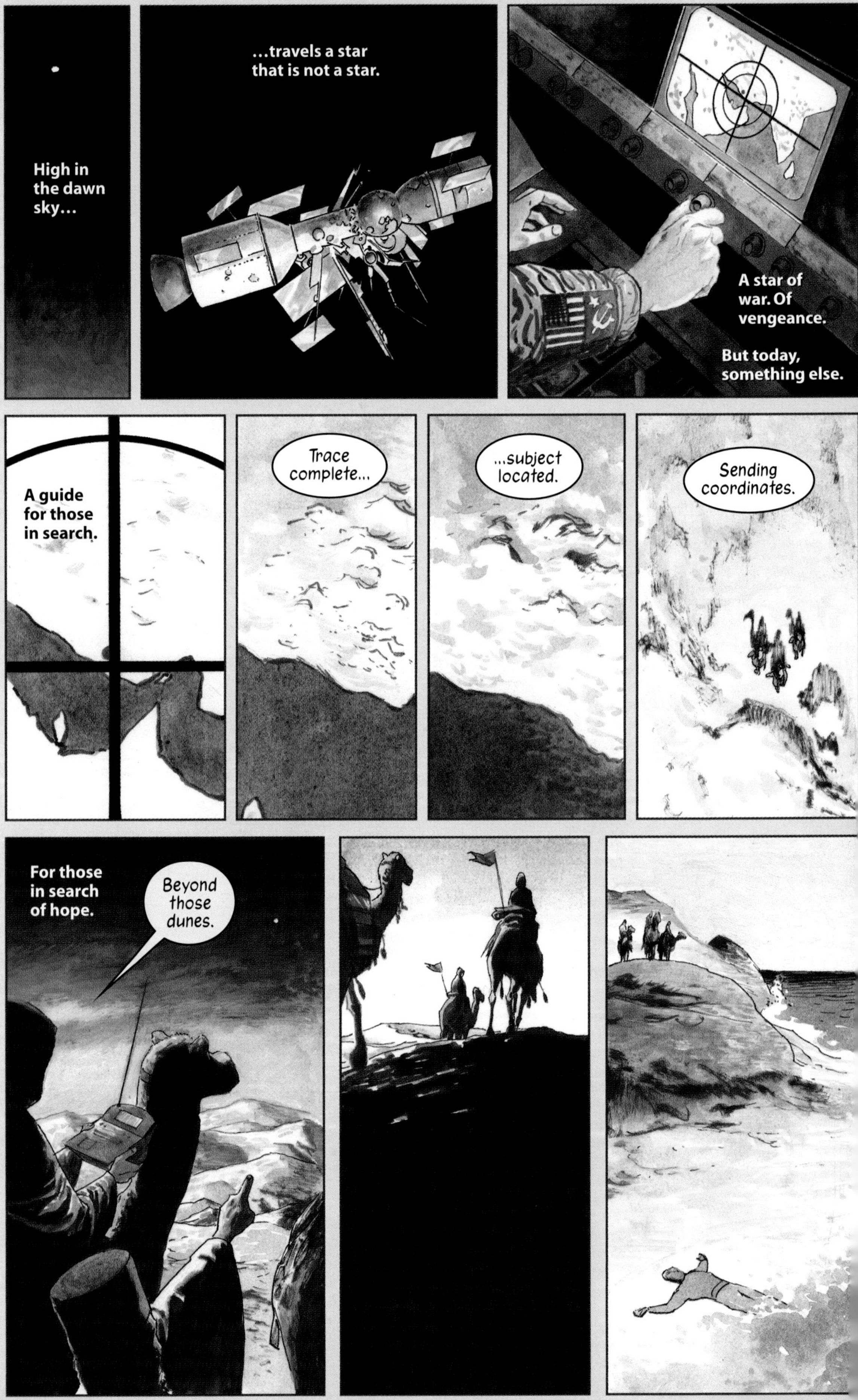
High in the dawn sky…
…travels a star that is not a star.
A star of war. Of vengeance.
But today, something else.
A guide for those in search.
Trace complete…
…subject located.
Sending coordinates.
For those in search of hope.
Beyond those dunes.

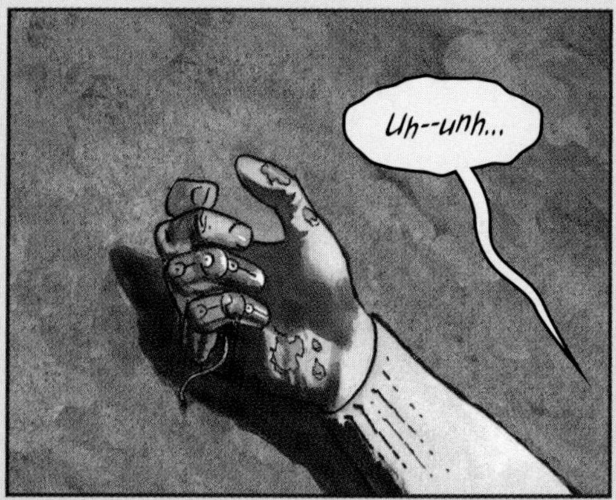
Uh--unh...

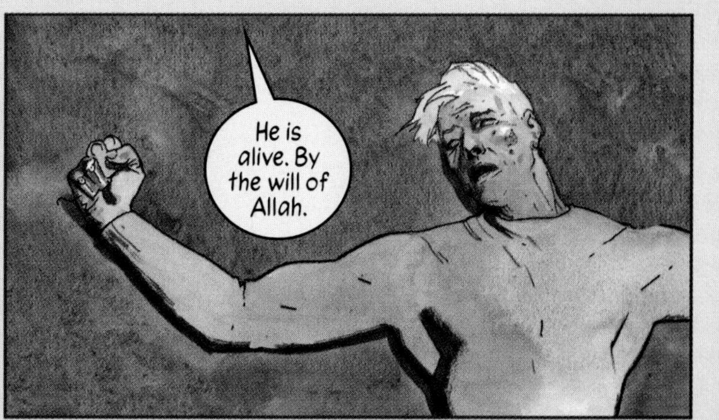
He is alive. By the will of Allah.

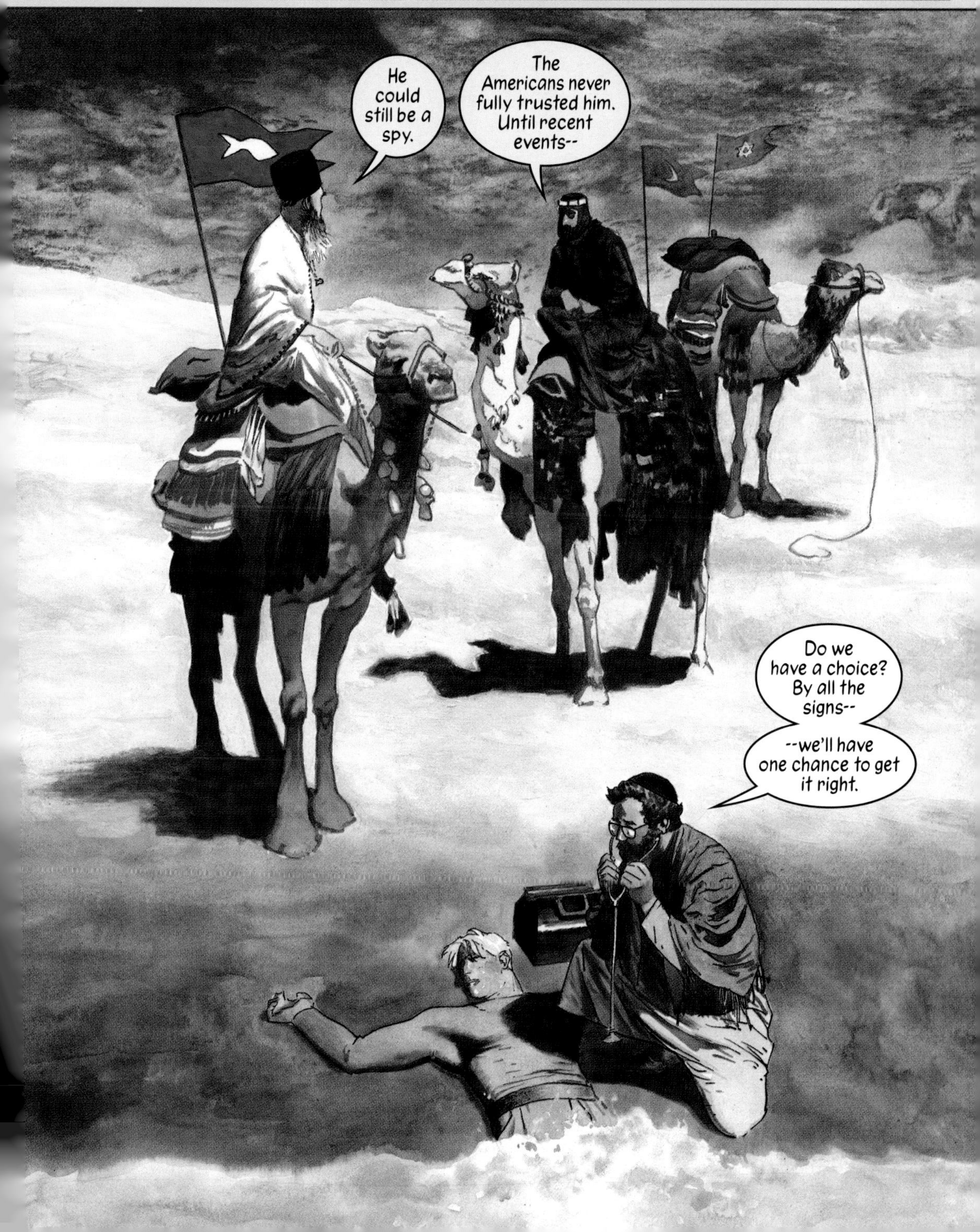
He could still be a spy.
The Americans never fully trusted him. Until recent events--
Do we have a choice? By all the signs--
--we'll have one chance to get it right.

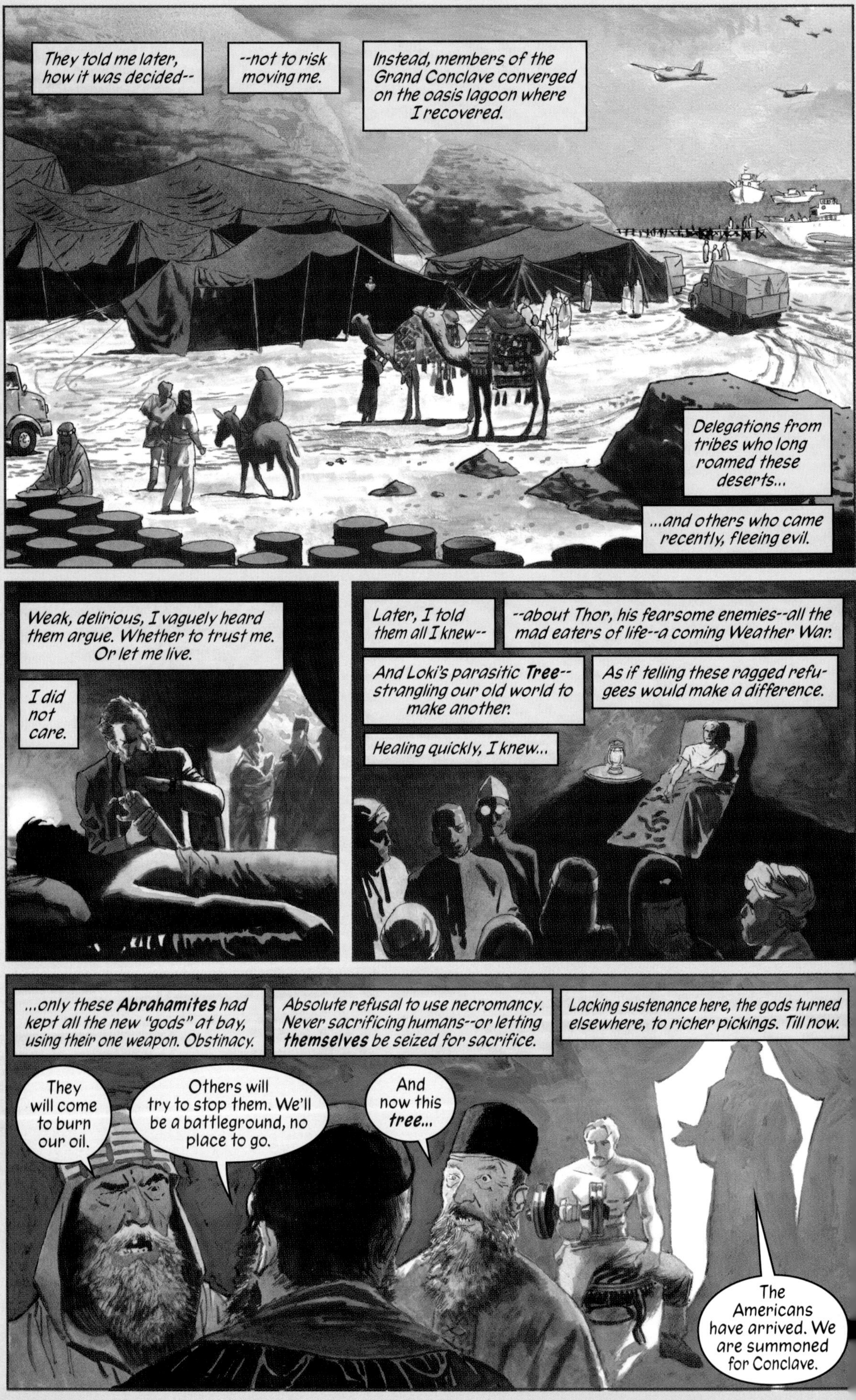

They told me later, how it was decided--
--not to risk moving me.
Instead, members of the Grand Conclave converged on the oasis lagoon where I recovered.
Delegations from tribes who long roamed these deserts...
...and others who came recently, fleeing evil.
Weak, delirious, I vaguely heard them argue. Whether to trust me. Or let me live.
I did not care.
Later, I told them all I knew--
--about Thor, his fearsome enemies--all the mad eaters of life--a coming Weather War.
And Loki's parasitic Tree--strangling our old world to make another.
As if telling these ragged refugees would make a difference.
Healing quickly, I knew...
...only these Abrahamites had kept all the new "gods" at bay, using their one weapon. Obstinacy.
Absolute refusal to use necromancy. Never sacrificing humans--or letting themselves be seized for sacrifice.
Lacking sustenance here, the gods turned elsewhere, to richer pickings. Till now.
They will come to burn our oil.
Others will try to stop them. We'll be a battleground, no place to go.
And now this tree...
The Americans have arrived. We are summoned for Conclave.

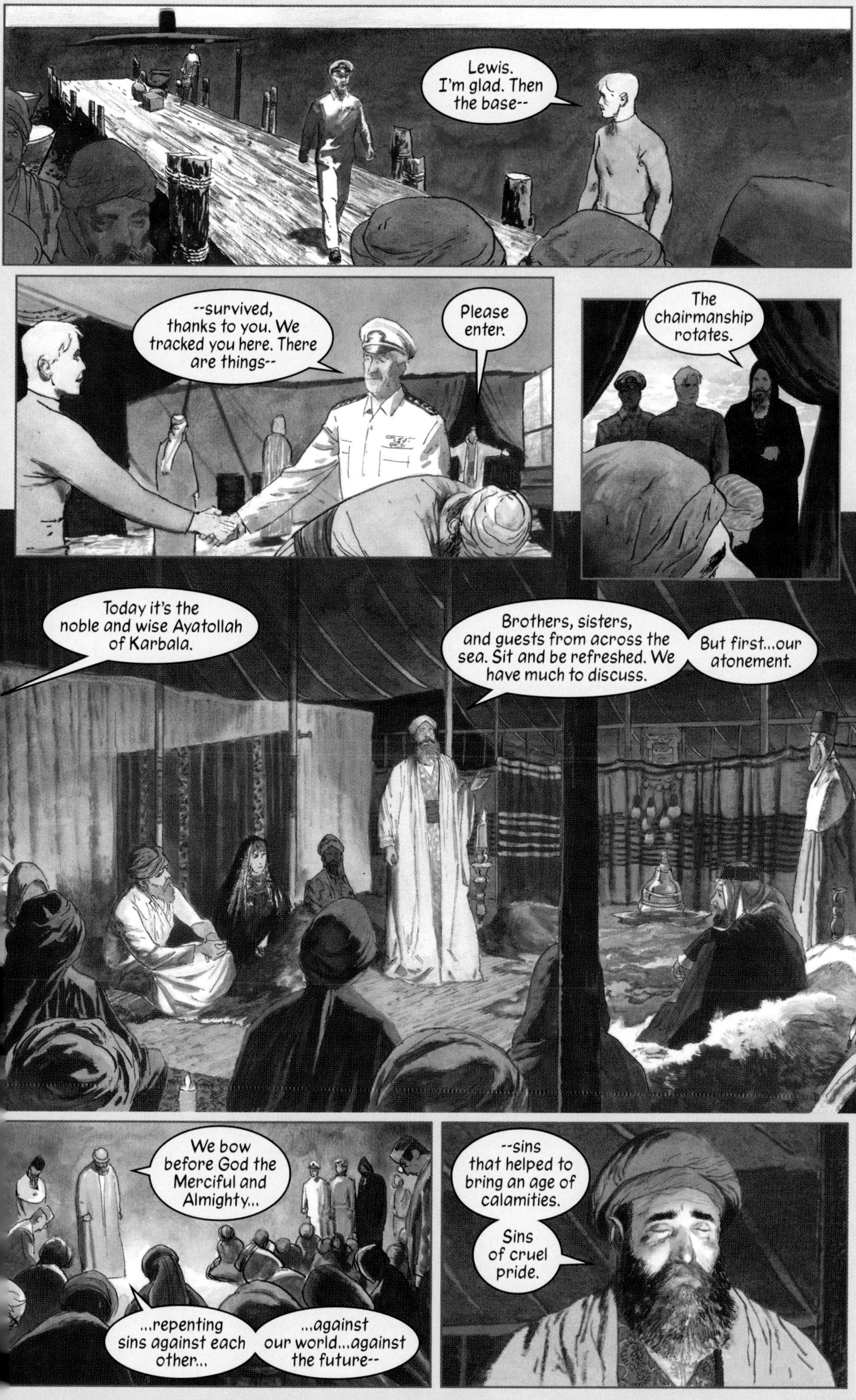

Lewis. I'm glad. Then the base--
--survived, thanks to you. We tracked you here. There are things--
Please enter.
The chairmanship rotates.
Today it's the noble and wise Ayatollah of Karbala.
Brothers, sisters, and guests from across the sea. Sit and be refreshed. We have much to discuss.
But first...our atonement.
We bow before God the Merciful and Almighty...
...repenting sins against each other...
...against our world...against the future--
--sins that helped to bring an age of calamities.
Sins of cruel pride.

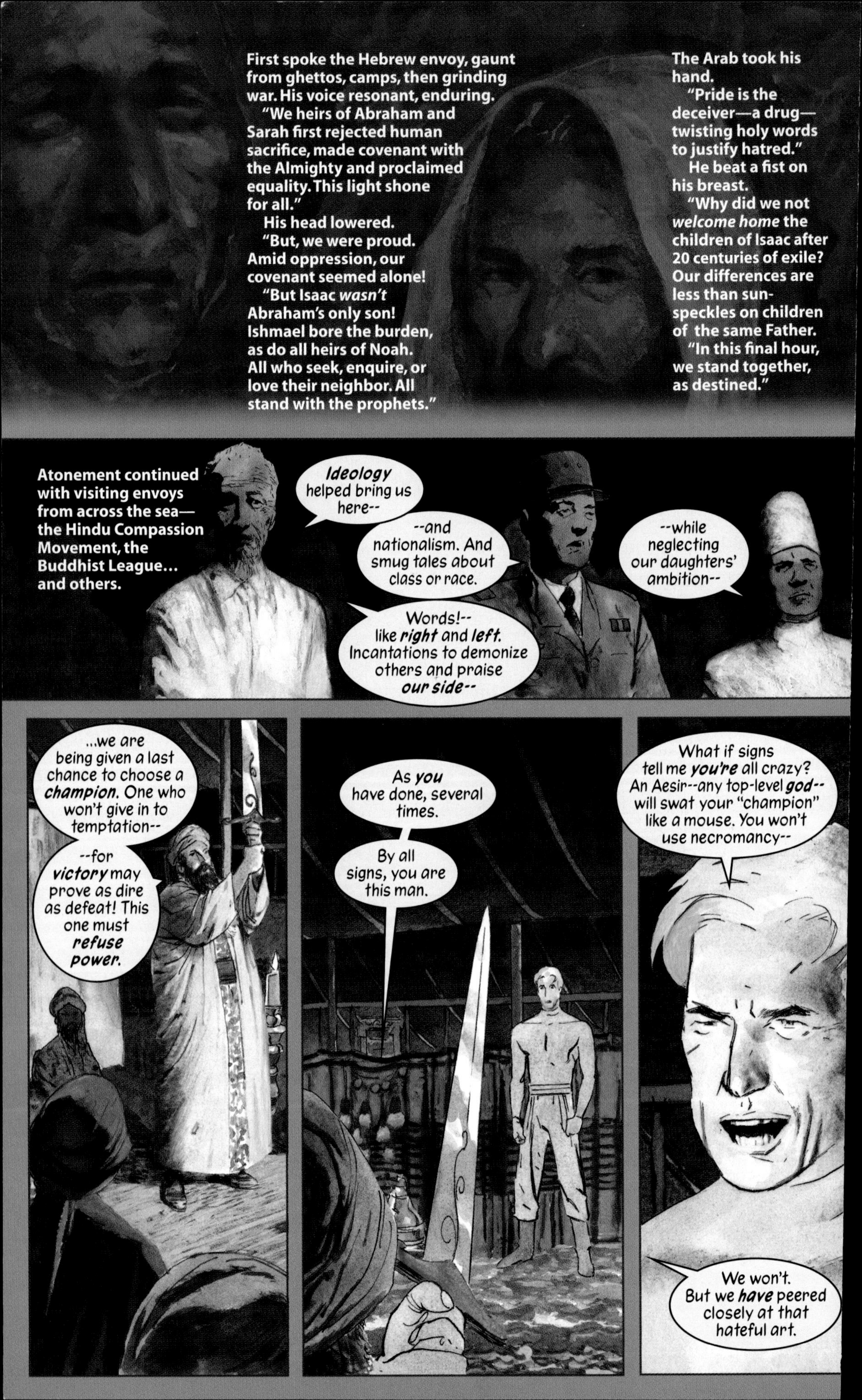

First spoke the Hebrew envoy, gaunt from ghettos, camps, then grinding war. His voice resonant, enduring.

"We heirs of Abraham and Sarah first rejected human sacrifice, made covenant with the Almighty and proclaimed equality. This light shone for all."

His head lowered.

"But, we were proud. Amid oppression, our covenant seemed alone!

"But Isaac *wasn't* Abraham's only son! Ishmael bore the burden, as do all heirs of Noah. All who seek, enquire, or love their neighbor. All stand with the prophets."

The Arab took his hand.

"Pride is the deceiver—a drug—twisting holy words to justify hatred."

He beat a fist on his breast.

"Why did we not *welcome home* the children of Isaac after 20 centuries of exile? Our differences are less than sun-speckles on children of the same Father.

"In this final hour, we stand together, as destined."

Atonement continued with visiting envoys from across the sea—the Hindu Compassion Movement, the Buddhist League... and others.

Ideology helped bring us here--

--and nationalism. And smug tales about class or race.

--while neglecting our daughters' ambition--

Words!-- like *right* and *left*. Incantations to demonize others and praise *our side*--

...we are being given a last chance to choose a *champion*. One who won't give in to temptation--

--for *victory* may prove as dire as defeat! This one must *refuse power.*

As *you* have done, several times.

By all signs, you are this man.

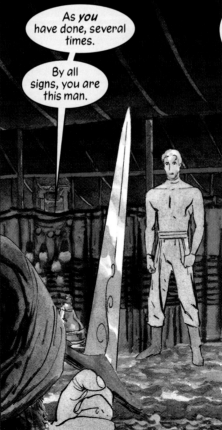

What if signs tell me *you're* all crazy? An Aesir--any top-level *god*-- will swat your "champion" like a mouse. You won't use necromancy--

We won't. But we *have* peered closely at that hateful art.

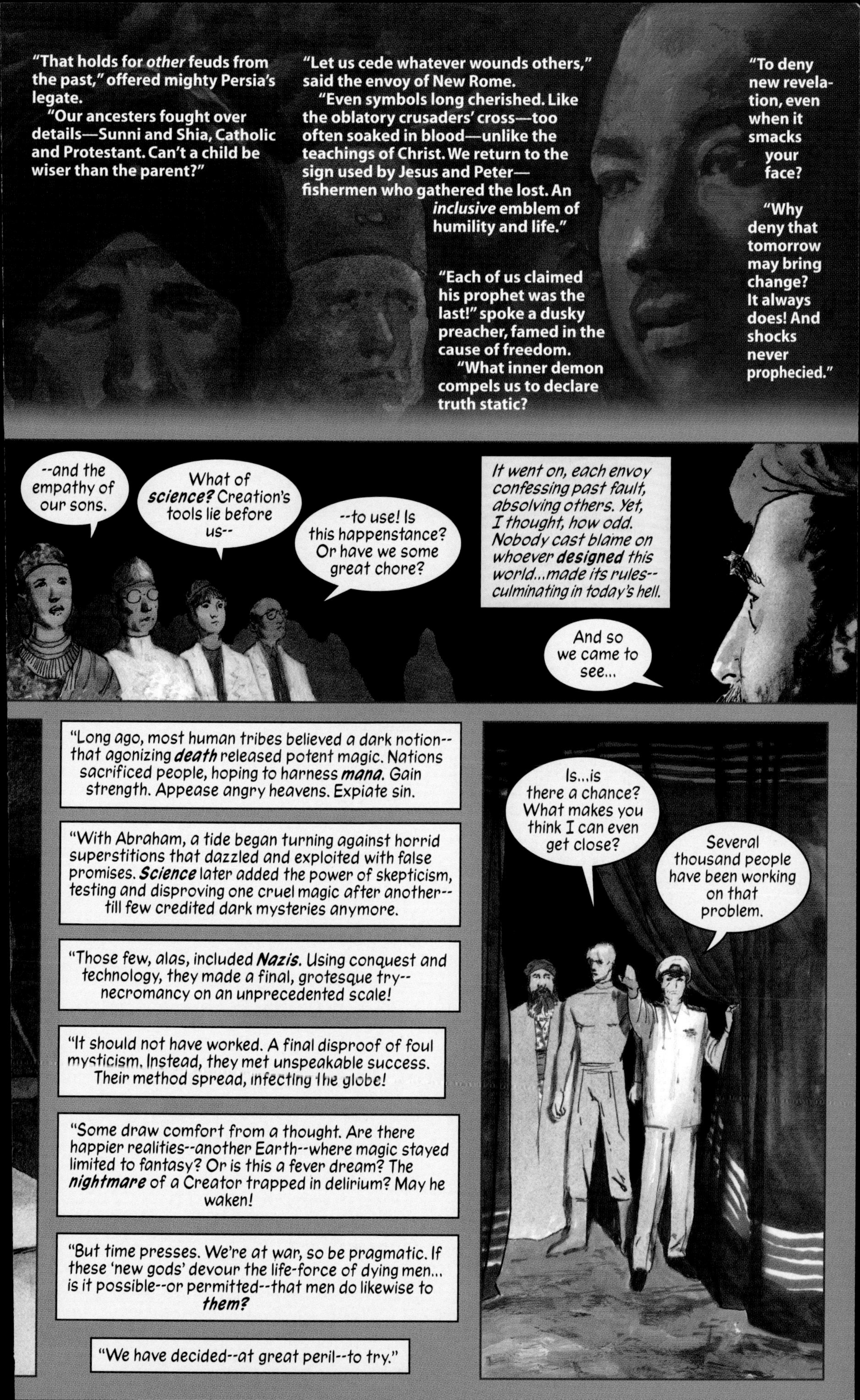

"That holds for *other* feuds from the past," offered mighty Persia's legate.

"Our ancestors fought over details—Sunni and Shia, Catholic and Protestant. Can't a child be wiser than the parent?"

"Let us cede whatever wounds others," said the envoy of New Rome.

"Even symbols long cherished. Like the oblatory crusaders' cross—too often soaked in blood—unlike the teachings of Christ. We return to the sign used by Jesus and Peter—fishermen who gathered the lost. An *inclusive* emblem of humility and life."

"Each of us claimed his prophet was the last!" spoke a dusky preacher, famed in the cause of freedom.

"What inner demon compels us to declare truth static?

"To deny new revelation, even when it smacks your face?

"Why deny that tomorrow may bring change? It always does! And shocks never prophecied."

--and the empathy of our sons.

What of *science?* Creation's tools lie before us--

--to use! Is this happenstance? Or have we some great chore?

It went on, each envoy confessing past fault, absolving others. Yet, I thought, how odd. Nobody cast blame on whoever *designed* this world...made its rules-- culminating in today's hell.

And so we came to see...

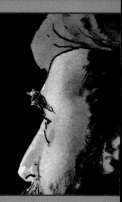

"Long ago, most human tribes believed a dark notion-- that agonizing *death* released potent magic. Nations sacrificed people, hoping to harness *mana*. Gain strength. Appease angry heavens. Expiate sin.

"With Abraham, a tide began turning against horrid superstitions that dazzled and exploited with false promises. *Science* later added the power of skepticism, testing and disproving one cruel magic after another-- till few credited dark mysteries anymore.

"Those few, alas, included *Nazis*. Using conquest and technology, they made a final, grotesque try-- necromancy on an unprecedented scale!

"It should not have worked. A final disproof of foul mysticism. Instead, they met unspeakable success. Their method spread, infecting the globe!

"Some draw comfort from a thought. Are there happier realities--another Earth--where magic stayed limited to fantasy? Or is this a fever dream? The *nightmare* of a Creator trapped in delirium? May he waken!

"But time presses. We're at war, so be pragmatic. If these 'new gods' devour the life-force of dying men... is it possible--or permitted--that men do likewise to *them?*

"We have decided--at great peril--to try."

Is...is there a chance? What makes you think I can even get close?

Several thousand people have been working on that problem.

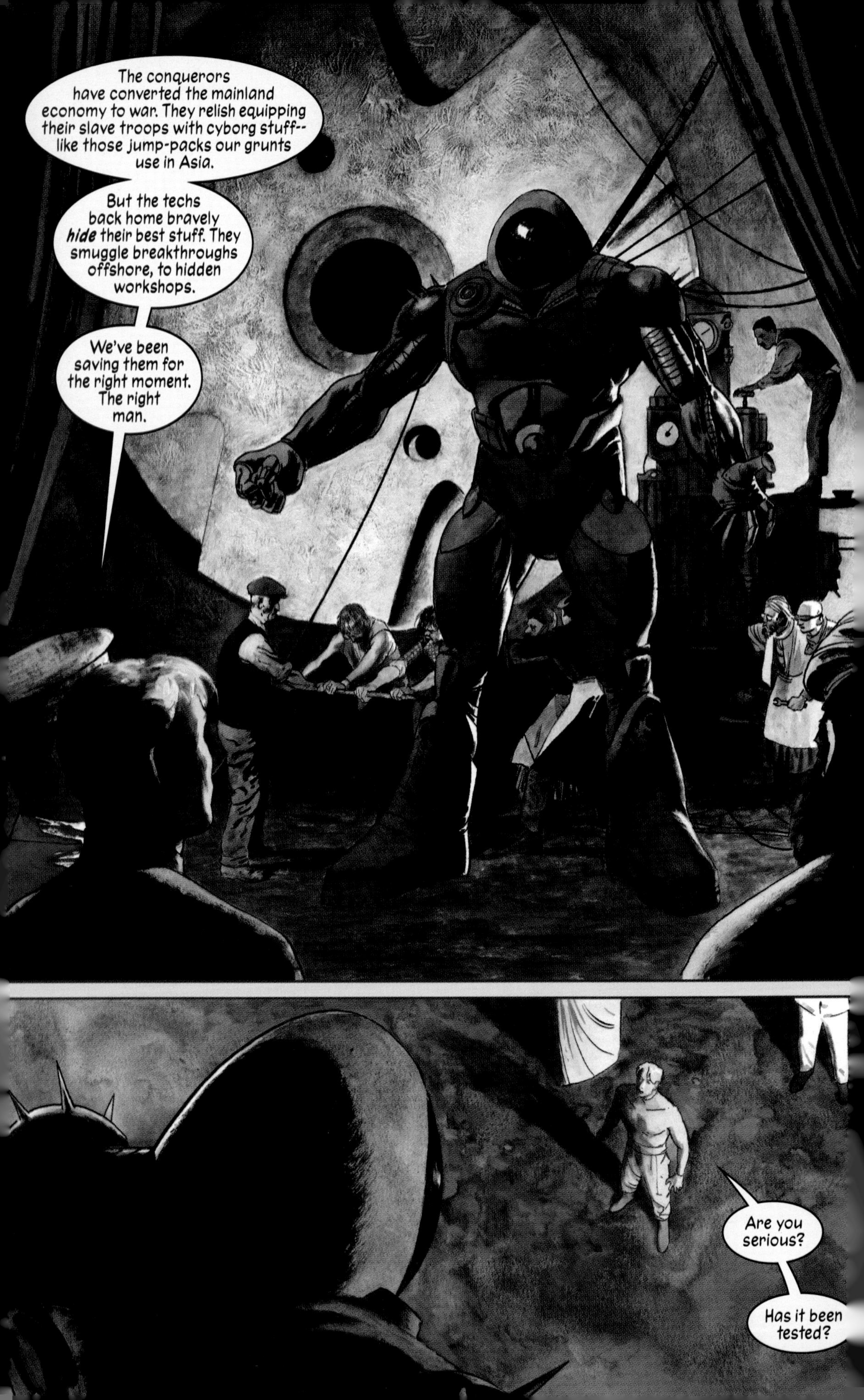
The conquerors have converted the mainland economy to war. They relish equipping their slave troops with cyborg stuff-- like those jump-packs our grunts use in Asia.
But the techs back home bravely *hide* their best stuff. They smuggle breakthroughs offshore, to hidden workshops.
We've been saving them for the right moment. The right man.
Are you serious?
Has it been tested?

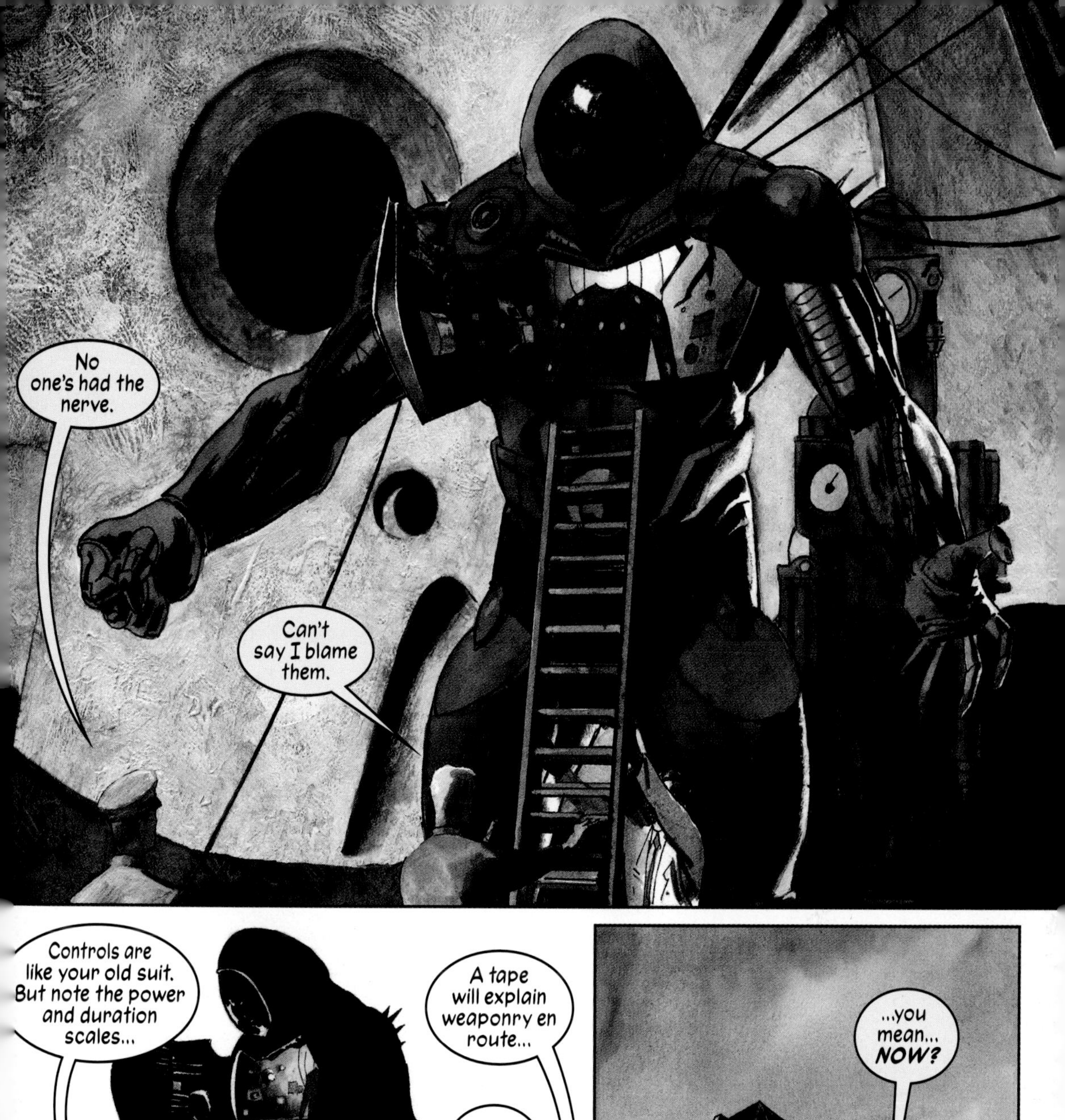
No one's had the nerve.
Can't say I blame them.

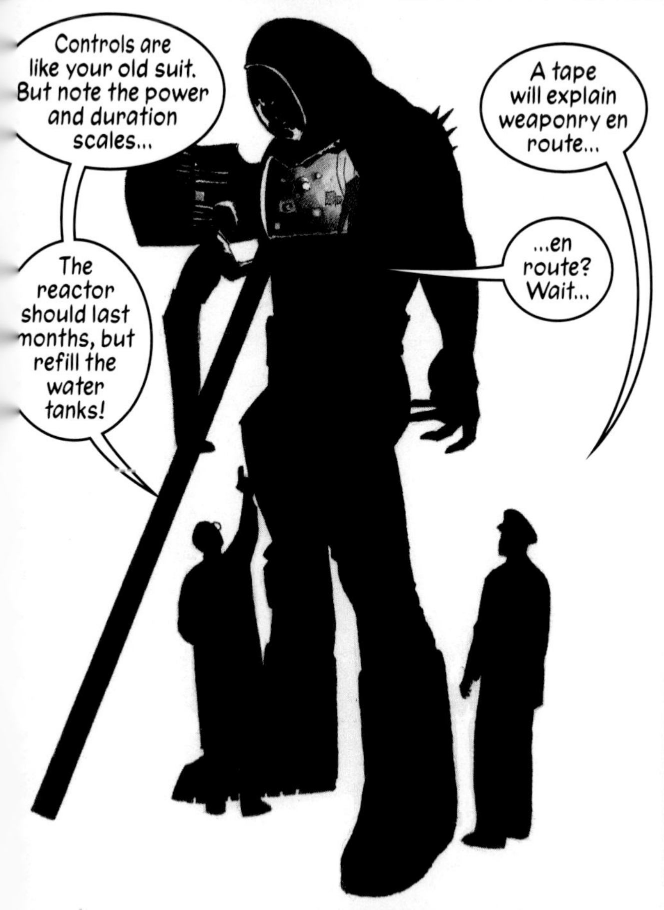
Controls are like your old suit. But note the power and duration scales...
The reactor should last months, but refill the water tanks!
A tape will explain weaponry en route...
...en route? Wait...

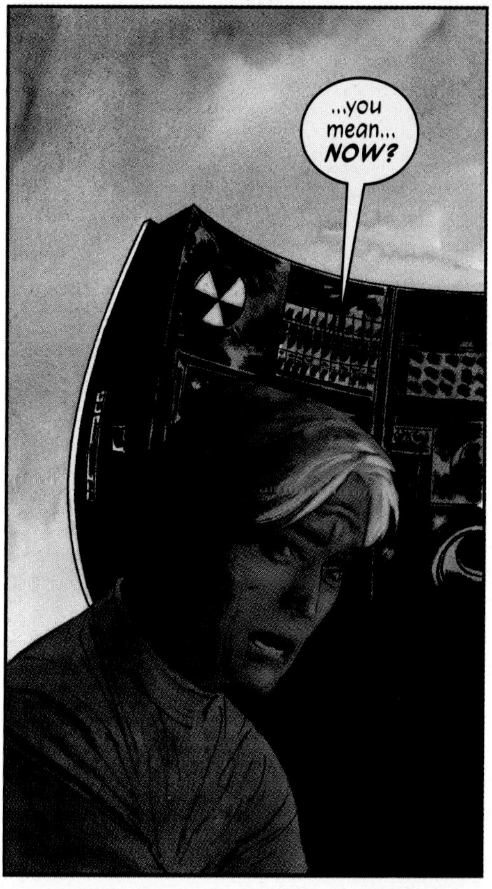
...you mean... **NOW?**

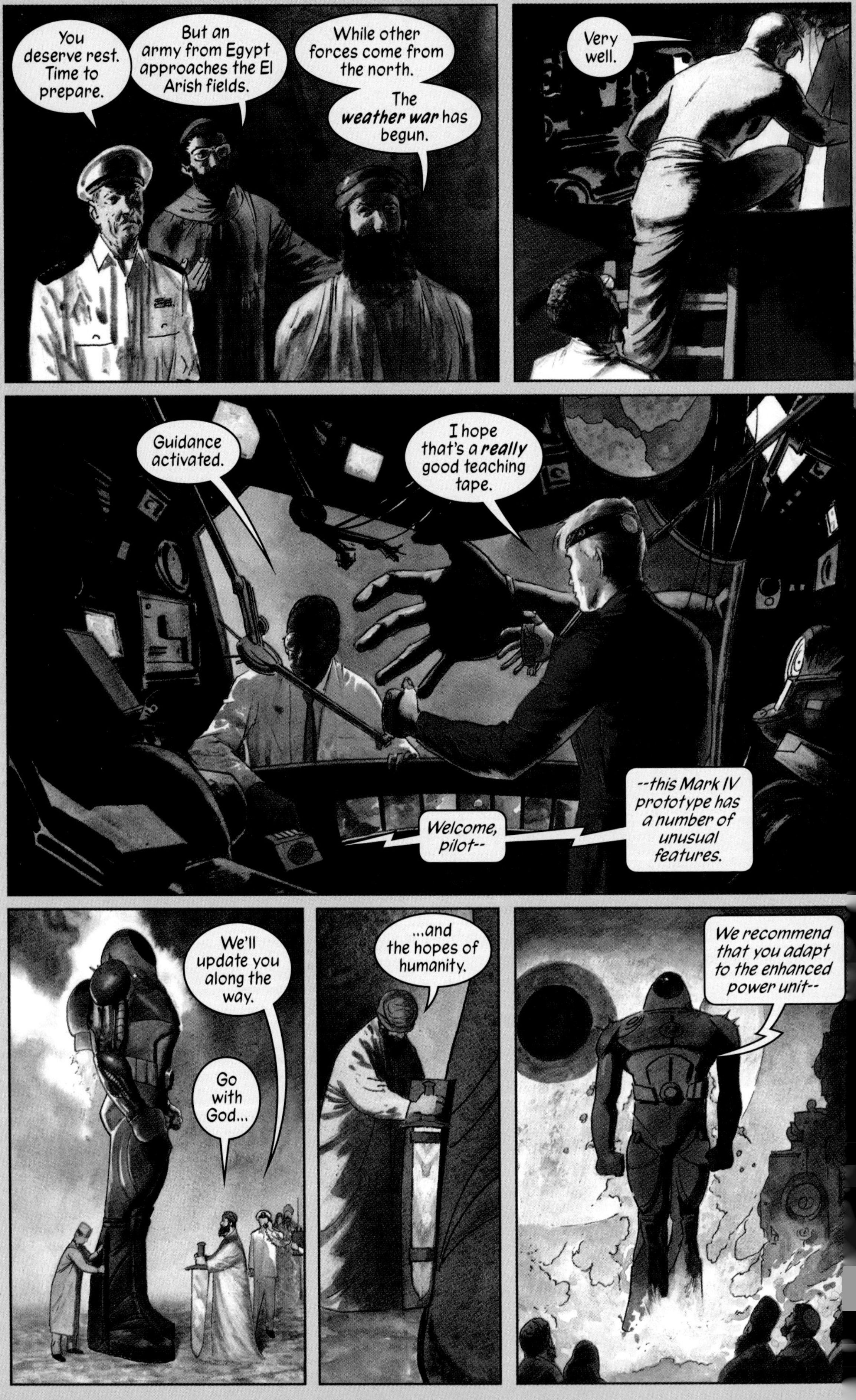
You deserve rest. Time to prepare.
But an army from Egypt approaches the El Arish fields.
While other forces come from the north.
The *weather war* has begun.
Very well.
Guidance activated.
I hope that's a *really* good teaching tape.
Welcome, pilot--
--this Mark IV prototype has a number of unusual features.
We'll update you along the way.
Go with God...
...and the hopes of humanity.
We recommend that you adapt to the enhanced power unit--

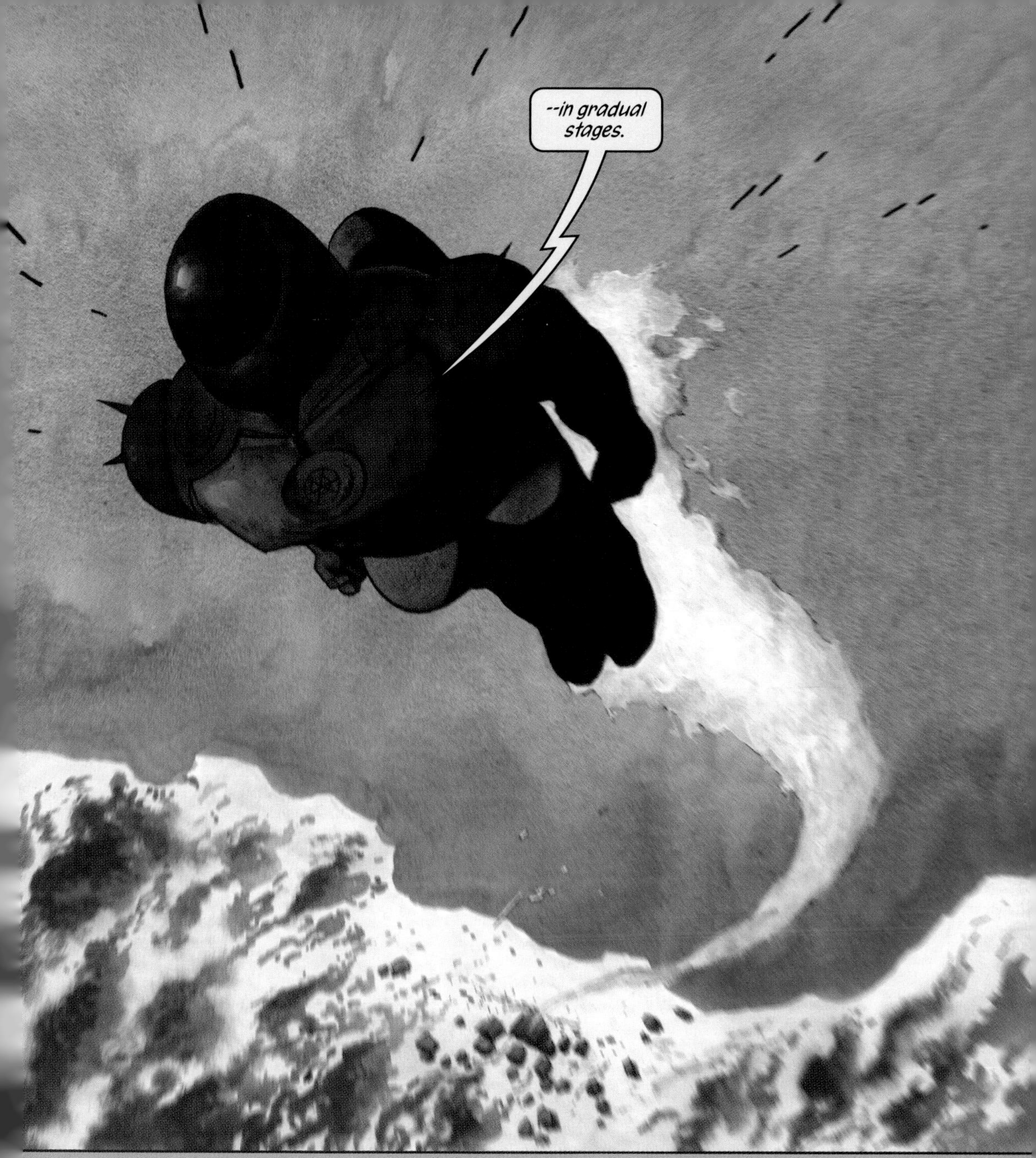
--in gradual stages.

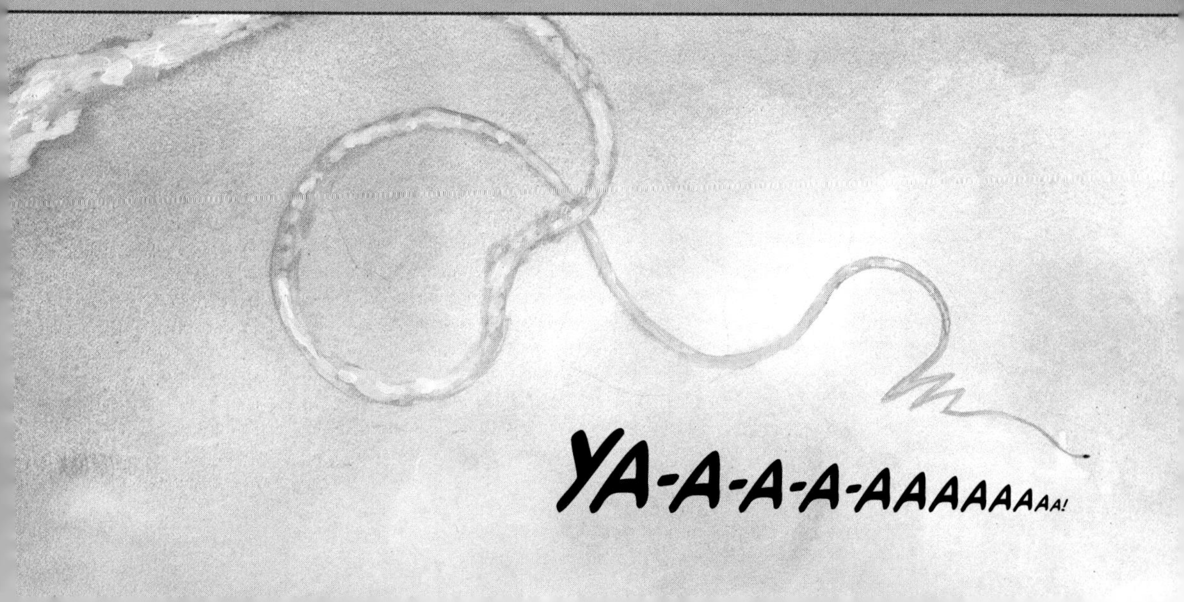
YA-A-A-A-AAAAAAAA!

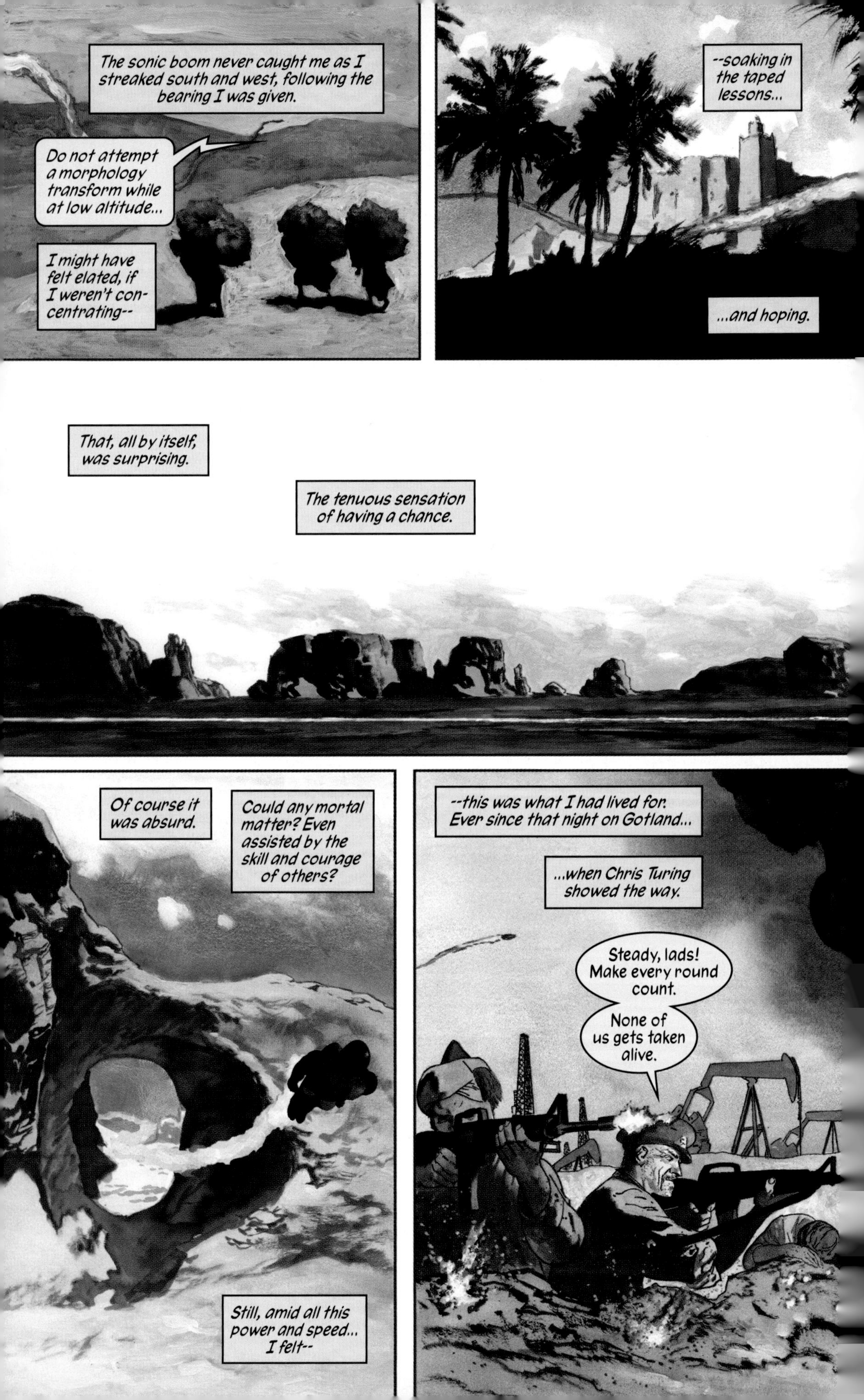
The sonic boom never caught me as I streaked south and west, following the bearing I was given.
Do not attempt a morphology transform while at low altitude...
I might have felt elated, if I weren't con-centrating--
--soaking in the taped lessons...
...and hoping.
That, all by itself, was surprising.
The tenuous sensation of having a chance.
Of course it was absurd.
Could any mortal matter? Even assisted by the skill and courage of others?
Still, amid all this power and speed... I felt--
--this was what I had lived for. Ever since that night on Gotland...
...when Chris Turing showed the way.
Steady, lads! Make every round count.
None of us gets taken alive.

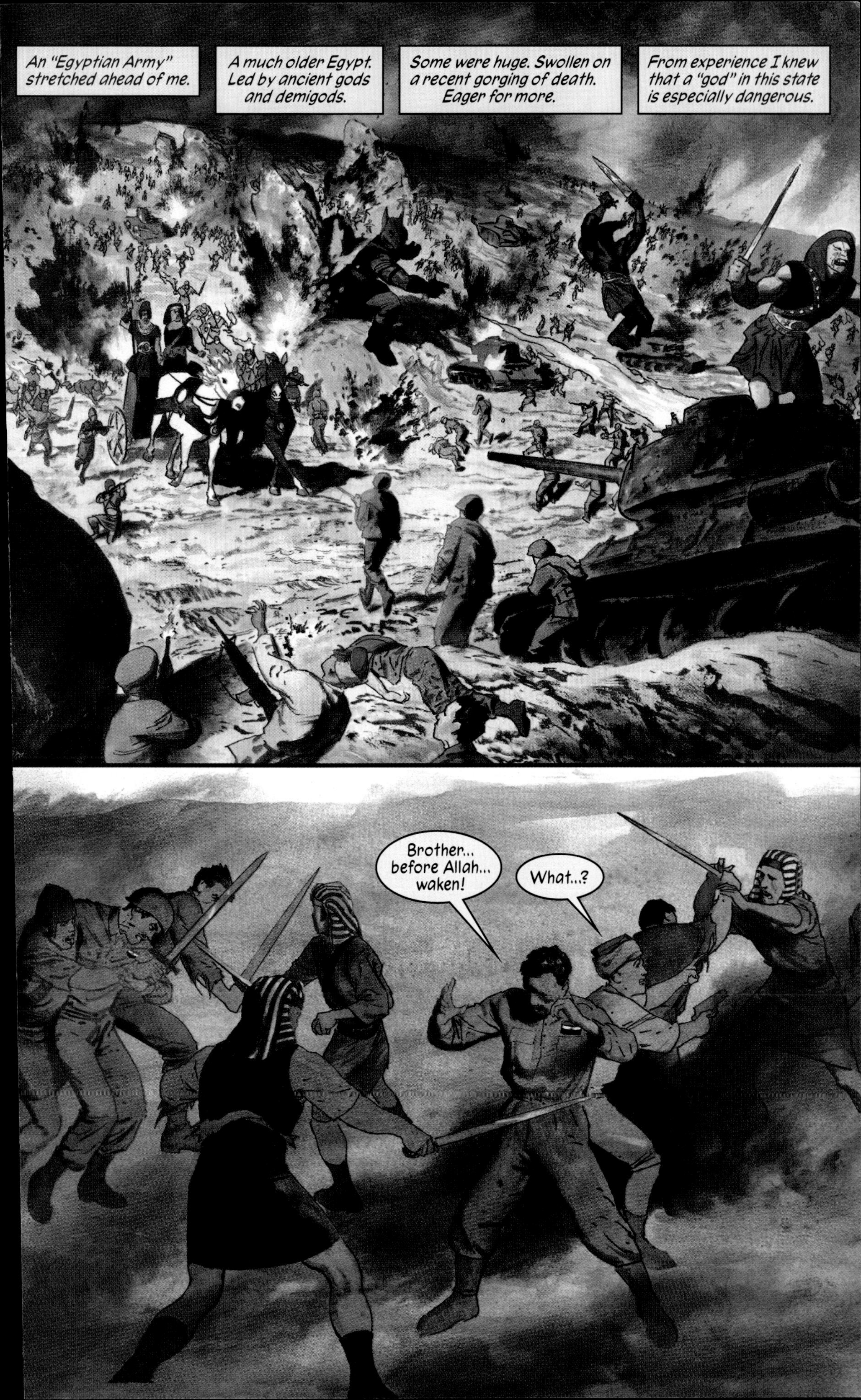
An "Egyptian Army" stretched ahead of me.
A much older Egypt. Led by ancient gods and demigods.
Some were huge. Swollen on a recent gorging of death. Eager for more.
From experience I knew that a "god" in this state is especially dangerous.
Brother... before Allah... waken!
What...?

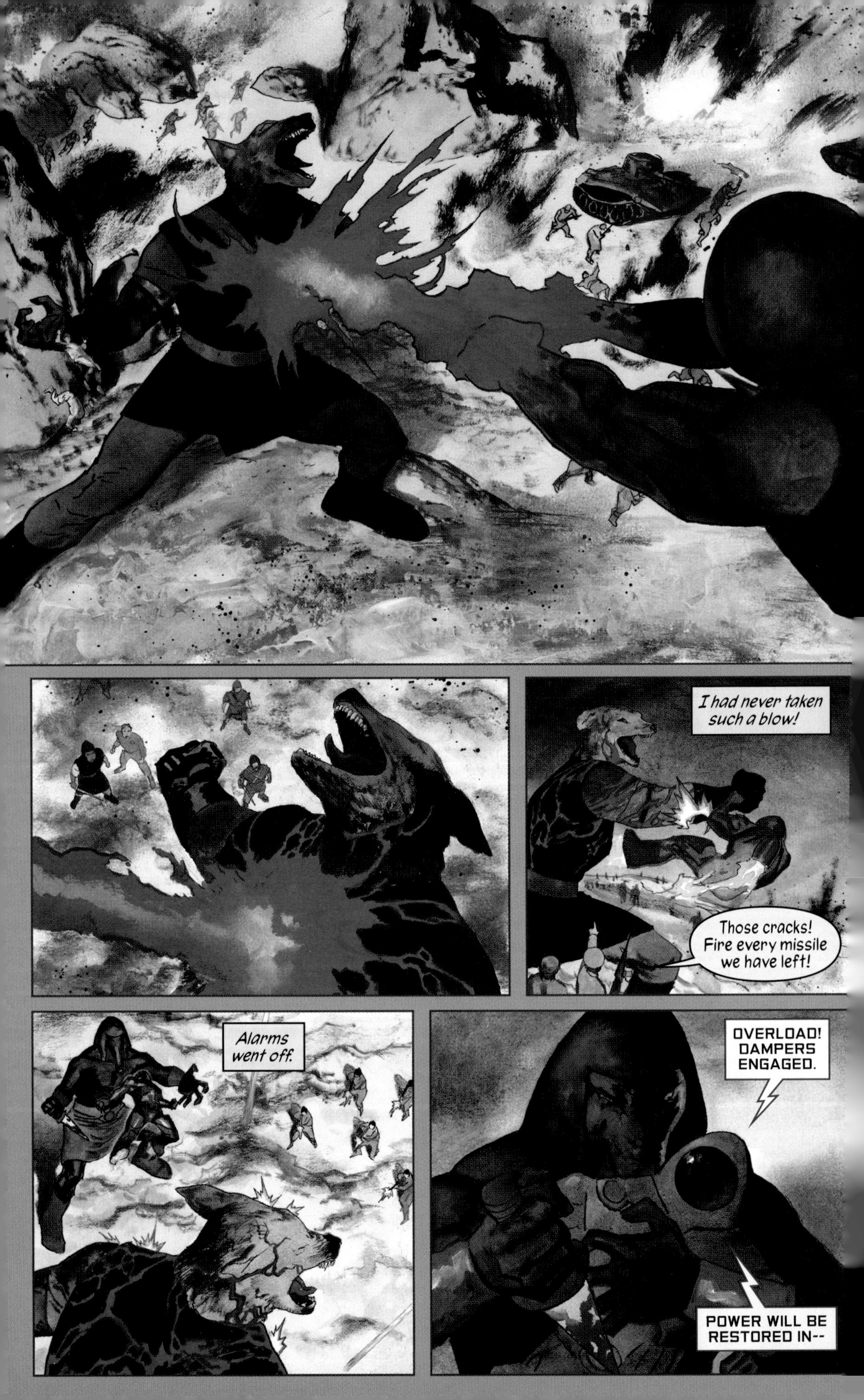
I had never taken such a blow!
Those cracks! Fire every missile we have left!
Alarms went off.
OVERLOAD! DAMPERS ENGAGED.
POWER WILL BE RESTORED IN--

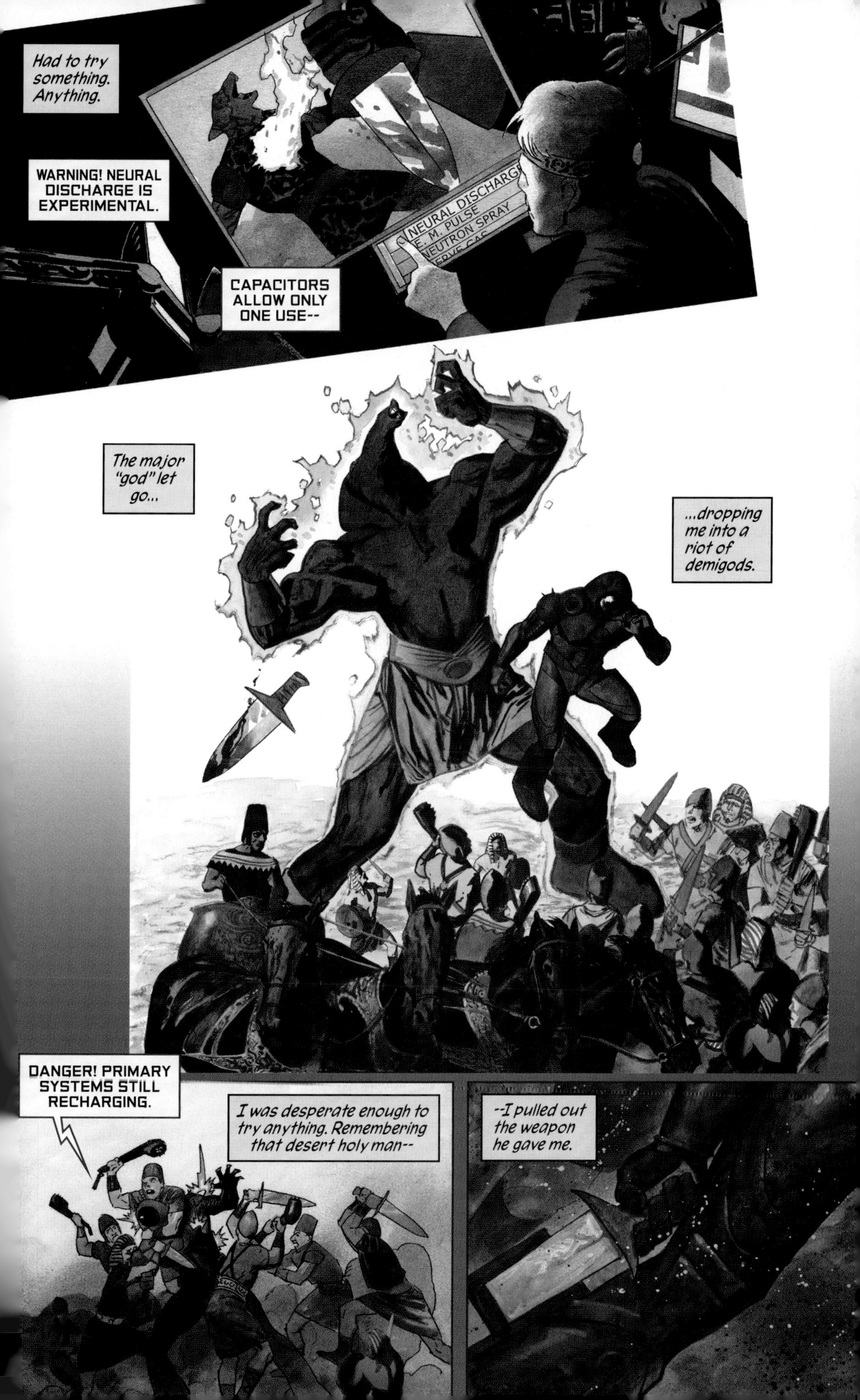
Had to try something. Anything.
WARNING! NEURAL DISCHARGE IS EXPERIMENTAL.
NEURAL DISCHARGE
NEURAL DISCHARGE
E. M. PULSE
NEUTRON SPRAY
CAPACITORS ALLOW ONLY ONE USE--
The major "god" let go...
...dropping me into a riot of demigods.
DANGER! PRIMARY SYSTEMS STILL RECHARGING.
I was desperate enough to try anything. Remembering that desert holy man--
--I pulled out the weapon he gave me.

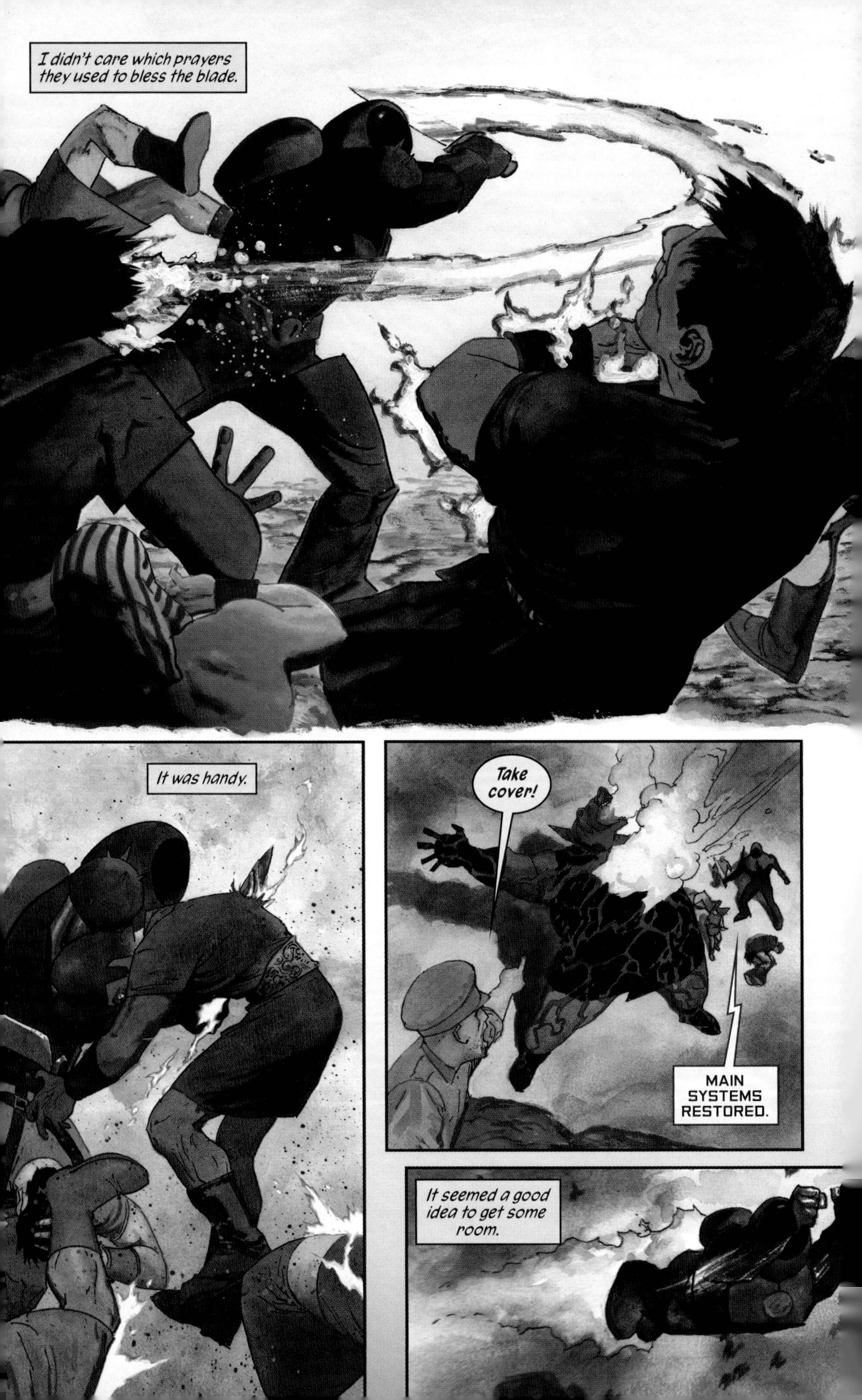
I didn't care which prayers they used to bless the blade.
It was handy.
Take cover!
MAIN SYSTEMS RESTORED.
It seemed a good idea to get some room.

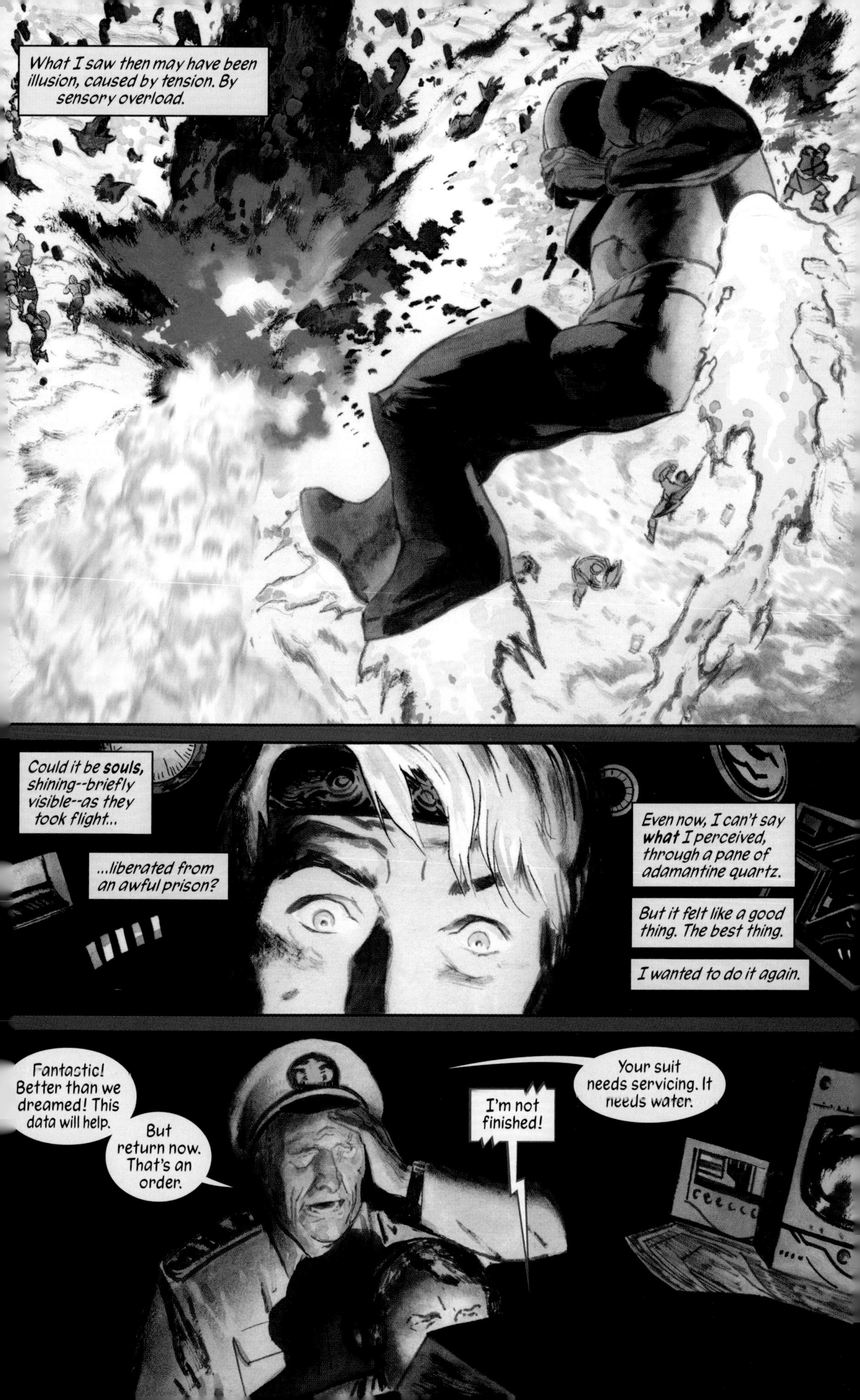

What I saw then may have been illusion, caused by tension. By sensory overload.
Could it be **souls,** shining--briefly visible--as they took flight...
...liberated from an awful prison?
Even now, I can't say **what** I perceived, through a pane of adamantine quartz.
But it felt like a good thing. The best thing.
I wanted to do it again.
Fantastic! Better than we dreamed! This data will help.
But return now. That's an order.
I'm not finished!
Your suit needs servicing. It needs water.

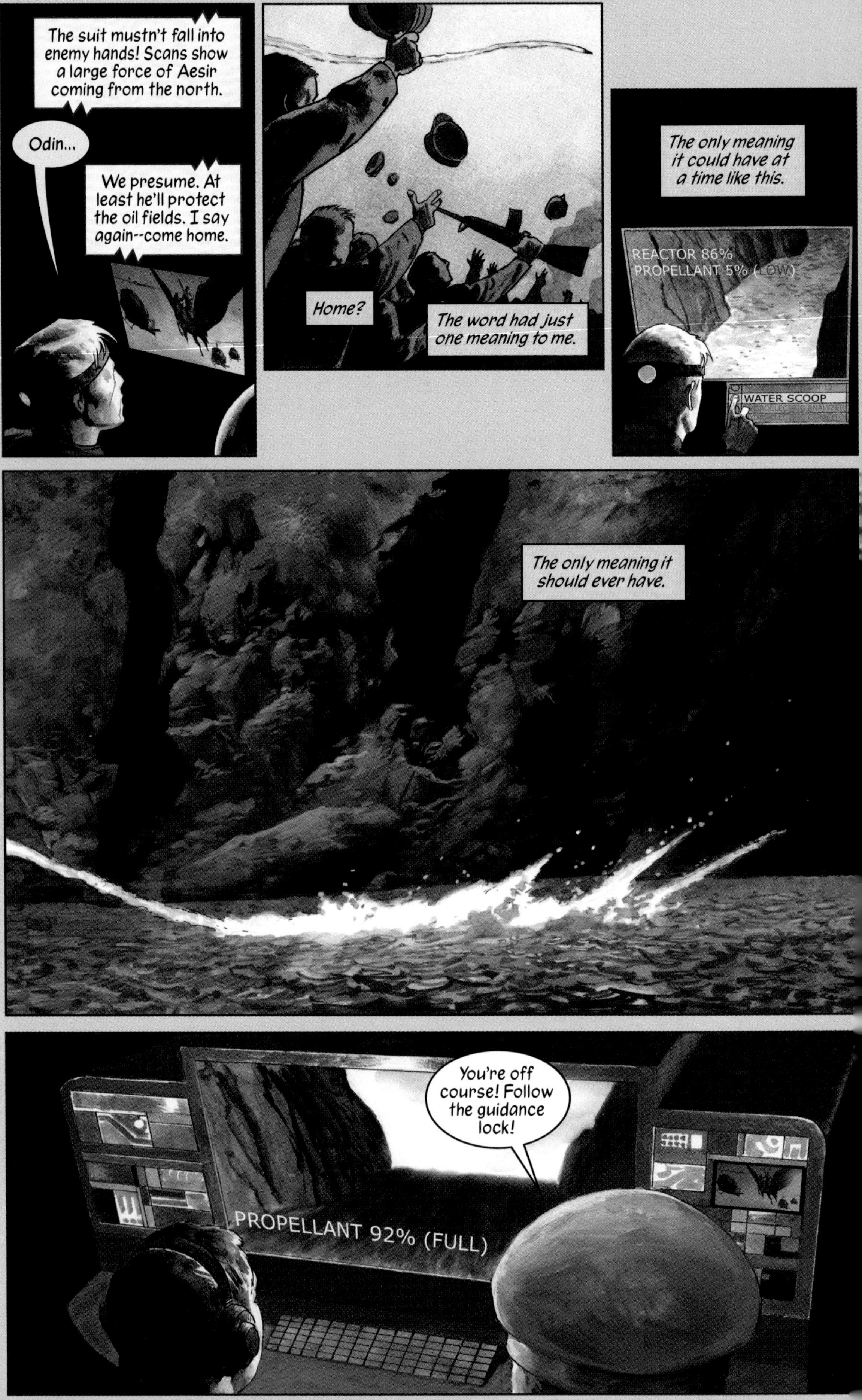

The suit mustn't fall into enemy hands! Scans show a large force of Aesir coming from the north.
Odin...
We presume. At least he'll protect the oil fields. I say again--come home.
Home?
The word had just one meaning to me.
The only meaning it could have at a time like this.
REACTOR 86%
PROPELLANT 5% (LOW)
WATER SCOOP
The only meaning it should ever have.
You're off course! Follow the guidance lock!
PROPELLANT 92% (FULL)

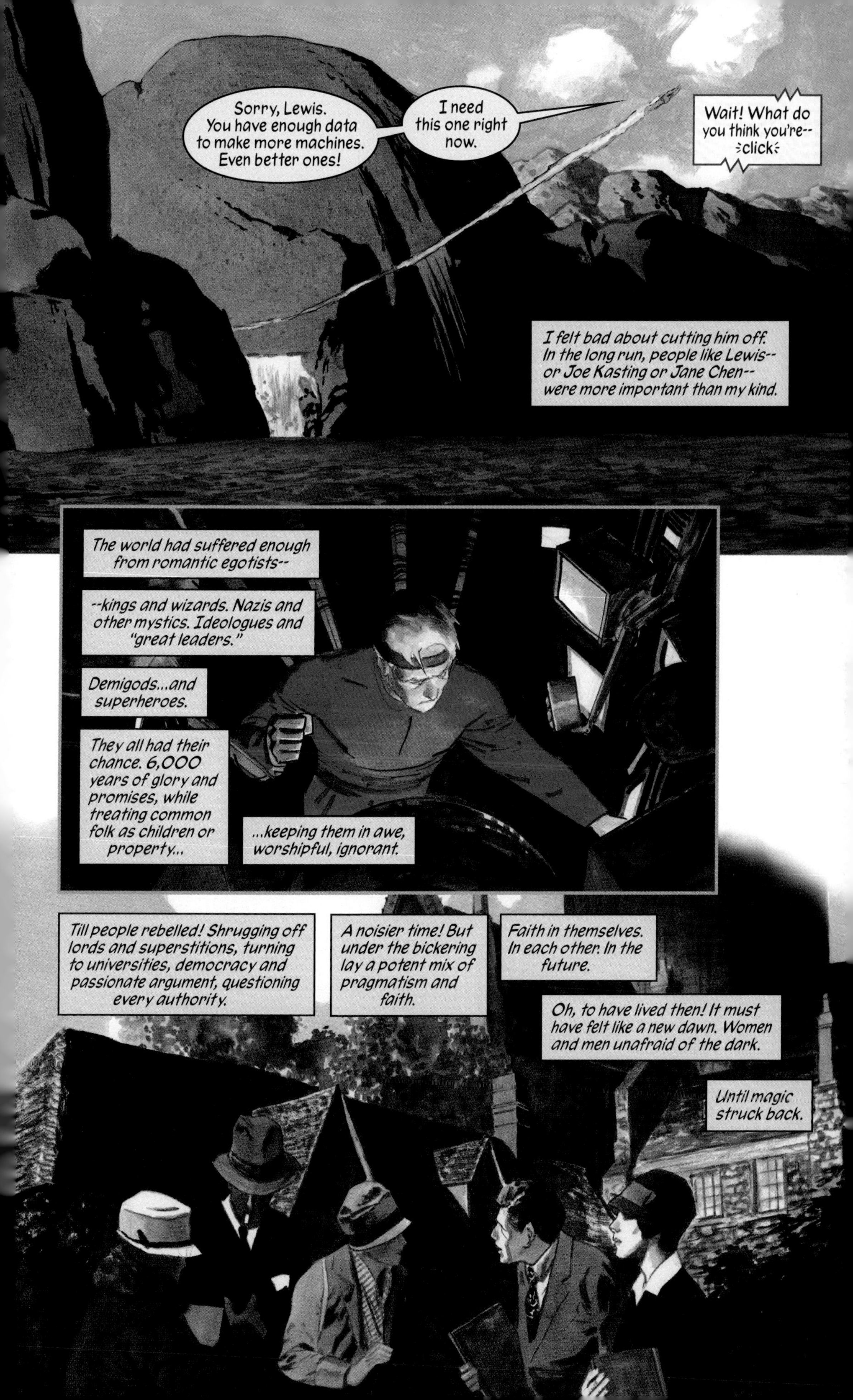
Sorry, Lewis. You have enough data to make more machines. Even better ones!
I need this one right now.
Wait! What do you think you're-- ≷click≷
I felt bad about cutting him off. In the long run, people like Lewis-- or Joe Kasting or Jane Chen-- were more important than my kind.
The world had suffered enough from romantic egotists--
--kings and wizards. Nazis and other mystics. Ideologues and "great leaders."
Demigods...and superheroes.
They all had their chance. 6,000 years of glory and promises, while treating common folk as children or property...
...keeping them in awe, worshipful, ignorant.
Till people rebelled! Shrugging off lords and superstitions, turning to universities, democracy and passionate argument, questioning every authority.
A noisier time! But under the bickering lay a potent mix of pragmatism and faith.
Faith in themselves. In each other. In the future.
Oh, to have lived then! It must have felt like a new dawn. Women and men unafraid of the dark.
Until magic struck back.

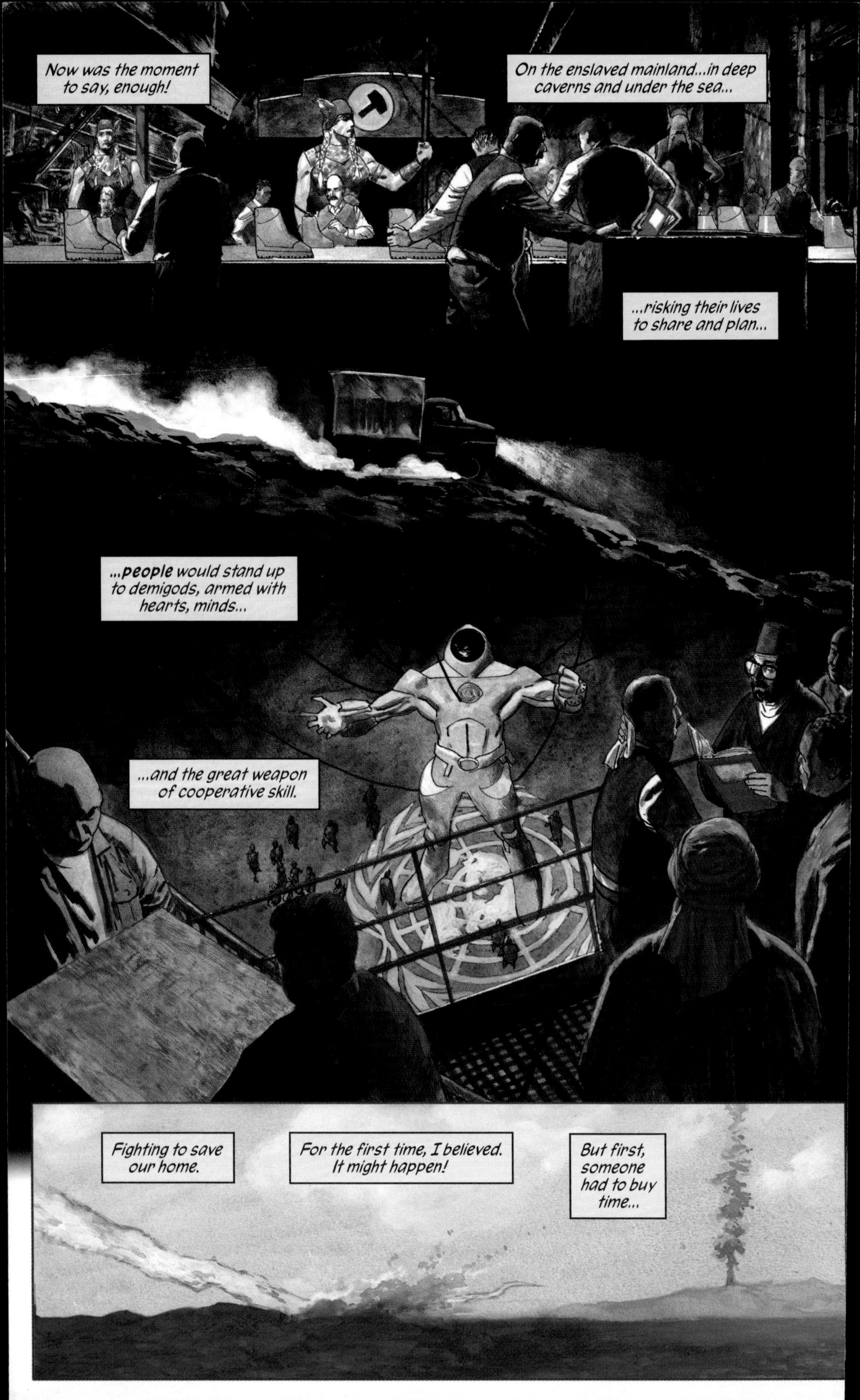
Now was the moment to say, enough!
On the enslaved mainland...in deep caverns and under the sea...
...risking their lives to share and plan...
...**people** would stand up to demigods, armed with hearts, minds...
...and the great weapon of cooperative skill.
Fighting to save our home.
For the first time, I believed. It might happen!
But first, someone had to buy time...

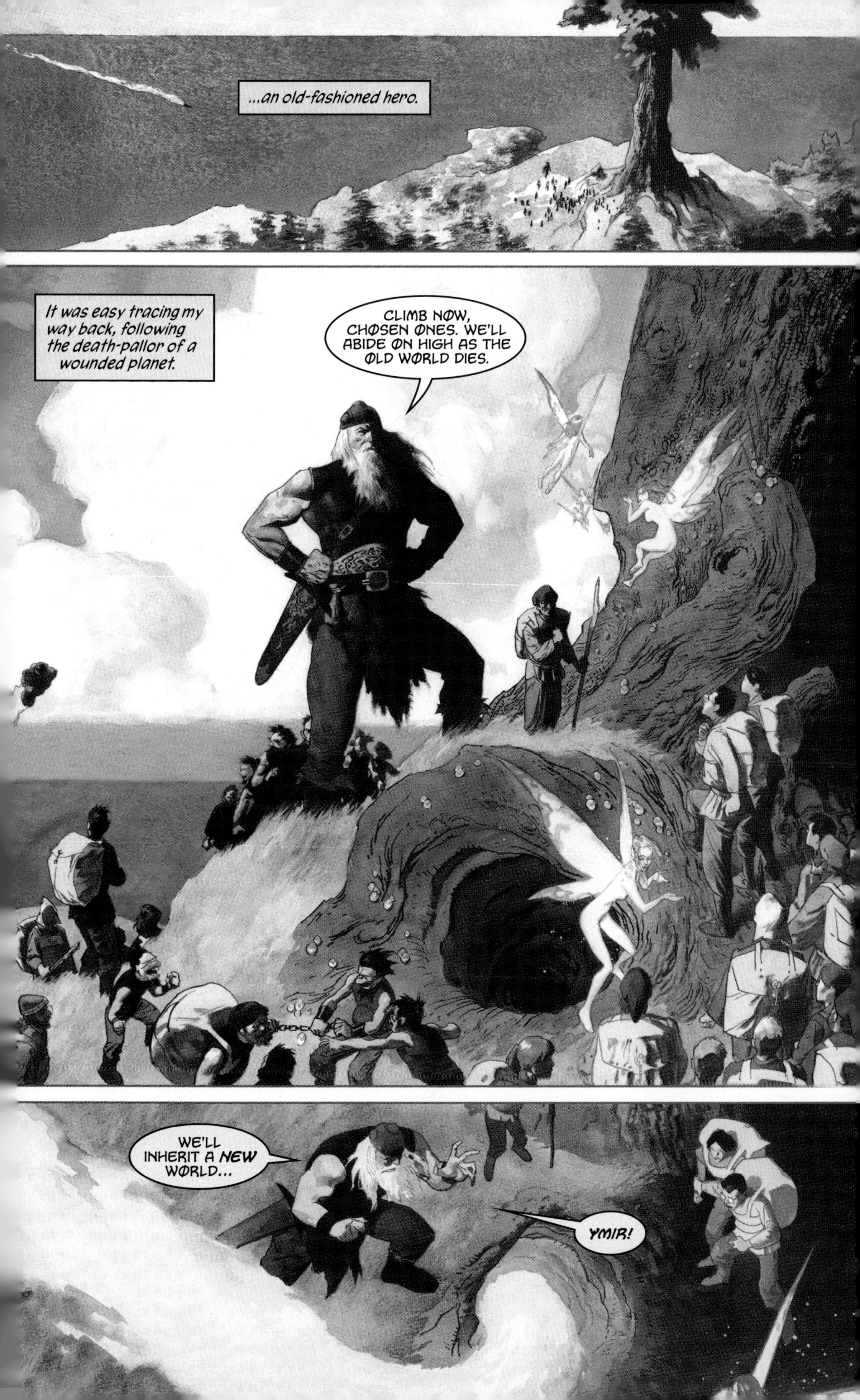
...an old-fashioned hero.
It was easy tracing my way back, following the death-pallor of a wounded planet.
CLIMB NOW, CHOSEN ONES. WE'LL ABIDE ON HIGH AS THE OLD WORLD DIES.
WE'LL INHERIT A NEW WORLD...
YMIR!

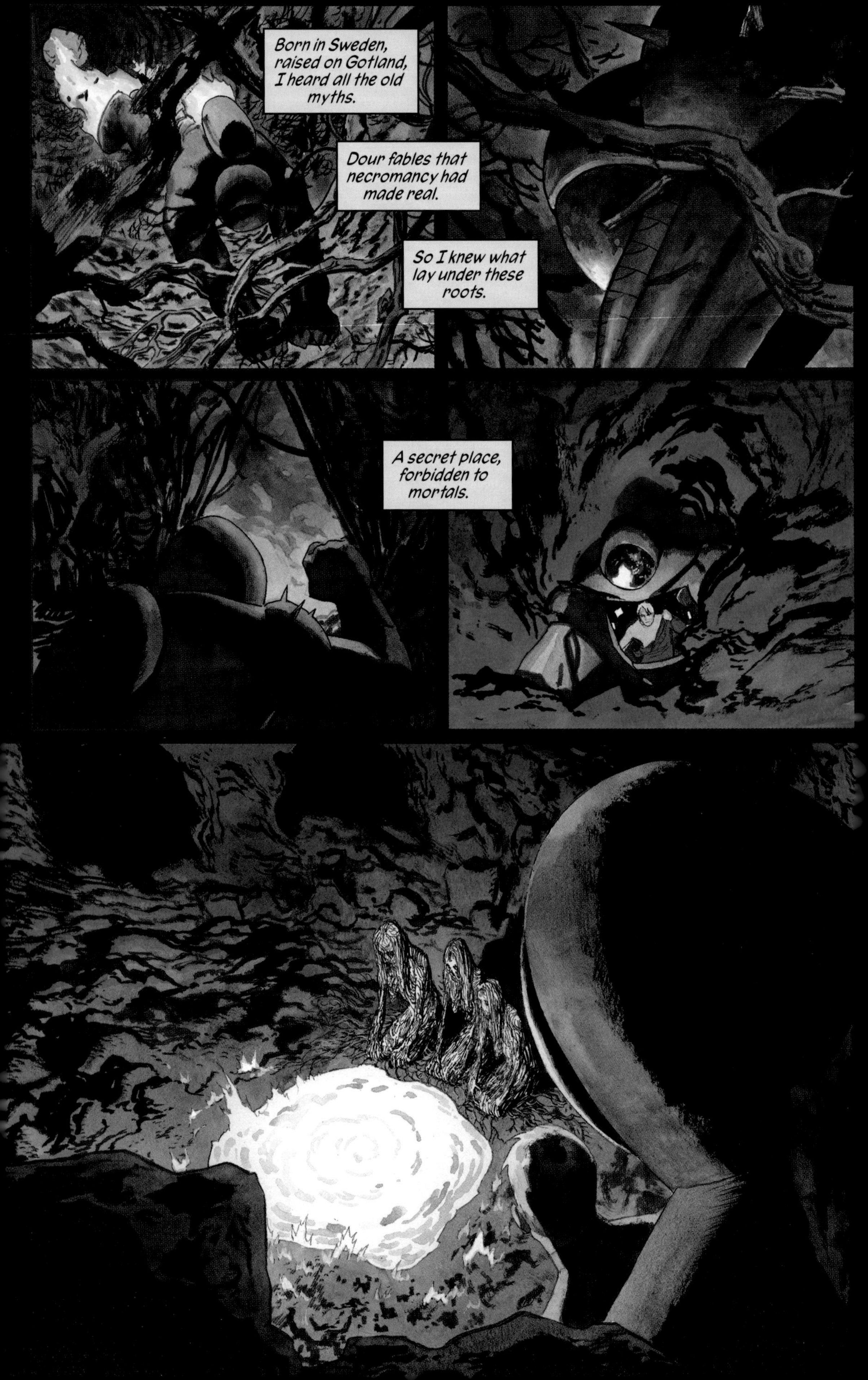
Born in Sweden, raised on Gotland, I heard all the old myths.
Dour fables that necromancy had made real.
So I knew what lay under these roots.
A secret place, forbidden to mortals.

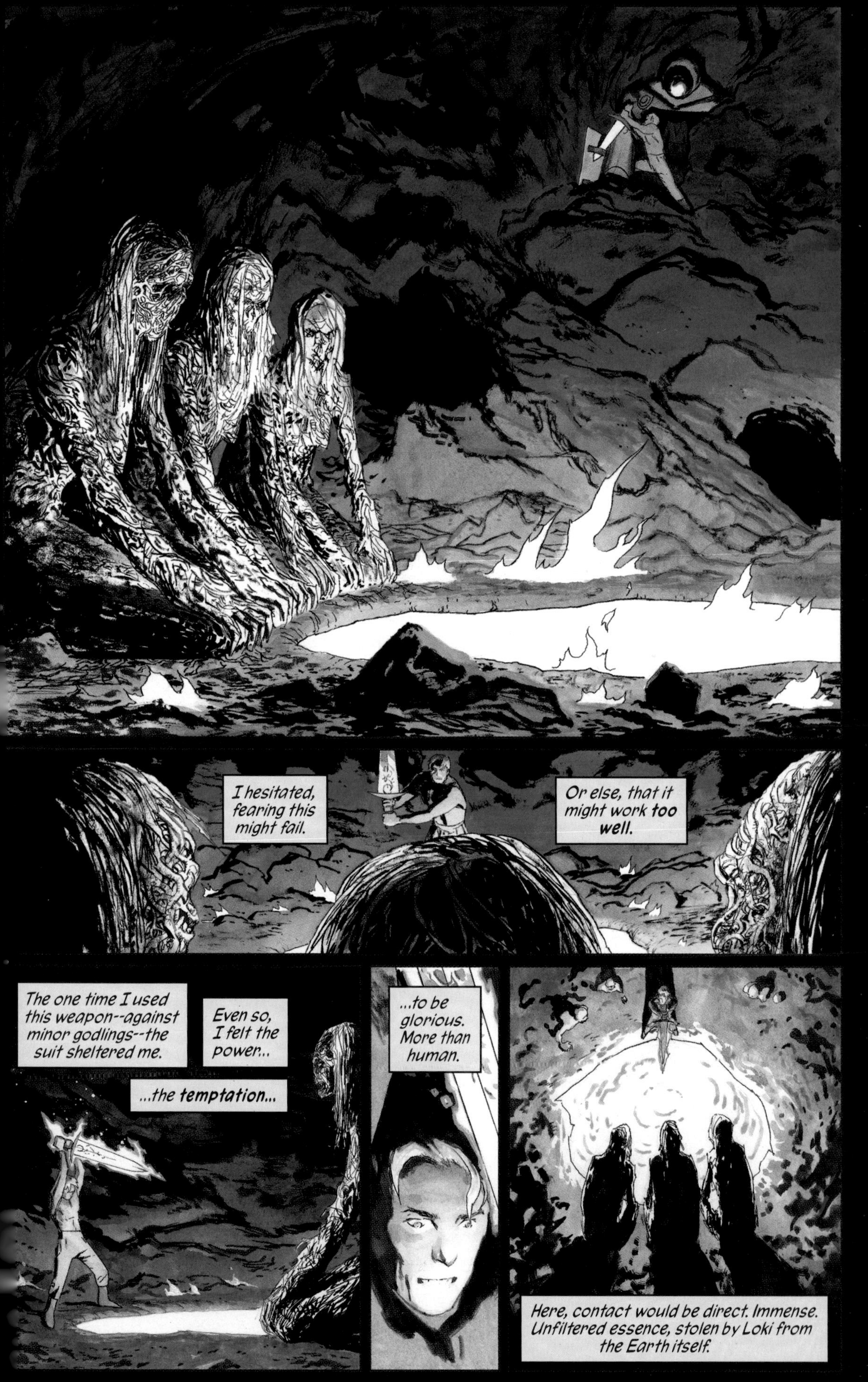
I hesitated, fearing this might fail.
Or else, that it might work **too well.**
The one time I used this weapon--against minor godlings--the suit sheltered me.
Even so, I felt the power...
...the *temptation*...
...to be glorious. More than human.
Here, contact would be direct. Immense. Unfiltered essence, stolen by Loki from the Earth itself.

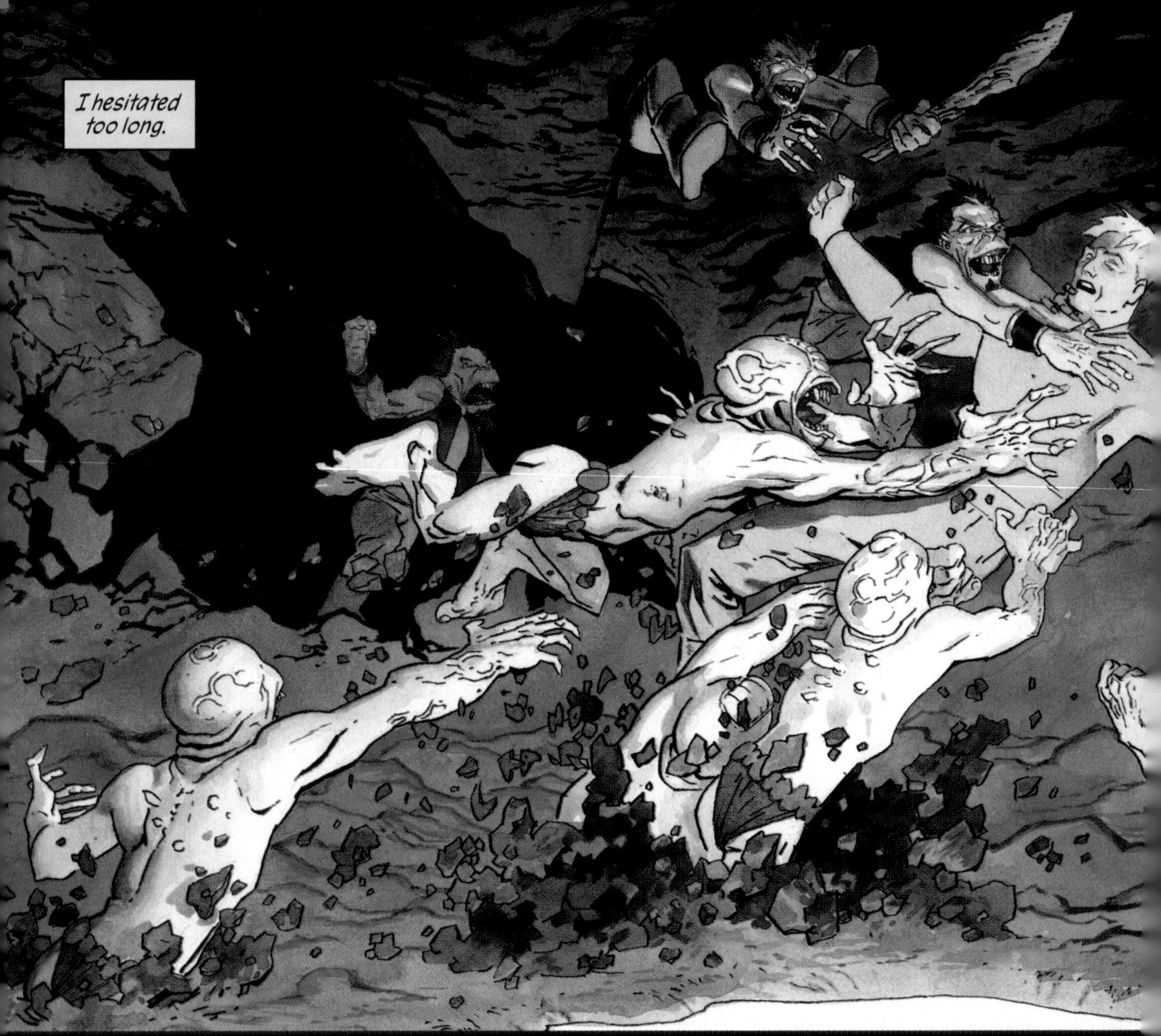
I hesitated too long.

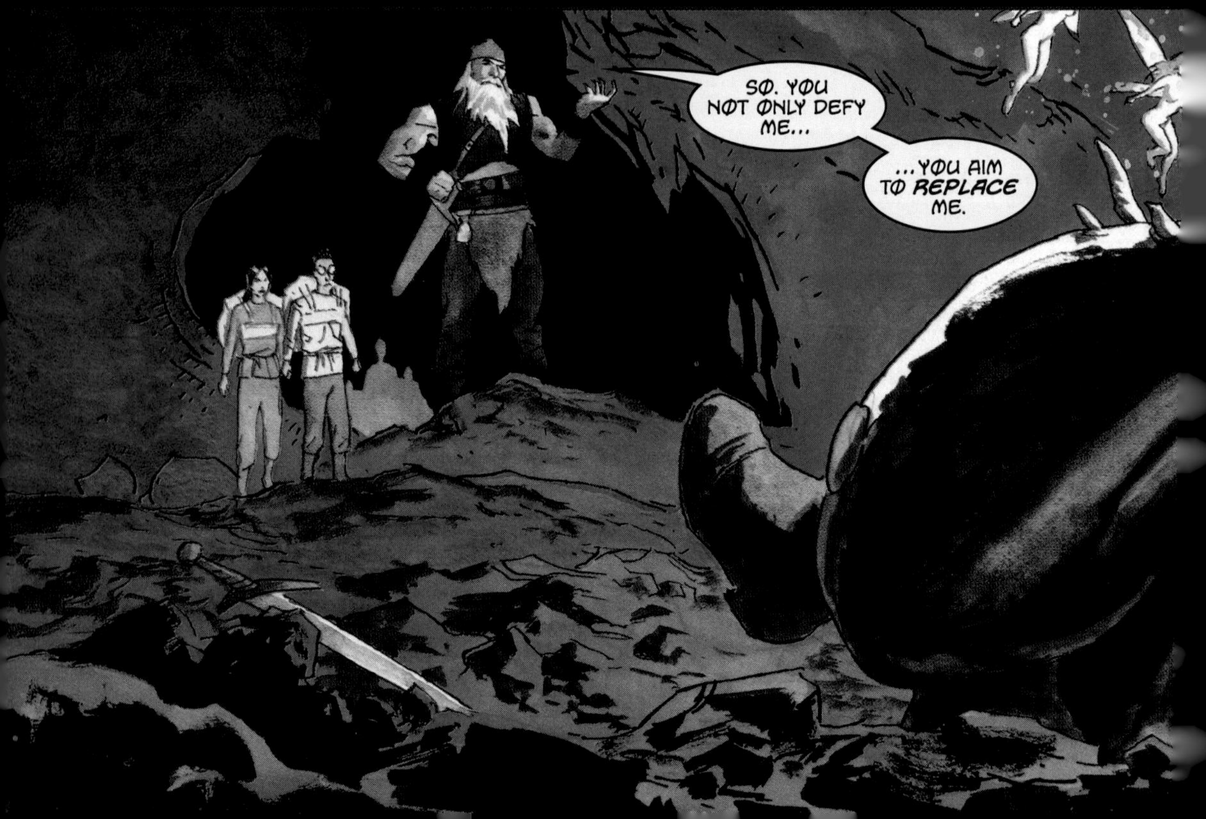
SO. YOU NOT ONLY DEFY ME...
...YOU AIM TO REPLACE ME.

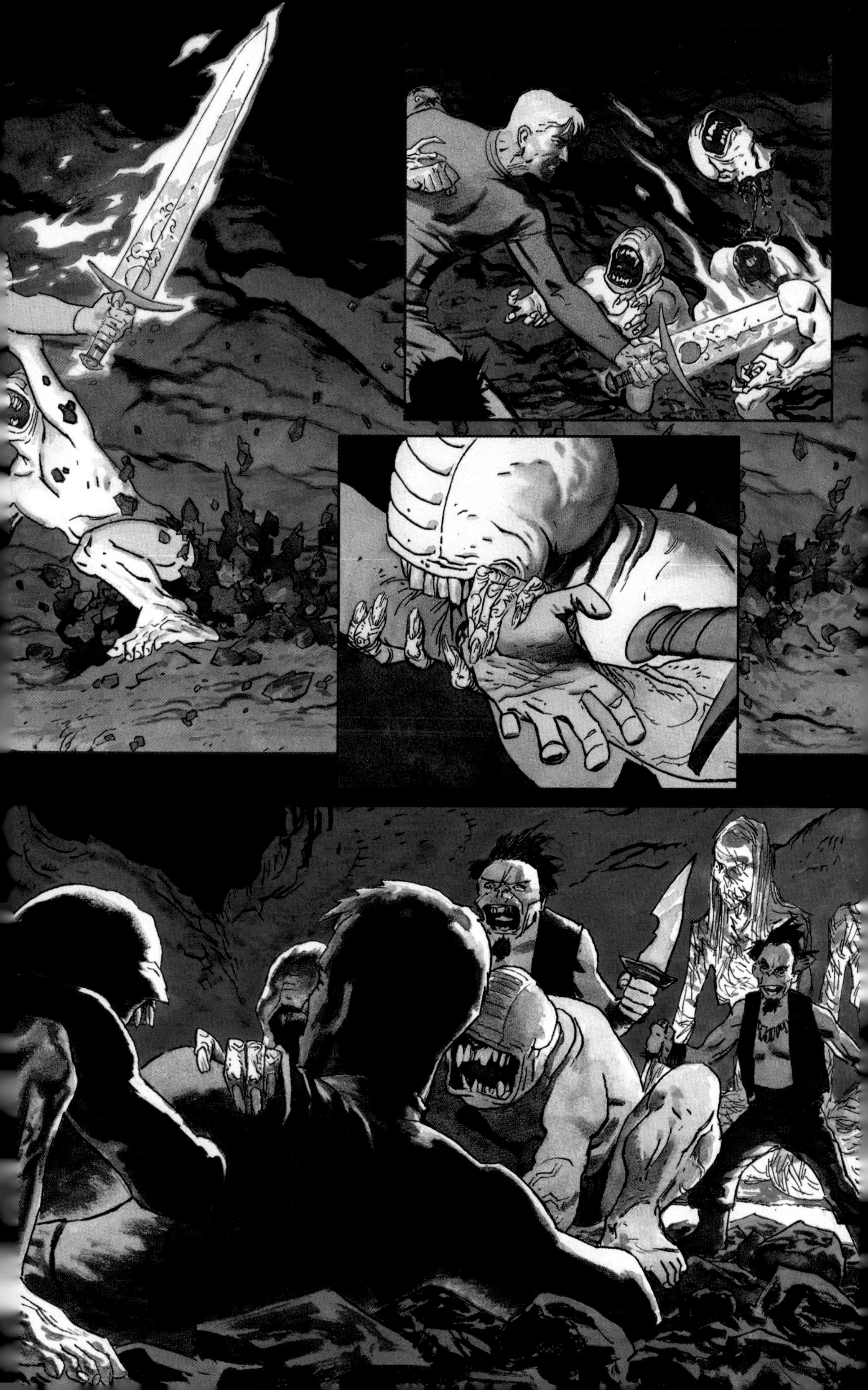

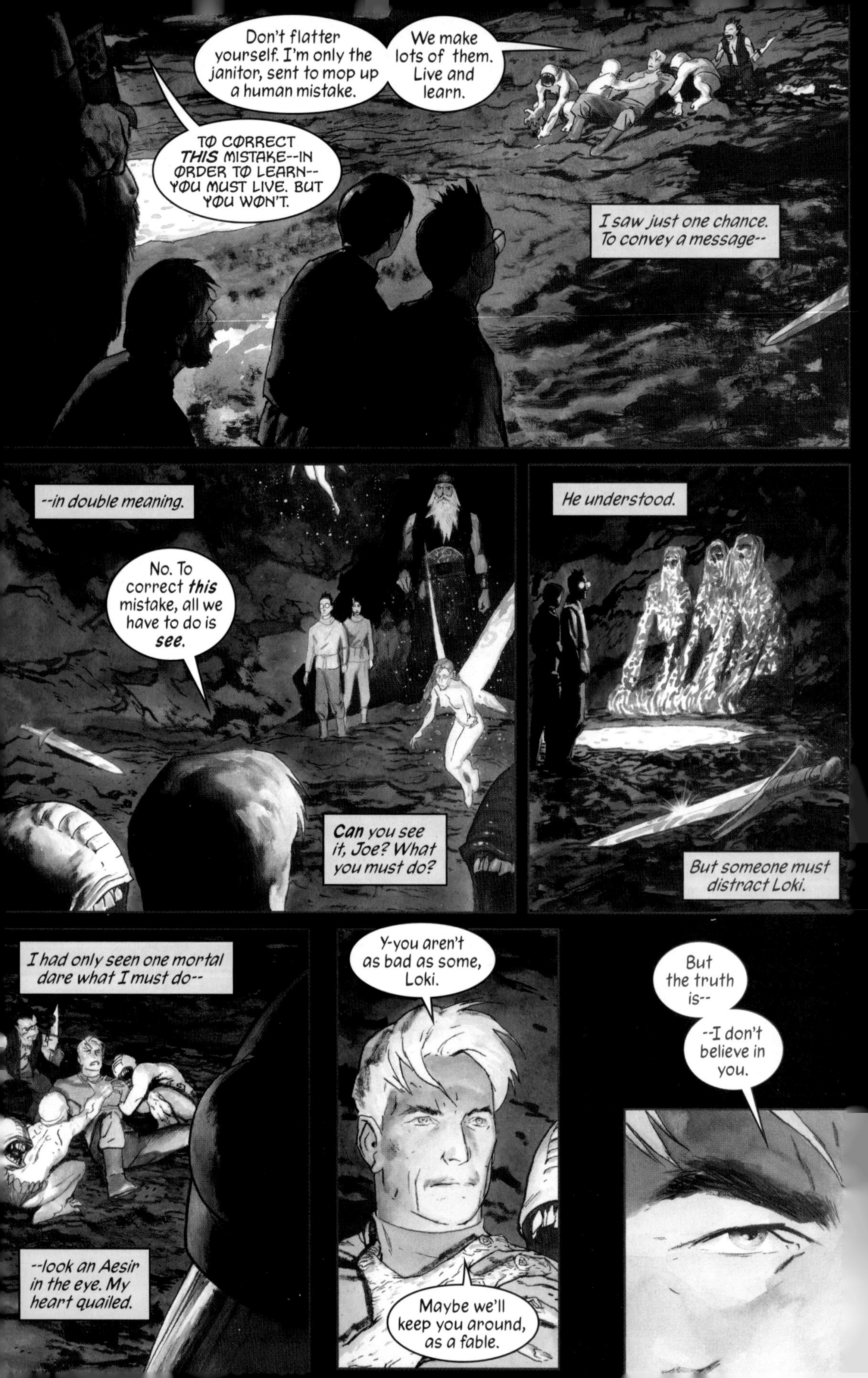

Don't flatter yourself. I'm only the janitor, sent to mop up a human mistake.
We make lots of them. Live and learn.
TO CORRECT THIS MISTAKE--IN ORDER TO LEARN--YOU MUST LIVE. BUT YOU WON'T.
I saw just one chance. To convey a message--
--in double meaning.
No. To correct this mistake, all we have to do is see.
Can you see it, Joe? What you must do?
He understood.
But someone must distract Loki.
I had only seen one mortal dare what I must do--
--look an Aesir in the eye. My heart quailed.
Y-you aren't as bad as some, Loki.
Maybe we'll keep you around, as a fable.
But the truth is--
--I don't believe in you.

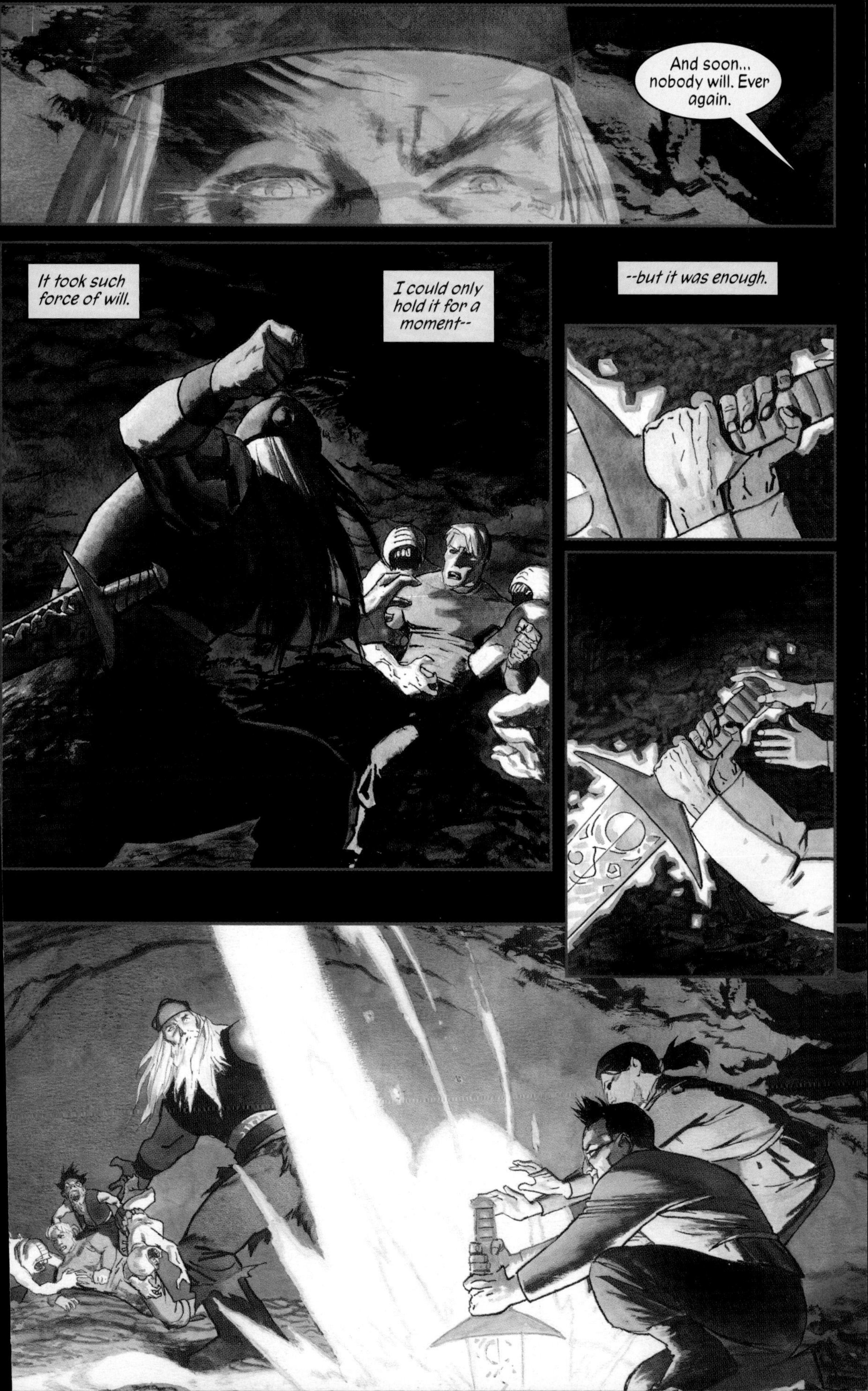
And soon... nobody will. Ever again.
It took such force of will.
I could only hold it for a moment--
--but it was enough.

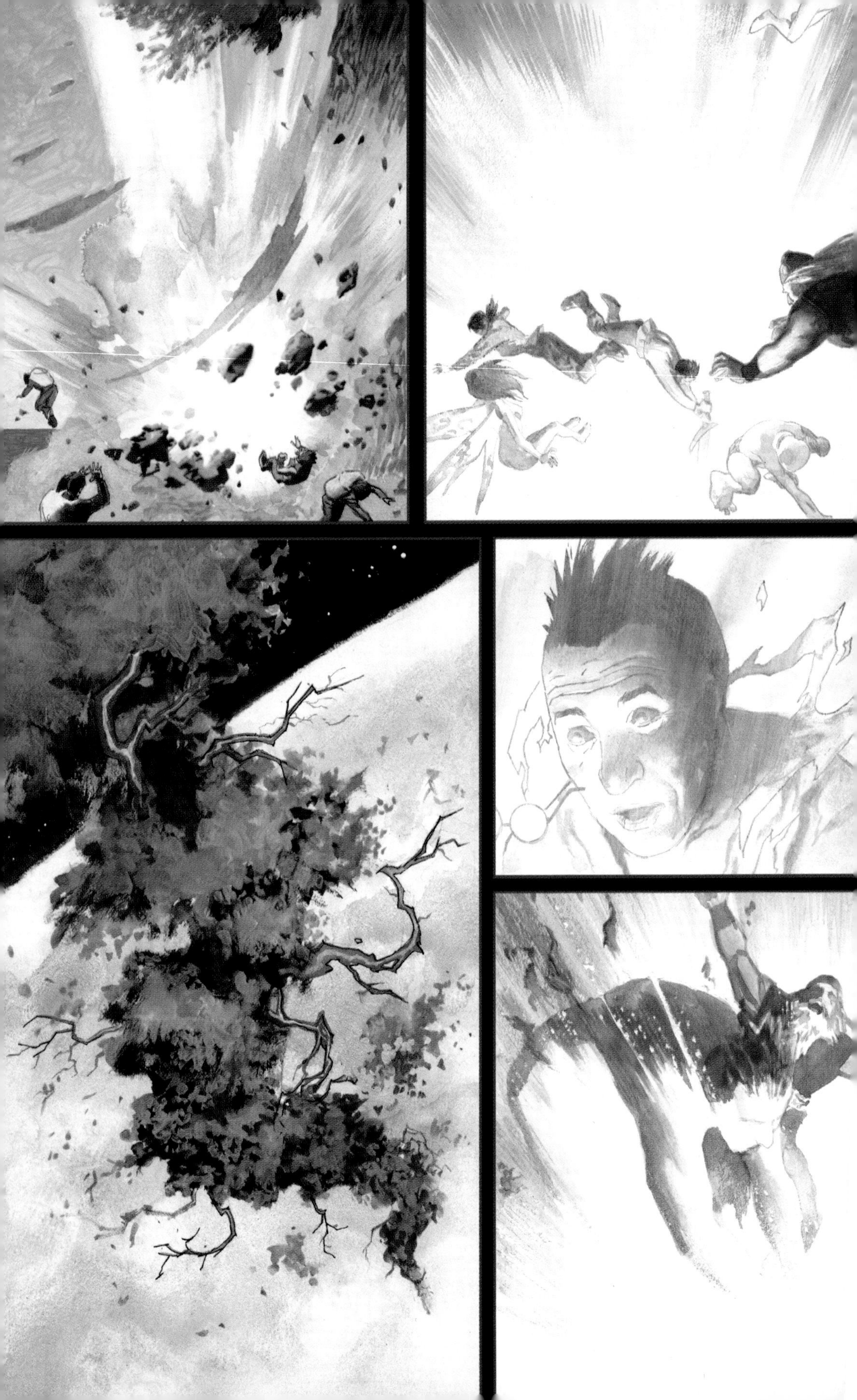

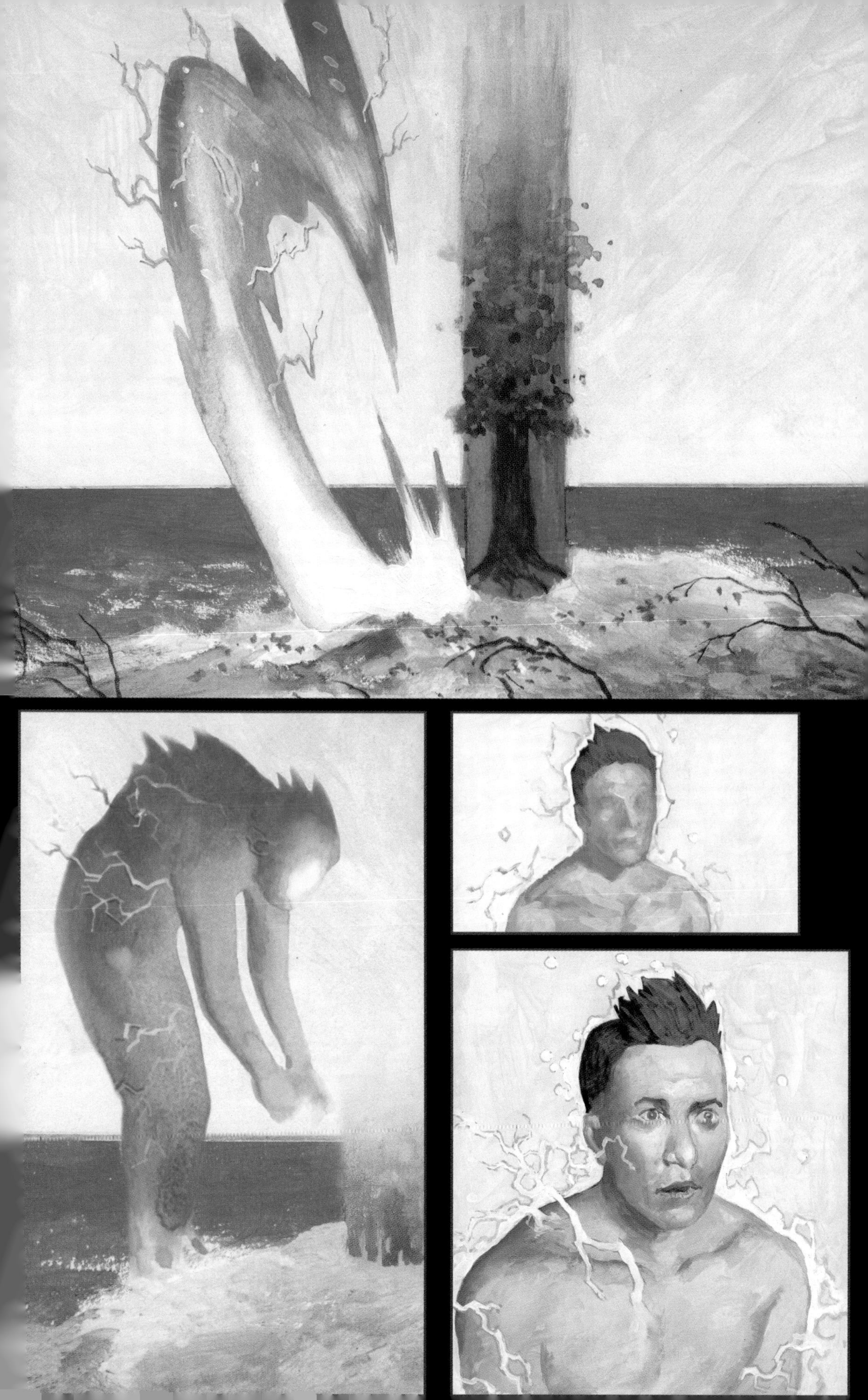

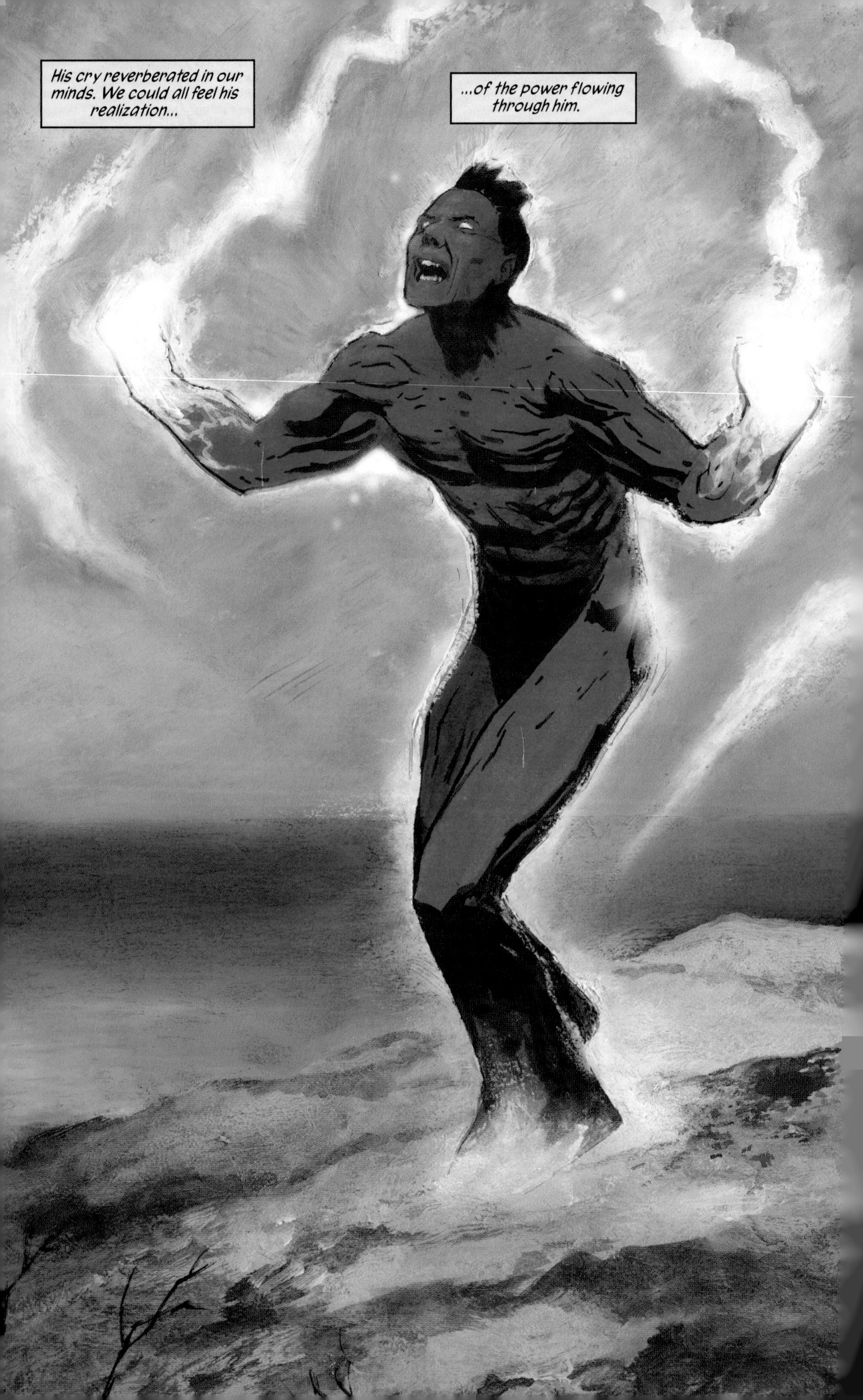
His cry reverberated in our minds. We could all feel his realization...
...of the power flowing through him.

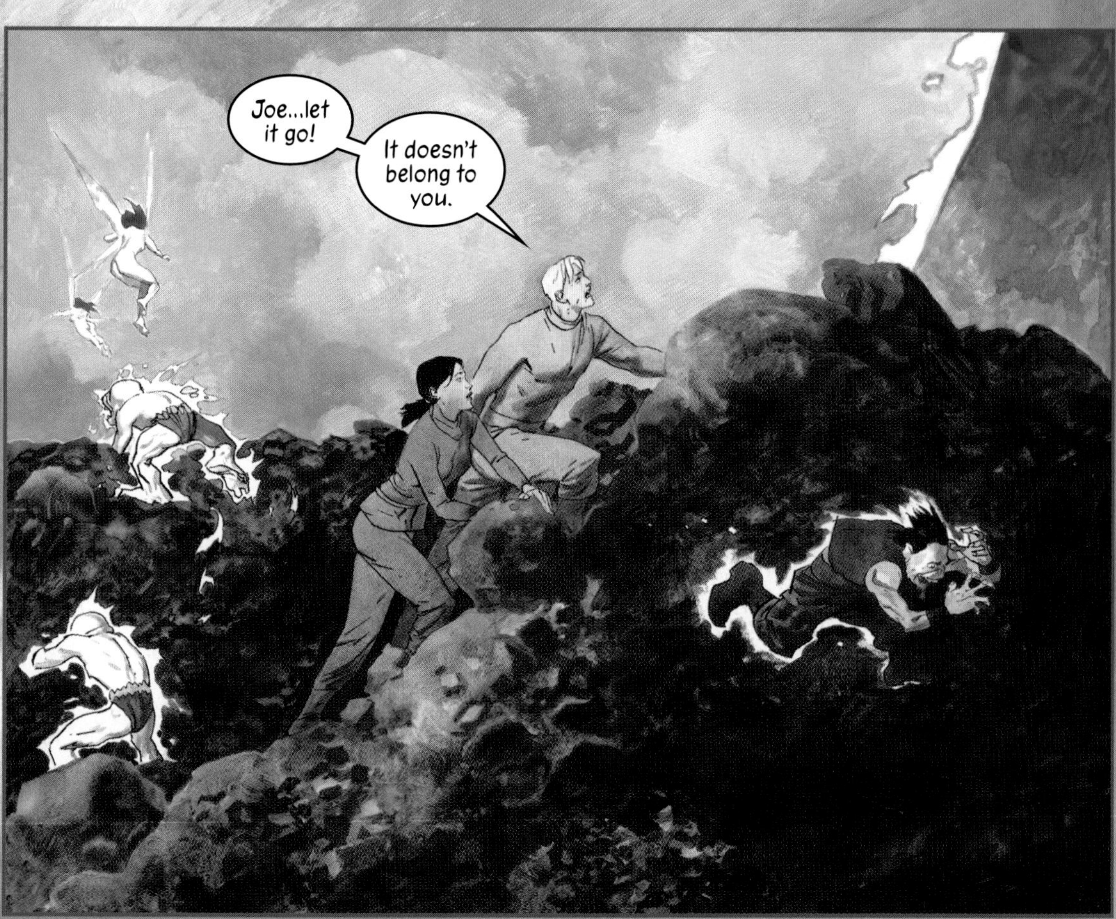
Joe...let it go!
It doesn't belong to you.

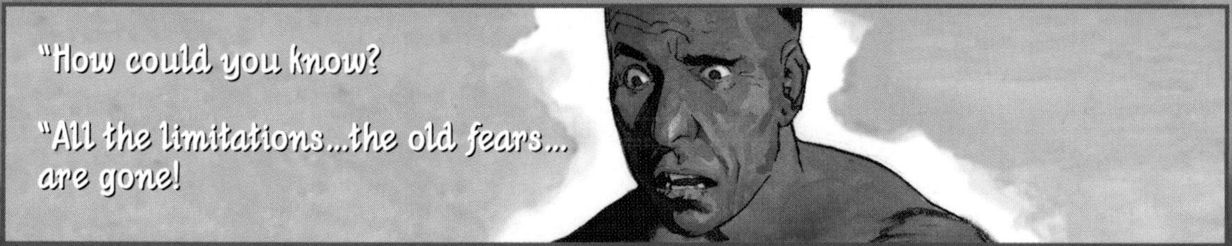
"How could you know?
"All the limitations...the old fears... are gone!

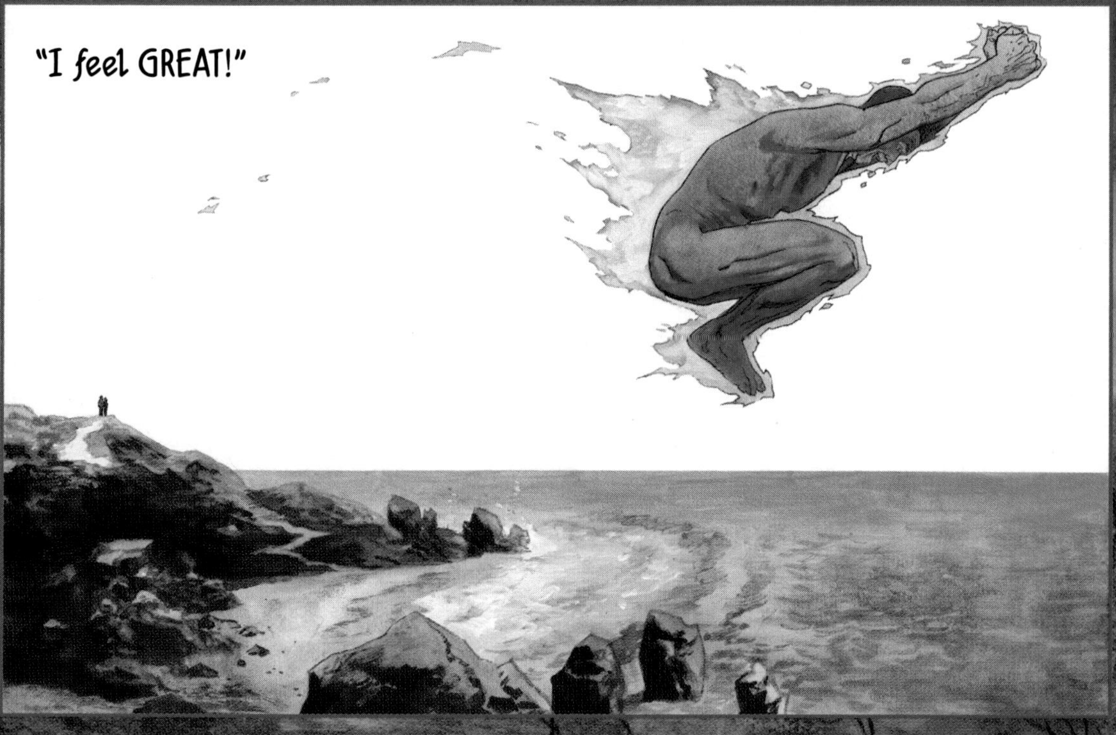
"I feel GREAT!"

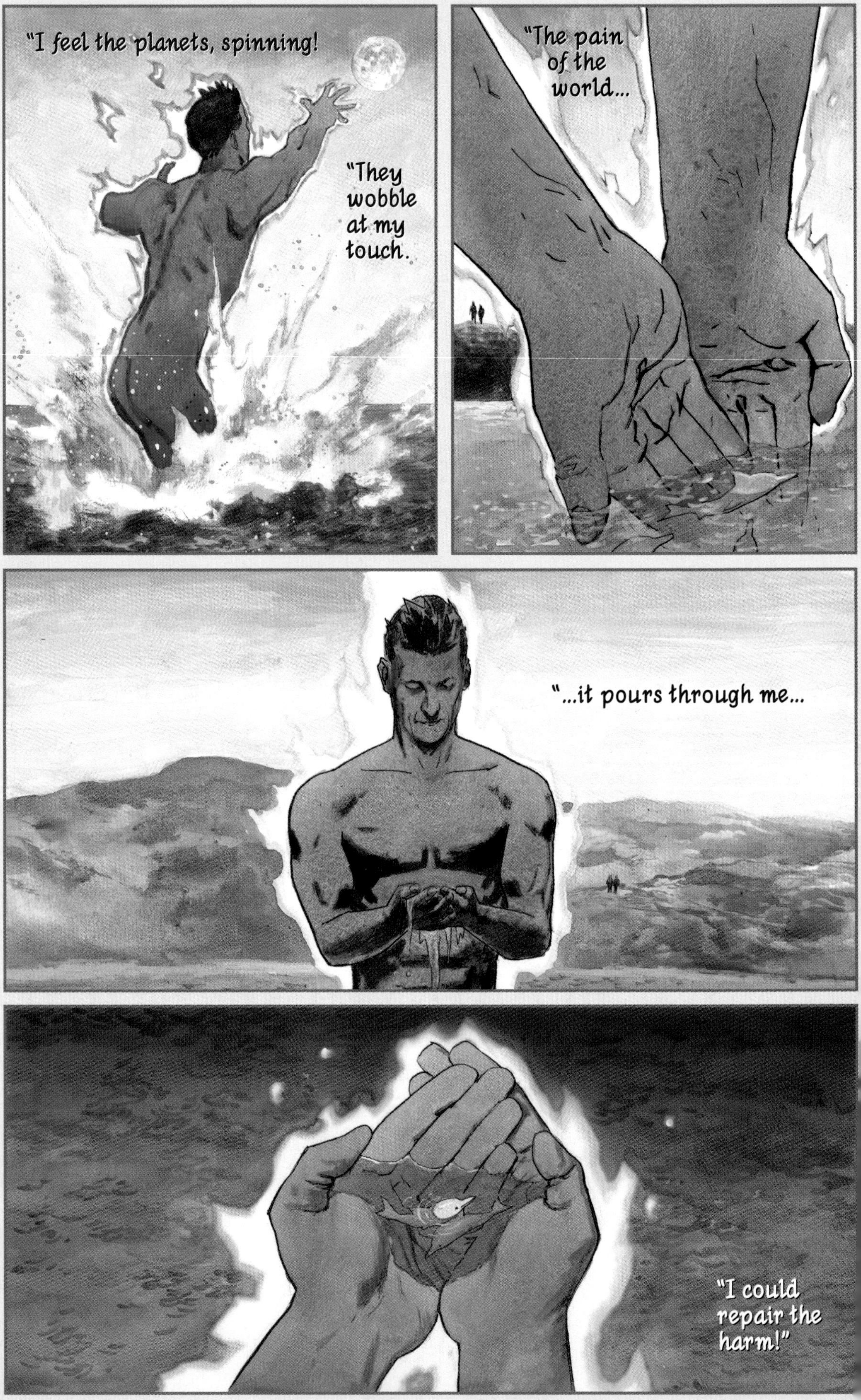
"I feel the planets, spinning!
"They wobble at my touch.
"The pain of the world...
"...it pours through me...
"I could repair the harm!"

Joe! You have to come back now.

I had tasted that power. Though a much smaller dose than Joe Kasting now experienced.

Power to do anything! To end the horror. To banish all the petty godlings.

Power to set things right.

What man could resist?

Only he **must** resist.

"Go back to what I was?

"Back to a quivering bookworm?"

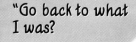

Back to a brave soldier...

...a scientist...

...a man.

Come back to me, Joe.

It doesn't belong to you. This isn't our way.

We stared as he grappled...

...with temptation we couldn't imagine.

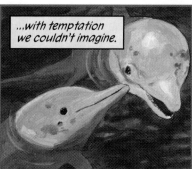

Holding our breath...

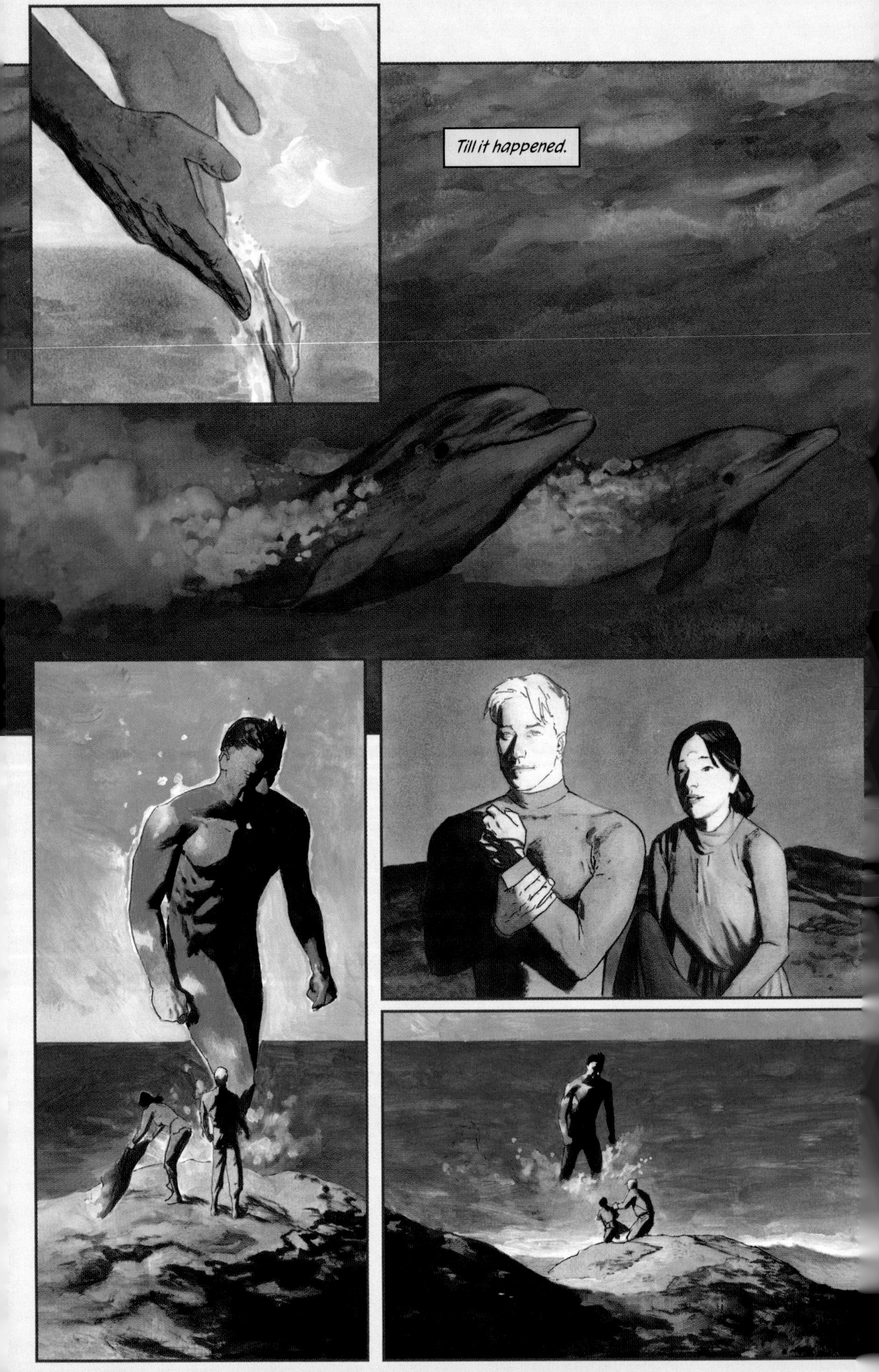
Till it happened.

The miracle.

Surrounding the pit, we found less debris than you'd expect. Most of the Tree's stolen essence had poured back into the Earth. Perhaps enough to help our home survive the coming battles.

No sign of Loki, though I knew we hadn't seen the last of the Trickster.

A "weather war"...

...and a war of freedom against magic.

Still, at long last, I felt cause for hope.

The holy man had been wrong. I wasn't the "champion."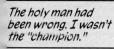

I saw another, now. A man. **Citizen.** One of us.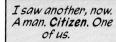

That very moment, I knew...

I've met two real heroes. The first showed me the way, years ago, defying evil.

...we would prevail...

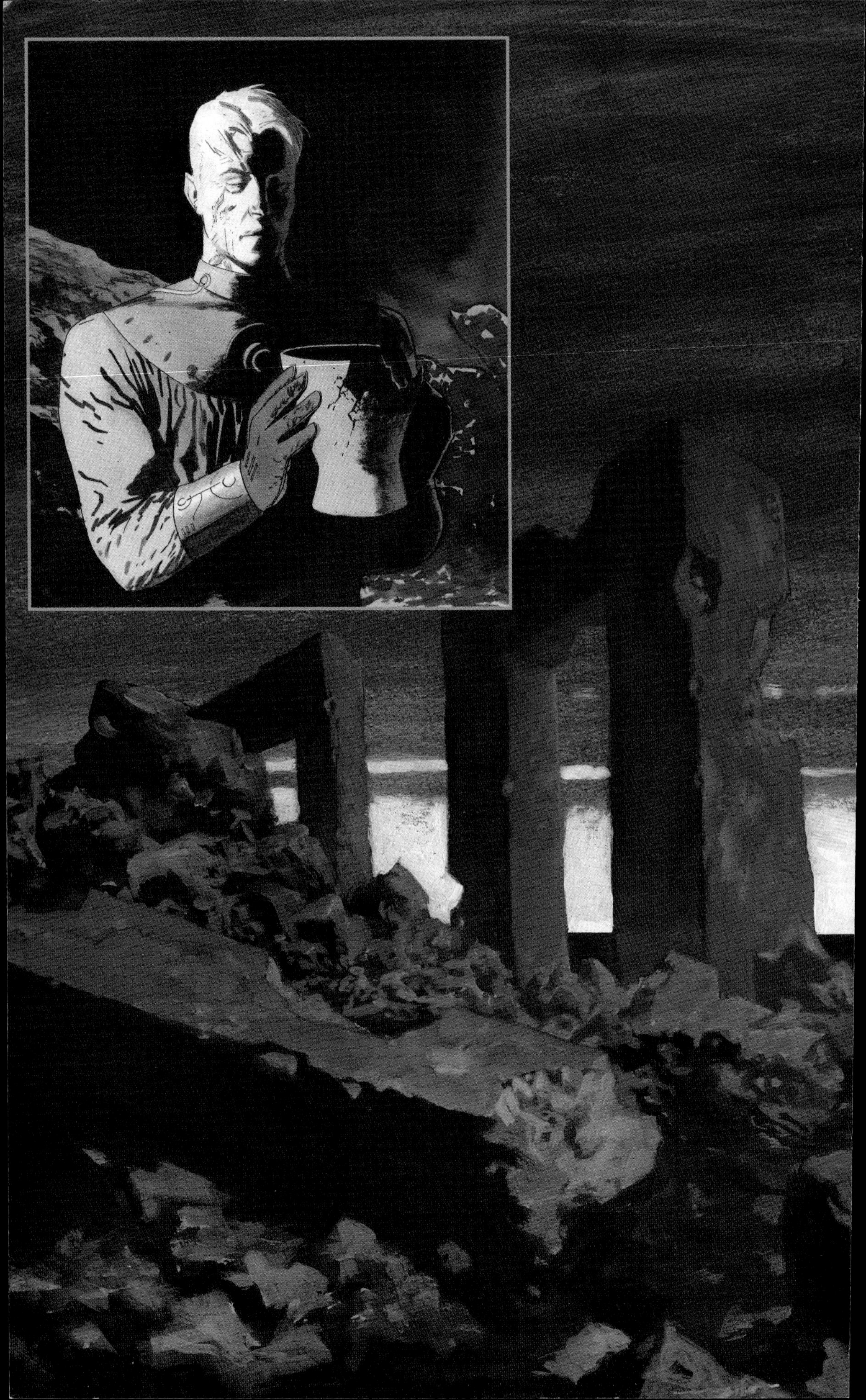

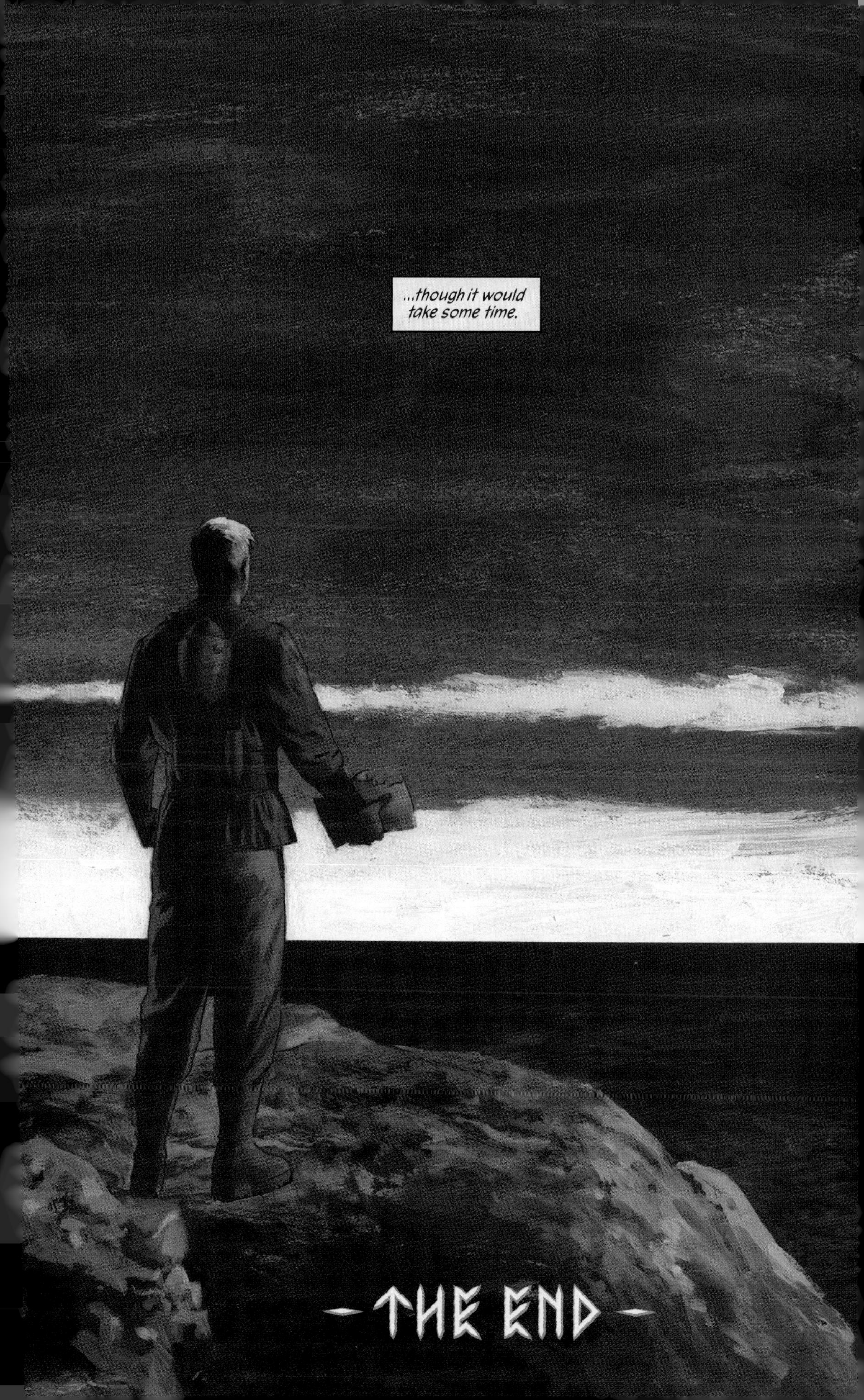
...though it would take some time.
THE END

Afterword

Science fiction was given the wrong name.

Only a small fraction of SF authors—and the tales they spin—have anything to do with *science*. What really compels us are twin notions of *change* and *transformation*—the world changing all around us, and humanity transforming from within.

Time is the essence. Time, like a juggernaut.

That's why more writers of SF study history than science. We devour legends and clues from the past, including tales of tragedy, triumph and lost opportunity. Our stories tend to be thought-experiments about that ongoing epic—either altering the past or extending the human saga into a future of possibilities. A much better name for the field might have been *Speculative History*.

Yes, a majority of our stories ask "what if?" Or ponder "if this goes on...." Tomorrow remains a popular playground. But sometimes it can be just as riveting to look at the present or the past—pondering how things "might have been."

The original novella behind *The Life Eaters* came about when I was invited by Gregory Benford, way back in the 1980s, to write for his anthology *Hitler Victorious*, a collection of tales about how the good guys might have lost the Second World War. It's been a fascinating sub-genre ever since Philip K. Dick wrote *The Man in the High Castle*—a great way to cause chills by imagining that history's worst bogeyman succeeded.

I never swallowed the common notion that "the Nazis almost won." *Ours* is the universe in which those delusional maniacs got amazing breaks, ruling and perverting a great nation instead of raving in lunatic asylums. We must never give murderous maniacs such a chance again.

Only that got me thinking. Might there have been even more to their delusions—their well-documented mysticism—than anyone figured? Steven Spielberg did a great job portraying Nazi obsession with the romantic and the occult in "Raiders of the Lost Arc." Himmler's SS practiced many weird rites. But did it go much deeper?

It occurred to me that the aim of the Holocaust cannot have *only* been death. Why transport so many people across great distances to be batch-processed in an industrial assembly line of horror? Why indeed, unless there was a sick hope for some product or result? The same result pursued by dark magic through the ages.

So much of popular culture nowadays seems eager to show the sweetly wise and benevolent side of a mystical tradition that spanned most cultures and almost every continent. Even in modern comics, there is a tendency to follow the old trope of Homer—the notion that super-empowered demigods matter more than the hard, cooperative work of skilled men and women.

The same women and men who built the universities and took us to the moon. Citizens who fought (and still fight) for freedom and the environment. The same people who roused themselves, rolled up their sleeves, and pounded Adolf Hitler's monsters back into mythology, where monsters belong.

True, there is still a world that needs saving, in myriad ways. We feel a chilling sense that everything is precarious. Sometimes it's so tempting to wish for *intervention*—by magical beings, by UFO grays, by cyberpunk supernerds or mighty mutants.

But honestly, who is likely to save civilization, or this planet, or our children's future? Meddlesome aliens? Mystic incantations? Superheroes?

Or us?

Forgive me, but I have to be optimistic. No other wager makes sense!

I'm betting on us.

David Brin
www.davidbrin.com.

From Pencils to Finish

Pencils

I like to keep my pencils fairly loose. This is tighter than usual for me since it's a pretty involved scene with the albino mole creatures erupting from the earth and the dwarf guys attacking from the rear, but it's still little more than a basic blueprint.

Inks

This is where the fun really starts for me. Roughs and initial pencils are work—when they go well, there's no part of a piece that I'm happier with; still, they strain the brain. Inking and painting, although they're by no means unconsidered, are more about instinct, where I get to turn on my Books on Tape or music and sort of bliss out.

Paints

Here's where the panel really starts to take shape, come into focus. Drawing problems I hadn't known about begin to stand out as the picture takes on weight and depth. This is always unhappy-making. I'll usually keep working around the problem areas hoping they'll just go away. (This almost never happens.) Finally, the panel is finished with that awkward hand (or whatever) either–A. cast in deep shadow ("when in doubt, black it out."*) or, B. obscured by a passing bird or leaf or flailing body or, C. fixed.

Sometimes I opt for C, but not without at least thinking about A or B.

Hey, babe–that's comics!

–Scott Hampton

*This is a piece of wisdom from the great Wally Wood.

Other books of interest

DAVID BRIN
STAR TREK
THE NEXT GENERATION
FORGIVENESS
SCOTT HAMPTON

Star Trek:
The Next Generation
Forgiveness

PLANETARY
2

Planetary
Books 1 & 2

ALAN MOORE
Book Four of the Transcendent New Series
PROMETHEA
J.H. WILLIAMS III
MICK GRAY
JEROMY COX

Promethea
Books 1 – 4

ALAN MOORE KEVIN O'NEILL
the LEAGUE OF EXTRAORDINARY GENTLEMEN
BEN DIMAGMALIW BILL OAKLEY
VOL. 1

League of
Extraordinary
Gentlemen, Volume 1

HOMAGE COMICS
He was a BAD MAN ... but if he wasn't GOOD ENOUGH, everything and everyone he cared about was going to DIE...
KURT BUSIEK'S
Astro City
The TARNISHED ANGEL
BUSIEK
ANDERSON
BLYBERG
SINCLAIR
ROSS &
COMICRAFT
Introduction by
FRANK MILLER
COMPLETE AND UNABRIDGED

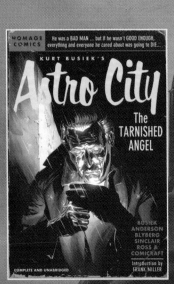

Kurt Busiek's Astro City:
Tarnished Angel

ZERO GIRL

Zero Girl
Volume 1

To find more collected editions and monthly comic books from WildStorm and DC Comics, call
1-888-comic book for the nearest comics shop or go to your local book store.